My Granddad knew Rasputin ...
and I met Elton John

My Granddad knew Rasputin ...
and I met Elton John

Stuart Linnell

This edition published 2025 by:

Takahe Publishing Ltd.

Registered Office:

77 Earlsdon Street, Coventry CV5 6EL

ISBN 978-1-908837-32-5

TAKAHE PUBLISHING LTD. 2025

Thank you to my wife and family for their encouragement whilst I've been writing this book. There was a time when health issues rather got in the way of making progress, but we got there. Thanks also to Steven Hodder for his professionalism in taking me through the publication process. Most of all it is dedicated to my beautiful grandchildren. I hope it will help them to learn and discover what my journey has involved, to understand our family story and the context in which it developed. I wish them much love and happiness in wherever life takes them.

Thank you to Franki Mills for the front cover illustration.

Contents

Preface

If you are fortunate to do the job you love you are fortunate indeed. So I have, indeed, been fortunate. Radio has provided me with that special opportunity. Whether playing records, meeting and interviewing people from so many different walks of life, talking to listeners taking part in phone-in debates or in competitions, whatever the format, radio has been my conduit to a life rich with interest, and what is referred to as job satisfaction.

You are also fortunate if you are able to enjoy the care and affection of a loving family. I certainly was, growing up with loving parents, a younger sister and two sets of grandparents who, in their own ways, doted on me, with two remarkable but very different Granddads. One of them was a war hero, the other was a gambler who met Rasputin.

My grandparents and, in the early part of their lifetime, my parents relied heavily on receiving information and enjoying entertainment from what they referred to as "the wireless". The term was first used in the late 19th century for the first radio transmitting and receiving technology. With many households owning radios that were not portable but were powered by being plugged into mains electricity, they continued to be referred to as wireless sets into the 1960s. The term was later revived in the telecommunications industry.

My mother neither shared nor understood my passion to work on the wireless. In many ways the word also summarises my Mum's worries for my future. She though I was rudderless or, maybe, "wireless" after emerging from my formal education with far fewer qualifications than I should have and, so far as she was concerned, no clear idea of what to do. My interests revolved around sport and popular music, but Mum could not even factor either into being part of substantial employment in my future.

When I started work at Birmingham City Council, as a clerk in what was then called the Welfare Department, she allowed herself a sigh of relief that I had a proper job. I understood her view that being a local government officer provided a route through which I could earn a meaningful living, but it was not long before things changed radically.

The word radio was now in common parlance in place of wireless, and a fundamental reorganisation of UK radio served to offer me, and many contemporaries, a wholly different future. First, the BBC restructured its networks, including the launch of local radio, and soon afterwards commercial radio arrived in the UK. My prospects looked significantly different, even thought they underlined my Mum's worst fears.

Memory does not serve to clearly identify at which point in my life I truly realised that the wireless, or radio, had made its mark so indelibly in my consciousness. It must have been a gradual process whereby the ability of one human being to communicate directly with another through intellectual discourse, or through the description of an event unfolding in front of the narrator, or by appreciation of music, became an integral part of my life. Whenever it was, or however it occurred, it created within me an enthusiasm bordering on sheer excitement that I could be part of that process. That is a feeling, an emotional perception really, that I still get whenever I enter a broadcast studio.

I am not sure my Mum was ever fully resigned to me realising my ambitions which, to be fair, initially extended no further than sitting at a microphone, playing records and maybe talking about sport. It is a great sadness to me that neither she nor my Dad saw me interview the likes of Elton John or Michael Parkinson, let alone the Prime Minister or the Archbishop of Canterbury. Pursuing my love of sport to commentating at Wembley and Lord's also occurred after they had died, as did the proud day that I followed in my Granddad's footsteps to be honoured by the monarch.

I hope they would have been reassured that it was a life that did have some purpose after all, and that it was not entirely wireless.

There are places I'll remember

All my life though some have changed

Some forever not for better

Some have gone and some remain

All these places had their moments

With lovers and friends I still can recall

Some are dead and some are living

In my life I've loved them all

John Lennon & Paul McCartney, 1965

©Sony/ATV Music Publishing LLC

My Granddad knew Rasputin … and I met Elton John

Chapter One

An Unexpected Hit

Because I'm happy

Clap along if you feel like a room without a roof

Because I'm happy

Clap along if you feel like happiness is the truth

Because I'm happy

Clap along if you know what happiness is to you

Because I'm happy

"I didn't expect to be in A&E at this time in the morning", I wrote, "but then I didn't expect to be knocked over by a police car".

It was shortly after six o'clock in the morning on Thursday, 16th January 2014. I should have been on air, hosting the Breakfast Show on BBC Radio Northampton. Instead, I sat behind the curtain of a cubicle in the Accident and Emergency Department of Northampton General Hospital, tapping those words into a Twitter message on my phone.

Within the hour, the online editions of the *Northampton Chronicle and Echo*, and the *Coventry Telegraph*, ran the story of the "Radio DJ Hit By Police Car". It was certainly not the way I had anticipated my day would start.

Crossing the road at Abington Square in Northampton, on my way into the radio station, I had been hit and knocked over by a car making an illegal right turn through traffic lights that only permitted vehicles to go straight on. It was a marked police car, manned by two officers.

The front bumper of the car made a direct hit on my ankles, forcing my torso up and over the bonnet, somersaulting across the fuselage like a Hollywood action hero. I crash landed, entirely unheroically, onto my back onto the road surface.

I can testify that tarmac is hard, particularly at five o'clock on a chilly January morning. Fortunately, I was carrying a bag, slung over my right shoulder. As I was catapulted to the ground, the bag swung round under my body and broke my fall, literally cushioning the impact. Had it not done so, the consequent injury of a hairline fracture of my pelvis would have been far worse, and the back of my head may well have smashed against the ground.

The damaged pelvis and the assault on my ankles were the visible results of the drama, although it later transpired that I also suffered skin trauma on both my legs. That continues to this day, years after the incident, causing discomfort and irritation. The impact of the police car's front bumper had caused a hole to open just above my right ankle, leaking a stream of blood. That took several weeks to heal, whilst a deep discolouration above my left ankle faded but even now remains visible.

As I lay on the road, the breath knocked out of me, one of the police officers jumped out of the car and called urgently for an ambulance to attend the scene. I was able to gulp in enough air to insist I didn't need an ambulance and that, actually, I had to get into the building to start work.

"What building?" he asked.

"That one", I gasped, nodding towards the imposing former bank premises which houses the offices and studios of BBC Radio Northampton.

I swallowed mouthfuls of air as I urgently attempted to restore normal breathing, and I managed to fill my lungs enough to add, "I present the Breakfast Show, and I'm due on air at six."

His obvious concern for my welfare now took on an anxious edge, his brow furrowing, as he realised who had been hit.

He helped me to my feet, whilst three youths raced across the road to assist. The trio, dressed in hoodies with scarves across their faces, had been walking behind me. They had engaged in quite loud, rapid conversation in a foreign, possibly Eastern European, language. I had been aware of them behind me and a glance over my shoulder had revealed three young men saying things I could not understand, getting closer to me. In that early hour, it had put me on my guard, but never judge a book and all that.

It was January, five o'clock in the morning and more than a tad cold. Hence the hoodies and the scarves. Those three young men raced to my aid when the police car hit me. They helped me to my feet, and they made sure that I was reunited with the bag which had saved me from more serious injury. Then they were gone, after showing me only care and concern.

At my insistence, the ambulance was stood down, and I walked extremely gingerly, assisted by the police officer, into the BBC Radio Northampton building. With the police officer at my side, I limped into the first-floor newsroom prompting breakfast news reader Andrew Radd to simultaneously raise his eyebrows and his suspicions. His face asked the obvious question, "What on earth have you done to be arrested at this time in the morning?".

I managed to explain what had occurred, only for Radders to immediately insist that I go straight to A&E. My protests that I could still host my show were instantly brushed aside as phone calls were made to organise a change of presenter. My producer, Ian Brown, got ready to host the first hour of the show, from 6 till 7, with lunch show presenter Helen Blaby rudely woken from her slumbers to arrive in time to take over for the remainder, between 7 and 9.

A cup of hot sweet tea was in my hands without being asked for, as the police officer who had guided me into the building took a very brief statement in his notebook, which I was then asked to sign.

By then, two more members of the Northamptonshire Constabulary were standing near me. One turned out to be the driver of the vehicle that had struck me. Obviously shaken, she was as white as a sheet as she offered her clearly heartfelt apologies. I asked if she was OK and if she wanted a cup of tea.

That offer was brusquely declined on her behalf by the third officer, standing next to her. He was a sergeant, and his response was that she must not consume anything until she had been to the police station to be breathalysed and interviewed.

By now, assistant producer Chaz Harrison had her coat on, ready to whisk me down the road in a radio station car to Northampton General Hospital.

* * * *

So it was that I sat in the A&E cubicle advising the world of my demise via Twitter.

That morning the hospital was undergoing an inspection by the Care Quality Commission, and the inspectors had paused next to my cubicle. The drawn curtain prevented me from seeing what was going on, but I could hear an apparently anxious senior nurse asking what they wanted to do.

There were reassuring words along the lines of "Just try to ignore us, we will just observe and ask questions if we need to" before they moved on out of my earshot. No great exclusive for me to reveal on my return to active duty, but just something to store and ask about when the opportunity arose.

X-rays revealed the hairline pelvic fracture, but thankfully nothing broken in my ankles, as had been feared. I was given extra strong painkillers to relieve my increasing back pain, and the open wound on my right ankle required cleaning and patching up.

A few hours later, my wife arrived by train. She retrieved my car from the car park and drove me home after a most unexpected start to the day.

The car radio was tuned in to BBC Radio Northampton, with my good friend and colleague Bernie Keith playing Pharrell Williams' big hit "Happy". Had Bernie realised we were listening at that moment, I am sure he would have wanted to ease my discomfort, and "Happy" was at least a cheery tune.

* * * *

The Police and Crime Commissioner for Northamptonshire, the county's first PCC Adam Simmonds, later revealed that he had been woken at 6am that morning by a call from a senior officer, alerting him to a "Polac", the force's term for a road accident involving a police vehicle, in Northampton town centre. Adam said that he'd rubbed the sleep from his eyes, as he responded.

"OK, have a report on my desk first thing."

"It's just a bit more serious than usual", the officer had said. "It involves one of the journalists from BBC Radio Northampton."

"Oh, really? Anyone we know?"

"It's the presenter of the Breakfast Show. Stuart Linnell."

By now, Adam said, he was sitting bolt upright in bed. As a man to whom his Christian faith was important, I doubt he utters profanities very often, but apparently, on this occasion, his instantaneous response drove him remarkably close to airing a four-letter expletive.

* * * *

The process that followed was protracted, to say the least. My legal advisers acted to seek compensation for the injuries and the anxieties that I had suffered. It was not a swift process.

The police officer who had driven the car was initially suspended from all duties, and was eventually found guilty of driving without due care and for disobeying a road sign. A friend who serves as a magistrate in a different place said that had the case come before him he would have asked that the charge be reconsidered. His view was that the lady in question was guilty of dangerous driving, which carries a potentially heavier sentence than that of driving without due care.

As it was, she was fined and required to pay costs, with three points on her driving licence. She was also disciplined and told to undergo a period of retraining by the Northamptonshire force before being allowed to return to her previous role behind the wheel.

It was nearly four years later that my claim was finally resolved. The skin trauma remains, but more than 45 years after my broadcasting career began, I was grateful to still be around to carry on for at least a little while longer.

So don't become some background noise

A backdrop for the girls and boys

Who just don't know or just don't care

And just complain when you're not there

You had your time, you had the power

You've yet to have your finest hour

Radio (radio)

All we hear is radio ga ga

Radio goo goo

Radio ga ga

All we hear is radio ga ga

Radio blah blah

Radio, what's new?

Radio, someone still loves you

Roger Taylor, 1983

Chapter Two

Two Granddads

Comin' in on a wing and a prayer
Comin' in on a wing and a prayer
With our one motor gone
We can still carry on
Comin' in on a wing and a prayer

Harold Adamson & Jimmy Mc Hugh, 1943
© Sony/ATV Music Publishing LLC

I had two quite remarkable grandfathers, each very different from the other, but both were hugely significant characters in my early life.

When I was born, in 1947 in Northfield in Birmingham, both sets of grandparents lived close by. In fact, my Mum lived with her parents for a time after she was married, whilst my Dad was away serving in the army during the Second World War.

My birth occurred, perhaps not surprisingly, within a year of his return to hearth and home. Thousands of couples across the UK enjoyed the arrival of babies in 1946 and 1947, and my parents welcomed me into the world on 22nd January 1947.

* * * *

My father had served in the Royal Warwickshire Regiment. He was a battery captain and, although he served overseas, he and his men were also assigned to the protection of industrial locations in the West Midlands. Ironically, given where my life would take me, the guns under Dad's command were sent, for a time, to guard the city of Coventry.

In 1940, most German air raids during the Battle of Britain and the early part of The Blitz concentrated on London and the South and East coasts, but the West Midlands also suffered badly. Birmingham and Coventry experienced heavy raids in August and October of that year.

On 4th November 1940 Dad's regiment received orders to go overseas. They left Coventry and ten days later arrived at the mobilisation centre at Southend-on-Sea. As a consequence, after providing part of Coventry's air raid defence, they missed the Coventry Blitz, the notorious bombing raid that destroyed the city on the night of 14th and 15th November.

Their mission should have taken them from Southend to either Malta or Port Suez in Egypt. Some of the regiment did arrive there, but Dad's battalion received orders to turn away from the coast and, instead, to travel back across the country to Wales. They set up camp at the foot of Cadre Idris, a mountain at the southern end of the Snowdonia National Park near the town of Dolgellau.

Wales was cold and wet, and the damp conditions wreaked havoc with my father's health. He contracted a severe bronchial condition that stayed with him for the rest of his life. He initially recovered sufficiently to go on an overseas assignment after all, his battalion being sent to Germany as the war neared its conclusion.

After his military service, he spoke very little about his time in the army, and the few facts he passed on had to be dragged from him. Amongst the things he did reveal was about entering Berlin soon after Hitler's capitulation. He told me that he was amongst those sent into Hitler's bunker, near the Reich Chancellery in Berlin, to seek out booby traps and other armaments that might be there.

He offered proof of the story by bringing home a brass statuette of a dachshund, about 12 inches high. It was an intriguing item, to say the least. Its base is embossed by a capital "H" above which sits a crown. The base unscrews, and attached to it is a long metal pin which lies inside the statuette but serves no obvious purpose.

My Dad said that it had been designed to be a stamp so that the "H" and crown insignia could be imprinted on the seal of a document. His theory was that the pin inside it suggested that it had been intended to be used as a booby trap, but one which had never been set.

Whether all that amounted to no more than a Dad's tale to satisfy his young son's curiosity I don't know, but the dachshund statuette survives to this day. My sister has it, and it sits as an ornament in her home.

* * * *

Dad returned to civilian life in Northfield, the part of Birmingham which was, at that time, dominated by the vehicle manufacturing factory at Longbridge.

It had been a printing works, founded in the late 1800s, but it was derelict when Herbert Austin discovered it. He decided to buy it and completed its purchase for £7,500. He did so in 1906, on 22 January, the same date on which I was born 41 years later. Austin went on to convert the building into the home of the British car industry.

Over succeeding years, the cars built there bore such names as Austin, Nash Metropolitan, Morris, British Leyland, and MG Rover. In 1959, it was the location where the brilliantly inventive mind of Alec Issigonis came up with a car which boasted front-wheel drive, a transverse mounted engine, a sump gearbox, and 10-inch wheels, not to mention what the sales brochures described as "a deceptively spacious interior for a small car ". It was the Austin Mini, later simply called "the Mini", built originally at Longbridge.

By the late 1960s, some 25,000 workers were employed at Longbridge, but before that, during World War 2, the main plant made munitions and tank parts, while the nearby East Works of Austin Aero Ltd at Cofton Hackett produced aircraft. The Short Stirling four-engined heavy bomber and the Hawker Hurricane single-seat fighter were both built there. Amongst the wartime workforce were the sisters Dorothy and Heather Swain, my Mum and my Auntie Heather.

* * * *

Decades later, in April 2005, after the surviving car manufacturer MG Rover went out of business, older sections of the factory were demolished and part of the site was redeveloped for commercial and residential use, but when I entered the world it was one of the main employers for local people. Percy Swain, father of Dorothy and Heather, was one of those who took advantage of living near the factory. He started one of the first, possibly the very first, car transporter companies in England.

Granddad Percy realised that the cars built at Longbridge had to be taken from their place of manufacture to their new owners, or at least to the dealers who were to sell them. He formed a business to do just that.

* * * *

Percy and his wife Maud had lived in a semi-detached house in a cul-de-sac in Northfield, but by the time I arrived, that house had become home to my Mum and Dad and me. Grandma and Granddad Swain moved literally just down the road to a smart little bungalow, located where Northfield joined the neighbouring district of Longbridge.

It was a bungalow with a long garden, temptingly long, in which a toddler could explore and lose himself. It had the additional fascination of the River Rea and a busy railway line sitting side by side, both visible from the bottom of the garden. Unfortunately, to obtain the best view of the trains as they carried people and freight to and from the Longbridge factory, you had to perch yourself adjacent to a regularly replenished, huge store of coal.

Coal was the basic fuel on which the bungalow depended. My grandmother's wonderful cooking range, which also maintained the hot water supply, relied exclusively on coal.

The range, shiny and black, occupying one entire side of the bungalow's large kitchen, and I loved it, especially when Grandma Maud was cooking a milk pudding. She always had a tapioca, sago or semolina pudding on the go, but my favourite was her rice pudding, topped with nutmeg. The aroma as you entered the bungalow was warm, comforting and mouth-watering.

Thus the coal on which the range relied was piled high at the bottom of the garden, alongside the perfect location from which you could watch the trains as they steamed and hissed their way past. It was too close for comfort for a small child, dressed proudly by his mother for a visit to his grandparents. Dressed, on one fateful day, all in white.

The anguish in my mother's outburst of horror when she saw that cherubic image emerge, covered from head to toe by black, ingrained soot, is lodged in my memory forever.

Indeed, I remember two things very clearly from that day. One was my mother's shriek of distress at the sight of my coal dust-covered hair, and my blackened face and clothing. The other was the reassuring embrace of

Grandma Maud, as a bowl of warm, sweet, rice pudding was served up. Grandma wiped away my tears and as much of the coal dust as she could, whilst Mum retrieved fresh clean clothing from our house, thankfully not far away.

We lived at the top of a hill at the far end of a cul-de-sac, Kemshead Avenue, which was literally across the road from my grandparent's bungalow. It was close enough for a new set of clothes to be swiftly provided for this errant child.

* * * *

Granny Maud was an important figure in my life. More so than my other Grandma, Jesse, my Dad's Mum. Jesse was much more aloof than Maud, preferring to spend her days with her friends playing bridge, regularly refreshed by a stiff gin or a tot of whisky, rather than enjoy time with her grandchildren. She certainly wasn't cold towards us, but her maternal instincts were the complete opposite of Granny Maud.

As her first grandchild, I was spoilt rotten by Maud. In her eyes, I could do no wrong, and I loved the cakes she baked in her beautifully ordered and spotlessly clean home, as well as those comforting milk puddings.

Maud had her own firmly-held notions and ideas. Most of them are quite quirky to look back on, but they came from a proud lady of Worcestershire stock, born more than ten years before the start of the twentieth century, and brought up in the Midlands countryside on the outskirts of a rural town. She had an honest heart and a very straightforward appraisal of what she saw around her.

At its most mundane, her domestic approach was typified by the fact that if we were served fruit for tea, tinned pears and tinned peaches being special treats on Sundays, we were expected to have a slice of bread and butter at the same time.

Similarly, if I ate a banana, a slice of buttered bread immediately appeared on a side plate in front of me. "To take the wind away," she said, with unquestionable Granny Maud logic.

The space age was something that troubled her greatly. I was 14 when the Russian cosmonaut Yuri Gagarin became the first person to fly in space. His single orbit of the Earth took 108 minutes in the Vostok spacecraft, on

12th April 1961. That was four years after the former Soviet Union had shocked the world by starting what became known as 'the space race', when they launched and recovered the unmanned satellite Sputnik 1 on 4th October 1957.

Granny Maud found all this difficult to comprehend.

"What are they doing, messing about in this space?" she said, before declaring firmly, "I don't believe in space."

She held that the space race, and in particular those who had started it, was entirely responsible for any bad weather that resulted thereafter. At the first rumble of a thunderstorm, or with a dramatically heavy downpour of rain, she was in no doubt about why it had occurred.

"I blame those Russians," she said. "It's all their fault, going where they shouldn't, in that space."

* * * *

I don't remember much about the house in Kemshead Avenue, other than it was near Granny Maud's bungalow. One very clear memory I do have though is that Mr. and Mrs. Dutton, who lived next door, looked after me sometimes if Mum had to go out on days when it was not convenient for me to go to my Grandma's. When that occurred, I was always ready to visit them because they had, in their entrance hall, a beautiful and fascinating Grandfather clock.

Its brilliantly coloured face, with its hourly illustration of the cow jumping over the moon, kept me fascinated for hours. It also taught me the basics of telling the time, the first example of me acquiring a skill that would prove useful for a broadcaster. That said, those who know me well will readily testify that it has not translated into good timekeeping in later life. My penchant for being late is a regular source of family frustration.

* * * *

Not far away, also in Northfield, my Dad's folks lived in rather more upmarket accommodation. They had a serviced apartment on Bristol Road South, the main route to and from the centre of Birmingham. It carried people to the edge of the city in their locally built cars, or by bus, or by what I regarded as the far more exciting mode of transport, the tram.

At that time, tram rails ran down the middle of the wide, neatly maintained, grass-edged, central reservation of Bristol Road, and were well-used by the factory workers and their families.

I loved sitting in the front bay window of Granddad Linnell's flat, looking directly out at Bristol Road South, waiting excitedly to spot each tram as it sped past.

Granddad Charles also had an additional feature adjacent to that window, a piece of equipment that was a magnet to a small child unused to seeing one. It was a telephone. Neither my parents nor my other Grandparents had a 'phone in their homes at that time. Apart from the novelty that he had one, my Granddad's 'phone had a special quality. It was within my reach.

I could, and often did, pick up the receiver from its cradle and pretend to talk to someone at the other end. My Granddad, who was otherwise infinitely patient with me, was seriously irritated by this and would scold me, warning that every time I picked it up it cost him threepence! Not that it did of course, but that was his stern rebuke.

Threepence had particular significance because in those days, long before decimal currency, there was a threepence coin, known as the threepenny bit. My Granddad knew that I was fascinated by the small, brass-coloured coin with its twelve flat edges, and I am sure that is why he used threepence when admonishing me for playing with his 'phone.

To twenty-first-century eyes, a black bakelite machine, which had a chrome dial, with letters and numbers picked out in holes set around it, seems like an antiquity. To make a call you had to turn the dial, with a finger in the appropriate hole for each letter and number required.

I say letters and numbers because each locality had its own name in the telephone system. My Granddad's was "Priory", so to call someone in the same area you had to dial "PRI" and then their number. To make a call over any distance, you had to dial "O" for the operator, who was based at the telephone exchange. She, and it was almost always a woman, would dial for you.

The 'phone sat on my Granddad's windowsill. There was no prospect of wandering around or going outside whilst having a conversation, as with a mobile 'phone. With the handset attached to the base, you had to sit, or stand, in that one place to chat.

For many, including my Mum and Dad at the time, using the 'phone meant going to the nearest public telephone box, located in a road nearby. Granddad Charles, who had been a salesman for a couple of companies, and would later become secretary of the North Worcestershire Golf Club, did live a somewhat more affluent life, and for him a 'phone in his home was essential.

* * * *

If having a telephone was a statement of relative prosperity, a television was not even on the agenda for my Mum and Dad. TV programmes, with the BBC providing the only channel available, were suspended during World War 2, from 1939 until 1946. When they returned, it was not until 1949 that a transmitter at Sutton Coldfield beamed pictures into Birmingham. I was too young to be aware of that, but I do recall, when I was four or five and first starting to take such things on board, that Granddad Charles had a TV set. He was, I think, the first in the family to own one.

It had a fairly small screen. The sound that accompanied the picture came from a loudspeaker that was slightly larger than the screen. The loudspeaker was located immediately below the screen, and the whole unit was housed in a mahogany cabinet with doors that closed over the set when it was not in use.

If TV was a novelty, radio was an ever-present. BBC news bulletins were listened to intently, as were concerts conducted by Sir Malcolm Sargent. He was associated with many choral ensembles, amongst them the D'Oyly Carte Opera Company, as well as the London Philharmonic, the Hallé, the BBC Symphony and the Royal Philharmonic orchestras. He was for many years the best-known English conductor, and he was chief conductor of the Proms from 1948 to 1967. Any radio show including music conducted by Sir Malcolm Sargent was a must-listen.

The popular songs of the day were sung along to regularly. They were often played by dance bands and their singers on the BBC Light Programme, which was launched at the end of the war in 1945. It was a radio station designated to provide easy listening, folk, jazz and light entertainment. What passed for pop music were usually tunes originally performed by American artists such as Tommy Dorsey, Glenn Miller and Bing Crosby, although the regular radio shows that made stars of English band leaders Jack Payne and Henry Hall were a staple diet of listening for my parents and grandparents.

There were some notable British singers, such as Vera Lynn, George Formby, Gracie Fields and Anne Shelton. One of Anne Shelton's hits was her cover version of a song that had been made famous by an American group called The Song Spinners, "Coming In On A Wing And A Prayer". It was one of my Dad's favourites and he was definitely an Anne Shelton fan. How he would have loved it when, many years later, I had the privilege of introducing her on stage in Coventry.

* * * *

I was born into a lively post-war world. My parents were, like so many others across the country, diligently putting their lives together following the end of the war. My father had to hang his officer's uniform in the wardrobe and get used to life in "civvy street".

The wider family gave me two quite remarkable men as Grandfathers in their own quite different ways. One, my Mum's Dad, an entrepreneurial mercurial man. The other, was my father's father, a businessman and a decorated war hero.

Neither would consider themselves rich. They would have laughed at being thought of as wealthy, but both were well placed to pass on a reasonable financial legacy to their offspring. Despite that, both saw fit, in very different ways, to deny that outcome.

* * * *

My Mum's father, Percy Swain, led quite a life. He was born in Altrincham in Cheshire, his father a railway engineer, and a very significant one. In fact, James T. J. Swain was a historic innovator. In 1829, when Robert Stephenson and his father George were designing and building the famous "Rocket" locomotive, the template for steam engines in the pioneering years of rail transport, James Swain played a critical role.

Whilst Stephenson and other engineers of the day fretted and poured over the means to make the locomotive move, James realised that a fundamental requirement was that the rails on which they ran had to be secure. He devised a solution to fix the steel rails to the ground. The rails sat in James's invention, called the "chair", which in turn was bolted to a wooden sleeper fixed to the ground. A series of sleepers extended from the beginning to the end of the entire length of the track, with the name 'Swain' stamped on the underside of each chair.

Whether James was rewarded well for his invention is rather lost in the mists of time, but it has long been assumed within the family that he probably was. So much so that his son Percy was able to lead a quite remarkable life.

He had grown into a tall handsome man, with a distinctively large, but by no means unsightly, nose. A dashing athletic young fellow, he went to Russia as an ice skating tutor to the children of the last Tsar, Nicholas II. Percy was probably just one of several tutors, and it is probable that not all of the Russian royal children were included, as it seems unlikely that Nicholas' heir and only son Alexei would have been a pupil.

Alexei was born with haemophilia, for which he was treated by the faith healer and mystic Grigori Rasputin. Alexei was rarely permitted to engage in any activity that might prompt bruising or bleeding, so ice skating was almost certainly not on the agenda of the last Tsesarevich of Russia. The presence of Rasputin in the Tsar's household meant that he may well have had contact, from time to time, with my Granddad.

The Tsar had other children, so it seems that Percy's pupils on the ice were the Grand Duchesses Anastasia, Maria, Olga and Tatiana, and quite possibly their mother, Princess Alix of Hesse.

Nicholas abdicated after the Revolution of 1917, and he and his family were all executed by their Bolshevik guards in July 1918. By that time, however, Percy was back in England, married with children of his own. One of them was my Mum.

* * * *

At the church of St. Michael at Stone in Stafford in 1910, Percy married 27-year-old Clara Maud Jones, who liked to be called Maud. Percy and Maud took on the running of a pub, "The Swan" at Burslem in the Potteries. That was where my Mum was born.

Percy and Maud had three daughters. The first, Hollis May, was born in 1911, but sadly as with many children at that time, she died in infancy aged just two in 1913. My Mum came next, Dorothy Mary, born in June 1914, and then my Auntie, Heather Joan, in January 1919. Percy was listed on the birth certificates of all three girls as "hotel keeper".

Not that Percy had moved directly from teaching Russian aristocracy to dance on ice to running an English pub. Not a bit of it. Somewhere in between, he had played a key role as a procurer of goods for the British Army. Sometimes based in Northern Ireland, sometimes at Epsom in Surrey, Percy's main forte was securing feed for the Army's horses. It fashioned his love of horses, which was to play a sad and sorry part of his later years.

It's not clear whether Percy was a serving member of the forces, but it was an accepted fact in the family that at some point in his life he had experienced severe trauma, possibly shellshock. I remember well observing the consequence of this.

He and Grandma Maud moved to a house in Kings Heath in Birmingham in their later years, and whenever there was a thunderstorm, I saw him hurriedly take refuge from the flashes of lightning and the noise of the thunderclaps. He would hide himself away in complete darkness, in a cupboard under the stairs, with the door firmly closed.

In his old age, Percy also became extremely intolerant of any loud noise. So much so that he became very agitated, even annoyed at times, if any of his grandchildren were noisy around him, as young children inevitably were. Visits to Grandma and Granddad Swain could therefore often become fraught affairs. However, for me, it was quite different once I was able to read.

* * * *

It was in that tall, semi-detached house in Addison Road, Kings Heath, that I first read the sports news. My audience was Granddad Percy. His eyesight was failing, and he used to sit in his large leather seat in the back room, actually the middle room of the house, where he could enjoy plenty of peace and quiet. The dining room was at the front, with the kitchen and what Grandma Maud called "the scullery" at the back. Granddad would hand me his morning newspaper, the *Daily Express* as I recall, and get me to read the sports pages out loud to him. Never any other part of the 'paper, just the sport.

This was long before the *Express* and other national newspapers adopted the tabloid size. The 'paper was designed in what is called broadsheet form.

It meant that the pages were really too big for a young boy to hold fully open, so I had to fold and organise the parts he wanted to hear into a manageable size. When I had finished I then had to refold and restore the pages to their original shape, all in the correct order by page number.

My sister, Yvonne, says that it was assumed later that it was from reading the sports news to my Granddad that my interest in following all sports, and wanting to report on them, developed.

* * * *

If my Granddad took delight in having his own, personal sports reporter, my mother was less than impressed when she realised that it involved me reading to him the runners and riders of the particular horse race meetings in which he was interested. Off-track betting was illegal in those days, so armed with the information I had helped him acquire, Percy would pop off to the hairdressers who surreptitiously accepted his bets, and those of others.

The process was made easier for Percy when, to bring in extra income, he and Maud let a room in their house to a lodger. The lodger was the very same hairdresser.

Those bets, and his regular visits to Kings Heath Greyhound Stadium, just a short bus ride from his house along Alcester Road South, required the pawning of the family silver to keep Percy in funds. The consequence was that pretty well every penny of any inheritance left by his railway engineer father, along with whatever capital Percy had amassed himself in his earlier, dynamic, entrepreneurial years, disappeared into the wind thanks to a gambler's whim.

* * * *

A short distance from the Swain's previous home, the bungalow in Tessall Lane, on the other side of Bristol Road South and its exciting tram tracks, lived my Dad's Dad, my other Granddad.

Captain Charles Goodman Linnell MC, was a man wrapped up in the role he had played in the defence of the nation. As I saw him as a small child, and as I grew to know him more during my adolescence, he was my hero.

He had fought for King and country and had been decorated for his courage and bravery. He won the MC, the Military Cross, at Passchendaele. According to the citation for his MC, Charles, then a Lieutenant with the South

Lancashire Regiment, is said to have displayed bravery and courage leading his men under enemy fire during a siege at a farm at Langemark in Belgium, during the third battle of Ypres, in November 1917.

Charles playing his role in the battle against the army of Kaiser Wilhelm II offers an ironic, but utterly tenuous, connection between my two Grandfathers. The Kaiser was the cousin of Tsar Nicholas II of Russia, for whom Grandpa Percy had been a royal ice-skating tutor. Small world, though not a fact that would stop the war.

* * * * *

Unlike many of his comrades and the tens of thousands of others who laid down their lives in those foreign fields, Charles thankfully survived. He returned home to his wife Jesse, whom he had married at All Saints' Church, Edmonton, Middlesex in July 1907, and to their son Eric, my Dad, born in January 1914, almost six months to the day before the start of the First World War.

They also had a daughter, Kathleen Esther, born six years before my Dad but, as with my other grandparents, their first child died at a very young age. Kathleen passed away, aged just 4, in 1912, two years before my Dad was born.

To provide for his family, with a somewhat demanding wife, Charles became a very successful salesman, first for the telecommunications company Edison, and later for the cooking equipment company Hobart. Later still, he established himself as an accountant, looking after the books of several families and businesses. His office was above a newsagent's shop in Northfield, roughly a mile along the tram track on Bristol Road South from his home in the serviced apartment where he lived with his wife Jesse and son Eric. He also became secretary of the North Worcestershire Golf Club.

It was essential for the family, and particularly for Jesse, that their home was a serviced apartment because it meant that they had a cleaner and a handyman-cum-valet on hand to look after the place. Agnes Jesse Stevens had clearly lived a privileged life before meeting and marrying Charles, and she saw no reason to alter her lifestyle simply as a consequence of becoming a wife and mother.

I am sure that she loved her husband, but Grandma Jesse's attitude to life was summed up one Christmas by inviting Charles, for his own present, to use his Hobart employee's discount to buy one of the revolutionary new ideas in kitchen equipment, a food mixer. Granddad knew better than to argue. He may have had the beating of Kaiser Wilhelm II's men at Passchendaele, but in Jesse he had met his match.

* * * *

Granddad Charles was, as I've said, my hero. He was a man of fascinating contrasts particularly politically, or so it seemed to me as a naïve youth. He exchanged correspondence with Winston Churchill and Anthony Eden, and he was a staunch supporter of the Royal family. So far as I could tell, he had all the trappings of a true blue Tory. Yet it turned out that he voted Labour, later endorsing the leadership of the party by Harold Wilson. All that despite taking as one of his morning newspapers the *News Chronicle* which supported the Liberal party.

Just as I'd become familiar with the *Daily Express* whilst reading the sports news and racing selections to my other Granddad, I also looked forward to reading the *News Chronicle*, particularly its feature devoted to its I-Spy Club, of which I became a member. Granddad Charles also read the local morning 'paper, The *Birmingham Post*, a sister to the local *Evening Despatch* which my Dad brought home every day. The two Birmingham papers were my introduction to local media, especially their sports pages.

* * * *

Before the First World War, the teenage Charles Linnell had lied about his age so that he could serve in South Africa, during the Second Boer War. Despite his youth, he emerged as a leader. So much so that, after the hostilities, he became first the Chairman and, later, the UK national President of the South African War Veterans' Association. For that work, he was made MBE in 1961. It was quite an adventure when my Dad and I went with him to Buckingham Palace for his investiture by Her Majesty, Queen Elizabeth II.

It turned into something even more exciting because it was 3rd November 1961, the day when the Queen's sister, Princess Margaret, gave birth to her first child. There was genuine joy amongst the staff at Buckingham Palace as they passed the word around to the honours recipients and their guests that "it's a boy!". The boy was David Armstrong-Jones, who became the 2nd Earl of Snowdon.

* * * *

I had been granted a day's leave from school to attend the investiture. The three generations of Linnells travelled First Class to London by train from New Street station in Birmingham, enjoying dinner as we went. Fish, chips and peas for me, on a moving train! I was in heaven.

An overnight stay and breakfast in a small hotel near the West End were followed by a taxi ride to Buckingham Palace, to see my Granddad standing tall and proud before the Queen as she attached his medal to the lapel of his jacket. Then it was a chilly stroll in winter sunshine along the Mall with this fascinated young teenager eagerly absorbing the media coverage of the royal birth.

There were only two TV channels in those days – BBC and ITV – so just a couple of cameras were in evidence at each key point, but the focal point of my interest came outside Clarence House, where the baby had been delivered. There stood a tall, distinguished figure who, with his familiar face and strident voice, was reporting for the BBC and, as it turned out, other parts of the English-speaking world. It was the doyen of cricket commentator, Brian Johnston, applying his wide experience and jocular presence to providing news of the joyous event.

'Johnners', as he became known to listeners of the BBC's cricket coverage, was at that time also the trusted and reliable commentator on major state occasions such as the funeral of King George VI in 1952, the Coronation of Queen Elizabeth II in 1953, and the royal weddings of Princess Margaret, Princess Anne and the Prince of Wales.

Here he was in the chilly, early afternoon sunshine in London, surrounded by an admiring, delighted and respectful public, as he reported on the arrival of the latest member of the Royal family. He was being recorded, as it turned out, for viewers in Canada at the moment we passed by.

To say it was a memorable day is a vast understatement, particularly for a 14-year-old who had seen his Granddad honoured by the Queen at Buckingham Palace, and had seen one of his broadcasting heroes at work, doing the job he dreamt of doing himself.

It never entered my head at any stage that day that 34 years later I would be in the same Royal palace, watched by my wife and my sons, as I stood before the same Monarch to receive the same honour.

* * * *

My Granddad's commitment to the South African War Veterans remained undimmed over the years, but the consequence of passing time took its toll. The numbers of his men inevitably declined, so that fewer of the veterans marched and stood alongside him at such events as Armistice Day parades and services. Those who were able to became increasingly frail, so I was often called upon to carry their colour, their standard, their flag, at those ceremonial events. If I felt something of an imposter, as a wet behind-the-ears youngster who had never served, I was nonetheless immensely proud to play my small part in keeping their bravery and their memories alive.

* * * *

Elderly though they were, as many as could do so still responded to the call to muster at, for example, Chelsea Barracks, where they were inspected every year by Her Majesty, Queen Elizabeth, the Queen Mother.

It was after one such parade in London, in 1969, that a combination of fate and wintry weather achieved what his opponents in wartime had failed to do, and conspired to deal Captain Charles Linnell MBE MC a fatal blow.

Leaving the coach that had brought the old comrades back from Chelsea, Granddad Charles slipped as he stepped down onto an icy pavement in front of the Hall of Memory in Birmingham's Broad Street. He broke his leg and was taken to Selly Oak Hospital. Whilst there he contracted pneumonia, and he died in hospital a fortnight later.

* * * *

Two years before that accident, the old fellow had sprung a family surprise. He announced that after ten years as a widower, he was going to marry for the second time. He was 86.

I say a family surprise, but I think my Dad knew that there was a new lady on the scene. Nonetheless, the announcement still caused eyebrows to rise to the heavens. My Mum, a very astute woman when it came to weighing up people, was particularly sceptical. She was always very diplomatic in what she said and to whom, but she never really took to Granddad's fiancée and was always suspicious of her motives.

The romance meant that I was invited to play another role for my Grandfather. Having been drafted in as standard bearer at the ex-servicemen's parades, he now asked me to be his best man. Thankfully, for a 20-year-old playing that part for his Granddad, there was no outrageous stag night. No cheeky speeches nor bawdy recollections about the groom and his past indiscretions were called for. I simply had to stand alongside him in church then later read the congratulatory telegram messages and propose the appropriate toasts.

The wedding took place on Saturday, 8th November 1969, with the event covered by "ATV Today", the regional ITV evening news programme for the West Midlands. The following evening's edition of "ATV Today" included a filmed report of the marriage at Edgbaston of 86-year-old Captain Charles Goodman Linnell MBE, National President of the South African War Veteran's Association, to 76-year-old Mrs. Annette Bond.

* * * *

I hope Annette made him happy. I found her a touch distant and rather dismissive of my sister and me, and we were very aware of her family being present at Granddad's home whenever we went to visit. Her grandchildren were often there, and while we were encouraged to get to know them there was no enthusiasm on either side for us to do so. What I had previously regarded as a warm and comforting home for my war hero Granddad had been transformed into an altogether different, unwelcoming place that I couldn't wait to leave.

After he died, two years later, many precious possessions went with him, or rather with her. I can't be sure what occurred; I was in my early 20s and had other things on my mind, notably pursuing sport, young ladies and Friday nights out with mates at a local hostelry. However, I do know my Dad was far from pleased when various items, including an inscribed solid silver tea service, framed photographs, letters and other personal messages to Granddad from Winston Churchill, Viscount Montgomery and King George VI, were all swiftly removed from the apartment simultaneously with his second wife moving out.

If that is not enough, it was always understood that Charles had shares in a gold mine in South Africa, an investment going back to the connections he had made when serving there. When he died, my Dad could find no evidence of that.

Granddad was certainly financially astute throughout his life. He purchased Premium Bonds from the date they were launched in 1956. That despite one of the politicians he came to admire later, Labour's Harold Wilson, then Shadow Chancellor of the Exchequer, describing the scheme as "a squalid raffle". I don't know how much Granddad invested in the first place, but he won quite often and always re-invested his winnings by purchasing more bonds, accumulating the maximum number that could be held by any one individual. Ironic then, perhaps, that the lady who became his second wife had the surname Bond from her previous marriage.

So when I say my father was far from pleased, it is actually an understatement. In effect, the home and contents, of personal and monetary value, that my Dad had grown up with and could reasonably have expected to inherit, were denied to him by his father's decision to re-marry in his 80s, and by his choice of bride.

* * * *

The tale of the two Granddads was the backdrop of my early life. One saw fit to donate a family fortune to gambling on horses and greyhounds. The other lost family heirlooms, and who knows what else besides, to a late-in-life romance and a tragic twist of fate.

Smile though your heart is aching

Smile even though it's breaking

When there are clouds in the sky, you'll get by

If you smile through your fear and sorrow

Smile and maybe tomorrow

You'll see the sun come shining through for you

Light up your face with gladness

Hide every trace of sadness

Although a tear may be ever so near

That's the time you must keep on trying

Smile, what's the use of crying?

You'll find that life is still worthwhile

If you just smile

Charlie Chaplin, John Turner, Geoffrey Parsons, 1954

© Bourne Co.

My Granddad knew Rasputin ... and I met Elton John

Chapter Three

Boomers

With His blessings from above
Serve it generously with love
One man, one wife, one love through life
Memories are made of this

Frank Miller / Richard Dehr / Terry Gilkyson, 1955
© Sony/ATV Music Publishing LLC, BMG Rights Management, Spirit Music
Group

When I was five years old Mum, Dad and I moved to a new house.

Still on Birmingham's border with Worcestershire, we swapped Northfield and its proximity to Bromsgrove, for the Maypole area of Kings Heath, close to Wythall, with Solihull just down the road.

32 Maypole Lane was a step up for my parents. A semi-detached house with three bedrooms and its own garage. It also had a very long back garden which played a significant role in the start of my love affair with radio.

The garden was laid out in two more or less equal halves. Nearest to the house was a fairly large lawn, with flower borders on either side and a round flower bed set in the middle of the lawn, towards its far end. A banked rockery acted as the halfway mark, and beyond that a vegetable garden allowed my Dad to proudly produce excellent potatoes, peas, beans, carrots, cabbages and rhubarb. Lots of rhubarb.

There was also a substantial apple tree, which delivered cooking apples for my Mum to include in her delicious apple pies, apple and raspberry tarts, apple crumbles, and the like. The rhubarb was tasty too.

All of that may sound like "Good Life" self-sufficiency, as in the TV comedy series. It wasn't quite like that, but we had a steady flow of healthy fruit and veg.

Apart from the apple tree's bountiful harvest, it served another purpose which I regarded as much more important. When I was seven or eight, my Dad bought me my very first radio set, a crystal set, so named because its most important component was a crystal detector. It required no external power, no mains electricity nor a battery. The signal received by the crystal detector produced the sound. The consequence was that the sound was not amplified so to hear it you had to wear headphones, but that was part of the fun.

Many crystal set owners will tell you that they built their own set, usually sold as a kit to be assembled by the user. I will confess that I didn't assemble mine. It came ready-made in a box. All I had to do was put on the headphones and turn the dial. That said, the secret to good crystal set reception is the length of the aerial plugged into the back of it. Another lesson learned that, in some instances at least, size can be important.

Dad rigged a blue, plastic-coated wire stretching from my bedroom window at the back of the house to the apple tree, some 75 to 100 feet away. Through that wire, via the crystal detector in its small plastic case, I listened through my headphones to news, sport, music, comedy and drama, supplied mainly by the BBC. What truly excited me was hearing the very different programming provided by the irritatingly fragile signal of Radio Luxembourg. There were other stations too, often broadcasting in languages I loved to listen to but couldn't understand.

It was such a thrill to hear the eclectic sounds of a world beyond the confines of my tiny Birmingham bedroom. If I said that, as a consequence, I instantly knew I wanted to be a broadcaster I would be lying, but I am certain that from the moment I lay beneath my bed sheets with magic filling my ears, I was hooked on the brilliant medium of radio.

* * * *

Before the world of wireless entered my life there was another, more tangible arrival. On 10th October 1952, Yvonne Mary Linnell turned up. My sister.

To say it was an unusual night is putting it mildly, particularly for a curious, and slightly bewildered five-year-old. My mother had opted for home confinement, so the midwife and another nurse moved in that evening to orchestrate what was to follow. The family doctor was also present. Admittedly his surgery was an annexe of his home, no more than two or three hundred yards up the road, but it was well after hours when our house went into full surgical mode.

To remove me from the gynaecological chaos, my father had put me to bed. However, Dad was apparently proving to be an otherwise utterly useless nuisance. The midwife helpfully suggested that he should find something to occupy his time whilst waiting to greet his new offspring. He decided to clean the goldfish tank.

Some twenty minutes or so later, a family friend popped in just in the nick of time. Dad, having started the process of emptying water from the tank, had wandered into the garden for a cigarette. The visitor was heard calling his name quite urgently.

"Eric! Eric! Your fish tank has no water in it and the fish are gasping for breath!"

There followed the sheer pandemonium of refilling the tank and rescuing the fish. That was played out to a soundtrack of my mother's raised cries and what sounded to me like inexplicably odd instructions from the medical team attending her in the bedroom next to mine. Unsurprisingly, I found it impossible to sleep.

I am pleased to report, by the way, that no goldfish were harmed in the birth of my sister.

* * * *

Once she was born, had met her Mum and Dad and had been washed and made presentable, Yvonne was wrapped in a pink blanket and brought in to meet me, cradled in the arms of the midwife. The baby, barely half an hour old, was gently placed alongside me as I lay bleary-eyed with my head on the pillow. The midwife said, "Stuart, this is your sister."

Ah, I thought, so this is what all the fuss was about.

Over the years my sister and I have not always seen eye to eye. Like many siblings, we have fallen out from time to time, but at that moment I loved her as much as I have ever loved anyone or anything.

* * * *

So, we were now a family of four, and 32 Maypole Lane, Birmingham was to be our home for the next thirty years. Yvonne and I grew up there. From there, we went to school and enjoyed life in a house that, as time went by, was filled with many happy memories and family occasions.

Our parents became worshippers at the nearby Immanuel Church at Highters Heath, where both Yvonne and I attended Sunday Schools. Whilst she joined the Brownies and later the Girl Guides, I became a chorister and altar server. In time I became head choirboy. Yvonne and I were both confirmed at Immanuel Church by the Bishop of Birmingham, and we made good friends amongst the congregation both as a family and as individuals.

* * * *

My cousin Stephen, who is seven months younger than me, often came to stay with us at Maypole Lane, together with his Mum, our Mum's sister, Auntie Heather. Not surprisingly as young boys, Steve and I had similar interests, football being one. Playing as cowboys, mimicking the popular TV shows of the day, was another. Whatever we did, we were required by our mothers to involve my sister.

We took our responsibilities towards the baby seriously, but we are still regularly reminded at family events of the time we went to the nearby spacious and rarely busy local pub car park to play football. We had to take Yvonne with us, tucked up in her pram for her morning nap.

Yes, seven-year-olds going out by themselves, with a baby in a pram. Such was the way of the world in the early 1950s.

It was just as well that it was like that. When we arrived back for lunch, sweaty and breathless from our game, the cry went up "Where's your sister?".

Stephen and I had forgotten all about her as she slept and we had left her behind. We raced back up to the pub car park, to find her safe and sound, her pram not having moved let alone having been investigated by anyone else.

She continued to be a presence in our playtime. A year or so later, playing in the back garden dressed as cowboys, we quickly resolved what to do with the toddler who was sent out to join in. Naturally, Yvonne was cast as the "baddie", taken prisoner and tied to the apple tree. That lasted less than five minutes, by which time she had worked out that her role in proceedings was not going to be terribly active. Her cries for freedom resulted in her parental rescue and a stern telling off for Steve and me.

* * * *

There were many happy times in that house, for Yvonne as well I should add. Sunday lunchtime was always something to look forward to. Mum's roast dinners were an essential part of Sunday, with chicken an occasional and special treat, unlike the regular event that it was to become.

If there were no guests we were allowed, while we ate, to listen to the wireless. We had a bakelite Marconi radio, in a cream case with a red carry handle, and red volume and tuning knobs. It sat neatly on the mantlepiece in the front room, where we also had the dining table and an upright piano.

Our Sunday was accompanied by the lunchtime variety show of the moment from the BBC Light Programme. We chuckled and often laughed out loud to the likes of "Round The Horne", "Beyond Our Ken", "The Clitheroe Kid", "Take It From Here", "Life With The Lyons", "The Billy Cotton Band Show", and my particular favourite "The Navy Lark", which starred Jon Pertwee, Ronnie Barker and Leslie Phillips.

When visitors came for Sunday lunch, however, the proceedings were quite different. The radio was silent, we were encouraged to join in the conversation, and lunch was often followed by our own musical entertainment. Yvonne or I performed rather inadequately whatever piece we were attempting to learn at piano classes. Sometimes my Dad sat at the piano stool, pumping pedals with his feet to allow a roll, punctured with tiny holes, to revolve in front of him as the piano played the tune without him touching the keys.

The instrument was a pianola, an automatic piano player, rather than just a piano, allowing great fun to be had by all. Some evenings I would sit, with the front room curtains open, apparently playing brilliantly as people walked by, hopefully impressed by my precocious talent. In fact, the music was actually created by the pianola rolls.

Neighbours and other passers-by turned their heads to look through the window to observe the burgeoning keyboard prodigy. Little did they know that, like the proverbial swan, my feet were paddling like mad, whilst my innocent childhood visage appeared enraptured in making beautiful music.

I did learn to play the piano properly but, to my huge regret, I allowed that to lapse. I can still pick out a tune if I put my mind to it, and it is a passion with which I am trying to renew my acquaintance in later life.

Those pianola rolls did not carry the latest, most popular music. They were of a distinct and distant vintage. So it was the good old radio to which we regularly turned to enjoy my Granny Maud's favourite, Perry Como.

"He was a barber, you know", Granny Maud would remind us when we heard Como's relaxed and casual crooning. We were also treated to the likes of Frankie Laine, Guy Mitchell, David Whitfield, Ruby Murray, Frank Sinatra and Dean Martin, often on the Sunday record requests show "Two-Way Family Favourites" broadcast on the BBC Light Programme.

Dean Martin's 1955 hit "Memories Are Made Of This" was one song my Dad often whistled around the house. It was a happy house. With music, the wireless and Mum's traditional Sunday lunch at its heart, it couldn't fail to be.

* * * *

Listening to the radio, and especially to music programmes, was a major influence in my life from my earliest days. Later I would hear fellow practitioners preach the significance of radio as the ultimate one-to-one medium, with the intimacy between broadcaster and listener high on the list of its qualities. That is a truism that I would never challenge, but I do not claim to be special or clever in regarding it as blooming obvious. I think I subconsciously absorbed and acknowledged that intimacy as a fact of life as I grew up with radio.

The wireless was as essential a part of everyday life in the 40s, 50s and 60s as mobile and wi-fi devices became in the 21st century. In my bedroom, as soon as I had my own record player, I became a broadcaster, even though my audience was only anyone within earshot elsewhere in the house. My sister would write out and post record requests under my bedroom door. She was not able to specify the record she wanted me to play as I was clearly limited to the extent of my personal record library, but it was the start of my journey as a presenter, and I whiled away many a happy hour in my own wireless world.

One of the programmes that became a particular favourite was "Two-Way Family Favourites", broadcast every Sunday morning. The notion of a show that united listeners in various parts of the world was particularly exciting. The fact that it focused on service men and women and their families, in the aftermath of the Second World War, made it even more so.

"Family Favourites" had several different presenters over the years, and in 1957 their ranks were joined by a former BBC staff producer turned announcer called Bill Crozier. When I first heard his voice I was ten years old. Seventeen years later, at Radio Hallam in Sheffield, I was beyond thrilled to realise that I was employed by the same radio station as Bill Crozier.

* * * *

My Mum – Dorothy Mary Linnell – was the strong one in my parent's marriage. Once I was born she stopped going out to work and focused on keeping a beautiful home and bringing up her children.

She became popular in the area by running a catalogue from a company that offered a whole range of items, from children's toys to adult fashion. Mum took orders from family, friends and neighbours, earning a commission from each completed order. In many ways, it was the forerunner of online sales, with our house the equivalent of the store you go to today for click and collect.

Mum also, literally, earned "pin money". The term originates from the 17th century, when a man gave his wife an allowance for dress and other personal expenses, which often included a clasp, or pin, to hold her hair in place or to attach a brooch to her dress. Mum came across a company that made and marketed hair grips.

They needed people to attach the grips, or pins, to the cards on which they were sold. Many an evening would see the four of us, Mum, Dad, Yvonne and me, slotting the grips onto the cards and packing them in boxes, which were then sent back to the company. I don't know how much Mum was paid for this, but I hope it was worth the endless nights we spent doing it whilst listening to the radio.

* * * *

When it came to holidays Mum did all the planning and made the arrangements. Amongst favourite places to go were Tenby and nearby Saundersfoot in Wales, and also the Isle of Wight. One sultry summer we spent ten days in Norfolk, near the Royal estate at Sandringham. A second cousin of my Mum's, Auntie Marjorie, ran the Post Office there with her husband Alan. Our holiday home was a caravan at a beautiful site near Sandringham village. I don't remember any Royal sightings, but that holiday lives long in the memory because during our stay Auntie Marjorie taught me to ride a bike.

I can therefore say, with absolute honesty, that I learned to ride a bike at the Queen's estate at Sandringham.

* * * *

In those post-war years, there was no debate about loyalty and support for the Royal Family. They were widely loved and respected, and in my teens, we went four or five years in a row to the Isle of Wight, always during Cowes Week, so that we could see if we could spot any of the Royals. Each time we stayed in bed and breakfast accommodation with the same family in Cowes. The elder daughter, a year or two older than me, did not have a boyfriend, which suited me fine. We spent a lot of time together.

Holidaying at Cowes was a delight in many ways. They were the heady days of the big transatlantic luxury liners that rounded the Isle of Wight to enter The Solent, as they sailed in and out of Southampton, returning from or en route to New York. I loved sitting on the front at Cowes with Yvonne, my Mum and Dad, and Granddad Charles, as we watched craft of many different shapes and sizes move majestically across the water. My Dad made regular checks of the sailing times of the big ships so that we were in position to see them come and go.

Even on holiday, my Granddad would dress in a collar and tie and a three-piece suit. He would position himself on a deckchair on the grassy promenade of Cowes seafront, with his morning newspaper. Between snoozes he would read his paper, carefully managing to open and fold the broad sheet-sized pages despite any breeze that might be blowing. Even when his eyes closed and you thought that he had drifted off for yet another nap, he would usually be the first to spot the notable ships passing along through the ever-changing nautical panorama.

Alongside the commercial vessels, Royal Navy ships would manoeuvre their way to and from Portsmouth. The Isle of Wight ferry would mingle with the yachts and other craft, some of which were engaged in sporting pursuits.

A few times each week there they would be, gliding in front of us, the giant ocean-going superstars. The SS France, the SS United States, the RMS Queen Mary, or most exciting of all, the RMS Queen Elizabeth, attracted huge attention from the Linnell family and the hundreds of others who were waiting to see them pass by.

From the beach, everyone would wave and cheer, not that anyone on board the liners could hear us. Mum would sit in her deckchair next to my Granddad, knitting a scarf or a jumper, occasionally joining in as we whooped, hollered, and waved till our arms felt ready to fall off. Such was the excitement created by those beautiful ships.

* * * *

I loved my Mum hugely. She was always on my case but in a good way. I know that she fretted over whether or not I was doing well at school, but she would only comment about things like my handwriting and the way I held my pen. We had to use a fountain pen at school, and Mum was firmly of the view that you should have a piece of blotting paper under your hand as you used the pen. I am sure it made absolutely no difference to the neatness of my work, but she insisted on it.

There was just one thing that made me cross with her. Occasionally, very occasionally, she would smoke a cigarette. It was usually on a Saturday night whilst watching television. You may consider that that is nothing to be upset about, but my Dad smoked heavily all his life and I hated it.

I hated the smell, the dirty ashtray, and the way the odour of second-hand smoke hung around his clothes. When he shaved first thing in the morning, he carried a fresh, healthy aroma, but that was soon spoiled when he lit the first cigarette of the day. So when my Mum, who would not normally smoke at all, decided every now and then that she would have one too, I used to leave the room. I just found it horrid.

I have never smoked, and I honestly do not understand why anyone would. To me the whole process, and the associated expense, is mind-numbingly pointless, the damage to your health rendering it an utter nonsense so far as I am concerned.

* * * *

It was from 32 Maypole Lane that I went to school. First to KHHS, or to give it its full title, Kings Heath High School for Girls, Preparatory School for Boys. My sister also went there when her turn came.

I was six years of age when I started school, wearing my KHHS gold and brown uniform, complete with short trousers, long socks and a very smart cap. The school was run by Major E.A. Dean-Davis and his wife, who lived in a big house on Alcester Road, Kings Heath in Birmingham. The school buildings stood on its grounds.

Why my parents decided on a fee-paying school for Yvonne and me, I don't know. It was not something I remember ever being discussed. They presumably believed it would provide us with a good start, and it certainly did that, but it also enabled Mum and Dad to live up to the perception of a middle-class lifestyle, even though their income fell somewhat short of that reality. Paying for their children to enjoy what they regarded as a better education than we would otherwise experience underpinned that. It was also a genuine statement of their determination to ensure we both had what they thought were the best opportunities for our futures.

It was at KHHS that I was encouraged to enjoy reading and writing, and in particular to embrace the beauty of the English language. I was not overly conscious of being more accomplished than anyone else, but my essays and compositions were read out loud to the class more often than those of most of my fellow pupils.

Maths however, or arithmetic as it was referred to, was something else. It is entirely due to the patience, forbearance and determination of my class teacher Mrs. Plant that the basic rudiments of addition, multiplication, division, and subtraction were embedded in my otherwise arithmetically adverse brain. I have no doubt that her perseverance played a huge part in ensuring that I went on to pass the eleven-plus.

Mrs. Plant, and the head teacher Mrs. Pearsall, also persuaded me, finicky child that I was, that I had nothing to fear from a cottage pie. I was shown that the beef that was minced in the school kitchen was just the same as the piece of meat which might be served up as part of Mum's Sunday lunch. They even allowed me to turn the handle of the mincer as cook prepared the food.

* * * *

KHHS also introduced me to sport, and specifically to cricket, the most wonderful game ever invented.

We were coached by a delightful man, Derief Taylor. He was born in Kingston, Jamaica, and had served with the British Eighth Army in the North African campaign in the Second World War. It was there that he met the Warwickshire batsman Tom Dollery who introduced him to Edgbaston and to life in England as a professional cricketer.

After his playing days, Derief became a coach for Warwickshire's youngsters. He was described as "probably the best coach of the under-18 age group in the country", with "an infinite capacity to understand the adolescent mind". Thankfully he extended what was said to be his unlimited patience with young players to the pupils of KHHS. Once a week he would devote an afternoon to coaching us in the basics of batting, bowling and fielding. More important than any of that, he endowed us with a love of the game.

Kings Heath Cricket Club was located immediately behind the school. Its facilities, and the patience of a wonderful coach, enabled a group of very young boys to develop a life-long devotion to the game.

Derief Taylor's son is Lord Taylor of Warwick, who was caught up in the Parliamentary expenses scandal in 2010. John Taylor studied English Literature and Law at Keele University and was called to the bar in 1978. He was made a life peer as Baron Taylor of Warwick in 1996. I will always be grateful for the generosity and encouragement that I, and my fellow pupils at KHHS, received from his father.

* * * *

My Dad played a huge part in fostering my love of sport. After leaving the army he worked for the Sun Life Assurance Society, guiding companies through the process of setting up pension schemes for the bosses and their employees. At weekends and on some evenings, however, depending on the relevant season, he was a rugby union referee or a cricket umpire.

Like many rugby union match officials in those days, he used his army rank whenever he was named as referee on a team sheet. It would read "Captain E. H. G. Linnell", the initials drawn from his full name of Eric Henry Goodman Linnell, and he was shown due respect, as has always been the case with rugby, with players calling him "sir" on the pitch in response to his decisions.

He refereed at regional and local level, sometimes at The Reddings, the then-home of Moseley Rugby Club. He never officiated at a Moseley first fifteen match, nor for any fixture of that status, but he took charge of many matches involving second teams and junior sides. He would often take me with him to sit and watch, leaving me full of questions afterwards, particularly about decisions he'd made.

"Why did you do that?", "What had that player done wrong?", and so on. One summer evening, after he'd umpired a particularly lively cricket match, during which some of his decisions had not been met favourably by either of the competing teams, he answered my questions by saying simply, "I can only give what I can see."

Perfect answer, even if some of those decisions did not always seem to be quite so perfect. I have always been sympathetic to the role of the match official who, as Dad told me, can only rule on the view that he has of any particular incident, and has to make an instant decision.

* * * *

In my school holidays, Dad also took me on some of his business trips. I loved sitting in the front passenger seat of the car alongside him, gazing out at the passing Midlands countryside. There were no seatbelts then. No motorways either, with plenty of green fields to look out on where houses have since been built.

Dad owned a series of cars during my childhood days, all of them Ford. He owned variously a Ford Consul, a Ford Cortina, and a Ford Anglia with the famous backward-slanted rear window. That was an American idea designed so that the rear window would remain clear in the rain. I am not sure if it worked, but the post-1960 Anglia was very popular.

Before the introduction of the flashing amber, red or white indicator lights located on the corners and often on the side of a car, to let other road users know you are about to turn left or right, vehicles had things called trafficators. They were amber-coloured arms, shaped like arrows, which emerged from the door pillars on either side of the car depending on which way you intended to turn.

One of the regular defects of the trafficators is that they got stuck, and you had to bang on the inside of the car to dislodge them. I am not sure which of Dad's cars had them, but the trafficator would regularly refuse to work properly, so I claimed the right to be the one who would hit the inside pillar of the car "to make the arm come out."

On those business trips with my Dad, I would wait in the car, often reading a comic like *The Beano*, *The Dandy*, or my big favourite *The Tiger*, which included the stories of *Roy Of The Rovers*. That weekly comic strip featured the exploits of fictional footballer Roy Race, who played for Melchester Rovers. The stories were poured over avidly whilst Dad went into the offices of whatever business he was visiting that day to secure another deal, or to resolve issues that had arisen since his last visit.

A regular port of call was Bromsgrove in Worcestershire where, instead of waiting in the car, I was allowed to sit on the platform of Bromsgrove station, the original station, which was to the North of the one that would replace it in 2016. I took my books of railway engine numbers and, like any good train spotter, carefully recorded those that stopped or went through the station. I was eight years of age, and before anyone concludes that my father was irresponsible to leave me there, bear in mind that this was the 1950s when the world was, in many ways, a more innocent place. He also ensured, by the way, that the station staff knew I was there and that he would be returning before too long. Yes, they had station staff then too!

Identifying the locomotives and their rolling stock was only part of the fascination at Bromsgrove. The real joy it offered was its location, at the foot of the two-mile Lickey Incline, with its gradient of 1-in-37.7. In other words, very steep.

It meant that ordinary trains ascending the incline, on their way up to Snow Hill station in Birmingham, needed extra power for the climb. Enter "Big Bertha", more accurately termed steam locomotive number 2290.

She was a beast of a railway engine, specifically designed for what were described as "banking duties". That meant she was attached to the rear of the train and pushed it up the hill, reinforcing the work of the normal engine which was pulling at the front. She also went on the front of some trains coming down the hill in the other direction, to act as a brake lest it gathered too much speed.

I felt real grief when Big Bertha was decommissioned in May 1956, and even more so when I learned that she was scrapped the following year. I was ten years of age then and I really failed to understand why such a giant machine had not been placed in a museum, or some similar facility, for the likes of me to continue to enthuse over her immense power. She was by no means a pretty machine, but her wholly functional appearance embodied what she was built to do. Sadly, she was disposed of once she reached the end of her useful life.

* * * *

From KHSS I passed the eleven-plus exam, and my next port of call was King's Norton Grammar School for Boys, KNGS.

I swapped the brown and gold of KHHS for a two-tone blue. the KNGS school tie having alternate stripes of sky blue and navy blue, and I was thrust for the first time into a boys-only environment. We had a Latin motto, Humani Semper Contendimus, which translates as 'we humans are always striving', and a school song, "To Be a Pilgrim", often referred to as "He Who Would Valiant Be", written by John Bunyan as part of 'The Pilgrim's Progress' in 1684.

All of the school's six hundred pupils were allocated membership of houses that competed for points across the school year. The house points were assigned based on academic, sporting and social achievements to individual pupils, and then accumulated into a grand total for each of the five houses. The houses were called Greves, Jervoise, Lyttleton, Middlemore and Mortimer, all named after distinguished local families. I was in Middlemore.

Whilst the award of house points across the term was only of partial interest, there was significant enthusiasm as the end of the academic year approached to see which house was leading the race to be the year's overall winner. The announcement and subsequent presentation of a trophy to the captain of the victorious house was a high point of each year's closing assembly.

* * * *

Amongst the school's former pupils, some well before my time, some after, are a few distinguished and famous names. Amongst them was the aeronautical engineer Harold Roxbee Cox, who became Lord Kings Norton. Others included the George Cross and George Medal holder Arthur Bywater, the radio TV and film scriptwriter Edward J. Mason, the MP Enoch Powell, and former Arsenal and England footballer Alan Smith. The broadcaster Adrian Goldberg, who would later become a colleague and acquaintance of mine at the BBC, is also listed amongst the school's alumni.

* * * *

King's Norton Grammar School for Girls was just around the corner from the boys' school, but far enough away to prevent any close encounters between pupils of the two establishments. During normal school hours anyway.

That did not prevent romantic liaisons, mind you. In the third year, for example, I fell hopelessly in love with Helen Golby. On the upper deck of the bus going to school each morning, I would pass her notes that included song lyrics of the day, such as Adam Faith's "How About That", "Do You Mind?" by Anthony Newley, or Gary Mills' "Look For A Star". She would read them before she and her classmates dissolved into a fit of giggles.

Helen always struck me as being slightly more sophisticated than her friends, and her giggling would end long before theirs. At that point, she would ask me if I had bought the record, or if I knew of any more songs by the pop star in question. Her apparent interest in my musical tastes inspired me to further lyrical endorsements of my affection.

It was not a romance that was destined to last, just an innocent adolescent liaison in those early teenage years.

* * * *

From the age of 14, I often rode my bike to school, a journey of just over three miles. Nothing to speak of in terms of distance really, but I doubt I would be as keen to venture on two wheels into the traffic of today as I was in 1961.

Part of the journey was vaguely rural, but the tough bit was negotiating the steep Parson's Hill. I say "steep" because it certainly offered a challenge, first to maintain control of your bike as it rapidly gained speed on the way down when going to school in the morning, but also to a schoolboy attempting to cycle up it on his way home in the afternoon.

* * * *

My academic achievements at KNGS were pretty insignificant. I excelled at English Language and English Literature, the latter leading me in the third year to a part in the school play.

It was Shakespeare's "Twelfth Night" and I had auditioned for the minor role of Curio, who has few lines but appears on stage at the start of the play. After Duke Orsino's opening monologue, "Let music be the food of love…", Curio asks "Will you go hunt my Lord?".

Orsino's reply "What Curio?" allows Curio to supply the punchline "The Hart", a Shakespearean joke that sets up the romantic ambiguity of the action that follows.

Despite the role of Curio being the height of my ambition the teacher producing the play, having heard my audition, asked me instead to read another much bigger part. To the delight and hilarity of my friends and classmates, I was cast as Lady Olivia, one of the play's main characters.

In contrast to the taunts of my school friends, my parents were both very proud as they sat in the audience in the school hall on the last of the three nights to hear me say:

"I will give out divers schedules of my beauty: it shall be inventoried, and every particle and utensil labelled to my will: as, item, two lips, indifferent red; item, two grey eyes, with lids to them; item, one neck, one chin, and so forth. Were you sent hither to praise me?"

Well, my parents praised me, as might be expected, and my teachers also took delight in my performance allowing me to accumulate a significant number of house points. However, I was not allowed to forget that 'inventory' for quite a few weeks, each time that unforgiving class of schoolboys assembled for lessons.

* * * *

Show business and local celebrity butted into life in those days in the King's Norton area. King's Norton runs almost seamlessly into the neighbouring district of Cotteridge, and it was there that a local celebrity had his day job. Singer Roy Edwards ran a TV repair shop in Cotteridge, and his wife had a hairdressing salon nearby, but most weekday lunchtimes Roy would be on television. He would be at the ITV studios in Birmingham appearing on a Midlands regional lunchtime show, called "Lunch Box".

Hosted by actress and singer Noele Gordon, the show would feature music by the Jerry Allen Trio, with vocals from Roy Edwards, and often by Noele herself. Before "Lunch Box" Noele, who had appeared in minor acting roles in a couple of films, had been a senior member of the production and management team at the Midlands TV company ATV, but became a star when she hosted a show intended to be no more than a filler in the afternoon schedules.

Called "Tea With Noele Gordon", it was the first popular ITV chat show, and Noele made history as the first woman to interview a British Prime Minister, Harold Macmillan. "Lunch Box" followed, and then Noele was cast in the starring role of Meg Mortimer in the soap opera "Crossroads". Amongst her close friends was the Nuneaton-born comedian and TV star Larry Grayson, who I would get to know many years later.

So it was in Cotteridge that one or two of us would hang out at lunchtime and after school. We were sometimes rewarded with the opportunity to have a brief chat with Roy Edwards and, occasionally, with one or two of his showbiz friends.

We were a diverse bunch at KNGS.

* * * *

Cotteridge was also the home of the Kings Norton Fire Station. It was an imposing building with three, large, bright red doors at the front. They opened out onto the Pershore Road to allow the fire engines, or fire appliances as they are now more appropriately called, to enter and exit the building.

The fire station's foundation stone bears the date 8th July 1929, the building being completed the following year. Behind the façade, a circular courtyard was surrounded by a block of offices and apartments, the latter being the homes of many of the fire officers. In one of those apartments lived one of my classmates, David, and his family.

Very occasionally a few of us would go there after school, all hoping that we would hear the bells and alarms that meant that one of the appliances had been called out so that we would then witness the drama and excitement of that moment.

We took our favourite records to play when we got together. I had started to amass a significant record collection by this time, and it was not solely chart hit singles and albums. I also acquired EPs and LPs illustrating the comic genius of Peter Sellers, Bob Newhart, Tom Lehrer, Victor Borge, Gerard Hoffnung and the surreal group the Bonzo Dog Doo Dah Band, who combined trad jazz with their comedy.

All appealed to my sense of humour, but it was Bob Newhart's monologue "The Driving Instructor" that I developed into my own party piece. Eight minutes long, and recorded live, Newhart recounts the story of how the eponymous driving instructor tries to teach 'Mrs. Webb'.

I listened to it so often I could recite it off by heart in a reasonably passable American accent. One afternoon I was persuaded to deliver it during one of our get-togethers at David's home at the fire station at Cotteridge. Instead of playing the record, I performed my own interpretation of the monologue, not realising that David's parents were listening in the next room. My face turned the brightest crimson when they emerged, leading the applause when I finished.

* * * *

In my first two or three years at KNGS, I often travelled on the bus to and from school with fellow pupil Brian Clarke, who lived around the corner from our house in Maypole Lane. Brian's Dad ran a cinema next door to St. Andrew's, the home ground of Birmingham City football club. We shared a love of sport, particularly cricket, and became good friends. Brian came on holiday with our family a few times. Later, at the end of our schooldays, my Dad arranged for Brian to have an interview at Sun Life, which led to him getting a job there.

Another KNGS pupil, Michael Baylis, also lived nearby. His uncle was Sir Stanley Rous, who was President of FIFA from 1961 to 1974, during which time England secured the famous 1966 World Cup victory at Wembley. Sir Stanley had previously been Secretary of the Football Association and, before that, an international referee. Michael went on to be the founder of the Baylis car dealership in Gloucestershire.

We all referred to each other by using our surnames, and others who figured in my schooldays in Kings Norton were Bache, Baker, Harris, Parker, Parkes, Lyne, March and Paddy Worth. Paddy surprised us all when our school days neared their conclusion by revealing that he wanted to be a chef, several decades before that became an occupation made glamorous and popular by the likes of Jamie Oliver and Gordon Ramsay.

An illustration of just how widely diverse we were was illustrated in a post made to a former pupils' online forum by one of my classmates, Ernie Barnhurst, who I remember shared my love of the pop hits of the day.

Ernie's post said:

"I was at the school between 1957 and 1965. I lived on a council estate in West Heath and joined the school in the days of the 11-plus.

"As a working class boy I found it difficult to fit in with the 'academic' culture of the school and participated in the delinquescent subculture, resisting the inculcation of middle-class mores. I believe I hold the school record for the longest detention. Of course, it was never fully served as no member of staff was willing to give up a complete Saturday to supervise it.

"I did however participate more fully in the extrinsic culture of the school, participating in house and school sports teams and school drama productions. I was also a vocalist in the college-based pop group 'The Orpheans'.

"I was gradually relegated to lower-level forms, year by year, but I must have learnt something, as I ended up with a hatful of O levels, far exceeding expectations, and entered the sixth form where, after gaining entry to Teacher Training, I'm sorry to say I decided to give up studying after the first year of A levels.

"Following school, I attended West Midlands College of Education, became a primary teacher for a few years, and did a year as an Educational Broadcaster for BBC Radio Bristol. Then, on the strength of gaining an Open University degree, became a sociology and education lecturer in a Bristol FE college.

"Since then I have been a senior manager in Further Education and Associate Lecturer for the Open University."

By no means does Ernie's experience precisely match with mine, but I can identify aspects of how his post reflected life at KNGS.

* * * *

Yes, we were quite a diverse bunch, brought together at the start of each school day in Assembly. The whole school gathered in the main school hall for a brief religious service, rooted in Anglican Christianity. We heard a bible passage, usually read by a sixth former, said a few prayers and sang at least one hymn, sometimes two.

From there we went to our classrooms where our form teacher took the register. All of that brought us to around nine-thirty in the morning when our lessons started. We would wander the school corridors in search of the relevant subject classroom, some wandering with greater haste and enthusiasm than others.

That brought us into contact with the various characters on the teaching staff. Mr. Braithwaite was, for his sins, my form teacher for three years. He also tried, in vain I regret to say, to teach me French. Oui, je le regrette.

I got on well with Mr. Braithwaite, possibly because he often umpired our house cricket matches. He encouraged my batting during a match with muttered comments of praise and constructive criticism. Whether or not he should have done so as a supposedly impartial match official was another matter. He no doubt did the same for others.

* * * *

Looming large amongst the KNGS teaching staff was Mr. Mapp, an effusive Welshman who taught English. He always wore a black academic gown, as did some of the other teachers, but it was easy to believe that Mr Mapp wore his gown at home, to the shops, to the theatre, everywhere! It appeared attached to him like the cape of a superhero or villain, depending on your perspective.

He always carried a black carbon rod. Twelve inches long, but with no markings of feet and inches, millimetres or anything of the sort. It was, simply, a twelve-inch long, black, round rod.

If he thought you were not concentrating, or worse still, dozing off, Mr Mapp would smack the black rod down, sharply and extremely loudly, on your desk, making the furniture shake. No one slept in one of Mr. Mapp's lessons.

The rod came into its own on one specific occasion when a boy, quite innocently, asked if it was a ruler.

The rod crashed onto the teacher's desk at the front of the classroom with unparalleled force. The collision of carbon road and the sturdy ancient wooden desk was so loud it made the classroom windows vibrate in their equally elderly frames.

"Ruler?" came the retort, the initial 'r' rolled vociferously, his voice rising to a crescendo from his natural basso profundo. The Welsh accent became more pronounced with each increasing decibel.

"Ruler?" he repeated. This time it seemed the 'r' might never stop rolling.

"This, boy, is a rule," he declared to the by now extremely red-faced unfortunate. "The 'ruler' lives in Buckingham Palace."

No one dared challenge the democratic weakness of the statement. In fact, it probably never occurred to any of us that we should. The point was made and never forgotten.

* * * *

KNGS was a football, rather than a rugby, school, which was a disappointment to my rugby referee Dad. He had attended King Edward's School, across the city in Edgbaston, and had wanted me to follow suit. To do so, however, I had to pass an entrance exam. Despite my eleven-plus success, I failed the King Edward's exam which I'm sure upset my Dad far more than he allowed me to see.

A few years later my sister made up for it by going one better, passing the entrance exam and going to King Edward VI High School for Girls which, although sharing the same site in Edgbaston as the boy's school, is managed separately. In those days though, rugby was not on the curriculum for girls, so my dad's dream of seeing his child play for his old school was not realised by either of us.

* * * *

A notable, regular feature of the playing fields that sat immediately behind the KNGS school buildings, was the smell. Chocolate. Cadbury's factory at Bournville was little more than a mile away, and when the wind was in the right direction the rich aroma of the company's product filled the air.

In 1878 the Cadbury brothers, Richard and George, sons of one of the company's founders, had acquired the Bournbrook estate in the countryside, 5 miles south of the outskirts of Birmingham. A newly established railway line and a canal ran alongside the land where George Cadbury built, at his own expense, a model village to provide homes for his employees.

It was designed to 'alleviate the evils of modern more cramped living conditions'. By 1900 the estate included 314 cottages and houses. The Cadbury family were Quakers, so there were no pubs on the estate which they renamed Bournville.

Part of the facilities provided for the workforce was an open-air swimming pool, Bournville Lido. It was located at one edge of the KNGS school playing fields, on the other side of a perimeter fence. A few times a year our PE lessons took the form of swimming lessons at the lido. Both the Boys and the Girls Schools' Swimming Galas were held there.

The lido was eventually closed in the 1970s after complaints of noise disturbance were made by residents of the newly built Oak Farm housing estate. Those complaints, coupled with new and stringent health and safety regulations applying to outdoor public swimming facilities, were enough for its demise.

The proximity of Cadbury's to the school also meant that at least once in your time at the school were the joys of a tour of the chocolate factory. No Willy Wonka, but chocolate galore. I went twice, though I am not sure why.

Ostensibly we were there to learn about the production process, the harvesting of the cacao tree seeds, processing cocoa, and so on. The bit we were all more interested in was the distribution of free samples at the end of the tour, packaged in metal tins branded by Cadbury's. The tins transformed within a few weeks into pencil cases for most of us, once the chocolate had been consumed of course.

The combination of the lido and the pervading aroma of chocolate provided lasting memories, thanks to the 19th-century entrepreneurial skills and philanthropy of the Cadbury brothers.

* * * *

Although I would never claim any great ability as a footballer, I was a regular member of the KNGS second eleven, playing either on the right wing, at centre back or right back, or occasionally in goal.

Second team trips to away matches at other schools saw talents other than those of football emerge as the team congregated at the back of the minibus. Everyone wanted to sit at the back.

During our journey, particularly on the return journey after the match, we gave voice to our repertoire of the hit songs of the day. Bobby Vee's "The Night Has A Thousand Eyes" was a particular favourite. The teacher to whom fell the onerous duty of keeping an eye on us on away trips, regularly brought his fiancée along on the coach. She would often comment on how impressed she was with our harmonies. She was a good judge. We were quite a decent choral ensemble, our vocal talents perhaps surpassing our ability as footballers.

* * * *

I played basketball for the school, encouraged by the assistant head of P.E., Malcolm Burgess, who was a coach with the England schoolboy team. I played right guard, and I tended to incur Mr Burgess' wrath by firing shots from a distance rather than pass the ball to a teammate. More often than not I scored, but Mr. Burgess wanted the ball to be passed so that the scoring opportunity would fall to one of the forward players.

"Bad habit Linnell", is what he used to shout when I chanced my arm, though always with a wry smile when my shot sank through the basket to add to our points tally. The change to the points system in the 80s, awarding three points rather than two for baskets scored from distance, thus encouraging the long-range shooting that I enjoyed, rather vindicated my approach. Well, I thought so anyway.

At the time my penchant for aiming at the hoop from further afield than Malcolm Burgess required, prompted the other members of the basketball team to follow the coaches' lead and give me the nickname "bad habit."

* * * *

It was the cricket pitch, however, where I was most at home.

My cricket education, which had started under Derief Taylor at Kings Heath High School, continued at KNGS. Mr. Knapman was the PE teacher with an ostensibly stern exterior for those who were not wholly engaged with his efforts to guide their physical development.

The general PE activity was not for me. Gym lessons, utilising wall bars, a pommel horse, a wooden vaulting box and uneven bars prompted anxiety, as much because I was worried about getting things wrong and scared of being hurt if I did.

My fears were intensified by those who appeared to have a natural gift for sport having more muscular bodies. Even at twelve and thirteen years of age some were developing biceps and pecs that gave them an obvious advantage in any physical activity.

* * * *

I was conscious of a widely published newspaper advertisement of the time promoting the body-building programme of Angelo Siciliano. Italian-born, he moved to New York as a schoolboy and, according to the legend he created about his life, he had sand kicked in his face on a beach as a scrawny weakling.

Siciliano visited strongman shows held at Coney Island in Brooklyn, and he studied the techniques and diets of the bodybuilders there. He went on to develop his own programme, which he called "Dynamic Tension", taking the name Charles Atlas after a friend told him his body resembled a statue of the Greek titan Atlas which stood on top of a Coney Island hotel.

The advertising campaign for his programme was one of the most read and longest-running campaigns of its time, all over the world. My Dad saw me studying it. The resulting conversation, in which I revealed my fears that I was destined to be the scrawny weakling of the Charles Atlas story, led Dad to have a word with Mr. Knapman.

I had no idea about that conversation, but at the next PE lesson, without making any fuss in front of my classmates, Mr Knapman came to my side every time it was my turn to go over the pommel horse or vault the box. Whatever the exercise he was there, with words of encouragement and occasionally a gentle push to guide me through the exercise.

After the lesson he took me to one side and, again doing nothing to alert others, he offered reassurance.

"Muscles are important Linnell," he said, "but we all develop at different speeds to one another. Having muscly arms does not make you better than the next man. We all have our skills and we don't all need built-up bodies to show them.

"Your father told me that you've been reading about Charles Atlas," he continued. "Mr. Atlas is obviously a very fit man, but you don't have to look like him to do well."

He continued to encourage me and guide me in his lessons, but it was in the Third Year that he asked me to join the after-school cricket nets with the school Second Eleven. Most of them were Fourth and Fifth Year pupils, so they were one or two years older than me.

I had no time to worry about that. Mr. Knapman told me I would be first to bat in the nets.

"I'm told that you have a good eye for the ball Linnell," he said. 'Put your pads on and let's see what you can do."

Leaving the other Second Eleven players to organise themselves, he bowled the first few deliveries at me himself.

"Don't try to be clever," he said. "Forget forward defensive and all that for now. Take one step back as the ball is coming to you to give yourself time to see it, and then just hit it back over my head as high and as hard as you can.'

I missed the first one completely and edged the second for what would have been an easy slip catch. The next one I connected with, and the next, and the next, and soon he had other players engaged in fielding practice chasing after my shots.

I did not make the Second Eleven that year, but I was the top scorer for Middlemore House in the Third Year inter-house cricket competition. In the Fourth Year, I was amongst the youngest to be picked for the Second Eleven and sent in to bat at number three. I became second eleven captain, regularly top-scoring, and taking a few wickets from time to time.

It led eventually to my selection for the first team, but sadly that did not last long. I was picked to play for just one fixture in fact, and I was sent in to open the batting. Keith Bland, the other opener, was the same age as me but he had already played a few times for the first eleven. A tall, elegant player, Keith had established himself as a first-team regular. With that in mind, I assumed that he would take responsibility and face the first ball, but instead, he sent me to the striker's end.

I wish now I had challenged that decision, but I was the new boy and pretty much unknown to the rest of the group. To my later regret, I did not argue, and duly took guard to face the first ball.

There was nothing special about the opening delivery of the match. It was fairly quick but otherwise simply straight and true, with nothing fancy or terribly awkward about it. I attempted what I thought was a stylish forward defensive stroke, seeking to return the ball to the bowler.

Maybe I took my eye off it, I don't know, but the bat and ball failed to connect. I winced as I heard the wicket tumble behind me as the ball found its way between my bat and pads. Why, at that moment, I had forgotten Mr. Knapman's advice to take a step back to allow myself time, I will never know. I was bowled first ball, and that was that.

A wretched afternoon followed, during which hardly anyone spoke to me. The next weekend I returned to captain the second eleven and scored a fairly swift fifty, satisfying myself that the events of the previous Saturday were an aberration. That conclusion was obviously not shared by others however and my first team days were over.

Despite that, I was selected amongst a group of boys from several nearby schools to go to Edgbaston for trials for Warwickshire County Cricket Club's Colts team. Foolishly, I failed to take it seriously. My performance was distinctly average, I was not chosen for further consideration, and any lingering thoughts of becoming a county cricketer were roundly dispelled.

* * * *

The head teacher in my time at KNGS was Geoffrey Sheen, a brilliant mathematician. Thankfully, for his sake, he never taught me. If he had, I am sure he would have been appalled at my failure to grasp what I regarded as the impenetrable complications of the subject that was his expertise.

Amongst his many gifts, Mr. Sheen was a musician and a man imbued with Christian principles. He was also a member of the United Nations

Association. He cared deeply about his pupils, something which to my great regret I only fully appreciated in my latter days at the school.

With my fellow classmates I was more concerned about avoiding any punishment that he might mete out to us, should any of our misdemeanours come to his notice. He used the cane, most often across the palm of one's hand, rather than the backside, but only if all other punishments had failed. In some cases, when required to deal with a serial offender, he aimed for the top of the thighs, which was said to be very painful.

I was never caned, although I am sure I came close to it. Those less fortunate would recount that he would say, "This will hurt me more than it does you", before delivering the blow.

In my final year at KNGS, I learned how I had misunderstood this slight, wiry man with crinkly grey hair and horn-rimmed glasses. It transpired one morning that a doctor had been called to Mr Sheen's office after he'd been found by his secretary to have been there all night, having fallen asleep at his desk. He was apparently suffering from exhaustion, after a series of very long days and even longer nights, dealing with paperwork in his office. No personal computers in those days, just reams of paper that had to be read and dealt with manually.

A few days later, back at school, he took the unusual step of coming into our classroom and sitting briefly with each one of us, quietly giving us his thoughts on our progress or lack of it. He was, it turned out, genuinely concerned at what the future held for one of the largest intakes of pupils in the school's history. We were the so-called "boom babies", all born in the immediate aftermath of the war, and Geoffrey Sheen spent a few minutes with each of us.

When he sat next to me, he looked me squarely in the eye. He spoke very quietly so that even for those elsewhere in the classroom, desperately trying to eavesdrop on the conversation, it was almost impossible to hear.

He leaned toward me and said, "Linnell, you are a bright boy, and I am told you are an adequate sportsman. If you apply yourself you will do well, but from what I can see you need to work harder at all your academic subjects. Put your mind to it and you will be alright, but I think you will have to work much harder than you do currently."

If ever there was a telling and accurate assessment of my school days that was it, from a man who had previously barely ever seen me one to one. That he spent a few minutes with each pupil of that large intake of "boom babies", delivering a personal assessment to each of us, was the measure of the man. It was an indication of just why he put in all those extra hours, to the possible detriment of his health.

On 5th June 1970, some seven years after I had left KNGS, Geoffrey Sheen died. He succumbed to a brain tumour. It was said by those paying tribute to him that he was the epitome of a man who gave and did not count the cost. He was concerned for the welfare as well as the education of the boys at his school, and he concerned himself about domestic troubles that any of them had when it was brought to his notice.

Some old boys have commented that in the 50s and 60s, KNGS had a "Greyfriars" or "Tom Brown's Schooldays" atmosphere and I suppose that is true. Geoffrey Sheen knew, I think, that he had to modernise it, but he also knew that the traditions of the school stood for something and needed to be preserved.

In many ways, I know I let him down. I let my parents down, too. I was not alone in my disappointing academic achievements, though that was of little consolation. A fair few of that huge post-war intake of schoolboys also failed to reach the standards required of them in the exam room.

Nonetheless, the school saw many of its number go on to University, some to either Oxford or Cambridge, with "Oxbridge" regarded as the educational holy grail. These were the days when most schoolchildren did not have that opportunity, and much was made of those who made it.

Later I allowed myself to consider that I had attended the euphemistic "University of Life", which is the excuse used by many of us for not doing as well at school as we know we should have. An excuse for guilt really. My scholastic failure was my own fault, but certainly not that of Geoffrey Sheen, nor his staff.

* * * *

My time at King's Norton Grammar School for Boys ended as ignominiously as my first-ball exit from the first eleven cricket team. Poor GCE 'O'-level results saw me enrol at a local technical college to try to make up for it, but it also led me to consider what career lay ahead for a bright, articulate young man who had only achieved passes in English Language and English Literature. I had only begun to properly grasp the unforgiving truth that life is a one-time opportunity with no rehearsal. Little did I realise that cricket would help provide the answer.

He who would valiant be 'gainst all disaster
Let him in constancy follow the Master
There's no discouragement shall make him once relent
His first avowed intent to be a pilgrim.

Who so beset him round with dismal stories
Do but themselves confound - his strength the more is
No foes shall stay his might; though he with giants fight
He will make good his right to be a pilgrim.

Since, Lord, Thou dost defend us with Thy Spirit
We know we at the end, shall life inherit
Then fancies flee away! I'll fear not what men say
I'll labour night and day to be a pilgrim.

John Bunyan, 1684. Modified by Percy Dearmer in The English Hymnal
©Oxford University Press

Chapter Four

I Gather You Play Cricket

Tell me when you feel a little blue
Tell me then I'll see what I can do
Just say the word and I'll be there
Anywhere, with lots of love to share

Les Reed & Geoff Stephens, 1964
©Southern Music

As a music-loving teenager in the 1960s, listening to hit records on the radio was an essential part of life. That prompted regular visits to the local record shop where most of my funds were invested to purchase the latest favourite discs.

In my mid-teens, whilst still at school, it was my obsession with my record collection and listening to them in my bedroom that got me into big trouble with my Mum. The fact that I played them more often and more loudly than she thought necessary and that I sang along to them at an equivalent volume, increased her irritation.

Not that it was solely noisy rock 'n' roll that I had on my bedroom shelves. True the list of artists included Elvis Presley, Buddy Holly, Cliff Richard, The Everly Brothers, and, as time went by, The Beatles and others that followed in their wake, but sitting alongside them was also an album by Glenn Miller, and a few records by one of the world's best purveyors of popular song, Frank Sinatra.

Sinatra's music arrived on my record player turntable when he recorded on his own label, Reprise, which he founded in 1960. I bought his album "I Remember Tommy", a tribute to bandleader Tommy Dorsey, which included new versions of songs that Sinatra had first performed or recorded with Dorsey early in his career. Sy Oliver, who had arranged many pieces for

Dorsey, arranged and conducted the album which features two of my all-time favourite Sinatra songs, "I'll Be Seeing You", and "Without A Song". I know many Sinatra aficionados will prefer his earlier recordings, but those swing arrangements and the mature Sinatra voice were my preference.

Discovering Sinatra introduced me to Tony Bennett, Sammy Davis Jr., and Dean Martin, who when he was not clowning around apparently under the influence of one or two Bourbons, was a fine singer and a very funny man. All of them, as composer and bandleader Henry Mancini once said, were performers who needed no studio help nor electronic gimmicks, they were simply great singers. Dean Martin's drinking, by the way, was apparently all part of the act. It's been revealed in biographies and in the testimony of friends and family that, while Dino enjoyed a tipple occasionally, it was no more than apple juice in the tumbler that he held on stage.

My record collection can therefore be regarded as eclectic, and I don't think it was the specific choice of music that upset my Mum. It was more that I played them loud and often. As a consequence, I did not respond as swiftly as she wanted when she called me to have my tea or to get on with my homework. So whatever prompted it, I had pushed my luck too far one particular afternoon when she stormed up the stairs and into my room. She grabbed my record player, which was plugged into a mains socket at the time and playing a seven-inch 45 rpm single. She picked up the whole thing and carried it out to the landing. The power cable stretched behind her, tearing the plug out of the socket as she went. She then threw the whole kit and kaboodle down the stairs.

"Now will you do what I tell you?" she yelled in exasperation.

Holding back the tears, I did not reply. I waited until she had gone back downstairs before I followed her and retrieved my pride and joy. Amazingly, when I plugged it in and placed it all back where it had been taken from, it still worked. The record that had been playing was slightly scratched but not so much. It still played.

It was a one-off clash which was not repeated, but my Mum had made her point. Important though music was, she tried to make me understand that I had to keep it in perspective alongside the rest of my adolescent life.

If you love music enjoying live performances is essential, and it was not long before playing records and listening to the radio led to concert-going. Whenever a concert tour brought the stars to town I was in the queue for tickets.

Birmingham was usually on the tour schedule for most of the top names. I went to see The Rolling Stones at the Birmingham Hippodrome Theatre, and at the same venue, The Dave Clark Five. DC5 vocalist and keyboard player Mike Smith would, many years later, become a good friend when he produced radio station jingles for me.

In my late teens and early twenties the Odeon Cinema in Birmingham staged concerts from time to time. Amongst those I saw there were Roy Orbison, The Kinks and Santana. In contrast to the Odeon auditorium, a tiny, intimate club located under a railway arch near Snow Hill station was the place where I saw and chatted with an early incarnation of Fleetwood Mac, then called 'Peter Green's Fleetwood Mac'. It had Peter Green on guitar and vocals, with John McVie playing bass, both backed by drummer Mick Fleetwood. Priceless memories.

* * * *

Watching the stars was one thing, meeting them was the icing on the cake. For a time, before full-time employment came my way, I had a Saturday job as a shop assistant at the Woolworths store in Kings Heath, a district near our home in Birmingham. Across the road from Woolworths, in a side street called York Road, there was a live music venue that gloried in the name "The Ritz Ballroom".

It was run by Joe Regan and his wife Mary, otherwise known as 'Ma Regan.' They ran three other venues across Birmingham which often took Joe away from The Ritz, but it was Ma who really ran the show. A PE teacher during the day, Ma selected and booked the acts for The Ritz, and by all accounts drove a hard bargain with the agents and managers who were keen to put their putative stars in front of the audience.

It was recognised that Ma knew what she was doing as she built The Ritz into a venue with an international reputation. One artist's manager with whom she got on particularly well was a young entrepreneur from Liverpool called Brian Epstein. He was pushing hard for exposure for his young four-piece group called The Beatles, who had a rapidly growing popularity.

Epstein had booked The Beatles into as many small local venues as he could around the country. He had originally planned for them to appear at The Ritz on 11th January 1963. The weather put paid to that. Snow, much of it in the form of heavy blizzards, made a trip to the venue treacherous for local people, let alone for the band.

It was rescheduled, and by the time they were due to play in Kings Heath The Beatles were on their way to the Top 10 with a record called "Please, Please Me". Despite their growing success and the clamour for this ground-breaking group of young men to play to larger crowds at bigger halls and theatres, Epstein showed commendable loyalty to the venues with which he had agreed deals. He stuck to the contracts he had signed and The Beatles duly honoured their booking at The Ritz, even though the demand to see them was much greater than the modest ballroom could hold.

Despite their famous haircuts, which made them highly recognisable, the four musicians were still able to stroll amongst Kings Heath shoppers that day without hindrance, at least to start with. That they were not instantly spotted was partly because afternoon shoppers were generally slightly older than their record-buying fans, and also because the last person you would expect to see as you went shopping for groceries and washing powder was a rising pop star, let alone four of them. They were apparently looking for nothing more than some fresh air, away from the tour van and the ballroom. It was Friday, 15th February 1963, and I was working an extra day at Woolworths to put some cash in my pocket.

The manager of the store had given me the delightful task of polishing apples when I saw a commotion on a nearby counter. A commotion that nearly turned into a riot.

Four young men had wandered casually into the store and were just browsing, particularly around the counter where Woolworths sold records on the store's own budget-priced 'Embassy' label. They were cover versions of the big hits of the day, recorded by people like Dick Jordan, Ray Pilgrim and Maureen Evans. They sold for a significantly cheaper price than the originals.

One of the group broke away from the others and decided to make a purchase at an adjacent counter. He selected a comb and offered the cash. The Woolworths mantra, stated clearly on a big label stuck to the side of each cash register in the shop, was "money must be registered before goods are wrapped." To comply, the girl behind the counter focused on doing just that without paying much attention to her customer.

When she looked up for the first time to hand him his change, she instantly recognised the handsome face of George Harrison. She let out a piercing shriek that threatened to shatter the windows. For a split second, as she struggled to get her breath back, the whole place fell totally silent. As one, the four looked at her, then at each other, before they ran back into the street as if their lives depended on it. They probably did.

The young assistant, who had realised she was about to serve a Beatle, had collapsed in a faint and was being revived by one of her more mature, though equally flustered, colleagues. Someone shouted rather pointlessly, "It's them! It's The Beatles!"

Men and women of all ages and circumstances were caught up in the melee that followed, many totally bewildered by what was going on. The confused pandemonium, and the fact that the Fab Four had been the first to react, allowed the group time to escape and make it back to the relative sanctity of The Ritz, where Joe Regan had turned up to help Ma oversee what they rightly envisaged would be a lively night.

It was later reported that George caused even more mayhem when he went missing just before the band were due on stage. He had to be rescued from screaming fans outside the ballroom, thus delaying the start of the show. It started late in any event, because of the time it took to get everyone safely into the building to see The Beatles.

Once the afternoon's chaos settled down, Woolworths went back to its usual self. Pick 'n Mix was as busy as ever, and my apples were shining brightly in their baskets. That weekend I bought a copy of "Please, Please Me".

* * * *

The Beatles wrote a song called "Like Dreamers Do" for a band from Birmingham called The Applejacks. It made the Top 20 in the summer of 1964, as a follow-up hit after The Applejacks had made it into the Top 10 with "Tell Me When."

The band had six members, vocalist Al Jackson, lead guitarist Martin Baggott, organist Don Gould, rhythm guitarist Phil Cash, drummer Gerry Freeman, and the one member of the band who was not from the West

Midlands, bass player Megan Davies who came from Sheffield. Despite the later popularity of many female singers and all-girl groups, having a female band member in an otherwise all-male group was then something of a novelty, so Megan received a lot of attention as The Applejacks enjoyed chart success.

As a half-decent ten-pin bowler, I often went with friends to play at the Acocks Green Bowl bowling alley. It was the middle of the day, and the middle of the working week, so the place was otherwise empty apart from one lane. That was occupied by a group of six people, of similar age to us, five guys and one girl. The Applejacks.

We played on a nearby lane and fell into conversation with them, talking about music and life, as you do. They were really easy to get on with, and we met them there again a couple of times, on the understanding that we would not shout about the fact that it was somewhere they went to enjoy their free time, unfettered by fans. Needless to say, records by The Applejacks found their way into my collection.

* * * *

The generational change that occurred in the 1960s was profound. Young people in that decade had witnessed social injustices affecting their parent's generation and they were not prepared to let the same happen to them. The popular groups of the day transformed attitudes to music, fashion and more, and The Beatles would go on to be regarded as the most influential band of all time.

Nearly twenty years had passed since the end of the Second World War, but the Vietnam War now overshadowed everything. It had escalated hugely. The American President, John F. Kennedy, increased the number of what were described as "military advisers" sent to Vietnam from just under a thousand in 1959 to sixteen thousand in 1963. In America, the anti-war movement and the civil rights movement united in protest, with artists like Bob Dylan, Woody Guthrie, Nina Simone and Joan Baez applying political, social, philosophical, and literary influences to their musical expression.

In 1963 The Beatles were enjoying their first major chart success in the UK with "Please, Please Me", following up their first modest hit "Love Me Do". It showed the new generation that they could make and enjoy their own music in a manner totally contrary to anything their parents had experienced. At the same time, Bob Dylan, having made his mark on the protest movements with songs like "Blowing In The Wind", and "A Hard Rain's a-Gonna Fall", was writing and recording an album that put him front and centre of political challenge, "The Times They Are A-Changin'". Of the title song Dylan said, "This was definitely a song with a purpose. I wanted to write a big song, some kind of theme song, with short concise verses that piled up on each other in a hypnotic way. The civil rights movement and the folk music movement were pretty close and allied together at that time."

We were all caught up in it, inspired by the freedom to be creative as demonstrated by The Beatles, and we were influenced by the shrugging off of any acknowledgement of the established order of things by the music and attitude of The Rolling Stones. Just as The Beatles were the overwhelmingly influential mould breakers and were fast becoming the biggest name in popular music, The Stones developed into the greatest rock band of all time. Others, like Led Zeppelin, Pink Floyd and Queen would later rise to similar heights with their own variations of the genre, but the innovative creativity of The Beatles and the sheer dynamism and drive of The Rolling Stones made both bands a class apart.

The irresistible rise of The Beatles saw them dominate the American charts, just as the American acts that had so influenced the young Lennon and McCartney had previously filled the UK Top 40. In response, the California-based Beach Boys adapted their repertoire of songs, which had been aimed at the all-American teenager who wanted to go surfing and drive hot rod cars, into sophisticated complex harmonies culminating in one of the most iconic classic albums "Pet Sounds".

Elvis Presley, whilst remaining a hugely popular musical presence, and one still admired by The Beatles themselves, found himself having to make room for these new stars who had emerged from the global counter-culture phenomena. Just as Presley had succeeded Sinatra, claiming the title of "King of Pop", so The Beatles were now taking Elvis's crown.

Presley's star waned for many of us as his manager, Colonel Tom Parker, insisted that Elvis made a succession of poorly produced musical films, each including one or two hit songs, rather than allowing him to tour and perform live. Cinema audiences could see him, but he never toured and so was never seen on stage in America let alone in the rest of the world. Towards the end of his life, Elvis did appear in concert, but only in the USA. The rest of us could only watch his performances on television as a huge star was reduced to a parody of what he should have been.

* * * *

Many felt that '60s culture allowed us the freedom to find our voice. It was unlikely that anyone would emulate the unprecedented success of the four boys from Liverpool, but we could at least show what we could do in our own backyard. Immanuel Church, Highters Heath, was a world away from Shea Stadium in Queens, New York, where The Beatles played in 1965 and again in 1970, but as the Head Choir Boy at Immanuel Church, that was where my voice was heard. I had always enjoyed singing and in addition to the church choir, I often performed at local parish parties.

Encouraged by a friend of my mother, I auditioned for an agent who appeared excited by what he heard and thus started to lay out plans for my life as a pop star. He promised to put together a backing band and to find venues for me to build a reputation as the latest singing sensation.

He even found me a stage name, deciding that my own did not quite roll off the tongue. He said we needed something like 'Cliff Richard' and came up with a similar combination of two first names. He settled on Simon Peter and, because of the religious connotation that then (and only then!) occurred to him, my backing group would be called The Fishermen.

That backing group never did emerge, so Simon Peter and The Fishermen remained a project that failed to see the light of day. After securing three bookings for me at working men's clubs in the West Midlands, the agent disappeared taking with him whatever modest earnings I was due. It turned out he had also retained significant amounts that he owed to other artists, some of whom had been with him for years.

I have to say that although I was no doubt quickly, if not immediately, forgotten by the audiences that heard me, I hadn't gone down badly in my three performances. Despite having to rely on backing from the resident pianist at each club, which did nothing to enhance my singing nor help me win any fans, I received polite if not ecstatic applause. My repertoire included the Manfred Mann hit "Pretty Flamingo", Paul Jones' "I've Been A Bad, Bad Boy", and Cliff's "Congratulations".

My Mum and Dad came to my second show, at a working men's club in the Black Country. During my performance, I was apparently on the receiving end of some fairly firm and loud criticism from a lady sitting in front of my parents. On stage I was totally unaware of what was going on, but my Mum let the unfortunate critic know in no uncertain terms that she should keep her opinions to herself and "give the young lad a chance."

The defection of my agent brought an abrupt halt to my quest for stardom as a pop vocalist, but it failed to dent my enthusiasm for music and pop culture. That said, it reinforced my rapidly forming view that playing the recorded music of others on the radio was the preferable option.

* * * *

The 1960s were not only notable for the music and fashion that changed post-war Britain but also for one of the greatest sporting events the nation had ever known.

Between 11th and 30th July 1966, the FIFA World Cup tournament was held in England. Matches were played at stadiums across the country. They were Ayresome Park in Middlesbrough, Goodison Park in Liverpool, Hillsborough Stadium in Sheffield, Old Trafford in Manchester, Roker Park in Sunderland, Villa Park in Birmingham, and Wembley Stadium in London. An eighth ground, the White City Stadium in London, was used for a match between Uruguay and France which had been scheduled to be played at Wembley on a Friday. Despite it being part of the World Cup, Wembley refused to accommodate the match as it would have meant cancelling its regularly scheduled Friday night greyhound race meeting.

Three matches were played at Villa Park, and I went to all of them. I saw Argentina beat Spain 2-1, a goalless draw between Argentina and West Germany, and then a further 2-1 defeat for Spain, this time by West Germany.

England's 4-2 victory against West Germany in the Final is seared into English history. Even those too young to have seen it will know of Geoff Hurst's second goal being awarded despite the controversy over whether the ball crossed the line after hitting the crossbar. Hurst's hat-trick, and the great commentary by Kenneth Wolstenholme as Hurst scored the final goal: "Some people are on the pitch. They think it's all over ... It is now!" is the stuff of folklore. It is worth noting that the match was televised by both major TV channels, BBC and ITV, and although Wolstenholme's famous line has become part of football folklore, the ITV commentary by Hugh Johns is regarded by many fellow journalists as the better description of the match.

Those of us not at Wembley for the Final watched it live on television in black and white, although a colour film of it was also made. It was the last World Cup Final to be broadcast in black and white.

At Wembley Stadium that day, 96,924 saw England become World Cup winners. My Dad and I were amongst the British television audience of 32.3 million viewers, watching it on our rented black and white TV with a tiny 12-inch screen.

Very few people owned their own TVs in those days. Most people rented sets, as we did. There were two big rental companies across the UK, Rediffusion and Radio Rentals. Both rented radios at first and then, as television became popular, TV sets were also made available. They also rented other domestic appliances, such as washing machines and refrigerators. Radio Rentals supplied our TV, and as time went by I remember Mum and Dad discussing whether they could afford to change the set for one with a larger screen, and eventually for a set that received colour pictures.

Renting domestic goods continues, but back then it was the route favoured by most families and the way that enabled most to watch the greatest day in English football.

* * * *

In addition to my part-time job at Woolworths, I was an ice cream man. I drove a van and parked at the kerbside of Birmingham streets to sell ice cream, ice lollies and the like, for 'Mr. V's', which took its name from the owner of the business, Severo Verrecchia. He was born in Glasgow to Italian parents and had lived in Bristol as a young man. There he met his wife and they relocated to Birmingham where they made their home. Severo started his own business reaching back into his Italian heritage, to serve delicious ice cream to the West Midlands.

The company was based in Ladywood in Birmingham. They had a huge garage in which the ice cream vans were stored. Negotiating their entry and exit, and parking them as close as possible next to each other, was difficult. We always managed it, even though on one occasion, reversing into a narrow space in the garage, I managed to dislodge one of the large glass ice cream cone signs from the side of my van. I say "dislodge" but it would have smashed to the ground had Severo, who was guiding me into the space left for me, not caught it as it fell.

One really hot sunny day, Severo sent me and my van to a public park in Handsworth where he knew a cricket match was being, quite literally, hotly contested. The rival teams engaged in the contest both came from the ice-cream-loving, local African-Caribbean community. Many local families had turned out in significant numbers to enjoy the occasion. The queue was constant from the moment I arrived, and Severo himself turned up during the afternoon to replenish my stock.

With a percentage of sales forming part of my remuneration, it turned into a very good day's work.

* * * *

I was now compiling quite an eclectic CV as a Woolworths' shop assistant, failed pop singer and Ice cream salesman, to which I nearly added the job of a male model. My Dad had allowed me to have his old khaki Army greatcoat. I had it dyed black, with the military insignia and gold buttons removed. When I wore it I reckoned I looked the bees' knees, and that was borne out one Saturday afternoon when I was window shopping in Kings Heath.

I had paused to look at the clothes on offer in the window of a gents' boutique. There were bright colours in psychedelic and paisley patterns, flared hipster-style trousers, and shirts worn open almost to the navel, all on view. Alongside them were black garments, some similar to my dad's old greatcoat.

My black hair was long, to my shoulders, parted down the middle, and I wore a full beard. As I looked at the wares in the shop window, a guy came out of the shop and started to chat with me. He was older than me, probably in his late 30s, wearing a grey cheesecloth shirt and wine-coloured flares. He also had long hair and a thick moustache.

"Have you seen anything you like?" he asked, nodding towards the clothes in the shop.

"Most of it," I replied, caught a little off-guard by the unexpected approach.

"If you'd like to try some of them, we're looking for models," he said. "You fit the bill perfectly. You have style, you're tall, and you have a great look. Would you be interested?"

I hesitated, completely surprised by the turn of events, but eventually blurted out, "I might be. What would I have to do?"

He pulled a business card out of his pocket.

"Come to this address tomorrow night at seven," he said. "We'll be taking photos of a few people who we think have potential. People like you. There will be a job in it for at least two people."

I thanked him and thought about nothing else on my way home. My mother told me in no uncertain terms that I would need my head looking at if I were to go to the photo shoot. My Dad said nothing but smiled sympathetically in my direction, in recognition I think that the world had changed in a manner that was passing both my parents by.

The irony was that whilst both Mum and Dad would waste no opportunity to express their distaste at Mick Jagger's reported lifestyle, or at The Beatles' hairstyles, they clearly enjoyed the music. They would happily tap their feet and even sing along to hits like "She Loves You" and "From Me To You". When it came to other things, however, from fashion at one extreme to the hedonism of what the popular press referred to as "free love", it was all too much for them. Dad was very slightly more relaxed in his approach to it, but for Mum, it was just bewildering and made no sense.

Despite Mum's anxieties, I went to the photo shoot. To say I was nervous was an understatement. There were about a dozen or so of us, some guys, some girls, all measured up by the staff from the boutique before being handed clothes to change into. The strong aroma in the room partly came from the lazy circles of smoke drifting from liberally placed rows of joss sticks. It also seemed to emerge from some unusual cigarettes being smoked by many in the room. As an avowed non-smoker, I declined the offer to join in.

We paraded according to a photographer's instructions, before being thanked for attending. We were each handed gift vouchers to spend in the boutique as we left. I was told that I would be put on what was called a 'stand by' list of people who would be called on if circumstances warranted it. Apparently, had I relaxed a little more in front of the camera I would have been the first choice. Those at the top of the list were much more flamboyant, literally flirting with the photographer. I had not been relaxed enough to do that, so I readily understood why I was listed amongst the reserves. Had I been a smoker I would no doubt have been much more at ease, in more ways than one.

Some months later I did receive a call inviting me to go for a follow-up shoot in London, but by that time I had landed what my Mum regarded as a "proper job", working in the offices of the local council. A day strutting my stuff in the big city was not on. A case of "what might have been", I suppose, but I did not regret having my Dad's greatcoat dyed black.

At a gig in a local music club soon after the modelling audition a girl, also dressed from head to toe in black, came up to me and told me I looked "cool". We saw a lot of each other that night and for a few weeks thereafter.

* * * *

If you look up the name Leslie Sabel, you'll probably find it featuring prominently in the news items of 1987. It is the name of the man who was First Officer of the Herald of Free Enterprise roll-on roll-off car ferry operating between Dover and Zeebrugge, that sank killing 193 people.

Leslie Sabel was responsible for ensuring that the ship's bow doors were closed as it set sail. That they remained open was the reason why the vessel was inundated by the sea, causing it to capsize.

To hear that name in 1987 instantly took me back two decades. Nothing to do with that maritime tragedy but bizarrely the same name, some twenty-two years before, loomed large in my life. As far from the sea as the geography of England allows, a very different man called Leslie Sabel became my boss.

The Leslie Sabel I met in 1965 was the Deputy Director of the Welfare Department of Birmingham City Council. As such, he interviewed me when I applied for a job as a clerk at their city centre offices.

That was the general direction I had been pointed towards by the Careers Teacher at King's Norton Grammar School for Boys. He was actually the school's senior Geography teacher, probably in his 40s, but for all the world giving the appearance of someone a good 20 years older. He was weary and careworn and would doubtless have preferred to be somewhere else with someone else, rather than dispensing career advice to those who were academic failures, or at best, near misses.

The hand-sewn patches on the elbows of his pale green cardigan only added to his inability to hide his disinterest, as he made a vague attempt to secure reasonable futures for those of us who were leaving the establishment after delivering disappointing examination results. For the higher achievers, a few destined to make their way to some of the nation's better universities, he had far more enthusiasm and encouragement.

Nonetheless, my parents were eager that I should heed his words of wisdom, such as they were, and they made it clear that I had better play my part. No one was the least bit interested when I said that I wanted to work in the media, maybe as a journalist but preferably playing records on the radio.

"Journalism?" the careers master queried, his greying right eyebrow arched high across his sallow brow. "Do you really think that is a career worth pursuing? Late nights chasing 'the news' and mixing with quite unsavoury folk along the way? I don't think you'd enjoy that Linnell, would you? As for the idea of being a disc jockey, is that any sort of job? Really?"

The terms 'the news' and 'disc jockey' were spoken with near contempt, as if he was referring to something wholly unmentionable, something that should not be included in polite conversation.

I spluttered back an awkward response, suggesting that if the media was disapproved of, maybe being a teacher could be considered. That received a baleful look of utter disdain, and I was reminded that I had not secured anything like sufficient grades to qualify for teacher training college. He told me that something far more stable, secure and unadventurous, such as becoming a civil servant or a local government officer would be much more appropriate for little old, underperforming me.

In their despair at what I might become, my parents undertook to stump up the wherewithal to allow me to attend a local technical college to re-sit some of the exams I had failed and to steer me towards a job thereafter.

In time I successfully applied for the job of junior clerk at the Birmingham office of the Ministry of Pensions and National Insurance. I had to sign the Official Secrets Act. Reassuringly I was never privy to any secrets that, had I revealed them, would have threatened the security of the nation. Nonetheless, my signature was appended to the Act of Parliament that was intended to deter spies and corrupt civil servants. I fall into neither category and as much as I enjoy the exploits of James Bond, as portrayed by Sean

Connery, Roger Moore, Daniel Craig and others, I have to report that, sadly, I have never owned an Aston Martin. The task I was given after signing the Official Secrets Act, the filing of documents, was actually mind-numbingly boring.

I did not remain a civil servant for long. In seeking gainful employment, I had simultaneously applied for a post with Birmingham City Council. They were clearly in no rush to acquire my talents, so it was three months after that application, and three months after I became a man from the Ministry and had filed my first National Insurance document that the local authority decided it would consider what I had to offer.

So it was that I sat before Leslie Sabel. He was a slightly built man with dark tortoiseshell spectacles and, I noted, quite hairy hands presumably at the end of quite hairy arms. He would have appeared quite bald, too, had it not been for an exaggerated comb-over of dark, floppy hair.

In an almost distracted manner, he asked me about my schooldays and told me a bit about the work of the Welfare Department, which involved overseeing the City Council's Homes for the Elderly. Then he asked the question that ensured I got the job and, for the first time in the entire process, encouraged me to think that maybe doing a proper job wouldn't be such a bad deal after all.

"I gather you play cricket. What do you do, bat or bowl?"

Caught off-guard by this unexpected turn of events, I hesitated for a moment, before stammering out my answer.

"A b-bit of b-both".

"Good. Just what we need. When can you start?"

It was not the conversation I was expecting, and as job interviews go it was most definitely unusual. It turned out that almost every department of Birmingham City Council had a cricket team playing in the local NALGO league. NALGO, the National Association of Local Government Officers, was the trade union for council employees. It later became part of UNISON.

All the NALGO league cricket matches were played at a vast sports ground at Yardley in Birmingham, where at least two fixtures were played simultaneously each evening. The Council Departments feared most for their cricketing prowess were the Housing Department, which boasted a pair of demon fast bowlers, and the Rates Department. The latter had built its reputation on the skills of Neal Abberley, a fine right-handed batsman, born in Birmingham and educated at Saltley Grammar School.

Abberley's batting had propelled the Rates Department to the upper end of the League. Just before I was offered employment apparently because of my enthusiasm for cricket, rather than any testimony to my ability as a clerical officer, Abberley had left the Council to play professionally for Warwickshire County Cricket Club.

He made a half-century on his county debut, against Cambridge University, and went on to enjoy a successful playing and coaching career. Abberley made 3 first-class hundreds, with a best of 117 not out against Essex, and scored a one-day hundred, 113 not out, against Hampshire.

In the NALGO league I also made an immediate impact. I scored 50 on my debut against the dreaded Housing Department, and I turned out to be a half-decent close-to-the-bat fielder, but my achievements never came close to the dizzying heights reached by Neal Abberley.

* * * *

If my careers teacher was right about anything it was that life at Birmingham City Council, apart from the cricket, was certainly 'unadventurous'. The highlight of my working week was the Friday morning "pocket money" run.

It was my job to work out how much money was left over after the Council had taken what it required from the retirement pensions of each of the residents of its old people's homes. I then had to put the resulting small change, in cash, into small brown envelopes, one for each resident. A council-employed driver would then whisk me around the city in a Council-owned black cab, from one old folk's home to another, where I handed out their pocket money to each individual at each place.

The drivers each had their favourite home to visit, usually because of the extra slice of cake they got with their cup of tea from the cook. How much deeper some of those friendships went, I did not enquire, though one or two hinted at more than convivial associations, but I also had my favourite place on the route.

At one home, near Northfield, the Matron took a shine to me. She took her tea break to coincide with our arrival and insisted that I join her. She was Irish and was a huge fan of The Bachelors pop group. Her mind was made up that I looked like the group's lead singer Con Cluskey. To my horror, on one visit I let slip that I had once tried my hand at singing in local clubs. Thereafter our visits included an impromptu rendition of "Charmaine" or "Diane", or one of The Bachelors other hits. That was the closest that Council workday life came to being adventurous.

* * * *

A fellow would-be cricketer and local council employee, Edwin McNamara, became a good friend. Edwin invited me to join a cricket team playing in a local parks league, run by his brother. I opened the bowling and batted in the middle order. We played on public park pitches all over Birmingham, with our home matches at Billesley Common, a large open space situated between the suburbs of Moseley and Yardley Wood in the south of the city. Many years later, part of the park was annexed to provide a new home for Moseley Rugby Club, after its home ground The Reddings was sold for housing.

In the summer, I played cricket on a midweek evening for the Welfare Department, and for the parks team at weekends, as sport continued to play a significant role in my life.

* * * *

In the football season Edwin and I, and other friends from the parks cricket team, would regularly meet on a Friday evening at a local hostelry, the Robin Hood in Hall Green in Birmingham, just down the road from the slightly more upmarket town of Shirley, near Solihull. There we would enjoy a fairly typical lads' night out, the evening becoming more raucous the later it got and the more the beer flowed. It was not uncommon for each of us to knock back eight or nine pints across the evening, sometimes more.

The notion of a "designated driver", who would consume only soft drinks, was not hugely prevalent back then, but one or two usually took on a similar role, drinking a lot less than the others with a view to ensuring that all had a safe journey home. Occasionally we would all chip in and contribute to the cost of a round-trip by taxi.

On Saturday morning, I would stumble out of bed no earlier than half-past-eleven. Edwin was soon at the door, ready for us to go to whichever local football team had the best Saturday afternoon fixture. We went to watch Aston Villa, Birmingham City or West Bromwich Albion, depending on the likely standard of their opponents.

Mum proffered only the occasional murmur of reproach if we had appeared to have consumed slightly more beer than was good for us the night before. Regardless she would serve Edwin and me a full English fry-up of bacon, egg, sausage, tomato and fried bread, and a steaming mug of hot tea to set us up for the match. She enjoyed looking after us, and she readily welcomed Edwin into our home, often telling me what a nice, polite boy he was.

Those weekends were hugely enjoyable and worth looking forward to.

* * * *

My ability as a footballer was such that I could be labelled "enthusiastic" and occasionally "hard-working". Now and then I even showed a tantalising glimpse of having a modicum of ability. I thoroughly enjoyed playing it, but I was never going to be a regular in anyone's team.

I joined a couple of local parks teams, but it was over a chat in a local pub one evening with some friends who were much better players than me, that I resolved to form my own team. At this time, I was still living at home with my parents who had by now moved from Maypole Lane to the nearby Worcestershire village of Hollywood, near Wythall.

A local sports club had a spare field with no regular activities taking place on it, and they agreed to turn it into a football pitch. We paid a modest rent taken from match day fees contributed by the players. We joined a Sunday league, and through the winter months I drove the tractor that pulled both mower and roller over the pitch, and I marked out the white lines. On match days I was player-manager, usually listing myself as substitute.

The fact that the sports club had a more than decent clubhouse and bar was an added attraction.

* * * *

My life was focused on the two things that so far as I was concerned mattered most, sport and music. The latter was encouraged by a guy called Danny, who I'd got to know when working for "Mr. V". Mum didn't like Danny very much. He was a couple of years older than me and boasted friends who turned out to be roadies for some of the nation's top pop and rock bands. Danny's occupation was always a touch vague and mysterious, but it seems he worked as a roadie himself from time to time.

Danny would usually pop in on a Thursday evening to say that he was going "for a road trip" at the weekend if I fancied joining him. I rarely said "no", so he would pick me up in his transit van on a Friday or, more often, a Saturday night and we would head out to the M1 motorway, to have a meal and to see which stars we could spot at the Blue Boar Services, later renamed as Watford Gap Service Station.

It had become a meeting place for rock bands including The Beatles, The Rolling Stones, The Kinks, The Who, Pink Floyd and Jimi Hendrix. They were usually travelling back south to London from whatever tour location they had just played, and the Blue Boar was a useful stopping-off point for them to break their journey and have something to eat in the early hours of the morning.

Inevitably, there were quite a few young ladies present as well, keen to see and, if possible, meet the rock stars. Their presence was another part of the attraction of the place for Danny. I would be lying if I said I didn't find them interesting too. However, like Danny, they were slightly older than me, and they certainly did not appear to be ladies you would want to take home to meet your mum. In any event, I was not a rock star nor even a part-time roadie, so my presence was largely irrelevant.

We never did see The Beatles there, but we saw The Kinks and The Who a couple of times, and on one occasion, The Stones. It was exciting and fun, but frowned on by Mum, particularly when I got home very late, or very early, depending on how you looked at it. It only went on for a few months, after which time Danny's visits stopped.

I heard that he'd been recruited as a roadie for an overseas tour, but it was never clear which band he was working for. Another story suggested that Danny had been detained "at Her Majesty's pleasure", but there was never any confirmation about precisely what had happened to him.

* * * *

A huge bonus of being a city council employee in Birmingham is that you could work in the evening as a steward at concerts at Birmingham Town Hall. It is a striking building that has survived various reconstructions of the city around it. The Town Hall looks like a Corinthian temple and was closely modelled on the Temple of Castor and Pollux in Rome. Its distinctive features include the great Palladian columns that surround the outside of the hall.

It was extensively refurbished in the early 2000s and relaunched as a concert venue in October 2007. It was officially reopened on 22nd April 2008 by their Royal Highnesses, The Prince of Wales and The Duchess of Cornwall.

Many years before that, I was fortunate enough to be employed as a steward, checking tickets and showing people to their seats, and then staying on to watch the show. Not only did I see the concerts for free, but I was also paid a small remuneration for doing so.

I watched a wonderfully eclectic range of stars perform on that Town Hall stage. In no particular order, they included Joan Baez, Julie Felix, Tom Paxton, Don McLean, Manfred Mann, The Spencer Davis Group, Roy Wood's Wizard, The Osmonds, The Sutherland Brothers & Quiver, Pink Floyd, Delaney & Bonnie & friends, Neil Sedaka, Elton John and David Bowie. Imagine that lot at one festival. They gave me the festival of my youth.

There was a bar in a huge space on the floor below the main auditorium. There you would often find Robert Plant and Roy Wood together, alongside other local musos, enjoying refreshments before the main act. Steve Gibbons and Mike Sheridan were just two of Birmingham's musical aristocracy who would also turn up to gigs.

* * * *

The Spencer Davis Group had Midlands connections. Spencer Davis himself was born in Swansea, and drummer Pete York is from Redcar in North Yorkshire, but the two other members of the band were both Birmingham lads. Bass player Muff Winwood, who later went on to produce albums for others including Dire Straits, was born in Erdington, whilst his brother Stevie, who was to enjoy a successful solo career and was part of the bands Traffic and Blind Faith, was born in Handsworth.

When The Spencer Davis Group played in Birmingham they therefore attracted a large local following. In 1968, when they were the support band for a tour headlined by Manfred Mann, that local support prompted the bill to be swapped. That night the Manfreds went on first and The Spencer Davis Group was promoted to the top of the bill.

That did not go down well with Mann or his band, which at that time included Paul Jones as lead vocalist. They did play in the first half, but insisted on completing their full set, even though it meant overrunning their allotted time. The Town Hall manager, an irascible little man with horn-rimmed glasses and a rather pointless single-strand comb-over haircut, who often enjoyed at least half a glass of liquid refreshment more than he should whilst working, determined he would cut their set short. He ordered that the house lights be switched on just as Manfred Mann was starting their big hit and closing number 'Semi-Detached Suburban Mr James'.

They finished the song and acknowledged the applause and cheers of the packed Town Hall audience before leaving the stage ready for a fight with whoever had tried to spoil their routine by putting the lights up. The manager had locked himself away in his office, and so avoided an immediate confrontation, only to be faced with Manfred Mann and his manager before the night ended. How that was resolved I don't know, but I do know that The Spencer Davis Group were brilliant in the second half, proving beyond doubt that they deserved to be top of the bill, in Birmingham at least.

* * * *

Reflecting now, I consider it quite extraordinary that I saw the original line-up of Tyrannosaurus Rex – Marc Bolan and Steve Peregrin Took. That was on Saturday, 15th February 1969, with a mime artist as a supporting act. His name was David Bowie.

Just as extraordinary were the successive nights three years later, when Bowie returned to Birmingham Town Hall in the guise of Ziggy Stardust. He had already played at the Town Hall earlier in the tour as he and his band promoted the album 'The Rise and Fall of Ziggy Stardust and the Spiders from Mars', and its follow-up, 'Aladdin Sane'. After taking the show across the UK, the USA and Japan throughout 1972, Bowie returned for more UK dates the following year and played two more nights at Birmingham Town Hall, on Thursday and Friday, 21st and 22nd June 1973.

Back then, to maximise ticket sales, promoters would schedule two shows per night, usually at 6.30pm and 8.30pm. So it was for Bowie, with more than 1,000 seats sold for each performance.

On stage, the Town Hall's mighty pipe organ behind the podium was effectively hidden by the atmospheric and dramatic lighting effects as Bowie took the stage as Ziggy Stardust. His band were cast as The Spiders From Mars with Mick Ronson on lead guitar, Trevor Bolder on bass guitar, and drummer Mick 'Woody' Woodmansey.

Working as a steward, I saw all four performances and marvelled at the musical brilliance, stagecraft and courage of Bowie. Courage particularly, because at some point on the first night, he injured his left ankle. Despite an obvious and no doubt painful limp he returned the following night for two more shows, the affected ankle heavily strapped and bandaged.

* * * *

One of the best nights of all for me was 3rd December 1969 when the star turn was Delaney and Bonnie and Friends.

The 'Friends' were a band of top musicians put together and led by Eric Clapton. Seeing Clapton, one of the all-time great rock guitarists play live, was quite something in itself, but that was topped by my mate and fellow steward Paul Luton nudging my elbow to point out another star guitarist playing anonymously at the back of the stage amongst the 'friends'. It was none other than George Harrison of The Beatles, who had turned up for a one-off guest appearance simply to play as part of the band.

Once more there were two shows that evening, one at 6.30pm, with very few seats occupied for the early start, followed by a full house for the 8.30pm performance. Paul and I blagged our way backstage between shows and found ourselves milling around next to the musicians, including Eric Clapton and George Harrison. We were both star-struck, neither of us getting up the nerve to say anything to them. George, sensing our nervousness, nodded his head towards us and said, "Alright lads?".

Ten years later, I was to interview George, but not in a music or concert setting. By then, the four Beatles had gone their separate ways and George was indulging in his love of motor sport. In 1969, however, Birmingham's concertgoers were in for a treat with that surprise guest appearance on the

Town Hall stage. The local newspaper, the *Birmingham Evening Mail*, ran a photo and interview of him the following night under the headline "The millionaire who came to jam".

* * * *

Earlier that year I delighted my Mum by declaring that I was going to spend the weekend on the Isle of Wight, one of her favourite holiday locations. I told her that I was going with my friend Martin who I had got to know at one of the Town Hall gigs. Not true, but if I told Mum I was going on my own I would never have heard the end of it.

Martin was actually a sound engineer, who often assisted with the sound system at the Town Hall. He had tickets for that year's Isle of Wight Festival at the end of August, where the likes of Joe Cocker, The Who and The Moody Blues would be playing. Best of all, top of the bill was Bob Dylan.

Martin had been planning to go with some friends, but a family issue had intervened, and he wasn't going to make it. He knew how much I loved going to the Town Hall concerts and how much I enjoyed live music, so he offered me the ticket free of charge.

When I protested that he should sell it, with the distinct possibility of making a tidy profit, he just raised an eyebrow and smiled.

"I didn't pay for it in the first place," he said. "One of The Who's roadies got it for me, and in any case, I know you like your music. So, do you want it or don't you?"

I gratefully accepted and set off for the Isle of Wight on the morning of Thursday, 28th August 1969, with sun cream in my backpack as well as sandwiches that Mum had insisted on making. She'd made enough for two of us, for which I was grateful because it meant I could eat what Mum had intended to be Martin's share as well as my own.

After arriving on the island on the ferry from Southampton, I made my way with thousands of others to the festival, which was held at Woodside Bay, near Ryde. My memories of the event are a touch hazy, and not because of the effects of the substance, you could smell everywhere on the festival site. The fact that I don't smoke anyway, not then nor since meant that I had no interest in the experiences that others seemed to enjoy from doing so.

What I didn't know was that I was developing the first stages of a bad dose of flu, but a steady though not excessive intake of alcohol kept me going.

Though never totally wasted, I consumed enough to ensure that I was "happy" throughout. Even happier after I stumbled, quite literally, across a Swedish girl called Sissel. Tall, slim and blonde, with brilliant blue eyes, she had unwittingly stretched out across my path as I was trying to find a vantage point to see the stage. I fell forward, just avoiding a couple of blokes who, it later emerged, had positioned themselves for both a view of the stage and a view of Sissel and the girlfriends that she was with.

She got to her feet straight away and was full of apologies. When she realised that I was alone she insisted, in her broken English, that she made it up to me by inviting me to have a drink with her and her friends. That her friends were attractive too there was no doubt, but there was something special and quite magnetic about Sissel.

The two guys that I had almost collapsed on top of were not slow in seizing the moment either. Whilst Sissel and I got to know each other, they took the opportunity to move closer to her friends. It was one of those incidents from which international liaisons are born.

I do remember the performance that weekend of the Bonzo Dog Doo Dah Band, although it stretched my vocabulary to try and explain them to Sissel; she understood 'eccentric', so that helped. I can also recall seeing Tom Paxton, The Pretty Things and Free. Then there was Dylan. He didn't have The Beatles on stage with him after all, despite rumours that have suggested he might, but John, George and Ringo were all there to meet him and watch from backstage.

Dylan's set started at about 11.00pm and finished a few minutes after midnight. The attendance at the festival was put at 100,000, although it felt like much more. We were crammed in tight, which delightfully meant that Sissel and I became very close, very quickly. Dylan included songs from his album "John Wesley Harding", which is a personal favourite of mine, and two that Sissel knew the words to, "Lay Lady, Lay" and "I'll Be Your Baby Tonight."

Her English was certainly passable, though not extensive. It was more than satisfactory for us to be able to communicate, and she made it clear, gently but firmly, that her vocabulary included the word "no."

Sissel and her friends stayed on the island after the festival. The last I saw of her before making my way to catch the ferry back to the mainland, was her smiling and waving goodbye before the three of them gathered their things ahead of looking for somewhere to stay in Ryde. I had said words to the effect that we should keep in touch, but she just laughed and said "Maybe."

I never saw nor heard of her again, but I remember much more of being with Sissel than I do the musical performances of the 1969 Isle of Wight Festival, Bob Dylan's performance apart.

Whether my mum had imagined that I would bring back a souvenir vial filled with layers of different coloured sand from Alum Bay, I don't know, but if she did she was disappointed. She put the fact that I didn't say much about the weekend down to me probably feeling tired from the travelling. I was very tired. Tired and happy, but about to hit my bed for a fortnight after the doctor diagnosed that I had full-blown flu.

* * * *

Another festival, the following year, took on an altogether different turn. This was the Bath Festival of Blues and Progressive Music, held at the Royal Bath and West Showground in Shepton Mallet in Somerset from 27th to 29th June 1970. Pink Floyd performed, and so did one of my all-time favourite bands, Led Zeppelin.

Three mates went with me on a very hot weekend. The liquid refreshment was consumed quite freely, although I was aware that I had to drive back home afterwards. As a consequence, my beer intake was limited and replaced for the most part by Coca-Cola.

Led Zeppelin's performance at that festival lingers in the memory. They were sensational, starting with "Immigrant Song", and ending with "Whole Lotta Love", "Communication Breakdown", and a medley of classic rock and roll songs as an encore.

The festival was also memorable for having the feel of being wholly mismanaged, which oddly added to the frisson of it all. Near to where we pitched ourselves in the main field was a makeshift gents' toilet. It consisted of a rectangular space surrounded by a large Hessian wall, held in place every three or four yards by metal poles, each up to five feet high.

Inside the wall was a row of large metal buckets, each heavily coated inside by heavy-duty disinfectant. The Hessian was not tall enough to hide the whole of the individual blokes who were relieving themselves, so as they were urinating their heads could be seen by all and sundry, and they could see over the wall. It meant that they could still see the stage whilst having a pee.

As dusk set in one music lover decided to add to the ambience by putting out his cigarette, or similar, adjacent to the Hessian wall. Except he didn't extinguish it completely, and within a few seconds a wall of flame, encouraged by the extra strong disinfectant, travelled at an alarming rate around the outskirts of the makeshift urinal, exposing the private parts and activities of those inside. I am sure some pubic hairs must have been singed before the fire was extinguished.

On the way home, in the early hours of the morning, we sang Beatles songs to ensure I stayed awake at the wheel. We also spent a little while debating with great amusement the consequences of the fire that destroyed the makeshift gents. We concluded that a new rock band would surely take the world by storm with the name 'The Blazing Urinals'.

* * * *

I have always enjoyed going to gigs. A friend of mine, a student at Lanchester Polytechnic in Coventry, included me in the guest list for events there, when opportunity and circumstance allowed. One such evening was Thursday, 3rd February 1972. He had secured tickets for me and two or three other mates to go to a concert that was part of that year's Lanchester Arts Festival.

The big attraction for me that night was Slade, who had emerged from the Black Country and had just enjoyed their first top 10 hits with "Coz I Luv You" and "Look Wot You Dun". Billy Preston, who had made his mark playing keyboards on Beatles' records, was also on the show, and top of the bill was the American star Chuck Berry.

I was not well that night. My first marriage was falling apart, and yet again I had the start of what turned out to be 'flu. However, my spirits were lifted by being in the audience that joined in when encouraged to do so by Chuck Berry in the song "My Ding-A-Ling". The performance was recorded, with Chuck Berry rehearsing us in what he wanted for nearly 20 minutes before launching fully into the song. Released as a single, that live recording topped the UK charts, so, together with some 3,000 others, I appeared on a No.1 hit record.

* * * *

In 1968, I took my first steps towards doing something about my love of radio by joining the Birmingham Hospital Broadcasting Network (BHBN). Its studios were then at the Edgbaston County Cricket Ground so, learning as I went from the highly experienced BHBN team, I started to cover sport. That included commentating on Warwickshire's county championship cricket matches.

I also hosted a weekly record request show. That meant visiting the wards at the local hospitals to interview patients. It occurred to me that I could also take advantage of my evening job at Birmingham Town Hall to interview stars performing there and include those interviews during my show.

Most of the artists were ready and willing to sit down and chat with me and often recorded a message for the audience listening in their hospital beds. Amongst those I spoke to were Neil Sedaka and Elton John.

* * * *

I was privileged to meet Neil Sedaka a couple of times when he came to the UK on tour, but it was at Birmingham Town Hall in 1973 that he generously gave me his time to record an interview. He indulged this young, wet behind the ears interviewer, as I asked him first to tell me about how his musical career began.

NS: "I started as a concert pianist. I was studying to be something in the serious world at the Juilliard School of Music in New York."

SL: "But you're first British hit single was 'I Go Ape' in 1959. That was quite a transition, wasn't it?"

NS: "I would think so. The teachers were very shocked at Juilliard in fact. I was embarrassed to play that one. I used to play 'Stupid Cupid' instead."

SL: "That was the one you wrote for Connie Francis", I added, trying to sound knowledgeable, and then asked, "had you been playing pop music while you'd been studying?"

NS: "I started playing pop music when I was about 13, and I didn't leave Juilliard until I was about 19."

SL: "What did your parents think? They would have encouraged you towards classical music, I would imagine."

NS: "They were horrified when I started to play pop things because they wanted me to have adopted music, but as soon as the first record came on the radio, they changed their opinion. All the neighbours opened the windows and said, 'Neil's on!'".

SL: "Of course, a string of hits followed – 'Breaking Up Is Hard To Do', 'Happy Birthday Sweet Sixteen', and probably the biggest of all 'Oh Carol'. You wrote that for Carole King, didn't you? What was the story behind that?"

NS: "She was my girlfriend, and I brought her into the business."

That came across as a slightly defensive answer as if he was saying "Don't go any further into that", so I didn't.

The interview with Neil Sedaka occurred as he enjoyed a return to chart success in the UK. Many of his songs that became worldwide hits in the 70s were not released initially in his native America, but 'That's When the Music Takes Me', 'Standing On The Inside', and 'Our Last Song Together' all registered in the UK charts. In addition, he wrote 'Love Will Keep Us Together' which gave The Captain & Tennille a US number one.

Meanwhile, other established artists were making a significant impact with new versions of old songs, which prompted my next question.

SL: "We have people like David Cassidy and Donny Osmond doing their versions of old, classic pop hits, and The Carpenters have devoted an entire side of one album to the hits of yesterday. What do you put this nostalgia thing down to?"

NS: "I don't know. I think it's a passing fad and it won't last very long."

SL: "But aren't your audiences wanting to see the old Neil Sedaka?"

NS: "No. I'm thankful that it's to the contrary. They come to hear the new ones".

SL: "You are, though, very firmly re-established again, aren't you? 'Solitaire' is a big hit for Andy Williams. There were a few other versions of that, weren't there?"

NS: "Yes, some good ones too – Petula Clark, Tony Christie, The Searchers…"

Foolishly I rushed in with a question that received a very firm retort, albeit delivered with a smile.

SL: "You wrote Solitaire for Petula Clark, didn't you?"

NS: "No! I wrote it for Neil Sedaka".

The next question was the obvious one that all singer-songwriters are asked, so why not ask it?

SL: "Which do you find the most rewarding – writing, recording, or performing live?"

NS: "They're all very different, and you have to be able to do them all. I suppose performing is the most taxing, because it's one thing to be able to write a song in the privacy of your living room, and then to go out in front of two or three thousand people takes a great deal out of you. Today, though, you have to be able to do it".

SL: "Which comes first for you – the words or the music?"

NS: "I write the music, and then either I put the lyric to it or Phil Cody or Howard Greenfield does, or maybe Roger Atkins".

More than 20 years later Sedaka returned to Birmingham to perform at Symphony Hall and was reported as falling in love with the place and its renowned brilliant acoustics. That evening in 1973, however, as we sat in his dressing room at Birmingham Town Hall, he was full of praise for the old building.

NS: "It's wonderful! Some person, who will remain unmentioned, said 'Oh, you're not going to like the hall'. I said, 'Really?'. They said 'Yes, the sound is very bad. I saw Ray Conniff there'. Well, I must say I'm pleasantly surprised. I think it's wonderful".

As I thanked him for the time he'd given me – much longer than I had anticipated – I asked what song most reflected Neil Sedaka at that time.

NS: "Good question. One off the new album – either 'Going Nowhere' or 'Laughter In The Rain'.

The latter was not only a big hit in the UK, but it was also the song that took him back to the top of the charts in the US, his first American number-one since 'Breaking Up Is Hard To Do' in 1962.

Ooh, I hear laughter in the rain

Walking hand in hand with the one I love

Ooh, how I love the rainy days

And the happy way I feel inside

Neil Sedaka & Phil Cody 1974

©Sony/ATV Music Publishing LLC, BMG Rights Management

Chapter Five

This is Elton John Speaking

Blue jean baby, L.A. lady, seamstress for the band
Pretty eyed, pirate smile, you'll marry a music man
Ballerina, you must have seen her dancing in the sand
And now she's in me, always with me, tiny dancer in my hand

Bernie Taupin & Elton John, 1972
© Universal Music Publishing Group

I met Elton John in 1971 when he played at Birmingham Town Hall just as his 'Madman Across The Water' album was released. That album included probably my favourite Elton John song, 'Tiny Dancer'.

Whenever possible I arrived at the Town Hall for my stewarding shift early enough to see the sound check. This particular evening, Friday, December 3rd, 1971, was one such. Elton's fifth single, 'Your Song', had made it into the UK Top 10 and it was also a Top 20 hit in America. He followed that with more chart success in the US, but "Tiny Dancer" only made it into the lower reaches of the Top 100.

At more than 6 minutes in duration, the record proved to be too long for inclusion on most radio shows and so it did not receive as much radio airplay as it deserved, which may account for it failing to hit the heights in the singles chart. Radio stations were not keen to play songs that were substantially longer than the usual average of 3 minutes, so "Tiny Dancer" sadly fell foul of that yardstick. It has nonetheless become a big favourite within Elton's repertoire.

After the sound check, Elton came off stage and just mingled and chatted with those of us who had been watching. He was really likeable, keen to chat and happy to pass the time with people who obviously enjoyed listening to his music. There was nothing then to suggest that he would become the exuberant, larger-than-life showman that would emerge later.

Two years later at the Town Hall, it was a much more flamboyant Elton John who played there for two successive nights, Sunday and Monday, 16th and 17th December 1973. His seventh album, the iconic 'Goodbye Yellow Brick Road', had just been released and singles like 'Rocket Man', 'Daniel', and 'Saturday Night's Alright For Fighting', had firmly established him as a worldwide hitmaker.

* * * *

Elton sat alongside an eclectic mix of hit records and artists in the UK charts. The Partridge Family, Peters and Lee, The Carpenters, Clifford T. Ward, Paul Simon and The Osmonds were enjoying Top 10 success, as were solo releases from former Beatles' George Harrison and Paul McCartney.

There were also the so-called "glam" acts such as The Sweet and Gary Glitter, then one of the nation's best-loved entertainers. Years later Glitter, under his real name Paul Gadd, saw his fame shatter and his reputation irreparably tarnished, when he was convicted for downloading child pornography. Later still, he was convicted of historical child sex offences. In 1973 however, there was not even a hint of those issues. So as far as Elton John was concerned, Gary Glitter was at that time a hugely popular, rival hitmaker who enjoyed great chart success.

* * * *

Despite now being a big star, Elton had no hesitation in saying "yes" when I asked him if I could record an interview for hospital radio in Birmingham.

In fact, as well as the interview he also recorded a special message for those listening in hospital.

EJ: "Hello. This is Elton John speaking. I'd like to say hello to everybody in hospital in the Birmingham area. I hope you're feeling not too bad, and I hope that you're going to get well soon and get out of that hospital soon and get home. So, from Elton John and my band, and everybody else connected with me, we'd like to wish you all the best."

That message, and the interview that followed, was recorded after the second show on the Monday evening.

SL: "You've just performed for more than two thousand fans. How does that feel?"

EJ: "Oh, very elated. This is one of my favourite gigs. We've only done two nights in a couple of places, Glasgow and Birmingham, and this is one of my favourite halls. I really like it. I'm knocked out tonight. I'm really pleased."

SL: "Touring must be a very exhausting experience. Do you find it so?"

EJ: "It is at the moment because we've been on the road since halfway through August. We've been ten weeks in America, and we came back and started on an English tour. I've got things to do in between, like produce Kiki (Dee) and record myself, so I've really not stopped since August. In fact, I'm not stopping till June next year, so ask me in June and I shall be a frazzled wreck!"

SL: "You obviously enjoy it though, although do you do it to repay the loyalty of your fans for buying the records?"

EJ: "Oh no, I would never do it if I thought that. I do it because I enjoy it. I would never do it if I didn't enjoy it. I wouldn't do it to say 'We've got to do it to sell records'. It's something I like doing. I thought after I'd been doing it for three years the novelty would wear off, but I'm enjoying it even more now than I did when I started out. That's really incredible because I thought I'd be really fed up with it by now."

SL: "It's four years now since your first album was released, 'Empty Sky'. You've reached the stage now where every record you make is a guaranteed hit before it's released almost."

EJ: "I wouldn't say that. Album-wise we do alright, but with singles this country's dodgy. We've had some pretty good years here, but I never think any single, or any album, is set for success because you never can tell. If you go along thinking like that you can come unstuck. When the next album or single comes out I'm always on the 'phone asking "How's it doing?". I get very paranoid about how it does".

SL: "Why do you say, 'this country is a dodgy scene'?"

EJ: "Well, I've never had a number one over here. I've had a number-one album. Two number-one albums actually, but in America, I could sing the national anthem and put it out, and it would sell."

He laughed before continuing.

EJ: "That's a bit of a drag, in some senses."

SL: "What do you put that down to?"

EJ: "I don't know. I just think it may be because we've toured America a lot and we've become very popular over there. There's a different sort of scene in America. It's different to here. There's not the teenybopper scene as such in America. There's not people like Gary Glitter or The Sweet. The groups that sell are Grand Funk and groups like that, and I think that's probably why. I think the audiences are that much older in the States."

I was also interested in the way that Elton was different at this point in 1973 from the performer I'd seen two years before. Now he was much more elaborate and dazzling in his stage persona.

SL: "There are lots of gimmicks appearing in your act now. Flashing lights and so on. Where does all this come from?"

EJL "We've always had flashing lights I think. No, it's not gimmicks, it's just stage presentation. We've always concentrated on that."

SL: "But this is something that pop music is developing these days. There's more and more of it, isn't there?"

EJ: "Well, I think you have to give value for money. I think kids like to pay money and see something. That's why Gary Glitter is so popular because they know they're going to see a show. The Faces always travel around with a good lighting system. I think the groups feel more at home with a good set-up on stage, and they like to give value for money."

After successive nights in Birmingham, Elton was scheduled for three nights the following week at the Hammersmith Odeon in London, before taking a short break from his tour over Christmas and the first few months of 1974. Then it was a benefit gig in May at his beloved Watford Football Club, nine more nights in London, including a guest appearance at a Beach Boys concert, before going off round the UK once more, taking in Leeds, Manchester, Preston, Liverpool and a whole lot more.

Finding time to relax from a schedule like that prompted my next question.

SL: "How do you unwind after a concert like this?"

EJ: "Usually by going to have something to eat. It's very hard to unwind. In America, all you do is go to bed, because you're getting up the next morning at eight o'clock to go somewhere else."

SL: "A short break from touring after Christmas though. What are your plans?"

EJ: "We've got a new album to do in January. I don't know how that's going to come out, but if next year is half as good as this year's been for me, I won't complain."

That new album was 'Caribou', which became number one in the UK, the USA, Australia and Canada, and it included the hit singles 'The Bitch Is Back' and 'Don't Let The Sun Go Down On Me'. So, as he had said, there was nothing much to complain about from a prolific singer-songwriter well on his way to becoming one of the world's biggest pop superstars.

* * * *

We never got around to chatting about our mutual love of football. In 1976, Elton became Chairman of Watford, proving to be one of the club's most passionate fans. He appointed Graham Taylor as his manager. Together they took Watford from the Fourth Division to the First. Taylor went on to manage England.

Elton's birth name was Reg Dwight. His cousin Roy Dwight was a professional footballer, famous for his role in the 1959 FA Cup Final. Playing for Nottingham Forest against Luton Town, Dwight scored the opening goal. 23 minutes later with Forest winning 2–0, he broke his leg and was carried off the Wembley pitch. With only 10 men, Forest held on to win the match 2–1.

Music played such an important part in Elton's life. He was hired at the age of 15 as a pianist at a pub near his home at Pinner in Middlesex, but anyone observing him supporting Watford, wearing their black, red and yellow colours, will know just how much he loves football.

And you can tell everybody this is your song

It may be quite simple, but now that it's done

I hope you don't mind, I hope you don't mind that I put down in words

How wonderful life is while you're in the world

Bernie Taupin & Elton John 1970

Chapter Six

On Air

They say it's gonna die but please let's face it
They just don't know what's a goin' to replace it.
Ballads and calypsos they got nothin' on
Real country music that just drives along
Well, move it.

Ian Samwell, 1958
© EMI Mills Music Inc

The sixties began in October 1958. In the UK, anyway.

Until then American stars, led by Elvis Presley, had dominated the UK charts. The Everly Brothers, Paul Anka, Buddy Holly, Pat Boone, Connie Francis, Jerry Lee Lewis and Ricky Nelson were other American performers who enjoyed a regular flow of hits.

A few English stars, like Marty Wilde, Tommy Steele and Frankie Vaughan made it into the Top 10, but it was on 29th August 1958 that a record was released that was widely regarded as being one of the first authentic rock and roll songs produced outside the United States. It made a star of an 18-year-old called Harry Webb, who had changed his name to Cliff Richard.

The song was called 'Move It', apparently written on the top deck of a London bus by guitarist Ian "Sammy" Samwell while he was travelling to Cliff's house for a band rehearsal. It became the first hit record for Cliff and his backing group, then known as The Drifters, who were to be re-named The Shadows. 'Move It' reached number two on the UK singles chart.

John Lennon later said, "Before Cliff and The Shadows, there had been nothing worth listening to in British music."

Four years after 'Move It' provided a lift-off for Cliff, The Beatles released a single, written by Lennon and fellow band member Paul McCartney, called 'Love Me Do'. The next phase of a huge cultural revolution was underway.

* * * *

I was, and remain, a huge fan of Cliff Richard, but in the firmament of the musical stars I admire, The Beatles are also right up there. My affection for them began in an uninspiring, dour classroom at King's Norton Grammar School when one Thursday morning in mid-September 1962, my form mate Roy March came up to me, obviously bursting to pass on critically important information. Roy and I were big fans of Radio Luxembourg, which transmitted to the UK from the Grand Duchy. Each night you could hear the current hits and, on a Sunday evening, listen to the *New Musical Express* (NME) Top 40, hosted by the Australian-born DJ Barry Alldis.

The UK number one that weekend was 'She's Not You' by Elvis Presley and The Jordanaires, but Roy was not concerned with that. He was falling over himself to tell me about this new English group he had just heard.

"They're called The Beatles", he said, almost breathless with excitement, "and this is their first record. They're brilliant!"

In his hand, Roy held a seven-inch vinyl single with a red Parlophone label, that gave the title of the song as 'Love Me Do', credited the composers as 'Lennon – McCartney', and named the performers as The Beatles. We had no means of listening to the record there and then in school, but Roy said I could borrow it, take it home to play it, just as long as I promised to bring it back the following day.

I did return it to him, but not before almost wearing it out as I played it over and over again on the record player in my bedroom. The B-side, featuring a song called 'P.S. I Love You', was played just as much that evening as I was introduced to The Beatles.

That weekend I purchased my own copy of the record, which reached a relatively modest number 17 in the charts. It was the start of a musical phenomenon.

* * * *

Soon other British bands made their mark, but there were battles to be won along the way. One band that faced a big challenge to be heard was Georgie Fame and the Blue Flames. They had been formed originally as the backing group for singer Billy Fury but found it difficult to get their records played, even on Radio Luxembourg. "The station of the stars", as it was called, broadcasting on 208 medium wave, was the only game in town for artists to get airtime and for the mainly teenage record-buying public to hear them.

Georgie Fame's manager at the time was an Irish businessman called Ronan O'Rahilly. His efforts to put Fame's music on Luxembourg were frustrated because the radio station's main programmes were sponsored by the major record labels EMI, Decca, Pye and Philips. Each label had their own shows promoting just their records, each deciding which of their artists to promote. Although Georgie Fame recorded for EMI Columbia, his records were not being chosen for broadcast.

For pop music in the UK, there was no alternative to Radio Luxembourg. The BBC had a very staid, very formal network of just three stations. They were The Light Programme, The Home Service and The Third Programme. Little opportunity there for pop records.

Lunchtime shows on the BBC Light Programme did include songs that were listed in the current charts. They were played live, but not by the artists on the records. Two Birmingham-born singers, John Carter and Ken Lewis, who were both also songwriters, performed the latest hits as recorded by groups from the emerging Liverpool Sound in the early 60s. Augmented by jazz singers such as Marion Montgomery and Marion Ryan, and backed by session musicians, they appeared on Light Programme shows Easy Beat and Saturday Club.

For Carter and Lewis it was a crucial first step on the road to their own success. They went on to write hit songs for other artists, and they also recorded some songs of their own. Initially recording under the name Carter-Lewis and The Southerners, they then formed The Ivy League before being responsible for a string of hits, using group names The Flowerpot Men, White Plains, and First Class.

Carter and Lewis were not alone in singing the hits of the day on the Light Programme. Some were performed by a dance band with their own resident vocalists. One of the best of those was Ross McManus, whose son Declan would later become the huge star Elvis Costello.

I have a very clear recollection of hearing one such show when Ross McManus sang the Procul Harum hit 'A Whiter Shade Of Pale', accompanied by Jack Parnell and his Orchestra. It was an accomplished, professional performance, but it was definitely not what the record-buying kids wanted to hear. They wanted to hear the actual record.

The result of all that was defiance from Ronan O'Rahilly. He bought a 702-ton former Danish passenger ferry and had it converted to house a fully operational radio station on board, capable of transmitting from the open sea. At noon on Saturday 28th March 1964, Radio Caroline introduced pirate radio to the UK.

Calling itself "Your all-day music station" it initially broadcast from 6 a.m. to 6 p.m., seven days a week, and not only played the records people wanted to hear, but it also made stars of the DJs who played them. People like Simon Dee, Tony Blackburn, Johnnie Walker, Dave Lee Travis, and Keith Skues, who would later become my boss at Radio Hallam in Sheffield, all became well-known names. The Fortunes recorded the station's theme tune 'Caroline', and Ronan O'Rahilly had established a platform on which Georgie Fame and The Blue Flames could have their records played.

* * * *

In the 1960s UK Broadcasting was controlled by the GPO, the General Post Office. Its main preoccupation, as its name suggests, was the sending of mail across the country, essentially letters and parcels. This was construed as the sending of items from a specific sender to a specific receiver, so as new forms of communication were added they too came under the authority of the GPO.

The GPO granted exclusive radio broadcasting licences to the BBC. Television licences were also granted to the BBC and additionally, after intense pressure from various interested groups, to 16 commercially funded regional ITV companies. Many also wanted to see commercial radio introduced but they were thwarted by a succession of governments.

Radio Caroline initiated a change to all that, and it was soon followed by other offshore pirate stations such as Swinging Radio England, Britain Radio, and Wonderful Radio London, or "Big L" as it became known. The popularity of these stations demonstrated a public demand that would not go away.

* * * *

The pirates were exciting to listen to. Apart from playing the records that the BBC were not playing, they also featured new, exciting artists ignored by the BBC. The reception was not great, but in a way that made it even more fun. Throughout my career, I have often heard the mantra that "quality of content is more important than quality of reception", and up to a point, that is correct.

Certainly, in the days of those 60s pirate stations, you had no alternative but to put up with variable reception. The signal often faded in and out, but it was what you had to listen to if you wanted to enjoy the current pop hits. Radio Caroline was the station I could hear best, but only after placing my transistor radio at an odd angle in the corner of my parent's bathroom window. Not an ideal place to listen by any means, but with the volume turned up much louder than was acceptable to my Mum I could enjoy the music I wanted to hear.

Radio Caroline brought me many hits that the BBC didn't. They included the records of Crispian St. Peters, "You Were On My Mind" and "The Pied Piper", Len Barry's "Like A Baby", The Small Faces' "Sha-La-La-La-Lee", and "Wild Thing" by The Troggs.

It was original, vibrant and compelling, and just what teenagers wanted to hear. The term "teenagers" was used by popular newspapers whenever young people were involved in something untoward. It was used disparagingly about a generation that, for the first time in decades, was making the change from childhood to adulthood without being required to sacrifice itself in a war. It was a generation seeking a new identity and finding it in new, brash and confident musical expression.

* * * *

The challenge for the GPO and the Government was that although the pirate radio stations maintained perfectly legal sales and management offices in mainland Britain, their transmitters were not under British law. In addition, in most instances, the ships on which they were located were registered in other countries.

There followed lengthy debates in Parliament in which several reasons were listed as to why this unlicensed broadcasting should be stopped. They included allegations of the misappropriation of military installations, such as abandoned Second World War Sea Forts in the Thames Estuary. A station called Radio City, using the tagline "the tower of power", was housed in one of the forts.

Other objections were the use of wavelengths allocated to other legitimate users and the unauthorised playing of recorded music. The vessels themselves were said to pose a danger to shipping, and it was claimed that the broadcast signals could interfere with aircraft as well as police, fire and ambulance services.

An incident in 1966, when one pirate radio operator killed another in a dispute over sub-standard transmitting equipment, provided a spur for Parliament to take decisive action. On 15th August 1967, it passed the Marine Broadcasting Offences Act. Ireland, France and the Netherlands all passed similar legislation over the next few years.

The offshore stations were silenced, although Radio Caroline continued for a while after moving to the Dutch coast, where it was later joined by the rival Radio North Sea International.

In the UK, the success of the pirates and the demand for a new different style of radio programming prompted a major shake-up of BBC radio stations. The old, staid Home Service, Light Programme and Third Programme stations were scrapped. In their place, in September 1967, came four new national networks.

The Home Service was replaced by a speech-based channel to be called Radio 4, and the Third Programme by one for serious music and drama called Radio 3. There was also one replacing the Light Programme, geared to providing lighter music, mostly pop, as well as sport and a few talk-based shows. This service was split in two during the day, using the names Radio 1 and Radio 2, with shared evening programmes. It was the end of the 1970s before 24-hour broadcasting began.

Radio 1 was intended to fill the gap created by the offshore pirate stations, and it recruited many of its DJs from the likes of Radio Caroline and Radio London. Tony Blackburn, previously a star of Caroline, was the first voice on Radio 1, famously playing 'Flowers In The Rain' by The Move as the station's first record.

The new station line-up proved popular and successful, but it was also criticised by some who regarded Radio 1 as a pale, homogenised version of the pirate stations. However, for the majority of people who simply wanted to hear the current pop hits of the day it delivered just what was wanted.

* * * *

The man behind the concept and design of the four new national networks was a distinguished former Second World War correspondent called Frank Gillard. He had been made Director of Radio and was allowed to implement his plan, but he realised that there was another element that was missing from the new set-up. Gillard recognised that the pirate stations had, in some cases, been local to specific areas of the country as a consequence of the relatively limited range of their transmitters. He therefore introduced BBC Local Radio, which began as an experiment, initially co-funded by the BBC and local authorities.

The experiment actually began in Portsmouth on 29th November 1961. Gillard envisaged 150 BBC local stations such as this, each depending on local news agencies for news content and, as he put it, "under the charge of an independent highly paid manager, and staff of about 12".

The local authority funding was intended to play a significant role in helping to pay for the new service and to encourage local interest. That idea fell flat when only a few Labour-controlled local councils were willing to get involved.

After the 1961 Portsmouth experiment, the first properly established BBC Local Radio station was launched in 1967. On 8th November, BBC Radio Leicester went on air. It was followed by stations at Leeds, Stoke, Durham, Sheffield, Merseyside, Brighton, and Nottingham. By the early 1970s, the requirement for local authority funding was dropped, and the BBC Local Radio network spread across the country, funded by the licence fee.

* * * *

Whilst Gillard's work established the new shape of the BBC, there was another significant change in the nation's cultural and political scene. Before the Second World War the voting age in almost all countries was 21 or higher. In 1946 Czechoslovakia became the first state to reduce the voting age to 20 years, and by 1968 a total of 17 countries had lowered their voting age. In 1969, the UK had reduced its voting age to 18.

The general election of 1970 saw 18-year-olds having the right to vote for the first time. 1.1 million more people voted in 1970 compared to the previous election in 1966. Despite that, turnout actually fell to its lowest level since 1935.

Regardless of poor electoral turnout 18, 19, and 20-year-olds had now been empowered like never before. They were a force that politicians and decision-makers had to take account of.

* * * *

On 9th November 1970, BBC Radio Birmingham went on air from the newly built BBC Midlands broadcasting centre at Pebble Mill, located on the Calthorpe Estate in Birmingham. Like the other early BBC local stations, it broadcast on the newly introduced VHF waveband, later labelled as FM, rather than on the popular and then widely used medium wave, or AM, frequencies. Few VHF radios existed at the time, so the new local services attracted very small audiences until they were given a place on medium wave in addition to VHF a few years later.

Within a few weeks of the launch of Radio Birmingham, thanks to a recommendation from my friend and mentor at BHBN David Wigley, I found myself sitting in the newsroom at Pebble Mill talking to the station's first Sports Editor, Roger Moody. I was recruited to help on the Saturday afternoon sports show. That meant that I made the tea for the rest of the team, as well as keeping a check on scores coming in from some of the local non-league football matches. It was only one day a week, but it was my first job in proper radio.

* * * *

I was in my element, thoroughly enjoying rubbing shoulders with the radio station's full-time broadcasters and unashamedly trying to learn from them. One, who became a close friend, was a young news reporter called Ian Rufus. Ian was two years younger than me, but he had worked in newspapers, starting at his hometown's paper the *Rotherham Advertiser*.

He had many attributes, but I realised early in our friendship that Ian had a great ability to be one step ahead. Whilst living and working for the day, Ian always had an acute awareness of the future and what his next step might be. He was amongst the first to work out what opportunities were waiting and whether they were worth pursuing.

It, therefore, came as no surprise to me that Ian stayed little more than a year at BBC Radio Birmingham, before securing a senior reporter's job at what would be the UK's first legal, land-based, commercial radio station, LBC in London. When he left Pebble Mill, he made a point of coming over to me, shook my hand and looked me in the eye. "Let's keep in touch", he said. We did.

* * * *

Radio Birmingham Sports Editor Roger Moody was an excellent role model for a young hopeful broadcaster, and he generously gave of his time to guide and advise me in those early days. Exciting days they were too, with many characters who were to become household names making their mark.

One was Leslie Meakin, Birmingham born and bred, who hosted Radio Birmingham's weekday Breakfast Show, called "On The Move". Under the name Les Ross, he became a radio DJ by winning a competition run by a local newspaper. The runner-up in that competition was another locally-born would-be radio star. His name was Peter Dingley, better known as Johnnie Walker. Les and Johnnie both became well-known locally by securing gigs in local bars and ballrooms.

Whereas Les was younger, Johnnie was born two years before me. He went on to work on pirate radio ships before joining Radio 1.

Les also appeared on one of BBC Radio Birmingham's most popular shows, "The Ross And Henry Show", on Saturday morning, co-hosting with fellow Brummie John Henry. A recording of that show was sent to Radio 1, but word came back that it wouldn't work on the national station because it was "too slick".

Local sports journalist Tony Butler wandered in and out of the newsroom, providing tips and stories for Roger Moody. Tony was then a freelance reporter covering greyhound racing, speedway and other sports for the *Daily Telegraph* and other outlets. He would later become a star on Birmingham's first commercial station BRMB, before eventually returning to the BBC.

The Radio Birmingham News Editor was a man called Stan Jones. He took me to one side one day and said that he'd heard some of my interviews.

"You're very good," he said, making me feel ten feet tall, before giving me an outstandingly simple piece of advice.

"You're good, but you should remember that there is only ever one question when you interview someone," he said. "You look them in the eye and say, 'Joe Bloggs, what's it all about?' And then, you listen".

"The best interviewer," he added emphatically, "is a great listener".

That's advice that I've always remembered and tried to take with me throughout my career.

* * * *

BBC Radio Birmingham's Saturday afternoon show was imaginatively titled, "Sport On Saturday". It was hosted by a Midlands broadcasting legend of the time. A rumbustious, larger-than-life, journalist who could only be considered "old school" even by the perspective of those days. Barney Bamford.

Before local radio arrived, Barney was well-known across the Midlands for both sports and news features. Examples of his versatility, which also highlight how things used to be, are from Saturday, 17th November 1962, when Barney and his colleague John Camkin, provided live commentary on the Light Programme "on the second half of one of today's English League matches", as it was listed in the *Radio Times*. Not the whole match, just the second half.

Barney's eclectic workload extended to the Home Service where, every afternoon, separate regional programmes were scheduled and simultaneously broadcast to each different part of the country. It was regional radio, if not local.

On Friday, 29th October 1965, in a programme broadcast solely to the Midlands, Barney found himself talking to an American businesswoman about the beauty business. That show was listed in some detail in *Radio Times*:

16.45: HOME THIS AFTERNOON

including:

A Canal Restored: KEITH ACKRILL talks to people who remember the heyday of the Stratford-upon-Avon canal. those who watched its decline, and the helpers who were engaged in its reconstruction

A Change of Home: DAVID FRANKLIN on moving from town to village

Let's Take a Pub: TONY CHURCH talks to people who have decided to go over to the other side of the bar about the problems they have discovered

Sixty-eight Years of the Beauty Business: BARNEY BAMFORD talks to American beautician ROSE LAIRD

Introduced by DAVID STEVENS from the Midlands.

* * * *

So it was, when BBC Radio Birmingham began, the versatile Barney Bamford was the host of "Sport On Saturday". Barney had an idiosyncratic approach which began immediately before going on air, when he placed, on top of the broadcast desk in front of him, a bottle of brandy. Unopened, but with the seal removed from the stopper, so that the drink could be readily poured. Next to the bottle, a white porcelain teacup.

Not all presenters operated or drove, the desk themselves. Barney was one who did not. A technical producer in the next-door production studio where I was based did that job, switching on Barney's microphone and turning the controls.

In a modern studio, when you switch on your microphone you automatically activate a red light which shows that the mic is working. Not so in the Radio Birmingham studio in the early 1970s. The red light had its own separate switch, and sometimes the producer would switch on the presenter's mic but forget the red light.

On one afternoon, Saturday 14th April 1973, the red light was not switched on at the same time as Barney's microphone.

"I'm waiting for a red light", he said, live on air, to an audience innocently oblivious to what he meant. "Ah, there it is. Good afternoon, and welcome to Sport on Saturday on BBC Radio Birmingham."

Barney then hosted the show, seamlessly linking from football match reports to rugby commentaries, and reading other results and the latest scores along the way. The show ran from two in the afternoon until five o'clock. By five, Barney's bottle of brandy was empty, its contents consumed from a porcelain tea cup by a presenter who showed no obvious signs of having touched a drop.

At five o'clock BBC Radio Birmingham carried "Sports Report", in those days from Radio 2. That live re-broadcast from the national network ran for its full hour. The local output resumed for a further half-hour at six, with reports and interviews from local matches. I was part of that show, reading local results, or sometimes reporting from one of the local football clubs, usually Walsall or West Bromwich Albion.

On that day in 1973, I was in the studio. Barney was also the duty Midlands reporter for BBC network news that weekend, providing input if and when required to the national bulletins on Radio 2 and Radio 4. His habit, after the Radio Birmingham show, was to make his way through the Pebble Mill corridors to the Midlands Club and its bar on a floor above the studios. The rest of us joined him at half past six.

Barney's evening post-show tipple was a bottle of Guinness. Even though you might buy it for him he insisted on pouring it into a glass himself. That, he insisted, was the one way he could be sure the head on his drink was just as he wanted it.

That evening, during his first sip of Guinness, a message came through for him to urgently contact the newsroom in London. He used the phone in the bar and was heard to curse and mutter with some annoyance as he returned to his drink.

It transpired that late the night before a 22-year-old man had violently murdered three children in Worcester. The victims were a 4-year-old, a 2-year-old and a seven-month-old baby. After being killed, their bodies were impaled on the spikes of a wrought-iron fence. The London newsroom needed Barney to go to Worcester to interview police there and report back on the appalling tragedy.

Barney, having already polished off his brandy during the afternoon, now knocked back his Guinness and proceeded to drive down the M5 from Birmingham to Worcester. In those days the M5 was effectively no more than a dual carriageway, with just two lanes and a hard shoulder on either side of the central reservation.

Barney got there and back, fulfilled what had been asked of him, and returned to the Midlands Club just as the rest of us were preparing to go home. Someone bought him another Guinness, which he again poured himself before recounting the events of his journey.

No one was really surprised to learn that he had been stopped on the motorway by police who, he said, told him that one of his rear lights was faulty. As he told the story we looked at each other before one of the older members of the party asked the question that we were all burning to ask.

"Did they ask if you'd been drinking Barney?"

"No", he snapped back, almost triumphantly. "And do you know why?"

We looked at one another again and simultaneously shook our heads.

"Because", he said, almost glowing with pride, "I got out of my car and I walked to them. Perfectly capable."

Whether or not he was "perfectly capable", it transpired that the police officers had recognised him as he approached them. They knew what had happened in Worcester and understood why he was going there. So much so that they told him to follow them. They escorted him there and then waited to do so on his return journey, to make sure that he got back safely to Pebble Mill.

According to Barney, he had advised the officers that he was on duty for 'Her Majesty's British Broadcasting Corporation'.

Who knows if they really were impressed, let alone influenced, by that? It is more likely that the appalling nature and severity of the crime meant that they were concerned with ensuring that the BBC's man in the region was able to do his job and report the story.

* * * *

Barney retired soon after the start of BBC Radio Birmingham, with up-and-coming sports presenter Jim Rosenthal replacing him as host of the Saturday sports programme. Jim later became one of the nation's top presenters and commentators, enjoying a hugely successful career fronting sports shows, including coverage of football, boxing and Formula One, for ITV.

Other notable contributors to the station's sports output included Denis McShane, who would later become the Labour MP for Rotherham and a government minister. When Labour formed the government with Tony Blair as Prime Minister in 1997, Denis served as Parliamentary Private Secretary to a succession of ministers before being appointed Parliamentary Under-Secretary of State for Foreign and Commonwealth Affairs. In 2002 he was appointed Minister of State for Europe. Before turning to politics, Denis had been a reporter for BBC Radio Birmingham, including covering West Bromwich Albion, Wolverhampton Wanderers, and, occasionally, Coventry City.

Another significant character was Barry Lankester, a Coventry-born actor who became a well-known West Midlands news and sports reporter. He regularly covered Coventry rugby club's matches, and he was the first presenter of the West Midlands regional TV news programme, 'Midlands Today'.

* * * *

I worked briefly in the 1970s on a Friday evening sports programme on BBC Radio Birmingham, which previewed the weekend's action. Sports Editor Roger Moody had the excellent idea of recruiting local sports stars to host it.

It was presented first by the Northern Ireland international striker Derek Dougan, who had played for Aston Villa in the '60s, and later for Wolverhampton Wanderers. "The Doog", as he was called, had been one of my schoolboy footballing heroes, from his days at Blackburn Rovers when he was part of their famous "3-D" forward line, alongside Peter Dobing and Bryan Douglas.

Dobing, Dougan and Douglas were a formidable unit, although The Doog later said of his time at Blackburn, "the dourness of the club matched that of the town. I could not shake off the depression that caused me to wake each day regretting that I had to go to the ground. Life was grey and monotonous."

As a young fan, unaware of such anxieties affecting sports stars, I simply knew Derek Dougan as a top player who had a record of scoring in every other game. To work years later on a radio show that he presented was magical, even though my role was very minor, escorting his guests in and out of the studio.

When The Doog moved on, Roger Moody turned to one of that rare breed, a man who did well at two different sports, cricket and football. He was Jim Cumbes, who played First-Class cricket for four different counties as a right-arm fast-medium bowler and lower-order right-handed batsman. A Mancunian, by the time he came on board at BBC Radio Birmingham he had played for Lancashire, Surrey, and had then joined Worcestershire. He later played for Warwickshire before enjoying a highly successful career as chief executive of Lancashire from 1998 to 2012.

Jim was also a professional footballer. He was an accomplished goalkeeper for West Bromwich Albion and Aston Villa, amongst other clubs.

Whereas Derek Dougan was an urbane smooth talker with his charming Belfast lilt, Jimmy Cumbes was equally eloquent, but down to earth and unquestionably determined to do well. Both were keen to learn and understand how radio worked and about the part they were required to play.

The Friday evening show was a huge success, drawing a large listening audience and teaching me a lot about how to showcase local sport, and about the role and power of personality. Roger Moody's ability to attract these two charismatic characters to host the show was not lost on me.

* * * *

Common to many of the men and women I got to know in those early days in broadcasting was, as in the case of Barney Bamford, a propensity for drink. Several of them enjoyed a glass or two, and there was more than one senior manager at the BBC in Birmingham who kept a bottle of something strong and rejuvenating in a desk drawer.

My taste for beer had been developed socially alongside my friends and acquaintances, but when Roger Moody eventually sent me to report on matches on a Saturday afternoon I soon found that several pints on a Friday night out with the lads was not ideal preparation. Not for me, anyway.

Those Friday nights at the *Robin Hood* in Hall Green were no longer part of my weekly routine. In any event love and marriage intervened, but not in the best of circumstances.

When I find myself in times of trouble

Mother Mary comes to me

Speaking words of wisdom, let it be.

And in my hour of darkness

She is standing right in front of me

Speaking words of wisdom, let it be.

Let it be, let it be.

Whisper words of wisdom, let it be.

John Lennon, Paul McCartney, 1969

© Sony/ATV Music Publishing LLC

Chapter Seven

Options

Sail on silver girl

Sail on by

Your time has come to shine

All your dreams are on their way

See how they shine

Oh, if you need a friend

I'm sailing right behind

Like a bridge over troubled water

I will ease your mind

Like a bridge over troubled water

I will ease your mind

Paul Simon, 1970

© Universal Music Publishing Group

I have been married three times, not a record to boast about but it happened. The first time was in 1970.

Amongst the friends our family made at Immanuel Church were two sisters, both really lovely people. Their father had extremely strict, somewhat Victorian, views of how his daughters should behave and how their friendships should be conducted. I had no quarrel with that, though it certainly made dating difficult. Still, the day came when I married his younger daughter.

Immanuel Church was packed with family, friends and members of the wider congregation, all there to wish us well. Edwin McNamara, my old friend and work colleague from Birmingham Social Services Department, was my witty and trusty best man.

Waiting at the front of the church, wearing a morning suit with a white carnation in the buttonhole of my jacket, I looked down the aisle as my beautiful bride approached on her father's arm. It was a delightful and memorable start, yet our previously happy relationship went downhill all too quickly after we became husband and wife.

We honeymooned in the southwest of England, where we had previously enjoyed a few more than pleasant holidays, stopping at Minehead on our first night as a married couple. To say that it did not go well is an understatement. When it came to my bedroom performance, my bride found me wanting, and it was not long into the marriage before she sought solace elsewhere. Her assessment of me that night may have been right, but if others in my life ever had similar complaints they were never expressed. Not to me, anyway.

I readily admit that I was an innocent abroad when it came to carrying out my wider duties as a husband. There had been no consideration of us living together beforehand. That had never been part of the equation, as her Dad would never have sanctioned such an idea. So when we set about making a home and domestic lifestyle, we were making it up as we went along.

That no doubt applies to many couples, but we seemed to flounder in the process, with confrontation and attrition swiftly coming between us. She found solace with someone else, and the last I saw of her after we parted was when I was travelling back from watching a West Bromwich Albion match at The Hawthorns and I glanced across the carriageway of the M6 motorway. As I was driving towards Birmingham, she was en route somewhere north, to wherever her new life was going to be. She was driving my tiny yellow Fiat 500 that she had decided to take as a tangible asset from the wreckage of our relationship.

Within a couple of years, we separated, and I found myself living alone. "Easy to prepare" ready meals sustained me and away from work I became a very lonely soul. With no one to talk to at home, I took some consolation from my record collection. One of the biggest-selling and widely acclaimed albums of the time, Simon and Garfunkel's "Bridge Over Troubled Water", was regularly played.

My parents were upset and disappointed, and my mother constantly hoped for a reconciliation. It was not to be, and I would often go alone to Barbarella's nightclub, then one of Birmingham's most popular venues. I could easily have found consolation in a glass, but fortunately, my finances prevented that, so at Barbarella's, I made a vodka and lime, just one, last all night.

Unhappy as I was at that time, nearly fifty years later circumstances brought my first wife and I, briefly, back together. Her sister died after contracting breast cancer, and I was notified of the arrangements for the funeral. Her sister had kept me in touch with their family, though never once in all the passing years did she mention my ex. As she had been a friend of all our family, my sister Yvonne and I attended the funeral together.

As we waited outside the crematorium, among the first people we met was my first wife. Probably because of the bad terms on which we had parted all those years before, it never occurred to me that she would want to see me again, let alone chat. I had no knowledge of how her life had panned out, so I really had no clue of how things would go if we came face to face once more.

With many people wanting to pay their respects and offer condolences there was never any likelihood of a prolonged reminiscence, but we were able to spend a few moments together. It was hardly private, with others milling around at the post-ceremony wake in a local pub. There was, though, just enough time for a few words to be said that allowed the healing of any scars that still lingered after so many years. Things were said that needed to be, including the word "sorry". Fences were mended, and we parted this time on good terms, albeit with a tinge of regret that things had gone so wrong in the first place.

* * * *

When that marriage broke down, my main preoccupation was my work. Alongside the day job with the local authority, I had a burgeoning career in broadcasting.

Partly because I wanted to move on from bad personal memories in the Midlands, I applied for a job advertised by Granada Television in Manchester. They were recruiting new continuity announcers and a move from one big city to another held a lot of appeal. The audition tape that they had asked for resulted in me being invited for an interview and a studio test.

The manager who interviewed me was extremely pleasant and helpful, explaining that he was seeing four of us that day, with two posts available.

"You should be pleased to have got this far," he told me. "We have had more than a hundred applications."

Trying for a job in television offered a buzz of glamour and excitement, and that was encouraged when I realised that the office in which I was being interviewed overlooked a set that was used for the soap opera *Coronation Street*. The manager gave me a sheet of notes about forthcoming programmes. I had to turn the notes into a script, which I then had to read in a sound studio.

He said he had seen the other three candidates already and he promised that no decision had yet been made. After a chat, in which I probably spent too much time rambling about my love of Coronation Street, I recorded my continuity test. As I was the last of the candidates to be interviewed, he asked me if I would wait in his office so that he could tell me how I had got on. After nearly twenty minutes, he returned to say that he and his boss had reviewed all four applicants. It had been a very difficult decision he said, but this time I was not successful.

"Do not let this put you off Stuart," he said. "It was a very close call between the four of you. You did very well. I have no doubt that you will have other openings. Thank you for giving Granada the opportunity to consider you today. I now have to telephone the others. I hope we meet again."

Disappointed, but not deterred, I returned to Birmingham to take stock of what I wanted to do with my life. I was about to discover that, unexpectedly, I had a remarkable array of choices.

* * * *

Midway through 1974 I had, without really noticing, completed almost ten years in the employment of Birmingham City Council.

It was an anniversary that would mean I could increase my annual leave entitlement from three weeks to four, and I was being encouraged to seek promotion within the council. The Welfare Department that I had joined originally had become part of the new, much larger, Social Services Department, which embraced childcare and other services alongside those for the elderly. It was suggested to me that there was a middle management role in Social Services for me if I wanted it. At the same time, a friend at the Rates Department told me that an even higher-ranked job was probably mine for the asking there if I wanted to apply and did well at the interview. Hints were also dropped, half in jest, about a role in their cricket team.

I had compensated for my disappointing academic achievements at school by successfully navigating my way through the Diploma of Municipal Administration, or DMA, regarded as a degree-level qualification geared to local government officers. I studied through a scheme called "day release", which did what its name suggests. It allowed me to spend one day of my working week at college, attending lectures on subjects including Public Law, Public Finance and Use of English. I also went to evening classes.

So a career in local government beckoned, with the prospect of significant job security, a very reasonable salary and an excellent pension to look forward to at the end of it. My Mum could relax that I had a job she could relate to. All very good, but in the back of my mind the question persisted: was I destined to pursue my school career master's mantra of an "unadventurous" working life after all?

As I pondered that, the BBC held out the prospect of what appeared to be a potentially more exciting alternative.

* * * *

My broadcasting career had progressed well, ironically in no small degree because of the introduction of flexible working by Birmingham City Council. The council called it "flexitime", and it meant that so long as you put in the hours and did the job required, you could adjust the timetable of your working day to suit yourself.

With nothing and no one at home to offer any form of distraction, I spent my time between the offices of the City Council and the broadcasting studios at Pebble Mill. There I was variously a reporter, a producer, an assistant producer and, occasionally, a presenter, for BBC Radio Birmingham. Whatever was required by the radio station, I adjusted my Council hours accordingly and lived two parallel working lives.

As I pursued that double life my ambitions and aspirations for the future were suddenly tested. At precisely the same time that I received clear indications of the career on offer to me at the City Council, I was taken to one side at Pebble Mill and told that a full-time staff position at BBC Radio Birmingham was about to be advertised. I was told that I was regarded as one of the favourites for it if I was interested.

* * * *

Dilemma? Possibly, but local councils are not renowned for moving quickly. In the time it took to process the advertising of the various council posts that I had been pointed towards, the BBC job was made available. I duly applied. I was interviewed and I was told that a decision would be made quickly.

Then came another twist. At around half past nine the morning after that BBC interview, I received a phone call offering me a job in radio, but not from the BBC. The call was from someone I had met in the early days of Radio Birmingham. On the other end of the line was Ian Rufus.

Ian's parting shot after he'd left his reporting job at BBC Radio Birmingham to join LBC was for us to keep in touch. LBC had launched in October 1973 as the news and talk station for London, and Ian was part of the day one team at LBC, the very first station in the new Independent Local Radio network. Ian's intervention would prove crucial, although I had already flirted with the new commercial network.

* * * *

There had been so much political debate about whether or not legal commercial radio should exist in the UK, there was distinct anxiety that everything was done correctly. Testimony to this was demonstrated by a letter sent to LBC on 4 February 1979.

John Thompson, Director of Radio at the Independent Broadcasting Authority (IBA), showed the perceived importance of referring to the new network in the approved way when he wrote:

"Could you please try and get your folk on air not to talk about 'commercial radio' – unless that outdated phrase is needed for reason of clarity in a particular context – and instead to talk about Independent Radio or Independent Local Radio."

Nonetheless, the name was abbreviated to ILR by those in the radio industry, and a few months after LBC, in February 1974, ILR arrived in Birmingham in the form of BRMB, a local rival to BBC Radio Birmingham. It set up home in what had previously been the studios of the ITV company ABC, in Aston Road North, near to the HP sauce factory. It was in close proximity to the 17th-century Jacobean mansion Aston Hall, and to Villa Park, the home ground of Aston Villa Football Club.

One of ABC TV's most successful programmes was 'Thank Your Lucky Stars', a pop music show hosted by Coventry-born broadcaster Brian Matthew, which featured such stars as The Beatles, The Rolling Stones, Adam Faith, John Leyton and The Brook Brothers. That TV show had been broadcast from the same studios that were now converted for the purposes of BRMB radio.

Many of the local BBC team at Pebble Mill were obviously keen to move across town to seek the apparent riches that commercial radio could bring. Those that were successful in doing so celebrated loudly and at length, whilst many of those that were not required by the new station played down the fact that they had any interest in it at all and, rather, would pointedly talk up the values of working for the BBC.

I had applied for the job of Sports Editor at BRMB, without really considering that I had any real chance of securing it. It was, therefore, a pleasant surprise to be invited for an interview by the station's Managing Director, David Pinnell. He was temporarily based in the offices of the *Birmingham Post & Mail* newspaper in the city centre, the newspaper group being shareholders in the new radio company.

Mr Pinnell was generous with his assessment of what I had done at the BBC, surprising me by knowing far more about me than I could have imagined he would. Despite that, I did not get the job.

Instead, it went to a man who I had first met in the newsroom at Pebble Mill where, as a local freelance sports reporter, he flitted in and out offering tips and stories. He was Tony Butler. At BRMB Tony would go on to become a local broadcasting legend, proving that David Pinnell had made the right choice.

* * * *

In being rejected by BRMB I was in good company. The same applied to Les Ross, who had made it clear that he was ready to jump ship from BBC Radio Birmingham. It was quite a shock to many of us that Les was not part of the presenter's roster when BRMB launched.

Instead, he made the move to commercial radio in the North-East of England, at Radio Tees, based at Stockton-on-Tees, hosting the breakfast show when that station launched, also in 1974. Twelve months later, however, Les was ensconced in what became his natural home, having returned to Birmingham to present the Breakfast Show at BRMB. He replaced Adrian Juste who had joined Radio 1.

* * * *

After being part of the newsroom at the launch of LBC, Ian Rufus had quickly moved on. Within twelve months of LBC going on air Ian had made another decisive move. Born in South Yorkshire, he had seized on the chance to return home, successfully applying to be the News Editor of another new ILR station, Radio Hallam, based in Sheffield.

The 'phone call Ian made to me added another job option to those currently in front of me. Would I like to go to Sheffield to meet him to discuss the possibility of becoming Sports Editor of Radio Hallam?

* * * *

My Auntie Heather, my Mum's sister, had now moved from Liverpool to Sheffield where she lived with her husband, Uncle Len, and their daughter Jane. Cousin Stephen, their son, was living in Sweden and after establishing a living as a professional musician, he was on the way to becoming a prosperous and successful businessman in the world of aviation.

Auntie Heather was very excited at the prospect of me going to visit her, both on the day of my meeting with Ian and, thereafter, if I went to work at Hallam. The context of my three-way career contest – the local council, versus the BBC, versus this new, unproven idea of commercial radio – was too involved to contemplate introducing it as a family debate or conversation. It was, in any event, for me to process for myself the rationale behind those options. The family connection in Sheffield was, inevitably, an additional element as I made my decision.

* * * *

I met Ian at the building site in Sheffield that was to be the home of Radio Hallam. It was an annexe of the offices of the *Sheffield Star* and *Morning Telegraph* newspapers. The local print media, as in Birmingham, had taken up the option to become shareholders in this brash new radio business.

The building was full of craftsmen, including builders, electricians, plumbers and decorators, weaving their way around each other, negotiating breeze blocks and partly constructed partition walls, with suspended ceilings being fitted precariously above their heads. All concerned were trying to meet the deadlines set for them so that the radio station could hit its scheduled on-air date.

Amidst the chaos, Ian took me into what passed for an office, in that it had a desk and three dusty office chairs. He clicked on a rather elderly kettle in the corner, made us both a cup of coffee, and told me that he knew I had tried to get a job at BRMB, and he had heard whispers about Granada Television. Having missed out on both, how did I feel about becoming Sports Editor at Hallam?

We discussed how I might approach the job, what sports and clubs we would cover, and how it might fit into the station's output. Then we got down to talking about money.

Some years later, Ian admitted that I had not been his first choice and that before meeting me he had discussed the job with a much more experienced journalist than me, Ron Gubba, who had turned him down. Ron went on to enjoy a successful career with the BBC and the *Daily Telegraph*. His brother was the TV sports commentator Tony Gubba, alongside whom I would work in future years, and Ron's son is the TV and film director John Gubba. A talented family.

Ron, it turned out, had proved to be too expensive for Ian, but he then correctly guessed that my remunerative expectations might be more modest and that I would fit his budget. We agreed on a salary of £3,200 a year, significantly more than what I earned from my current City Council employment, and certainly more than would be on offer from BBC Radio Birmingham.

My mind was well on the way to a decision, but I said what I thought was the appropriate thing and asked if I could think it over and respond in a day or two.

The next day, after returning from Sheffield, I was asked to contact a senior producer at Pebble Mill. The message was that they had not been able to decide between me and another Stuart, a talented broadcaster called Stuart Roper, for the BBC Radio Birmingham vacancy for which we had both applied. As a result, the decision had been made to create two posts and to recruit us both.

Again, I asked for time to think about it. Within three days, I had been offered two quite different but exciting opportunities to follow my dream and do what I had always wanted to do in broadcasting. Alongside that, there was the distinct, but not yet specified, prospect of career progression in local government.

Full-time professional broadcaster or local government officer. That was the first choice to make. Did I want to ignore what the latter might offer, such as secure employment, a clear career path, reasonably well-paid, and a more than decent pension with which to eventually enjoy retirement? Saying "yes" would mean I would be able to continue broadcasting in a part-time, freelance capacity alongside that if that was what I wanted.

Clearly that warranted due consideration, but I did not entertain it as a serious prospect for very long. I certainly did not spend much time weighing up the benefits of a comfortable retirement that would follow from extending my career in local government. Foolish? Probably, but at 27 years of age, the notion of being paid to play records, talk about football and much more, was distinctly more attractive.

It then came down to the choice between the BBC, again with apparently more secure prospects, or the flamboyant, ostentatious, new world of commercial radio. The latter would also allow me to make my own mark, setting out my own way of doing things as Sports Editor at a brand new station.

In the background was the reassurance of Auntie Heather being ready to offer me a roof over my head in Sheffield, not to mention the benefit of home cooking and all that goes with family support. She could also reassure my Mum that she would keep an eye on me.

* * * *

In my head, the decision was made, but I held off confirming it with anyone until I had spoken to my parents. At 27 years of age, I knew that it had to be my decision rather than anyone else's, but whatever I did, I wanted them to hear it from me before it reached them in any other way.

Neither was in the best of health. All those years of smoking had caught up with my Dad, and that coupled with the after-effects of the respiratory illness he had sustained in the damp of a wet, wartime camp in Wales, often made his breathing difficult.

In his late fifties, he had lost all his teeth, at least in part because of the damage nicotine had caused. He never got used to wearing his false set and so his cheeks became sunken into his face. The gaunt appearance that resulted added to a general demeanour of him being unwell.

My Mum was suffering from the beginning of kidney trouble, an illness that dogged the later years of her life.

So neither was in the best of condition to hear me say that I was considering leaving a solid, safe career in local government for what was, to them, this strange uncertain world of broadcasting.

"It's not a proper job, is it?" said my anxious Mum, who made up her mind there and then that I was kissing goodbye to any chance of a normal future.

My reassurances about the professionalism of those with whom I would be working made only marginal headway. They were more than sceptical about me achieving the success and prosperity they had hoped for me.

"Let's face it," said Mum, going on to refer to her favourite Midlands regional news presenter of the day, "you are no Tom Coyne, are you?"

The rationale I presented to them left them far from convinced, but they did acknowledge that I had to make my own way. I did not get their blessing entirely, but I had not really expected to.

"Well, if you go to Sheffield," Mum said, "at least you will have Auntie Heather and Uncle Len there."

* * * *

As if to put the final seal on the decision one of my female colleagues at Birmingham Social Services Department, to whom I had grown close, turned out to have been born in Sheffield.

About twelve months before that career choice became an issue, I had moved in with her to share the bedsit she lived in at Warley, in Sandwell. I had become part of a group of friends who all lived along the same street, Barclay Road, directly opposite Warley Woods Park, which ran down the full length of the other side of the road. Saturday night house parties were a common occurrence, and I discovered a personal home life that had barely existed in my failed marriage.

When I raised the prospect of moving to Sheffield, she immediately identified that it was surely where my ambitions lay, and she was hugely encouraging when I talked it through with her. So, encouraging that, later, she would become my second wife.

* * * *

In that whirlwind week I had been offered two jobs in broadcasting and had been encouraged to pursue the promotion that I was assured was on the way at the City Council. By the end of the week, I had handed in my notice at Birmingham Social Services Department, phoned BBC Radio Birmingham to say "thanks, but no thanks" for the job offer there, and had called an enthusiastic Ian Rufus to accept his offer to join Radio Hallam.

At the start of August, I took the train to Sheffield and moved in with Auntie Heather and Uncle Len. Radio Hallam went on air on October 1st, 1974. Before it did, I found myself at the heart of one of the biggest stories to ever hit English football. The story revolved around one of the most remarkable men I have ever met – Brian Clough.

He's a man

With a plan

Got a counterfeit dollar in his hand

He's Misstra Know-It-All

Playin' hard

Talkin' fast

Makin' sure that he won't be the last

He's Misstra Know-It-All

Makes a deal

With a smile

Knowin' all the time that his lie's a mile

He's Misstra Know-It-All

Must be seen

There's no doubt

He's the coolest one with the biggest mouth

He's Misstra Know-It-All

Stevie Wonder, 1974

© Jobete Music Co.

My Granddad knew Rasputin ... and I met Elton John

Chapter Eight

Sheffield

When will I see you again?

When will our hearts beat together?

Are we in love or just friends?

Is this my beginning or is this the end?

When will I see you again?

(When will I see you again?)

When will I see you again?

Kenny Gamble & Leon Huff, 1974

© Warner Chappell Music, Inc

Radio Hallam went on air in Sheffield on 1st October 1974. I left my job with Birmingham City Council at the beginning of August and moved in with my Auntie Heather and Uncle Len, in their house at Cruise Road, Ranmoor in Sheffield.

With Ian Rufus and other new colleagues assembling to be part of Hallam's initial workforce, I was also planning and preparing for the big launch. Early on the morning of Thursday, 12th September, with just three weeks to go to the big day, Ian took a call from one of his old mates at LBC. Alongside the LBC team in London sat the editors and reporters of Independent Radio News (IRN) whose job it was to provide the new commercial network with national and international news. Local stations used the material from IRN alongside their own local material.

Ian's friend in London ran the sports news for IRN and asked if there was anyone at Hallam who could help out with a rapidly developing story in Yorkshire. Brian Clough, the controversial football manager, had been sacked by Leeds United Football Club after only 44 days in charge. As there was at that time no ILR radio station at Leeds, they wondered if anyone at Hallam could cover the story.

A few minutes later, I was driving up the M1 to West Yorkshire, with "Hang On In There Baby" by Johnny Bristol playing on my car radio on Radio 1.

By the time I got to the Leeds United stadium at Elland Road, a large number of reporters had already gathered. Also very much in evidence was a band of Leeds fans that was growing by the minute, as news spread of Clough's departure.

Keen to be brought up to date with the details and developments of the story, I fell into conversation with four reporters who knew Yorkshire sport inside out and back to front. They included John Sadler, one of the finest sports writers it was my privilege to meet, Peter Cooper and Michael Morgan, who was to become a personal friend. Sadler was on his way to becoming the top sports reporter at *The Sun*, Cooper worked for the *Daily Mirror*, as well as being well-known as a presenter with BBC Radio Sheffield, and Mike Morgan was then with the *Daily Express*. Bill Mallinson of the *Daily Mail* made up the quartet.

They knew far more about the intricacies of Leeds United and Clough's brief tenure there than I did, and they generously brought me up to date. They did not, however, tell me everything. They kept to themselves the plans that they were trying to lay to meet with Clough later in the day to obtain his side of the story. Not including me in that proposition was fair enough, as I was very much the new kid on the block and they had no reason to trust me that far.

John Sadler was quite close to Brian Clough and, indeed, became the latter's ghostwriter. Together, they later produced two books: 'Clough: The Autobiography', published in 1994, and 'Cloughie: Walking On Water' in 2002. There were also many ghosted newspaper columns. All that was a result of Clough keeping his word after telling Sadler when they first met: "If you're prepared to get off your arse and come to see me, then I promise that in one hour, I'll fill your newspaper for a week."

So I was the new boy, and although the group of Yorkshire reporters allowed me to briefly intrude their circle, there was only so much that they were going to indulge to this upstart from a radio station that had not yet gone on the air and, in any event, was not in Leeds.

What they did point me towards was that some of the players that Clough had brought to Leeds were staying in a hotel in Leeds city centre. Clough reasoned that he had to try to break up what he saw as the dressing room cabal that would obstruct his attempts to change the club. Billy Bremner, Johnny Giles and Norman Hunter were part of that established group, and it appeared that they had now conspired to unseat him.

That the players who had become Leeds legends under their previous manager Don Revie had turned against Clough was not entirely surprising after he had said in his first training session with them, "You can all throw your medals in the bin because they were not won fairly."

* * * *

Two of Clough's new signings were staying at the Dragonara Hotel in Leeds. I made my way to the hotel in Neville Street in the city centre to find John McGovern and Duncan McKenzie both ready to have their say. They sat down with a gaggle of journalists who had turned up to hear their perspective on the dramatic turn of events at Leeds United.

McGovern, who had previously played for Clough at Derby County, told me, "This has all become very difficult for me in a very short time. I know and respect Brian Clough and I followed him here with the best of intentions, but it appears my association with him has made me unwelcome in the squad."

Duncan McKenzie was more optimistic about having become a Leeds player, so it's perhaps not too surprising that he stayed at Elland Road for a further two years and was successful there. McKenzie, a very articulate man, spoke to me at length about Clough and about his own, personal ambitions. Others, like striker John O'Hare and coach Jimmy Gordon, avoided reporters and kept their counsel. They were all reunited with Brian Clough less than four months later when the outspoken manager signed them for his next club, Nottingham Forest.

* * * *

My debut in commercial radio was via my interviews with John McGovern and Duncan McKenzie, recorded that day in a Leeds hotel. The interviews were heard on LBC and also during the sports shows of the other new ILR stations that were already on the air, like BRMB, elsewhere in the country.

As for Brian Clough, his path and mine would converge on more than one occasion.

* * * *

Unwittingly, Brian Clough was party to a memorable meeting I had when I first met one of Yorkshire sport's greatest heroes.

It was a meeting that was set up for me by a guy called Brian Kirkham, who worked for the bookmakers Ladbrokes. Brian was keen to provide Radio Hallam with a daily supply of racing tips, in return for the occasional mention of the company he worked for. Advertising of gambling was not allowed at that time, but an occasional, appropriate acknowledgement of Brian's credentials was acceptable.

I soon discovered that Brian was well-connected when he asked if I would be interested in an interview with Geoffrey Boycott. I gave him a positive answer before he'd even finished asking the question.

Boycott had been granted a benefit year by Yorkshire County Cricket Club and wanted publicity for the events he was holding across the county. Perhaps not surprisingly it turned out that Brian Kirkham was a close confidante of a good number of sportsmen and women, most of whom enjoyed a flutter now and then. Amongst his contacts was a member of the Geoffrey Boycott benefit committee who arranged for me to visit and interview the great man in his home.

Boycott lived with his mum in a terraced cottage in Milton Terrace, Fitzwilliam, a mining village near Wakefield in West Yorkshire. Located just north of Barnsley, it was one of the South Yorkshire towns served by Radio Hallam. Geoffrey's father, Thomas, was a miner, as his father had been, from Shropshire. Thomas Boycott had moved his family to Yorkshire to find work at the Fitzwilliam Main Colliery, later renamed as Hemsworth Colliery.

Geoffrey's dad had died in 1967, from the aftereffects of an accident at the mine nearly twenty years before, leaving Geoffrey to care for his mum, Jane. He had two brothers, but Geoffrey was the one who remained at home and took on the responsibility of looking after their mother. Soon after Thomas had died Jane developed rheumatoid arthritis, which grew progressively worse.

It was Jane Boycott who answered the door when I arrived at her modest but beautifully kept home. Immediately in front of the property, and the neighbouring houses in the long terrace row, was a wide green space. Sadly, the grass had become knee-high, preventing any young would-be Boycotts from practising their skills there.

I introduced myself to Jane, who warmly welcomed me in. The front door opened straight into the front room. A man, obviously her son, one of the nation's leading sportsmen, sat with his back to me talking on the phone. He sat with his feet on a coffee table apparently oblivious to Jane and me. She apologised that Geoffrey was engaged in conversation and asked if I'd like a cup of tea. I had long since learned that it's the height of rudeness to decline the offer of a cup of tea, particularly in Yorkshire. Jane disappeared to make the brew, while I sat patiently and waited for her son to finish his call.

It allowed me to observe my surroundings. In this front room of the two up, two down, house there were photos all around the walls. They were of Boycott in action, receiving caps and cups, and posing in the playing kits of both Yorkshire and England. In those days before newspapers ran colour illustrations as a matter of course, these pictures were almost all in black and white. There was barely a space on the wall not covered by this monochrome display of the best of Boycott. On the sideboard and other pieces of furniture were placed yet more Boycott memorabilia. Cricket balls, batting gloves, and a stump all added to a remarkable collection of souvenirs of a true sporting hero.,

Mrs. Boycott brought me my tea, just as her son appeared to be finishing his phone call, so she simply smiled at me and said "I hope you enjoy your tea. I'll leave you to it."

Geoffrey said his goodbyes to the person he had been talking to, put the phone back on its cradle, and turned to face me for the first time.

"Sorry about that," he said. "That was my friend Brian Clough. He's offered to help me with my benefit year."

I mumbled something about there being no need to apologise and asked if he would mind moving to sit next to me so that my microphone cable would reach.

It was around 10.30 in the morning, and Geoffrey was in pyjamas and a long dressing gown, his attire just making the entire exercise of interviewing one of the world's greatest batsmen in his own home that little bit more bizarre.

The interview went well, but Geoffrey firmly steered me away from the politics of Yorkshire cricket, particularly relating to his captaincy of the county side. Those issues were to pursue him for some years, but he did not want to talk about it, other than making an oblique acknowledgement that the County had things it needed to resolve. Being still relatively new to the area, I was not sufficiently aware of the minute machinations of it all to prompt a more telling response. It was a firm reminder that I should be more diligent in doing my homework. I was, nonetheless, pleased with the recording that I was able to take back to the radio station.

For the first week on air, I had an exclusive interview with Geoffrey Boycott talking about plans for his forthcoming benefit year, whilst clearly stating his disappointment at having had to withdraw from England's winter tour to Australia and New Zealand. That was developing into a major sporting story that autumn and Geoffrey had just written to the selectors explaining why he could not travel.

He made clear his sadness at having to make that decision.

I had my big sports exclusive with which to mark Radio Hallam's sports content. It was enthusiastically edited and prepared for day one. More than that, I had actually visited one of England's best, and certainly one of the nation's most enigmatic, sportsmen in his own home.

* * * *

Before a radio station goes on air, test transmissions take place. They make sure all the technical arrangements work as they should and that all the associated legal and contractual requirements are complied with. The commercial radio regulator in 1974, the Independent Broadcasting Authority (IBA), allowed the radio company to use those test transmissions to inform prospective listeners what the new service would include.

Part of the Radio Hallam test transmission included the station's Programme Director Keith Skues saying:

"Something else which plays a very large part in the life of the South Yorkshire man and woman is sport. Here's Stuart Linnell, our Sports Editor, to tell you the score."

That was my cue…

"In South Yorkshire and the North Midlands, sport is big, and here on Radio Hallam we treat it in a big way. Every Saturday throughout the soccer season, our outside broadcast teams will be reporting on the matches involving Sheffield United and Wednesday, Rotherham, Chesterfield, Barnsley and Doncaster, the Hallam Big Six! And that's not all. There'll be news and results from all the other big games wherever they're being played. But sport's not just soccer. It's motor racing, angling, and during the summer it's cricket. It's even knurr and spell, and if you're not familiar with that game, tune in to Radio Hallam because we'll no doubt get around to covering a contest at some time. And, at two-thirty every Saturday, this is the sound that will turn you on to Hallam Sport, Sportacular!"

On came the up-tempo big band sports theme tune, specially composed as part of the station's jingle package. I loved that music, and it did what it was intended to, providing an exciting, driven introduction to the show.

I do not remember us ever fully covering knurr and spell. Having included it in that test transmission, I had to appear on Roger Moffat's mid-morning show one day and explain to him that it was a bat and ball game, originating in the North of England, dating back to the beginning of the 14th century. It had enjoyed a revival in the 1970s, but there was no live coverage of a knurr and spell contest, mainly because we never heard of one taking place.

* * * *

Test transmissions over, just before 7 o'clock on the morning of 1st October 1974, I was at Auntie Heather's house in Ranmoor with my bedside radio tuned in to 194 medium wave. The station also had VHF (FM) transmitters, but medium wave, or AM as it became known, was still the most popular way that people listened to radio and, like many other people, the radio at my bedside did not have VHF.

Former Radio 1 DJ Johnny Moran was the first presenter on air, hosting the Breakfast Show and he kicked off with a really smooth, confident start, playing the station's first record, "I've Got The Music In Me", by Kiki Dee. There was no computerised play-out back then, it was an actual vinyl record, and 90 seconds in, the record stuck!

Not the best start for a new station or its breakfast show host, but Johnny, cool as you like, quickly and smoothly calmed the troubled waters and reminded us that the station was there to be a friend to all who might listen across South Yorkshire and North Derbyshire. Thus, the next record was destined to be something of a station theme song, "You've Got A Friend" by James Taylor.

The James Taylor track should have been played first, but the inevitable "Sod's Law" played its part, with the record turntables failing just as Johnny was lining up that first piece of vinyl. With two sound engineers crouched behind the studio desk, frantically wielding soldering irons whilst trying to fix the problem, Johnny quickly switched his attention to turntable two where Kiki Dee was ready to go. Johnny presided over it all serenely as mild panic set in around him. One hitch followed another until things eventually settled down.

Johnny admitted afterwards that he'd been nervous the night before that first Breakfast Show, fearing he would not wake up in time to go on air. He said that he was calm once he got there, but that he was as anxious as everyone else in the studio when it became clear that there was an issue with the turntables. As a listener, you would never have guessed that he had the slightest concern, thanks to his professionalism and the swift remedial action of the engineers.

* * * *

Whilst "You've Got A Friend" became an adopted theme tune, Radio Hallam's own station identification jingles in those early days came in for some sharply focused criticism from some listeners. A recurrent musical riff was based on the tune of "On Ilkla Moor Baht 'at".

That song is understood to be a county anthem for Yorkshire. All of Yorkshire. However, we are talking Local Radio with a capital "L". Ilkley Moor is in West Yorkshire, whilst Radio Hallam was geared to serving South Yorkshire. There were more than a few who felt that it was, therefore, inappropriate to hear jingles based on a folk song referring to another part of the county being used on their new local station.

Soon after James Taylor, Johnny played the song that will always remind me of Radio Hallam, "When Will I See You Again?" by The Three Degrees. It had been released in the UK that summer and had gone to Number 1. It was one of the best songs written by Kenny Gamble and Leon Huff for the Philadelphia label, the Philly sound at its best. Whenever I hear it, it brings back memories of those heady days in Sheffield.

* * * *

1974 was not the most auspicious time to start a business. Faced with a strike by coal miners which threatened the nation's electricity supply, the Conservative Government under Prime Minister Edward Heath had imposed a three-day working week. That ran from January until March, during which time Heath called a General Election.

A hung Parliament resulted, with the Conservatives losing their majority. Supported by other parties, notably the Liberals and the Ulster Unionists, the Labour leader Harold Wilson formed a government and called another election in October, just as Radio Hallam went on air. The miner's dispute was big news in South Yorkshire with coal mines throughout the area. Immediately after winning the 1974 General Election, the Wilson Government awarded the miners a pay increase, with another the following year, but the market for UK coal was in decline. Collieries closed and tension between the miners and the government increased. All of that was covered in the news bulletins and programmes on Radio Hallam. It meant that the newsroom was never short of stories, but it made for an economic environment that offered great uncertainty.

To add to that equation, Radio Hallam had local competition. BBC Radio Sheffield was approaching its 7th birthday by the time Hallam arrived, so there was an immediate comparison to be made between an established BBC local station and its new-born upstart commercial cousin. Some listeners disliked Hallam's music because there was "too much pop." Others thought that hearing a music mix that was more up-to-date than that of Radio Sheffield as well as a strong alternative to the BBC's national networks, was just what they wanted.

The on-air team at BBC Radio Sheffield was well known to local people and, even presenters who weren't actually from South Yorkshire or North Derbyshire were regarded as part of the local family. Almost all the Hallam crew, on the other hand, were new to the patch, many arriving with the "from London" tag. That said, some were known from national stations which went a long way towards generating an audience from the very start.

Programme Director Keith Skues moved to Hallam from BBC Radio 1. Before joining the BBC in 1967 Keith had worked on the pirate ships Radio Caroline and Radio London, as well as a spell on Radio Luxembourg. For Hallam, he recruited colleagues he'd known and worked with at the BBC.

Johnny Moran worked for Luxembourg for a while and then hosted a weekly record review show on Radio 1, called "Scene and Heard." Johnny was recruited to present Hallam's weekday breakfast show.

Bill Crozier had been the voice of Sunday lunchtime on, first the Light Programme, and then BBC Radio 2. He broadcast from Cologne in Germany, with a co-presenter, who for many years was Jean Metcalf, in a studio in London. It was a hugely popular record request show called "Two-Way Family Favourites", with the two presenters alternating in reading the dedications of families at home in the UK, and those of British Forces serving in West Germany or elsewhere overseas. The show's theme tune, "With A Song In My Heart" played by Andre Kostelanetz and his orchestra, was as popular as the show itself.

Few, if any, radio broadcasters will have navigated their career without someone declaring "You don't look like what you sound like." That was certainly true of Bill Crozier. His unmistakable, deep brown, seductive voice came from within an elderly persona, barely five feet tall with grey hair and tiny peering eyes just visible above tiny half-framed glasses that sat at the end of his nose. Every day he wore an all-encompassing long black cloak, fastened by a silver chain that sat just below his neck, giving him the appearance of a priest, or maybe a diminutive version of Batman. He certainly did not look like what he sounded like.

Bill was a nationally known star turn, synonymous with the nation's most popular record request show. Unsurprisingly then, when recruited by Keith Skues he was asked to present a record request show on Radio Hallam, scheduled at 6.30 every weekday evening.

Another name to arrive with London and BBC connections was the man who became Hallam's big star, Roger Moffat. Roger had also served an apprenticeship at Radio Luxembourg, but after moving to the BBC he adopted an irreverential attitude to authority. It was never quite documented just how many times Roger was relieved of his duties whilst in the employ of the BBC, but his cultured, gentle voice kept him in constant demand from listeners, despite his apparently deliberate knack of crossing the line when he was least expected to.

For the Light Programme, and later Radio 2, he was the regular presenter of live music shows featuring the BBC Northern Dance Orchestra, conducted first by Alyn Ainsworth and later by Bernard Herrmann. The resident vocalist on those shows was Sheila Buxton, with whom it was rumoured that Roger was more than just a good friend. Roger clearly enjoyed occasional gentle banter with the musicians in the band, but for the most part, it was one programme that he handled with a straight bat, avoiding the impetuous, often quirky, frivolity that pervaded some of his other work.

Roger was the host of what became the Radio 2 Late Show after the demise of the Light Programme. It was Roger who announced the closure of the Light Programme at 2 a.m. on Saturday, 30th September 1967. He played the last piece of music heard on the station, 'That's Where It Is' by Woody Herman and His Orchestra, and he announced the closure of the station without fuss or undue fanfare.

"Well there we end broadcasting on the Light Programme," he said, "not just for today but, as it seems, forever. The Light Programme, as it's known now, is closing down, but in only a few hours, the BBC, with Paul Hollingdale, will open up Radio 2 on 247 metres, and 1500 metres, and VHF. That's at half-past five. Then, at seven o'clock, on 247 metres, Tony Blackburn will open and swing into our new Radio 1 network."

That was it. The end of twenty years of the Light Programme, and the dawn of the new era that also saw the Home Service become Radio 4, and the Third Programme transform into Radio 3.

* * * *

With Roger Moffat at the microphone, the Radio 2 Late Show would, before 24-hour broadcasting began, end each day's programmes at 2 a.m. Roger would then start up again, around ten minutes later, to read the Shipping

Forecast. One night, either through his typically heightened sense of mischief, or maybe boredom, or because of the excesses of late-night refreshment, or a combination of it all, Roger went too far.

The Beaufort Scale, which is used during the Shipping Forecast to describe the intensity of wind speed, goes up to force 12. That applies to a hurricane. Roger significantly increased the numbers he was reading, making it appear that cataclysmic conditions were about to disrupt the oceans and destroy the planet. It is a golden rule that you do not mess around with the Shipping Forecast, a rule that Roger either forgot or decided to ignore that night.

It was the final straw. After a series of indiscretions and practical jokes that were frowned on by BBC management, it was decided that enough was enough. From the BBC, exit Roger Moffat.

Aware of his old friend's availability, Keith Skues wasted no time in hiring him for Radio Hallam, where Roger found an audience who loved his cheek and charm and took to him instantly. Not, however, before he'd made national headlines with apparently disparaging comments about the city of Sheffield.

Roger had enough of a profile that his departure from the BBC had been widely reported in the national newspapers. When Keith Skues first took him to South Yorkshire for a look around the city in which the new station would be based, Roger was met by a reporter who asked him what he thought of Sheffield.

It was a cold, wet and windy day, and Roger's first look at Sheffield was somewhat coloured by the weather conditions.

"It's a bloody awful place," he said, before adding, "on a horrible day like this."

The latter part of that comment was somehow lost in the reporting that followed, with banner headlines, quoting Roger as describing Sheffield as "a bloody awful place", in the following day's edition of *The Sun*.

* * * *

Keith Skues knew Roger's serious weakness and scheduled his daily show accordingly, from 9am to 12 noon, Monday to Friday. The 9am start was to ensure that Roger would go on air well before the pubs opened and that he had enough time to sleep off the effects of the night before. It worked. Roger was a palpable hit.

He still did things his way. On this new station, with a music policy of playing current hits and golden oldies, all geared to the Top 40 past and present, Roger would nonetheless start his show each day with the overture to a musical.

Every morning a different show, "West Side Story", "Oklahoma", "My Fair Lady", "The Sound Of Music", "South Pacific", and the rest, had its introductory overture played as the first record on Roger Moffat's programme. One lunchtime, in the pub, I asked him to tell me why, on a pop music station, he would start with a huge piece of orchestral music like that.

His unchallengeable answer was instant. "If I don't," he said, "who will?"

* * * *

That first morning, 1st October 1974, Roger inadvertently caused chaos at Radio Hallam. This time he created a faux par that was neither deliberate nor mischievous. He opened his show, as became his habit, with an overture and then, between records, introduced himself and his on-air partner Brenda Ellison to the listening audience. Roger spent much of that first hour expounding how bemused he was at being called "duck" and "love" by Sheffield's bus conductors and shop assistants. It was terminology that he was not used to in London.

"I may be from Aylesbury, but I am not a duck," he exclaimed, "and I will decide if I am anybody's love".

Brenda for her part tried to steer him towards an understanding that people were just trying to be friendly and welcoming, and Roger slowly warmed to that.

All this was very entertaining and went on for about 35 minutes when there was a sudden commotion in the offices and corridors. I had arrived to start work just after 9 o'clock and I was sitting at my desk in the Newsroom scheduling the material I needed for the day's sports bulletins.

The rush of bodies towards the studio prompted all of us to pause from our labours as we tried to work out what was going on. An exasperated Sales Director Darryl Adams, explained, as he passed by the newsroom.

"Bloody Roger has forgotten to play any ads," he said calmly, though clearly annoyed. "I don't know whether to laugh or cry."

His mind was made up for him when the reporters simultaneously burst out laughing.

At the time, ILR stations were allowed to sell and air a maximum of nine minutes of advertising per hour. On Day One, Radio Hallam's inventory was fully sold, but Roger Moffat, getting into his stride in his first show, had completely forgotten to play the commercials. Despite rehearsals and practice technical run-throughs he ignored the fact that, unlike the BBC where no such concerns exist, Radio Hallam had a requirement to play the ads, and within the permitted time.

The ads were scheduled in four or five blocks, usually spread across the hour, between the records and the chat. Keith Skues went into the studio to oversee the problem, joined in the on-air rescue and gently took the rise out of Roger. Around the presenters, members of the sales team re-organised the breaks into some semblance of order and nine minutes of ads were played within a twenty-minute window.

To add to the pressure, Ian Rufus had devised a system whereby Radio Hallam's news bulletins started at five minutes to the hour, rather than on the hour. Local news would fill the first five minutes, followed by a world and national news bulletin from IRN, which began precisely as the hour struck. The station boasted its news was "five minutes sooner," with BBC Radio Sheffield responding by saying that Radio Hallam's news was "fifty-five minutes later." Whatever way you looked at it, the ads that Roger had forgotten to play had to be broadcast before 09.55, which was when the news bulletin was due to start.

They did, just about. That drama averted, Roger had at least one more notorious moment of madness, or maybe mischief, up his sleeve.

* * * *

On Tuesday, 16th August 1977, the King of Rock 'n' Roll, Elvis Presley, was found dead on the floor of the bathroom at his Graceland mansion in Memphis, Tennessee. Elvis was said to have had an addiction to painkillers, and his diet was understood to have been based on high-cholesterol fast food, particularly burgers.

From being arguably the most attractive man on the planet, with a slim body and the swivelling hips that saw him branded in his early days in America as the bad boy of rock 'n' roll, Elvis had become physically bloated and hugely overweight. Despite his failing health, he continued to accept bookings for live performances and had been due to set off on another tour across the States when he died.

The golden voice that had seduced millions of record buyers around the world, had declined into that of a struggling crooner, sometimes unable to hit the high notes, and often failing to remember the words of his biggest hits.

Elvis died in mid-afternoon US time, with the news reaching the UK just as that night's "News At Ten" was ending on ITV. ITN newscaster Reginald Bosanquet ended the programme with the words "There are unconfirmed reports that Elvis Presley has died. Well, let's hope they're not true. Good night."

Confusion reigned in the ITN newsroom because the flashed report that Elvis had died had taken priority on the news wires over other reports, sent minutes earlier, that the singer was being treated after being taken ill. Hence Reggie Bosanquet saying, "Let's hope they're not true."

News At Ten was followed by an ad break, and as that ended regional ITV stations across the country were told to hold their scheduled output and return to ITN for a national news update. There was Reggie again, this time more somberly announcing that the reports had been confirmed and that Elvis had, in fact, died.

The following day Presley's tributes and the entire catalogue of his hits could be heard on radio stations around the world, including Radio Hallam. At Hallam, however, things were to take a slightly different, unexpected turn.

Elvis' records were scheduled across the day, in all programmes, by the station's Head of Music, Beverley Chubb. Knowing my love of music, and with other reporters busy on other stories, Ian Rufus asked me to compile a brief obituary of Elvis Presley for the evening news programme. The sports schedule was fairly light so I had time to do it, and I set about my task of telling the Presley story, starting with the first 15 seconds or so of Elvis singing "Rags To Riches".

Long before my piece was aired, however, the death of Elvis Presley put Radio Hallam onto the pages of the tabloid press. At around half-past-nine that morning, after doing what was required of him and playing a carefully selected Presley hit, Roger Moffat drew breath and added his voice to the growing global tributes to the King of rock 'n roll.

"All this fuss," he started, immediately alerting all listening amongst the Radio Hallam staff that something was about to happen.

"He wasn't a bad singer, I suppose, but what a lot of fuss. He was just another crooner, really."

He went on to propose that as local people seemed to be so bothered by it all, Elvis' body should be shipped to Sheffield, stuffed, and put on display in a glass case in Radio Hallam's reception area at the entrance to the building.

Elvis "stuffed and put in a glass case". TV and newspapers jumped all over it and, once again, Roger Moffat was news.

A busload of Elvis fans turned up at the radio station the following day to protest against this outrage. Even a vague on-air apology by Roger failed to calm the gathering storm. Fortunately, by now, most of Roger's regular listeners had tuned into his sense of humour. The initial indignation died down, and the general view that emerged was that it was just another example of Moffat mayhem. Not that it did Radio Hallam any harm. The station's listening figures were already ahead of target, and the publicity merely enhanced its popularity and that of Roger Moffat. People were tuning in each day to hear what on earth he was going to say next.

* * * *

If the political unrest of the miner's strike and the General Election had dominated the news headlines at the start of the year in which Radio Hallam was launched, they were joined by accounts of civil disobedience and violence caused by the Irish Republican Army, the IRA. The Provisional IRA, as it was called, was an Irish republican paramilitary organisation which aimed to end British rule in Northern Ireland.

On 21st November 1974, bombs exploded in two pubs in the centre of my home city of Birmingham, killing 21 people and injuring 182 others. It was the deadliest act of terrorism to occur in England since the Second World War. The Provisional IRA never officially admitted responsibility for the

Birmingham pub bombings, although a former senior officer of the organisation confessed to their involvement years later in 2014.

Six Irishmen were arrested within hours of the blasts. They were found guilty and subsequently sentenced to life imprisonment. They became known as the Birmingham Six, and they continually maintained their innocence. In 1991, their convictions were declared unsafe and unsatisfactory, and quashed by the Court of Appeal.

That November in 1974, news of the Birmingham bombings was carried extensively on all radio and TV stations, including Radio Hallam. It was the biggest story of the moment. For me, it produced an odd spectrum of emotions. I felt relief that I was now living and working in Sheffield, as I could easily have been in the vicinity of the two pubs, the Mulberry Bush and The Tavern In The Town, had I still been in Birmingham. I was conscious of feeling angry, no doubt shared by millions of other people across the country at such a callous, cowardly disregard for human life. There was also an element of embarrassment that the city of my birth should feature so prominently in the national news.

I was not at all proud of the Birmingham I had left behind. It had become the archetypal concrete jungle, with a profusion of ugly, modern buildings, not even striking in the way that brutal architecture can be. They were often awkward and clumsy structures, with few redeeming features, overshadowing and hiding the city's Victorian heritage. Birmingham also had a brusque, almost aggressive image. I knew that Brummies were good, hard-working, honest people, but Birmingham had often thought of itself as Chicago and was home to some faux gangsters who provided a pale imitation of Al Capone.

Birmingham had been good to me in many ways. It had educated me, taught me how to play cricket, and pointed me towards the career I had always dreamt about. Despite that, it was not a place I was too keen to relate to let alone admit to having been born there, its image having become brash and unpleasant. It was a perspective that was to change markedly when I went back home some years later.

* * * *

Before Radio Hallam's launch day, I had introduced myself at Sheffield's local football clubs and had made the required arrangements to maintain contact with the managers and other key people on the local sports scene. We covered both Sheffield clubs – United and Wednesday – as well as Barnsley, Chesterfield, Doncaster Rovers and Rotherham United.

We had no commentary rights in those days, but I devised a schedule of match coverage adopted from those of the other ILR stations that were already on air. Tony Butler had generously allowed me to spend a couple of days shadowing him at BRMB, including sitting in the studio while he presented a Saturday afternoon show in his unique, idiosyncratic way.

At BRMB, Tony also covered six clubs – Aston Villa, Birmingham City, Coventry City, Walsall, West Bromwich Albion and Wolverhampton Wanderers. He took two or three brief match reports in each half from each club, interspersed with music.

The music tracks were from the BRMB playlist, so they were current hits and golden oldies, but I realised that not one track was referred to on-air by Tony. He ignored them. They appeared between batches of reports, which also included Tony's personal perspective, but none of the records were credited by him as the show's presenter. They simply filled time.

I decided there and then that my style would differ from that. I took the view that as we could not provide match commentary, playing music was a necessity to break up the chat and keep the show moving. However, if you were going to play a record you should present it properly. I introduced and back-credited the artists and title. I was there as much as a DJ as I was a sports journalist, and that gave the show its style and format.

Our reporters provided reports of 30 seconds duration each time, and we went "round the grounds", taking all six match reports in turn, three times in each half. As well as pre-match previews and team news, half-time and full-time reports, we carried out post-match interviews with the managers and key players.

It was a fast-moving show and, like other programmes on the station, it needed a title. That was decided, as many things were, in the pub.

Peter Donaldson was another of Keith Skues' recruits from the BBC, joining Radio Hallam from Radio 4. He had a beautiful, commanding voice, one that told you he had something important to say and that you had better listen.

As we sat in The Dove and Rainbow, the pub next door to the radio station, we searched for a name, throwing around ideas of what the show would be like and what it might sound like. Peter looked up from his drink and delivered the answer.

"It's going to be a sports spectacular," he said," so what about 'Sportacular'."

Sportacular it was, and that was Peter Donaldson's single most important contribution to Radio Hallam.

Few, if any, of us knew what happened, but the night before Hallam was due to go on air for the first time, Peter was back in London, where he re-joined Radio 4 and became their Chief Announcer and Head of Continuity. Later he was the station's principal news reader. Why he left Hallam after no more than a month, immediately before it launched, was never spelt out, but he had quit the BBC and moved to Sheffield after leading something of a revolt against BBC management in London. It's possible, then, that after holding his ground, he had been offered, at the eleventh hour, the opportunity to return on his terms.

* * * *

Peter had publicly criticised newsreaders, not necessarily at Radio 4, who "clearly have no understanding of what they are reading", saying that consequently the quality of the broadcast suffered.

Regrettably, Peter was absolutely right. On far too many radio stations you can hear the news being read by people who clearly do not have the first idea of the meaning of the story they are presenting to their listeners. The fact that Peter Donaldson railed against it during his career shows it is nothing new, but I fear that it has become worse as a consequence of news being marginalised by station managers and programmers in pursuit of so-called "fun and personality". Nothing wrong with the latter, but it should not be at the expense of the clear and accurate presentation of news.

Peter Donaldson died in November 2015, aged 70. In tribute to him the then Director-General of the BBC, Lord Tony Hall, described him as "the quintessential voice of the BBC". That is exactly what he was, and he was also the man who came up with the title of my Saturday afternoon sports show at Radio Hallam.

You just call out my name

And you know wherever I am

I'll come running, running, yeah, yeah, to see you again

Winter, spring, summer or fall

All you have to do is call

And I'll be there, yes, I will

You've got a friend

You've got a friend

Carole King, 1971

© Sony/ATV Music Publishing LLC

Chapter Nine

Argentina

Well, the rain exploded with a mighty crash

As we fell into the sun

And the first one said to the second one there

I hope you're having fun

Band on the run, band on the run

And the jailer man and sailor Sam

Were searching every one

For the band on the run

Band on the run

Band on the run

Band on the run

Paul McCartney/Linda McCartney

© Kobalt Music Publishing Ltd., 1973

Covering sport in South Yorkshire and North Derbyshire in the mid to late 1970s was certainly not dull. All of the local football clubs spent much of the time in the lower leagues of English football, the two Sheffield clubs, United and Wednesday, were for a time both in the Third Division, as it was known then. None of the other four – Barnsley, Chesterfield, Doncaster Rovers and Rotherham United – ever made it higher than Division Two.

Despite that, we were by no means without drama and excitement. England 1966 World Cup winner Jack Charlton arrived to manage Sheffield Wednesday, whilst the ever-jovial Harry Haslam made his mark across the city at Bramall Lane.

Local derbies between United and Wednesday attracted attendances of a size that was more usually seen in the First Division, and they were full of goals and incidents. They had top players too, with the likes of the great Tony Currie and the veteran Alan Woodward at United, whilst Gary Bannister and the enigmatic Terry Curran were at Wednesday. Curran would later play for United after I'd left Sheffield, but while he was at the Hillsborough club he delivered skill and guile in equal measure. Jack Charlton had persuaded him to drop down two divisions to join Wednesday, and big Jack then went on to describe Curran as "the most exciting player in English football at the moment."

* * * *

Cricket in Yorkshire and Derbyshire was always high on the agenda. Geoffrey Boycott was never far from the top of the sports news during my time in South Yorkshire, and in front of his home supporters at Headingley on August 11th 1977, he became the first batsman in history to score his hundredth 100 in a Test match. It was his second Test after returning from a three-year self-imposed exile. He scored 191 to help England beat Australia and retain the Ashes with an innings victory. In the aftermath of that remarkable achievement, he made many guest appearances at events and sporting venues across Yorkshire, thanking the county's cricket fans for backing him throughout his troubled times and when he was at the crease.

"If I wanted to do it anywhere, I would always have wanted it to be in front of my own Yorkshire public," he told me. "The way they applauded and cheered and sang my name, was the sort of reception they've given me throughout my whole career, really. I'm really pleased for them, as well as myself. It's a dream come true."

A celebratory dinner was held at Sheffield City Hall to mark the occasion, the dinner itself breaking records for its formidable array of speakers and for the duration of the event. The master of ceremonies was Michael Parkinson, who made the first speech before introducing three more speakers, as well as Geoffrey himself. The speakers were, in the order in which they appeared that night, Michael Parkinson, Brian Clough, Geoffrey Boycott, the Liberal

Democrat MP, broadcaster and raconteur Clement Freud, and the BBC newsreader Peter Woods.

After the speeches from Michael Parkinson and Brian Clough, Geoffrey was presented with a cake, baked to look like a pyramid of cricket balls, 100 of them, to represent each century. He then spoke to express his gratitude, to thank the speakers and other VIPs who had turned out to mark the occasion, and to thank his mother for her continuing support.

It had by now turned 10.30pm and Parky announced a comfort break. Excursions to the toilets and the bar, usually in that order, followed. Around half an hour later, the formalities resumed, Clement Freud was introduced and embarked on a hilarious speech, made even funnier by his famously dour, lugubrious expression and delivery.

By the time he concluded, the clock was edging towards midnight, but we still weren't done. Peter Woods was introduced as the final speaker. Twelve months before, Peter had made the front pages of the national newspapers when he slurred his words whilst reading the news during a late evening BBC TV programme. So much so that he was faded off-air with the host, Robin Day, saying "And there we leave the newsroom, earlier than usual".

The newspaper reporters took delight in speculating on the reason for what had happened, all of them inferring that Woods was drunk. The official BBC explanation, blaming it on medication for sinus problems, simply made it worse as the speculation turned to the nature of the medication.

His speech at the Geoffrey Boycott dinner was therefore awaited with great anticipation, enhanced by the extreme lateness of the hour which meant there had been plenty of time for Woods and his audience to enjoy substantial quantities of liquid refreshment. It was a witty, intelligent and hilarious speech which saw the evening end with a standing ovation for all the speakers. There was great applause, particularly for Geoffrey Boycott.

* * * *

I made many friends in Sheffield, not the least of whom was the footballer Ken Knighton, who was captain of Sheffield Wednesday when Radio Hallam launched in 1974. Ken was born near Barnsley, but his career had taken him to Wolverhampton Wanderers, Oldham Athletic, Preston North End,

Blackburn Rovers and Hull City before signing for Wednesday in 1973. When Ken joined the club one of the all-time legends of Sheffield football, Derek Dooley, had been Wednesday's manager, but by the time Hallam arrived on the scene, things had changed dramatically.

The board of directors at Sheffield Wednesday had undergone major changes in December 1973, including the appointments of a new Chairman and a new Vice-Chairman. Despite showing signs of recovering from a poor run of results, Derek Dooley was sacked on Christmas Eve.

He had joined the club as a player in 1947, becoming a popular goalscoring fan favourite. In a match at Preston in February 1953 Dooley broke his leg, an x-ray revealing that he had sustained a double fracture. Despite successful treatment for the fractures, a small scratch on his leg became infected, and he had to have his leg amputated. He was 24 years of age when his playing days were so cruelly ended. In his playing career, from 1950 to 1953, he scored 62 goals in 61 league matches, and a further goal in the 2 FA Cup-ties he played in. Sheffield-born Derek had been devoted to the Owls, but when he was sacked he was so bitter he vowed never to have anything more to do with the club.

He even did the unthinkable by crossing the city to work for Wednesday's archrivals Sheffield United, becoming the Blades' Chairman and, later, Vice-President. It was 1992, long after I had left Sheffield before Derek Dooley returned to Wednesday's Hillsborough ground to watch a local derby between the two sides. That day he was given a standing ovation by both sets of supporters.

When he died in 2008, his funeral took place at Sheffield Cathedral. The cathedral was surrounded by thousands of fans from both Sheffield clubs who listened to the service on loudspeakers. Inside, the service was attended by England legend Sir Bobby Charlton, Yorkshire cricket umpire Dickie Bird and former United managers Neil Warnock and Dave Bassett.

* * * *

When Radio Hallam went on air, the man who had replaced Derek Dooley, Steve Burtenshaw, was struggling for consistency with Sheffield Wednesday, whilst across the city, Ken Furphy was the manager of Sheffield United. Burtenshaw always seemed to me to be passing through at Hillsborough, never really showing confidence that he was the man to show the leadership the club desperately needed. At Bramall Lane, under the combative Furphy, the Blades were a competitive outfit, always striving to secure top-dog status in the city. When I turned up to interview Furphy for the first time, I was the one on the receiving end of his questions, rather than the other way round, as he gave me the third degree about who I was and where I had come from. It was as though he was asking who I thought I was, daring to cover his team.

If United had gusto and something of a swagger about them, Wednesday was struggling in the aftermath of football's infamous betting scandal of 1964.

Ten years on, the club was still tainted with the fact that three of its players, Peter Swan, David Layne and Tony Kay, had been accused and found guilty of match-fixing and betting against their own team in an away game at Ipswich Town. Two of them, Swan and Kay, were England internationals. The three were sent to prison, and on release, banned from football for life. The bans were later lifted, and although Swan and Layne re-joined Sheffield Wednesday, their playing careers were effectively over, and the club they had let down still carried the scars.

Wednesday therefore needed whatever positive PR it could get, though that was not the reason why I recruited Ken Knighton to combine his career as a footballer with the role of presenting a weekly football phone-in show on Radio Hallam. I recalled the impact that I had seen the likes of Derek Dougan and Jim Cumbes enjoy in my days at BBC Radio Birmingham, and I wanted to recreate that effect in Sheffield.

My plan was to create an on-air double act with Ken Knighton and Sheffield United captain Keith Eddy co-hosting a radio show. I had no doubt that "The Ken and Keith Show" would grab the attention of the fans, and I am convinced that it would have been a winner.

For a start, the banter they could have enjoyed about the name of the show would have provided a lively backdrop, whether it should be "The Ken and Keith Show" or "The Keith and Ken Show". However, Ken Furphy could not be persuaded to allow Eddy to take part and flatly refused.

Whether it was because he was concerned that it would take the player's focus away from football, or because of a reluctance to have United linked to Wednesday, I don't know, but I have no doubt it would have been a great pairing at the microphone. Sadly it never happened. As it was, Ken's weekly programme was a big hit, and the fans of all the local clubs, including United, phoned in and loved talking to him.

* * * *

Ken also opened the door to football stories that may not have otherwise come my way. Like the weekend in 1976 when Fulham came to town to play Sheffield United at Bramall Lane. In the Fulham playing squad at that time was England's World Cup winning captain Bobby Moore, the flamboyant, ultra-gifted Rodney Marsh, and the one and only George Best.

Ken discovered that Fulham was staying at one of Sheffield's top hotels, the Hallam Towers, the night before the match, and he arranged that the two of us would go there to interview Best and Marsh together. George Best was quietly subdued, and although he joined in the conversation, he left it to his outspoken team-mate to dominate proceedings.

At the time Don Revie was England manager, famously distributing comprehensive dossiers on their opponents to each player in the international squad. Revie's time managing England was not a success, despite his record of achievements at club level with Leeds United. He was criticised by many pundits and players. Rodney Marsh made it clear during our interview in Sheffield that he thought Revie was the wrong man for the job.

"Don Revie should never have been appointed," said Marsh. "The players don't like him, the results are frankly rubbish, and his methods are not what's needed at international level."

Marsh's comments were very much in line with what others were saying. Derby Country defender Colin Todd had commented that Revie appeared not to know which players he wanted in his team and that his methods were more suited to day-to-day club management, rather than the politics and committee meetings required at international level.

Our interview was seized on that weekend by the national press, with the Sunday newspaper, *The News Of The World*, quoting what Rodney Marsh had said to us during our Radio Hallam interview.

* * * *

Ken Knighton and I became good friends, even to the point that he was my best man when I married for the second time in March 1976.

The Sheffield-born girl that I had met at Birmingham City Council Social Services Department, and with whom I had lived immediately before moving North, had decided to move with me to South Yorkshire. She had successfully applied for a senior management job at the Royal Hallamshire Hospital, and we bought a house together.

Our register office wedding was quite different to the church ceremony of my first marriage. No religious proceedings this time, despite my second wife's late father having been a local vicar in Sheffield, at a parish quite close to our new home.

Friends and family gathered at the register office in Sheffield Town Hall, including colleagues from Radio Hallam, as I took my vows for the second time. Newly married, we then drove down the M1 to Luton Airport where we boarded a flight to our honeymoon in Ibiza.

* * * *

When we returned, my work focus was heavily slanted towards the affairs of the six local football clubs, to which end I was ably assisted by Alan Biggs, a young reporter from Chesterfield who was keen to make his mark in sports journalism. Not that securing Alan's services was easy.

First, I had to persuade Ian Rufus that the radio station should invest in someone to support me. I succeeded, but only by agreeing that Alan's services would be shared with the news team. Alan was recruited as a general news reporter who would also spend part of his time covering sport. On 13th April 1976, not long before his 21st birthday, Alan received a letter from Ian offering him a job at Radio Hallam which included "...you will be required to carry out certain duties under the direction of the Sports Editor, Stuart Linnell."

Alan had been a trainee reporter at the *Derbyshire Times* in his hometown of Chesterfield and had briefly been the host of a weekly sports show on the fledgling local cable TV station, Sheffield Cablevision. It was there that I came close to saying a final 'goodbye' to this cruel world. Alan was interviewing me about my job at Radio Hallam when one of the studio lights exploded shooting fragments of glass and filament across the studio. I recall one sizable piece of studio light shrapnel whizzing only inches from my ear, whilst another landed on and singed Alan's jumper.

We both survived, and Alan went on to be part of the team in the Radio Hallam newsroom. Despite the condition that he reported on news as well as sport, Alan's supportive role to me at Hallam grew as time went by. He succeeded me as Sports Editor some four years after taking up his job at the radio station, moving on later in a highly successful career to work for BBC Radio 5 Live, and thereafter as a freelance reporter for talkSPORT.

Between us, we covered all local sport, including speedway, with hugely enjoyable evenings watching the Sheffield Tigers speedway team at Owlerton Stadium where greyhound racing was also staged. Occasionally we covered some of the higher-profile greyhound meetings.

We were also in attendance at County cricket fixtures, with some Yorkshire matches played at Abbeydale Park in Sheffield, whilst Derbyshire's home fixtures were occasionally played from time to time at Queen's Park, Chesterfield. Abbeydale and Queen's Park are both beautiful settings for first-class cricket.

Queen's Park was the starting point for one of the most remarkable days of sport I was privileged to cover. On 15th September 1975 one of the last professional sportsmen to play both cricket and football competed in both on the same day. He was Chris Balderstone, and after playing in a County Championship cricket fixture, he took part in a Football League match on the same day.

Balderstone played cricket for Leicestershire, and he was 51 not out against Derbyshire at the end of day two at Chesterfield. At the close of play, he changed into his football kit and drove the 30 miles to Doncaster Rovers' Belle Vue ground. There he played for the home side in a 1–1 draw against Brentford in League Division Four. The following morning he was back in his whites at Chesterfield to complete a century and take three wickets, helping Leicestershire secure its first ever County Championship title.

To follow Balderstone through all that was quite something. He made himself available to reporters throughout, despite having to focus on his two different roles. He was an accomplished sportsman, playing football during his career for four different football clubs, whilst being selected to play in two Test Matches for the England cricket team. He later became an international cricket umpire.

* * * *

Snooker became a huge part of what we did on air when Sheffield's Crucible Theatre became the home of the World Professional Snooker Championship. A Derbyshire businessman, Mike Watterson, had steered the game towards a sustainable future, with the Crucible destined to be the iconic home of its major championship.

The game was perfect for colour television, with coloured snooker balls set on the green baize. The first TV programmes to be transmitted in colour in the UK had been seen in 1967. Ten years later the first World Snooker Championship staged at The Crucible attracted coverage from BBC TV.

Alan Weeks was the first host of the television coverage, which in those early days was limited to highlights of the semi-finals and the Final. They were shown late at night on BBC2, with the legendary "Whispering" Ted Lowe as the main commentator.

Its popularity was quickly established, so much so that the following year there were nightly highlights programmes for each of the fourteen days of the tournament, as well as Saturday afternoon coverage on the BBC's flagship sports show 'Grandstand'. David Vine shared the TV hosting duties at The Crucible with Alan Weeks, with the ultimately knowledgeable and authoritative former professional snooker and billiards player Clive Everton introduced as a commentator, alternating with Ted Lowe.

By 1980 live daily TV broadcasts were introduced, with the urbane David Vine continuing in the main presenter's role for the next twenty years.

As a major event on our patch, I regarded it as essential that Radio Hallam covered the World Championship. My decision to maintain a reporting presence at The Crucible throughout the fortnight contributed to Mike Watterson agreeing to buy advertising for the tournament on the radio station.

We ran regular reports and updates from the matches, as well as associated stories about the players. These were the heydays of Alex "Hurricane" Higgins, Canadian stars Cliff Thorburn and Bill Werbeniuk, the enigmatic Welshmen Ray Reardon and Terry Griffiths, the gutsy Australian Eddie Charlton and the final flurry in the career of Fred Davis, brother of the legendary former World Champion Joe Davis.

Joe was an iconic snooker legend, but sadly he died just as the move to The Crucible saw snooker hit the big time. He had retired from competitive snooker in 1964, but his presence amongst spectators in Sheffield in the first couple of years of the World Championship making its home there always caused a stir among the fans. Joe collapsed whilst watching his brother play the South African player Perrie Mans in the 1978 semi-final and died two months later.

There was, therefore, always plenty to talk about when the snooker hit town. I even attempted the seemingly impossible by trying to commentate on snooker on the radio. One or two very late finishes saw matches going well into the early hours, and I was encouraged by my colleagues to describe the action and the late-night tension inside the theatre. The late show on Radio Hallam was, like the daytime programmes, a mix of music and chat so the reasoning was, if there is snooker to talk about, go for it.

The late ending to some matches helped, such as the 1979 semi-final when Terry Griffiths beat Eddie Charlton 19-17, with the match finishing at 1.40 am!

* * * *

On Saturday afternoon my sport and music show, using the title "Sportacular" coined by Peter Donaldson, focused on football for much of the year, with cricket during the summer. Throughout the year we also reported on horse racing from the Town Moor course at Doncaster. In 1978, the show came live from Town Moor to cover the running of the St. Leger, with Her Majesty the Queen attending the racecourse.

We had no commentary rights of our own, but once the race started we were allowed to rebroadcast the live ITV commentary, as heard across the country. I could talk right up to the start and then bring in the ITV commentary the instant the race got underway. That proved to be quite a test in 1978 when the horse Easter King hit its head in the starting gate and collapsed just before the start of the race. A tented screen was put around the stricken animal as it was humanely put down, with the start of the St. Leger heavily delayed.

That meant that my carefully prepared preamble had to be extended substantially and improvised until the race got underway. That year's St. Leger was won by a horse called Julio Mariner, ridden by Eddie Hyde, but it will always be synonymous for me with the tragedy of Easter King.

* * * *

Until the mid-1970s overseas players in British football were a rarity, but when the hosts Argentina won the World Cup in 1978 all that changed.

The headlines were grabbed by Tottenham Hotspur signing the brilliant Ricky Villa and Ossie Ardiles. It was big news, but few realised their arrival in England was largely down to the manager of Sheffield United, Harry Haslam.

Some 12 years before, at the 1966 World Cup in England, Harry had got to know the captain of the Argentinian side, Antonio Rattin. On the way to winning the '66 tournament, England had played Argentina at Wembley in the quarter-final. Rattin was sent off that day, with England manager Alf Ramsey calling the South American side "animals".

Despite Ramsey's outburst, with which many England fans sympathised, Harry Haslam became a good friend of Antonio Rattin. When they spoke soon after the '78 World Cup, the Argentinian told Harry that if English clubs were interested a number of his country's World Cup winning side were keen to play in England.

Harry was, without doubt, one of the best-connected men in football and he immediately called another friend, Arsenal manager Terry Neill. They arranged that the two of them would fly to Buenos Aires, meet Rattin and explore what deals could be done. Harry had only relatively modest financial resources to draw on at Sheffield United, but he knew that Arsenal's financial clout was very different. He planned to bring a player back to Bramall Lane off the back of a bigger deal for the London club.

At the last minute, for reasons never properly explained, Terry Neill cried off, leaving Harry to seek another partner for his venture. The man he turned to was Keith Burkinshaw at Tottenham who readily agreed. Harry's next call was to me.

"Happy Harry" had seized on the fact that I wore a beard, which influenced the nickname he gave me, hence the start of the 'phone call.

"Gillette", he said, when he got through, late on a Monday afternoon. "What are you doing on Thursday?"

Without waiting for a reply, he continued.

"Antonio Rattin has agreed to be our agent in Argentina. Keith Burkinshaw and I are flying out there to sign some players. Would you like to come with us?"

What an opportunity. I asked Harry if I could call him back, and with my head spinning I rapidly ran through everything I had planned, both at work and at home, over the following week. It quickly became apparent that my commitments meant that I couldn't make it work, so I called Harry and explained that much as I would really have loved to have done so, it just wasn't possible.

With the benefit of hindsight, I should have just ditched everything and gone. Unsurprisingly, I cannot now recall whatever it was that prevented me from doing so.

At Harry's suggestion, we agreed that I would call him, or he would call me, every day that he was away. That way we could record a daily interview and cover his trip in that way. Reporter Tony Pritchett from the local evening paper, the *Sheffield Star*, had no such complications and he travelled to Argentina with the two managers.

Harry was, as always, as good as his word with me, and our daily calls provided Radio Hallam with exclusive radio coverage of the trip. The penultimate call was one I will never forget as Harry told me about the player he'd signed, and about the one that got away.

"I'm bringing home," he said, "a young man called Alex Sabella. He's clever and really skilful, and I know the fans will love him. But there was one kid that Rattin tried to line up for me that they won't let me sign. Gillette, he's got everything. He can pass a ball better than anyone I've ever seen, he can trap it, juggle with it, dribble with it, shoot with it, and even take a throw-in better than anyone else. They won't let him go because they're preparing him for the next World Cup, but he's going to be a star, mark my words.

"What's his name, Harry?" I asked.

"Oh," came the reply, "it's er – Madonna or something like that."

He was talking, of course, about the young Diego Maradona.

Harry could not sign Maradona and I never went to Argentina, but Keith Burkinshow grabbed the headlines by signing Ardiles and Villa for Spurs, whilst Alejandro Sabella became a big favourite at Bramall Lane and later at Leeds United.

* * * *

My on-air style for Sportacular was very different from what I had observed from Tony Butler at BRMB. For a start, I introduced and credited all the music. Whereas Tony would use a record to fill time between match reports but totally ignore and fail to even acknowledge each disc, my approach was to credit both artist and title as I would expect from the DJ in any other radio show.

Possibly because I was reasonably competent in doing that, or that I could do it without making too many mistakes, Keith Skues would, from time to time, invite me to sit in for other presenters when they were away through sickness or holiday, or similar. That often meant hosting the Late Show when others were moved around the schedule, although I would also be called in occasionally to join Roger Moffat and Brenda Ellison when they had live guests in for an interview on their midmorning show.

One morning in 1975 their special guest was Michael Parkinson, then at the height of his popularity as the UK's number one TV chat show host. His eponymous show was a major part of the BBC1 Saturday night line-up which also included "The Generation Game", comedy shows such as "The Two Ronnies" and "The Morecambe and Wise Show", and the football highlights programme "Match Of The Day", hosted by Jimmy Hill.

As far as Radio Hallam was concerned, Michael Parkinson was the number one South Yorkshire celebrity. A national TV star, he was born in the village of Cudworth in Barnsley and had been educated at Barnsley Grammar School. He was a keen cricketer, and both he and his opening batting partner at Barnsley Cricket Club, Harold 'Dickie' Bird, had trials for Yorkshire together with Geoffrey Boycott. Whilst Boycott became one of the world's best batsmen, and Dickie Bird one of the world's finest umpires, Michael Parkinson's career path took him to the top in journalism and broadcasting.

So popular was 'Parky', as everyone called him, that he was one of a group of celebrities who posed for the cover photograph for the Paul McCartney and Wings' album "Band On The Run", the biggest selling album of 1974. On the cover, Paul and Linda McCartney, and the other member of Wings, guitarist Denny Laine, were caught in the beam of a prison searchlight alongside other celebrities dressed as convicts. The six were Michael Parkinson, singer Kenny Lynch, actors James Coburn and Christopher Lee, boxer John Conteh, and the MP and raconteur Clement Freud.

Parky was my hero as an interviewer. I watched his show every Saturday night and I knew of course that he was a big sports fan. A top sports journalist, he wrote a column in those days for the sports section of *The Sunday Times*.

Brenda Ellison knew of my admiration for him, so she asked if I'd like to join in when she and Roger Moffat interviewed Parky. She didn't have to wait for an answer.

Although it was their show, Roger and Brenda generously allowed me to ask most of the questions, particularly about sport. One of Parky's great friends was George Best, a sportsman whom he and most of the rest of us rated as one of the best footballers ever. Michael has had several books published about Best, describing the player's incredible skill and unique talent. The books also address how booze, the demon that was so devastating for Best, destroyed all that greatness and footballing genius.

My first question for Parky that day was, "Just how good was George Best?"

MP: "The sadness of George Best was that he went out of the game at 27 when, presumably, the next two years he was going to be a great athlete at his peak, so we'll never really know how magnificent he might have been, and good God, he was good enough as a kid. The finest player I ever saw.

"George Best's problems were those of a young man who, at the age of 15, was taken away from his home in Northern Ireland; a working-class boy, who became, overnight, at 17, the biggest thing in the world. I mean he was as big as The Beatles at one point. He had fan clubs in Tokyo and in Istanbul! I mean it was extraordinary.

"How he coped with it and didn't cope with it, that's the fundamental tragedy of George Best. I can't think of anybody who I've met, in sport, or any entertainment profession, who could have taken what he took at his age and come through it unscathed. I think it would have ruined anybody."

Parky had just had a book published called "Sporting Fever", a collection of articles that he'd originally written for *The Sunday Times*. I suggested to him that running through the articles was a resentment that, coming from the North of England as he did, the South was seen as better off.

MP: "I think that there is a very real, fundamental divide in sport in this country between North and South. I think quite a bit of it is myth, and I've helped promote the myth; more than most people, I will admit.

"I think there's a great advantage to being from the North. There was, when I went into television, a great advantage to having an accent, but I've been very happy working in the South, I really have. I've been very happy working with people who, if the myth were true, I couldn't stand the sight of."

Roger joined in at that point referring to himself as a Southerner, even though he, like me, was born in Birmingham. Roger at the BBC, and Michael at the *Manchester Guardian* (as '*The Guardian*' newspaper was originally known), had been media buddies in Manchester. In the exchange that followed, we were treated to reminiscences of a few late-night drinking sessions.

When the studio hilarity eased, I jumped back in with a question about Michael's chat show. An obvious question, perhaps, but I thought it was worth asking.

SL: "Who's the interviewee you've enjoyed talking to most?"

MP: "Professor Bronowski".

Michael had answered instantly, without a second thought.

The man he was referring to was Jacob Bronowski, a British mathematician and historian, best known for developing a humanistic approach to science, and as the presenter and writer of a thirteen-part BBC TV documentary series, and accompanying book, 'The Ascent Of Man'. That led to him being referred to as "one of the world's most celebrated intellectuals". Michael Parkinson was full of admiration for him.

MP: "He was the cleverest, most profound, most articulate man I've ever met in my life. I could have talked to him forever, and ever, and ever. It's also a sign that I'm enjoying an interview if I have my notes out on my knee but never look at them once in 20 minutes. In my view, that's a perfect conversation. I'm not saying that I was perfect, it was just easy with him.

"If you read the book I wrote of the interview, if you took my questions out, his script read as perfect prose. (Malcolm) Muggeridge is another one whose conversation is perfect prose. I enjoyed Dame Edith Evans, and people like that. I enjoy the older stars because it seems to me that they have a discipline, they have an attitude of going out there and doing their best that some of the younger stars palpably lack.

"You're rather like a traffic cop with an interview of that sort. Your job is to keep the flow going, and occasionally alter the course of it, and to be as unobtrusive as possible. I firmly believe that, in a show like that, people want to see whoever is my guest in a situation that perhaps they've not seen them in before. I always feel that if you give people the correct atmosphere and the time, particularly, to relax and let it all come out, you find out a lot more about them actually."

Parky then talked about the frustrations he had encountered with two particular Hollywood stars.

MP: "One of the most difficult interviews I ever had, and this goes back to what I was saying about younger stars, was with Elliott Gould and Donald Sutherland. For some reason, they'd decided they were going to take me apart and take Mr. Al Capp (the other guest, the cartoonist) apart. Well, they might well have done me but there was no way they were going to do Al Capp.

"When we asked them to come on the programme, they knew what was required of them, and they just weren't prepared to do it once they got to the studio, which I found rather silly. I take the view that if someone is as reluctant as they were, and as hostile as they were, all I have to do is sit back and let them come across like that. The person at home doesn't feel sorry for them and doesn't feel sorry for me, but they don't like them very much."

Michael Parkinson was a huge star on British television, and he was much loved. He was made CBE (Commander of the Order of the British Empire) in 2000 for services to broadcasting, receiving his medal from Prince Charles, and he became Sir Michael when he was made a Knight Bachelor in the 2008 New Year's Honours List. He remarked that he was "not the type to get a knighthood", coming as he did "from Barnsley."

* * * *

Parky often came home to South Yorkshire, and I would bump into him when Yorkshire came to Sheffield to play county cricket matches.

The county club had left its original Sheffield home, Bramall Lane, the home ground of Sheffield United football club, the year before Radio Hallam began. The last cricket match at the Lane was a three-day County Championship match played on 4th, 6th and 7th August 1973, a drawn game against Lancashire.

Sheffield United then built a new stand on the part of the ground where the cricket pitch once stood, leaving Yorkshire to concentrate its home fissures at its Headingley headquarters in Leeds. Some matches were still played in Sheffield but in the very different environment of Abbeydale Park. Michael Parkinson was a regular spectator there, and during one match I persuaded him to join me and the great Yorkshire and England fast bowler Freddie Trueman, to record a chat based on a book written by Freddie that had recently been punished.

It turned into an hour-long conversation, covering how the game had developed since Freddie started, and his concerns about how it was still riven with class status. Freddie talked about some players being working-class lads, as he had been, whilst others were from a totally different social and economic background. As we chatted in a pitch-side hospitality marquee, with match spectators gathered around us. They listened intently to what was being said, occasionally applauding and laughing at the comments. Recorded for Radio Hallam, it was broadcast as a one-off special show under the title "Abbeydale Conversation".

* * * *

Much as I would love to, I could never call Michael Parkinson a "mate", but the fact that I knew him at all, coupled with his obvious local association with the area, prompted a Hallam newsroom colleague to ask me to talk to Parky about a proposition for a radio programme.

Reporter Ralph Bernard had joined the Hallam news team twelve months after we went on air. It was clear that routine, general reporting was not where Ralph wanted to focus his radio career. He set about researching, writing and compiling a series of interviews on the theme of alcoholism. It took some time to put together, and it became obvious that Ralph had collated a huge amount of quality material.

His idea was lacking in one respect. It needed a narrator, and who better for a programme produced in Sheffield than the nationally known South Yorkshire broadcaster, regarded as one of the biggest names of the time, Michael Parkinson.

"You know him, don't you?" Ralph said, more as a statement than a question. "You could ask him if he'll do it."

Ralph wouldn't take "no" for an answer, so very reluctantly I went one evening with a mate to a pub in Rotherham where I knew Parky was likely to be. I had met the landlord of the pub, an old friend of Parky's, at one or two functions and he nodded in acknowledgement from behind the bar when my friend and I wandered in and ordered a couple of drinks.

Parky was standing at the bar with a group of friends, and he also nodded in my direction.

"Great," I thought. "I'm in".

One of Parky's friends excused himself and went to the Gents, causing a minor hiatus and break in their conversation. That gave me my opportunity.

"Evening Michael," I said, even though his back was half turned away from me.

He looked over his shoulder and raised an eyebrow.

"Hello," he said. "Stuart, isn't it? From Radio Hallam?"

Encouraged that he had remembered my name I pressed on, almost stammering out my apology and the reason for my interruption to his private time.

"Sorry to bother you with this Michael, but one of my colleagues at Radio Hallam is making a documentary about alcoholism and we, well he, wondered if you would be the narrator."

Any good humour in his expression quickly disappeared as he looked me full in the face before very firmly and deliberately saying "no". He turned back with a deep sigh, shaking his head dismissively, and resumed his evening with his mates.

The following morning I passed on the bad news to Ralph. To my surprise and my mild irritation, he did not appear overly concerned about missing out on Parky being his narrator. Nor did he seem particularly impressed at the effort I had made in tracking him down.

To solve his problem Ralph turned to one of the big stars and distinctive voices of those early days of Independent Local Radio, LBC presenter and newsreader Douglas Cameron.

The documentary, called "Dying For A Drink", featuring music by singer-songwriter Richard Digance, went on to win awards for Ralph and for Radio Hallam.

Ralph Bernard would go on to be one of the most influential people in the history of UK commercial radio. He became Chief Executive of GWR Group, which acquired several local radio stations as it grew as a company. That acquisition policy meant that our paths would meet again. Ralph also led the team that created the hugely successful national commercial station Classic FM, and would later be made CBE.

* * * *

Sometime later it emerged that Parky had been having his own battle with the booze at the time I had asked him about narrating that documentary about alcoholism. I have heard him admit as much since, saying "I was not far off being an alcoholic at one point." He said that to manage his drinking, he had established a routine whereby he didn't drink after a Thursday in any week. That meant that he was sober for his show on a Saturday.

He added that his wife Mary was the one who put him straight. She said to him "Do you know what your problem is when you're drunk? You're ugly." The last word of that sentence, he said, was what made him stop drinking.

Sir Michael added since that his enjoyment of a drink had stemmed from his early days on Fleet Street, where journalists were regular, heavy drinkers, as were those they mixed with from other branches of the media.

* * * *

161

Throughout the early years of Radio Hallam Roger Moffat's alcohol consumption was the stuff of legend, but it was also the cause of some concern. There was concern for Roger's health, and also for the radio station being certain that one of its front-line presenters would be on air, on time, each weekday morning.

Roger would indulge most, if not every, day. In the pub, his habit was first to buy himself a Barley Wine. It's referred to as "wine" because its alcoholic strength is similar to wine, but as it is made from grain rather than fruit it is actually a beer. A quite strong beer.

The next drink would be bought for him as part of someone's round, whereupon Roger would ask for a Scotch. He would then alternate between Barley Wine and Scotch.

The net result of that routine would initially be that Roger talked and entertained those around him with brilliant wit, laced with highly humorous anecdotes. Then without warning, as if a switch had been pulled, he would suddenly appear moribund, sad and deeply unpleasant. The transformation occurred in an instant.

Roger's association with booze became part of the legend of those early Hallam years, and the story goes that it was woven into the lyrics of a hit record. One of the pop stars of the moment, amongst the many who visited Radio Hallam, was Andy Fairweather Low who had enjoyed chart success as the lead singer of the group Amen Corner. After leaving the group Andy wrote and recorded as a solo artist. One afternoon he came to Hallam for an interview, after which he and Keith Skues popped into the Dove and Rainbow next door to the radio station, where Roger was well into his Barley Wine and Scotch routine.

Andy observed the Moffat phenomena first hand and, so we were told, wrote what became his 1975 Christmas top 10 hit "Wide Eyed And Legless", largely based on what he had witnessed. That song perfectly summed up Roger Moffat's association with the bottle, so if the story behind the hit isn't true it certainly should be.

Roger Moffat was a brilliant broadcaster with a sumptuous voice and a truly mischievous sense of humour, but a man flawed by a weakness for a drink, or several.

Wherever I go and whatever I do

I seem to spend all of my time

Trying to turn my black night, blue

Well I'm tired of it all

It's the same thing every night

But the rhythm of the glass

Is stronger than the rhythm of night

Wide eyed and legless

I've gone and done it again

Wide eyed and legless

This world is full of my shame

Andy Fairweather-Low, 1975

© Imagem Songs Ltd., Fair Music Ltd

Chapter Ten

A Late Lunch with James Hunt

It's nine o'clock on a Saturday

The regular crowd shuffles in

There's an old man sitting next to me

Makin' love to his tonic and gin

He says, "Son, can you play me a memory

I'm not really sure how it goes

But it's sad and it's sweet and I knew it complete

When I wore a younger man's clothes"

La la la, di da da

La la, di da da da dum

Sing us a song, you're the piano man

Sing us a song tonight

Well, we're all in the mood for a melody

And you've got us feelin' alright

Billy Joel, 1973

With the release of a new album, or the publication of a new book, promoting the work is top of the agenda. The recording artist or author sets off on a tour of the country for autographs and photo sessions at stores in the major towns and cities. At each location they would also often stop by the local radio station to be interviewed, usually live on air.

That all ended when technology made it possible for them to sit in a studio, usually in London, and do one interview after another "down the line", as it's referred to, without having to travel. That would allow six or seven radio interviews each hour. It was obviously a more efficient use of time, but it removed the personal, face-to-face, contact with the radio presenters, which often meant the difference between a 'good' interview and a 'really good' interview.

That technology was a few years away when Radio Hallam began, so in those early years, we were regularly blessed with visits to the radio station from the stars of the day. The likes of David Essex, Leo Sayer, Lyn Paul (of The New Seekers), Alvin Stardust, Suzi Quatro, Cindy Kent (of The Settlers), the beautiful Dana and the lovely Lulu, were amongst those that came in.

* * * *

It was clearly a radio station that the stars enjoyed visiting, in part because they knew Johnny Moran, Keith Skues and Roger Moffat from their previous BBC incarnations, so there was a huge element of trust and familiarity.

Cliff Richard came to Hallam more than once, and visiting American stars like Micky Dolenz and Frankie Laine would follow suit. Micky Dolenz, who I first remembered as the "Circus Boy" from the children's TV show of that name, went on to be drummer and vocalist with The Monkees, and it was in that guise that he was interviewed by Hallam presenter Ray Stewart.

Ray was a literally larger-than-life character, born in Sheffield with an established following from his DJ sets in local clubs. He had also had a weekly show on BBC Radio Sheffield and he was wooed across to Hallam by Keith Skues. Ray was a particular fan of Frankie Laine who had enjoyed a hugely successful career with hit records dating back to the 1940s.

Frankie Laine's hits included "That Lucky Old Sun", "Mule Train", "Jezebel", "I Believe", "Hey Joe!", and "Rawhide". The latter was one of several well-known theme songs from movie and TV westerns that he recorded, including "High Noon" and "Champion, The Wonder Horse".

Ray was thrilled to bits when he first interviewed Frankie when the singer was on a UK concert tour. They got on so well that Frankie made a point of visiting Radio Hallam twice more to be interviewed by Ray Stewart.

One of Ray's shows was on a Saturday night, from nine o'clock in the evening until midnight, after which he would go on to work into the early hours of the morning as the star DJ in a local club. I was, and still am, a big fan of Billy Joel, so it occurred to me that his first hit single, "The Piano Man", could be turned into an appropriate theme tune for Ray's Saturday night show.

The song begins with the lyrics "It's nine o'clock on a Saturday...", so I suggested it to Ray. He loved it and started the show every Saturday night at nine with the first few bars of that song.

Ray and I got on well as he was a football fan, a Sheffield United supporter. In fact, for some time, he dated the daughter of the then United Chairman.

Top stars being interviewed on the radio station regularly made you feel as if you were part of something quite special, and it was, therefore, no surprise to learn, some three months in, that the station's advertising sales revenue for its first quarter had easily exceeded its target and showed every sign of continuing to do so. Despite the extremely tricky economic environment, with the country living with the restrictions of the three-day week imposed by the Government, Radio Hallam was a business success story. Audience figures were also impressive and there was a great atmosphere of positivity amongst the staff.

Much of that was down to the enthusiastic approach of Hallam's Managing Director Bill MacDonald. Bill had worked in radio in America and had the image many would expect to see from a US businessman. Tall, but stocky, his grey hair cut in a sharp crew cut, he was always in a dark suit, thin dark tie and a white button-down collar shirt. Bill had also developed a slightly clipped American accent. He had a misleadingly tough, rugged visage, but it would dissolve into a broad smile accompanied by an unexpectedly gentle chuckle when something amused him, which occurred more often than not.

Bill rarely weighed into the on-air content, at least not in front of the staff, though he may well have had his say during management and board meetings. His attitude was one of constant encouragement and that bred a high level of morale amongst the team.

All that, plus sharing the lift in and out of the building with people like Cliff Richard, and locally born stars such as Dave Berry, Tony Christie and Joe Cocker, made it feel like you belonged to something to be proud of. Whilst Dave Berry and Joe Cocker were both born in Sheffield, Tony Christie came from Conisbrough, between Rotherham and Doncaster. Those strong local connections were seized on to emphasise the local roots of the radio station.

My cousin Steve, by now a successful musician himself, playing guitar in the orchestra for the touring production of the musical "Hair", was very excited, even a touch jealous, when I told him that Dave Berry had visited Radio Hallam together with Sheffield born guitarist Frank White from his backing group The Cruisers. Frank was a hero for many young guitarists, not least because he played a rare double-necked Gibson guitar.

Steve was not alone in raving about that guitar. One neck had six strings, and the other had twelve. It was purchased for £400 in 1964, but by 2019 it was priced at £50,000. Not that its monetary value was the appeal for Steve and his fellow musicians. They were genuinely in awe of the instrument.

Two entertainers who became nationally known stars in the mid-70s were the singer and comedienne Marti Caine and top funnyman Bobby Knutt. Both were born in Sheffield in 1945, Marti in January and Bobby at the other end of the year, in November.

Bobby was already becoming well known when Radio Hallam launched in 1974, as a regular on the ITV shows 'The Comedians' and 'The Wheeltappers and Shunters Social Club'. Both he and Marti Caine had served their apprenticeships by working for many years on the club circuit in Yorkshire, but Marti was regarded as an overnight success when she won the ITV talent show 'New Faces' in 1975. In doing so, she defeated both Lenny Henry and Victoria Wood.

Needless to say, both Bobby and Marti were in demand by both Sheffield local radio stations, and whilst Radio Hallam readily welcomed them, they were also regular guests on BBC Radio Sheffield, particularly on a show hosted by Tony Capstick, a folk singer and comedian from Rotherham. Tony had also made his way through live performances, in his case through folk clubs in Yorkshire and elsewhere across the country.

Tony had four albums released before he hit the charts with "Capstick Comes Home" in 1981. Even though he was a presenter on the rival BBC local station, Radio Hallam had no concerns about playing Tony Capstick's records. His double-sided hit singles, "The Sheffield Grinder" and "Capstick Comes Home" went to No.3 in the UK singles chart, and both tracks were played on Radio Hallam.

Bobby Knutt was a big fan of Sheffield United, and he provided a memorable moment at a local derby between United and Sheffield Wednesday at Bramall Lane. He was introduced to the capacity crowd at half-time, everyone well aware of his life-long allegiance to the home side.

Wearing jeans and a zipped-up black leather jacket, he waved to all parts of the ground as he strode to the centre spot. He was inevitably booed by the Wednesday fans and cheered by the United supporters. He turned towards the end of the ground occupied by the home fans, waved again, and then turned to the visitors and waved once more. The more he waved, the louder the jeers and cheers. To say it was a lively atmosphere was putting it mildly.

Bobby turned to face the United-ites and unzipped his jacket to reveal a football shirt with the red and white stripes of Sheffield United. It prompted a huge cheer, even louder than before, and they even sang his name.

Still facing the same direction he let the jacket slip off his shoulders and fall to his waist, showing that the back of his shirt was carrying Wednesday's blue and white stripes. That was only visible to the visiting fans, who responded in turn with a huge roar of approval

Bobby then turned around so that both sets of supporters could see the colours of the other side. Cheers and jeers mixed with laughter all around the stadium. It was a simple but clever comedy routine, delivered hilariously and entirely without words. Bobby's timing was immaculate. It lasted more than five minutes and he left the pitch to tremendous applause from all parts.

Another Sheffield-born character making it big in the entertainment world was Pete Stringfellow. His Mojo Club in Pitsmoor in Sheffield had been a huge success in the mid-60s, with a host of big-name acts and bands playing there. He brought a long list of stars to Sheffield including The Who, Pink

Floyd, The Brian Auger Trinity, The Yardbirds, The Hollies, The Merseybeats, the Spencer Davis Group, The Pretty Things, Manfred Mann, The Small Faces, Georgie Fame and the Blue Flames, and The Jimi Hendrix Experience. There were American acts too, such as Ben E. King, Tina Turner, and Stevie Wonder, then billed as "Little" Stevie Wonder.

By the time Radio Hallam went on the air, Pete Stringfellow's business interests had moved to Leeds, where he ran the legendary nightclub Cinderella Rockafella's, before opening the Millionaire Club in Manchester. He would later sell the Millionaire Club to Granada Ltd and move with his whole family to London where he became nationally and internationally famous with his club Stringfellow's in Covent Garden in London.

Stringfellow's was an immediate success with celebrities, international film stars, TV personalities, rock stars, models, paparazzi and national newspaper journalists partying together. He followed that by opening clubs under the same name in America. There were Stringfellow's clubs in New York, Miami and Los Angeles, and he took over the former London cabaret club, Talk of the Town. He re-opened the latter with its original name Hippodrome and branded it as the "World's Greatest Disco". Not bad for the son of a steelworker from Pitsmoor in Sheffield.

Although he no longer operated in Sheffield he visited Radio Hallam on a few occasions, taking the opportunity on air to suggest that local people should take a trip from his home city to his other venues for their live entertainment. The consequence was that rival South Yorkshire venues advertised on the station, including the Fiesta Club in Sheffield.

The Fiesta attracted top names to the city to appear on stage in a cabaret setting, in front of an audience enjoying the show whilst eating a meal, often the then trendy 'chicken in a basket'. It was, as the name suggests, fried chicken and French fries, served in a disposable paperboard container shaped and designed to look like a small basket.

Located at Arundel Gate in Sheffield, the Fiesta Club claimed to be the largest nightclub in Europe, with a 1,300-seat amphitheatre. The stars were usually booked in for a week at a time, and when it opened in 1970, the opening act was The Shadows. By the time Radio Hallam was launched four years later, it was established as a place where anybody who was anybody should play, with names like Matt Monro, Sandie Shaw, The Beach Boys,

Stevie Wonder, Roy Orbison, Ella Fitzgerald, The Four Tops, Cilla Black, Lynsey de Paul, Tony Christie and the Jackson Five all appearing there.

Comedians also often topped the bill, including Les Dawson, Tommy Cooper and Freddie Starr. TV favourite Bruce Forsyth was another star who appeared at the Fiesta.

The singer Frankie Vaughan starred there in 1975 and, during his week at the Fiesta, he agreed to support a local charity event at a working men's club in Rotherham. The event was built around a contest to find that year's "Miss Rotherham". I had been booked as the compère, and Frankie Vaughan was a judge.

All went pretty smoothly, and the lucky young lady was duly chosen and crowned, posing for pictures with Frankie. Whilst those photos were being taken a member of the working men's club organising committee came up to me and whispered in my ear.

"Do you think he'll do a turn?"

"What?" I said, taken completely by surprise.

"Frank," came the reply. "Mr. Vaughan. As he's here, will he do a turn for us? Now. Will you ask him?"

"Well," I said anxiously, not exactly keen to impose on the goodwill of the pop star, "I will ask him, but I can't promise."

That seemed to delight the committee man who turned towards the box in a far corner of the room where the club's entertainment steward sat and gave the thumbs up.

I quickly went to Frankie and managed to say, "They're asking if you'd sing for them Frankie."

Before he could answer, the steward rang his bell and announced across the room, "Thank you. Thank you, please. Seeing as he's here, mister Frankie Vaughan has agreed to sing for us. Thank you, please. Mister Frankie Vaughan." If you ever saw the ITV show "The Wheeltappers And Shunters Social Club", in which the comedian Colin Crompton played the part of the steward, it was exactly like that.

The packed club, with pints of beer adorning every table, burst into applause. Frankie looked at me, shrugged his shoulders and gave a reluctant grin.

The club's resident pianist, who had provided accompanying music whilst the "Miss Rotherham" contestants had been on stage, looked hopefully at Frankie who walked over to him and asked, "Do you know 'Hello Dolly'?"

The pianist nodded enthusiastically and launched vigorously into the tune. Gamely, Frankie picked up the microphone and sang his hit as brilliantly as if he'd been performing at a Royal Variety Show. He brought the house down, with everyone standing to applaud him, as the steward rang his bell and said "Thank you, Mister Frankie Vaughan. Thank you please."

I said, "Well done, and thank you; I didn't know they were going to assume that you'd do that."

Frankie looked at me at winked.

"Neither did I," he said, "but it happens. What can you do?"

He spent some time shaking hands and signing autographs, well beyond the time he could have been expected to stay. Frankie Vaughan's shows at the Fiesta Club were all sold out, and deservedly so. A nicer, more genuine man you couldn't wish to meet.

My six years at Radio Hallam were rich in memorable moments like that, and there were many more besides thanks to sport.

Sebastian Coe, later to be a Conservative MP and later still a Peer, lived in Sheffield when he emerged as one of the world's top athletes. A middle-distance runner, he set three world records in the space of 41 days in 1979. I was amongst the group of journalists waiting to interview him each time on his return to Sheffield.

After I'd left Radio Hallam, Coe set a world record in the 800 metres in 1981, which remained unbroken until 1997. His rivalries with fellow Britons Steve Ovett and Steve Cram dominated middle-distance running for much of the 1980s, and he won four Olympic medals, including the 1500 metres gold medal at the Olympic Games in Moscow in 1980, and again in Los Angeles in 1984.

From time to time, visiting stars provided added entertainment for those of us fortunate enough to spend time with them. One such was James Hunt.

He was more than just a motor racing driver. He was a hugely glamorous figure, with a playboy image. Public school educated, he was tall, blond, good-looking, very intelligent and extremely articulate. His close friends have publicly defended his lothario reputation pointing out that he was, for example, a sensitive animal lover, and that he always acted in a gentlemanly way. He nonetheless had "Sex, breakfast of champions" sewn onto his overalls, and that image was enhanced with a national newspaper report claiming that he'd been to bed with thirty-five British Airways hostesses at the Tokyo Hilton hotel in the run-up to the 1976 Japanese Grand Prix, the race that would win him that year's Formula One World Championship.

His son Freddie has since added to the story by saying in an interview with the *Daily Mirror*, "There were witnesses. There was a fresh supply of hostesses. They would come to the hotel, stop over, and then get on the plane the next day. There was a different one every night."

A book, ghostwritten for him, called "Against All Odds" was rushed into the bookshops immediately after the final Championship winning Grand Prix in Japan, Hunt securing the points he needed to take the title by finishing third in that race. He had won in Spain, France, Germany, Holland, Canada and the USA. Ironically, he failed to win the British Grand Prix, held that year at Brands Hatch, with his big rival Niki Lauda dominating proceedings to take the chequered flag there.

The publication of the book saw James sent around the country by the publishers to promote sales. He visited local media in each major town and city, and I recorded an interview with him at Radio Hallam.

It was early afternoon by the time we finished the recording, after which James said he was hungry, and did I know of anywhere to grab a late lunch. I knew that we needed to find somewhere that really would be worth going to. This was, after all, James Hunt, World Motor Racing Champion.

I called a friend whose judgement of such things I rated highly, and he suggested a particular pub on the edge of the Peak District, just outside the city, where he knew the landlord. My friend said he would meet us there.

When we arrived the said landlord was just closing up, this being long before the days of all-day licensing, but as soon as he recognised James Hunt, he readily agreed to serve us. My friend hadn't let us down. The food was good and, with the place empty, we enjoyed a very pleasant, relaxed lunch with a bottle or two of very good red wine, supplied on the house.

The pub was not empty for very long. How word got around I can only imagine, though it may have had something to do with the barmaid and the lady who had just arrived to give the pub its afternoon once-over with polish and a duster. They instantly recognised the good-looking blond guy who was with us and fell into immediate and earnest conversation. They giggled merrily before each of them made a call from the pub phone, located on the wall in a corner of the bar.

They had, of course, clocked that it was James Hunt, motor racing world champion, and one of the most attractive men on the planet. Within an hour, this village hostelry, which should have been closed and empty, was full. Full of local ladies, eager to catch a glimpse of the man for themselves.

Three years later I met James Hunt again, when he took part in the Gunnar Nilsson Memorial Trophy Meeting at Donington Park, an event geared to raising funds for cancer research in memory of the Swedish racing driver Gunnar Nilsson. Nilsson died from testicular cancer on 20th October 1978, at the age of 29.

James Hunt was amongst a star-studded lineup of drivers, including Jackie Stewart, Mario Andretti, Nelson Picquet and the legendary Argentinian World Champion Juan Fangio, who was then in his late sixties. It was a motor racing fan's dream to be there amongst such great names from the sport, but the overwhelming reason that took me there was the chance to meet and interview George Harrison of The Beatles.

The Beatles split up in 1970 after the release of their album "Let It Be", and all four members of the band pursued their own, separate musical projects. George also launched into film production, mortgaging his home to fund the Monty Python movie "The Life Of Brian" in 1978. He was also a big fan of motorsport.

That day, 3rd June 1979, George took part in a charity race which he described as being "very, very nice", even though he admitted to being wary of being on the same track as some of the world's top Formula One drivers.

George told me, "I've liked motor racing since I was a kid. It's a bit more interesting for me now, with friends like Jackie Stewart and John Watson. I understand it so much more, and I guess I'm a sort of privileged hanger-on. I love it."

For me, to meet a Beatle was a memory to treasure. To speak to him this time, after being star-struck and tongue-tied when seeing him unexpectedly at Birmingham Town Hall ten years before, made it even more so.

* * * *

Brian Clough, who had been the focus of my first story in Yorkshire when he was sacked at Leeds, bumped into my life again when a football roadshow, sponsored by the *Daily Express*, came to Sheffield. The newspaper staged forums across the country with a panel made up of local managers, an *Express* reporter, a major national football personality, and a local radio sports presenter in the chair.

In Sheffield, in 1978, on the stage were Sheffield Wednesday manager Jack Charlton, Sheffield United assistant manager Danny Bergara, Daily Express reporter Peter Jackson, me in the chair, and Brian Clough, who was then taking Nottingham Forest to new heights.

The forum was staged in a working men's club with a huge bar that ran the length of the room. Needless to say, it was packed with football fans, almost exclusively men, from both Sheffield clubs and a few from elsewhere. Whilst all were there to hear the insights of all the panellists, it was the presence of Brian Clough that was the main attraction.

The bar remained open throughout the evening, and from time to time the replenishing of empty pint pots made it a fairly noisy room. At one point, whilst Brian was in mid-flow answering a question from the floor, it was obvious that the hubbub from the bar was making it hard for some to hear what he was saying.

As Chair I felt I should do something about it, so I interrupted him, putting my hand on his arm as I did so.

I had barely uttered the words "Gentlemen, please – could we keep the noise down a little so that we can all hear what Brian has to say?" before he turned to look at me, clearly irritated, and I knew I was in trouble.

I had interrupted him, I had had the temerity to touch him in the process, and I had referred to him as 'Brian'.

"Mr Chairman," he said testily, "Who is paying you tonight?"

It was not a question I was ready for, and I regret that I did not respond quickly. Certainly not quickly enough. He took advantage of my hesitation and addressed the throng who were clearly amused and delighted at my embarrassment.

"You see," he said. "He's alright asking the questions but ask him one and he's stuffed!"

When the cheers, which were loud and prolonged, died down Peter Jackson from the *Daily Express* came to my rescue.

"As you know Brian," he said, "These are our Forums and we are footing the bill for this event. The radio station has helped us promote it and they are recording it."

Mr. Clough seemed satisfied by that and resumed the answer he was giving before my intervention as if nothing had happened.

Afterwards, as he prepared to leave he stopped and said to me, "Nice to see you young man. I know what you were trying to do earlier, and why, but you should have left it to me. I was about to tell the noisy buggers to pipe down."

He winked, shook my hand and was then on his way, signing many autographs as he went.

We included boxing in the list of sports we covered, Ken Knighton joining me and Alan Biggs to commentate on amateur boxing nights in Sheffield. We were encouraged to cover the bouts by boxing trainer Brendan Ingle, a former Irish professional boxer who had made his home in Sheffield. Brendan was a good man, genuinely keen to encourage young people to be the best they could be. He lived in Wincobank in Sheffield, just across the road from St Thomas' Church where he ran dances, and formed St Thomas Boys and Girls Club where he ran his gym.

Brendan became a good friend. He gave us access to the exciting emerging young talent Herrol "Bomber" Graham. Herrol was undefeated in ten years and became the European, British, and Commonwealth Light-Middleweight Champion, as well as holding the European and British Middleweight titles. Brendan told me that Herrol was "the best person to come out of our gym."

Despite the following he built up in Sheffield, Herrol was born in Nottingham, and he is widely regarded as one of the best post-war British boxers to have never won a world title.

We were visited by World Champions at Radio Hallam. With Ken Knighton, I interviewed Chris Finnegan, the British and British Commonwealth, and also the European, Light-Heavyweight Champion. Chris was an articulate and intelligent interviewee who both Ken and I enjoyed meeting.

I also interviewed John Conteh, also a light-heavyweight, who took the British and Commonwealth titles from Chris Finnegan. Conteh held the WBC World title for most of my time at Radio Hallam, from 1974 to 1978. A man with huge charisma, Liverpool-born Conteh was as bright and lively as an interviewee as he was a competitor in the ring. Our paths would cross again some years later.

As all local radio stations do, Radio Hallam regularly ventured out of the studio to events that put their image, their brand and their presenters in front of the public.

In 1975 the radio station took its weekend schedule to the city's Hillsborough Park, a huge recreational area near to the Sheffield Wednesday football stadium. The park has a fishing lake, a bowling green and pavilion, a walled garden and a playground.

The entire area of the park that hot and sunny weekend was the venue for the Sheffield Show, an event full of entertainment in many and various ways, from military displays, pony rides and a fun fair, to live music. Both local radio stations – BBC Radio Sheffield and Radio Hallam - were there, with much of the live music coming from the Radio Hallam stage.

I was scheduled to host my Saturday afternoon show 'Sportacular' live on air and to the assembled audience in the park, from our outside broadcast studio, which was actually a converted caravan. The show included live coverage of local matches as usual, but alongside that, we had to reflect the fun and frolics of the Sheffield Show.

At two o'clock, as my show kicked off, we had live music scheduled from a group called Guys And Dolls, who were in the Top 10 with a record called 'There's A Whole Lotta Loving'. So after setting the scene for the football reports to come, I then introduced Guys And Dolls who joined me on the live stage.

There were six of them, three boys and three girls. They included David Van Day and Thereza Bazar, who would later leave the group to enjoy chart success as the duo Dollar, and Bruce Forsyth's daughter, Julie Forsyth. A glamorous band, they looked good and sounded good. After a brief interview, they sang their hit live to a pre-recorded backing track.

After the song finished, and they took their bow, the group signed a few autographs before being whisked away in shiny, black limousines. Once they'd gone, many of the large crowd that Guys and Dolls had attracted to our stage wandered off to other parts of the showground, leaving some football fans, and one or two who appeared interested in how it all worked, to hang around as we returned to the regular format of our Saturday afternoon diet of sport and music.

That was until around a quarter to five. As we were taking full-time reports from our six matches, I was joined on stage by the brother of a Beatle. Paul's brother, Mike McCartney, was our live guest. Mike was then a member of the trio Scaffold, calling himself Mike McGear.

The other members of Scaffold were the poet Roger McGough and comic entertainer John Gorman. The group enjoyed chart success with hits including 'Thank U Very Much', 'Do You Remember', and 'Lily The Pink'. Mike was happy to talk about the group, but he was keener to have fun with what he understandably regarded as a very odd scenario of being interviewed about himself and his music career during a local radio sports show, broadcast live from a stage in the middle of a public park. His assertion that "this is crazy, man" was not lost on me.

The bizarre nature of it all was added to when he insisted on reading the classified football results, which in those days were carefully delivered to aid those checking their pools coupons. Mike asked me to coach him, on air, about where the inflections should be in your voice, and how, from simply hearing the manner of your delivery, listeners would know if it was a home win, an away win or a draw.

He then read the results, almost singing them in parts. Whatever the radio audience thought of it, the people in the park loved it, laughing when he added a comic touch, and applauding and cheering loudly when he finished.

Amongst the friends I made in Sheffield was local businessman Peter Gilder. He owned the Volkswagen car dealership in the city. We became good friends, and Peter supplied me with a sponsored car, a VW Polo.

He was a keen sportsman, a Sheffield Wednesday fan. Peter was well known to local sports celebrities, many of whom were his customers. One was Howard Wilkinson who had played for both Sheffield football clubs before going on to be a successful manager. Amongst other clubs, he managed Leeds United and Sheffield Wednesday, and he had two spells as caretaker manager of England.

Howard was a regular dinner guest at Peter's home just outside the city, to which I was also invited from time to time. Peter was great fun and really down to earth. He was a successful businessman with celebrity guests sitting around his table, but he still brought a loaf of bread to the table to mop up the gravy off his plate.

In the summer Peter ran a local cricket team. It did not have its own ground but was instead a nomadic club called Sheffield Casuals. It had a schedule of fixtures on Sunday afternoons at locations throughout South Yorkshire and North Derbyshire, with the Casuals always in the role as visitors.

They were all delightful, picturesque venues, and were always really lovely places to spend a summer Sunday afternoon. Without exception, the host clubs all laid on superb teas. There was usually a ham salad, with the ham hanging over the edge of your plate, often with new potatoes and as much bread and butter as you could eat. Mugs of tea and cake would follow, often a Victoria sponge cut into generous slices, and sometimes scones with jam and cream. Just splendid.

Peter recruited me to the ranks of Sheffield Casuals, although I really just made up the numbers because the team was populated by guys who had been members long before I arrived. Some were excellent cricketers who played on Saturdays at a very high standard for top local League clubs. League cricket in Yorkshire was a really big deal. I got on well with the Casuals, even going on tour with them for a week in Somerset.

Then in 1977 came the highlight of my cricketing career. The Queen's Silver Jubilee prompted a range of celebratory events across the country, amongst them a charity cricket match played at Shaw Lane, the home of Barnsley Cricket Club.

The match was between two celebrity teams, one captained by the BBC Test Match Special commentator Christopher Martin-Jenkins, CMJ as he was known, the other by chat show host Michael Parkinson. I was in CMJs eleven.

One of the umpires was 'Dickie' Bird, the international Test Match umpire who had started his life in cricket as a young player at Barnsley Cricket Club alongside Michael Parkinson and Geoffrey Boycott. Also at Shaw Lane that day, as a spectator, was Geoffrey Boycott in the role of guest star in the pavilion rather than performing on the pitch.

Boycott took great delight at having fun at 'Dickie' Bird's expense. The famous umpire's proper name is Harold Bird, with 'Dickie' an obvious nickname. Throughout the afternoon Geoffrey insisted on calling him Richard, to the irritation of the star umpire who would respond with "he knows that's not my name!" for the benefit of anyone within earshot.

It was a really fun but hot day, with blazing sunshine helping to draw a large crowd and boosting sales of ice cream from the vendor who had been allowed into the ground.

CMJ asked me to bat in the middle order, and when it was my turn to arrive at the wicket it was to face the bowling of M. Parkinson. I faced three balls, all tossed up high but gently. The first I returned along the ground to the bowler. The second I met fair and square in the middle of the bat, feeling really pleased with myself as it crossed the boundary for four.

The third ball confused me thoroughly. I remain convinced to this day that it bounced more than once in front of me. Whatever it did, I completely mistimed my stroke and gave Parky a dolly catch off his own delivery.

Not the most outstanding of innings by any circumstance, but I left Shaw Lane that evening after a thoroughly enjoyable day. If it's safely stored somewhere at Barnsley Cricket Club, there's a scorebook that reads:

Linnell, caught and bowled Parkinson, 4.

To say I was pleased with that is an understatement.

* * * *

Towards the end of my time at Radio Hallam, an initiative from Sheffield City Council saw me travel to the other side of the world.

The plan was to invite as many ex-patriots as possible from Sheffield and the surrounding area to come home for a special festival. To promote it, the plan was for Radio Hallam presenters and reporters to go to other countries where the ex-pats had settled and to interview the people in question for special programmes on Hallam.

Members of the team variously set off for France, Germany, Holland and elsewhere. I claimed Australia.

I made my pitch to News Editor Ian Rufus, "If anyone's going to Australia, I think it should be me. England's playing the Ashes Test series there with Geoffrey Boycott in the side, so I might get an interview with him, as well as talking to the ex-pats out there."

Ian agreed, as long as I made my own travel arrangements. He suggested I contact the Australian airline Qantas to see if they would sponsor my trip. The rules about the references that Qantas could receive on air in return for doing so were quite strict, but Sales Manager Darryl Adams said that he was sure it could be resolved.

Amid severe winter weather in South Yorkshire, on Monday, 8th January 1979, I left home, with the snow literally knee-deep at my house in Sheffield. I made it to Heathrow Airport in London in good time to board a Qantas 747 "Jumbo" jet, set to depart at five-thirty that evening, bound for Sydney. I had been warned by the generous folk at Qantas that I was embarking on what they called 'the milk run' to Australia, because it stopped at Damascus, Bahrain, Kuala Lumpur and Singapore, before flying across Australia to land at Sydney's Kingsford Smith airport at Mascot in New South Wales.

At every stop, those of us not disembarking from the aircraft were given a tissue to place over our nose and mouth as the crew moved down the cabin spraying insecticide. Each stop was for no more than half an hour, until we got to Singapore, when we were invited to leave the 'plane and stretch our legs in the airport terminal. That stop lasted about an hour, after which we re-boarded before the final part of our journey.

The flight arrived in Sydney at nine-thirty on the morning of Wednesday, 10th January, to temperatures of 90 degrees (Fahrenheit) in the shade, a huge contrast to the sub-zero temperatures and deep snow that I had left behind in Sheffield.

Through both Qantas and Sheffield City Council, I made contact with people in Sydney who had agreed to book hotel accommodation for me and to show me around. They met me at the airport, took me to the hotel and patiently provided me with advice about how to get to the places I needed to visit, to meet the ex-pat Sheffield folk who had agreed to talk to me.

They also asked the vital question that I had hoped might be raised. Would I like to go to the Test Match?

Would I? There is the rude answer about what bears do in the woods and the irreverent answer about the Pope's religion. I ensured that I fell back on neither expression but made it very clear that it was precisely what I would like to do. Arrangements were duly made so that after a quick shower and a change of clothes, I would meet my chaperones in the hotel reception for a rapid trip around the city. That enabled me to note the location of such Sydney landmarks as the Harbour Bridge and the Opera House, before being deposited at the Sydney Cricket Ground, the famous SCG.

In my room, I was grateful for the air conditioning, the outside temperature having now climbed to the upper 90s. Whilst changing I turned on the TV to catch up with the latest from the Test Match. I was very surprised to find that there was no live cricket coverage on any of the channels available in my room.

10 - A Late Lunch with James Hunt

When I went down to reception, I asked if the channel showing the cricket was available in the hotel. I was told that I could access all of Sydney's channels from the TV set in my room, including ABC which had the rights to the live coverage. The receptionist said she had heard that there was an issue of some sort at the ground which had apparently taken the coverage off air, but she knew no more than that.

En route to the ground, via the sights of Sydney, we heard a news bulletin on the car radio. The main story was that the TV coverage had been temporarily cancelled because a cameraman had passed out in the heat and humidity and had fallen twenty feet from a platform high above one of the sightscreens, breaking his collarbone and sustaining a suspected fractured skull.

Indeed, as I entered the SCG, the stadium announcer was advising all inside to take necessary precautions and to drink plenty of water, as the temperature had just edged above 100 degrees.

My helpful guides, who had secured main stand tickets for me, left me to find my way around the ground and enjoy the day's play. The staircase I climbed towards my seat took me to a level with a view I will never forget. Immediately in front of me was the Test Match arena, with play in progress, and beyond it the famous Hill, where thousands of Australian fans had watched cricket since 1894. The Hill is now long gone, replaced by the modern stands that have been constructed as the ground's capacity has increased to just short of 50,000, but then it was the home of Aussie fans who intrinsically loved cricket, but who were more concerned with excitement and spectacle than with the intricacies of the game itself.

The beer can and the portable cooler, introduced to sports crowds in the 1960s, had increased alcohol consumption at cricket matches which in turn fuelled questionable crowd behaviour. Limited overs cricket, developing during the 1970s, with some being played at least partially at night, had attracted a new crowd to cricket at the SCG. It's fair to say that those watching the Test Matches were less inclined to be quite so boisterous, but cheeky banter was always in play.

The view I took in for the first time that morning was captured almost exactly on the dust cover of the book "A Pitch In Both Camps", written by the distinguished sportswriter, the late Alan Lee, who I knew in passing from my earlier times in the West Midlands as he lived at Stratford-upon-Avon. Alan, in fact, proved to be a great help on my arrival at the ground.

As I stood taking in the arena before me, I heard a distinctive, beautifully spoken voice behind me say, "I say, old chap, can we help you? If you wouldn't mind awfully, you are rather blocking the view."

The perfectly modulated tones belonged to Trevor McDonald, the not-yet-knighted star of ITN. Sir Trevor, as he now is, was not only one of the UK's leading news readers, or newscasters as ITN prefers to call them, but he has always been a huge and highly knowledgeable cricket lover. Here was I, a UK local radio sports editor, being gently chided by this gifted, senior journalist for having the temerity of standing in the direct line of sight of the entire SCG press box.

Alan Lee came to my rescue. Recognising that I was something of a bewildered lost soul, far from home and rapt in awe at being at that famous venue, and thankfully recognising me, he said, "It's Stuart, isn't it? First time here? You can come and sit here until lunch if you'd like."

I needed no second invitation. Crimson with embarrassment, I nodded chastely at Trevor McDonald and accepted Alan's offer of a seat next to his, amongst the ranks of some of the world's finest cricket reporters.

I say "some of" because other members of cricket's press pack were elsewhere in Australia, following Kerry Packer's World Series Cricket.

Mr. Packer owned the television company Nine Network. Unable to win the rights to show the conventional Test series from the Australian Broadcasting Corporation (ABC) Kerry Packer decided to run his own breakaway competition, with his 'Supertest' Matches staged in direct opposition to the Ashes series. He also offered salaries to the cricketers that were significantly more than that on offer whilst playing for their country.

He enlisted leading Australian, English, Pakistani, South African and West Indies players. Amongst them were the captains of England, the West Indies, and Australia – Tony Greig, Clive Lloyd, and Greg Chappell. Former Australian Captain Ian Chappell and future Pakistani captain Imran Khan, who would later become his country's Prime Minister, also signed up.

The row that followed looked certain to end in bans from first-class and Test cricket for all the Packer players, but a court case ruled in their favour. However, the repercussions of Packer's intervention were felt across cricket for some time.

I had included a couple of days in my schedule to take in World Series Cricket, with a Packer Supertest due to start in Melbourne, immediately after the 4th Ashes Test in Sydney, but I had unfinished business first at the SCG. Geoffrey Boycott was top of the list of people I wanted to interview during my stay in Australia, and I made every effort to do so.

I found my way to the pavilion and the entrance to the SCG player's dressing rooms at the end of play on that first day that I was there. I left messages that I had newly arrived from Sheffield and that I would like a brief interview with Mr Boycott.

Circumstances conspired against me. In the last couple of months before setting off with England, Boycott's mother, to whom he was devoted and whom I had met at their home in Fitzwilliam just before Radio Hallam launched in 1974, had died after a long illness. Geoffrey was also locked in the increasingly acrimonious dispute with Yorkshire County Cricket Club, which had seen him deposed as the club's captain and replaced by John Hampshire. He had also missed out on being vice-captain of England on this tour, with Warwickshire's Bob Willis chosen in preference.

His form in Australia, by his own exceptional standard, had been wretched. At Sydney, he was caught Border bowled Hogg for a meagre eight runs in the first innings and was then out first ball in the second innings, lbw to Hogg.

Add to all that, he had a preoccupation with writing notes for a book he was preparing, writing articles for various newspapers and writing letters to the Yorkshire Reform Group. They were supporters of the county who wished, amongst other things, to see Boycott reinstated as captain.

No surprise then that I was kept waiting without response from the great man, until long after many others had left the ground.

Bob Willis and a couple of other players took pity on me, telling me that they thought Boycott had left the ground anyway, and asked where I was staying. It turned out my hotel was a block away from theirs, so I gratefully accepted their offer of a lift and enjoyed the banter in the car on the way back across the city.

As for Geoffrey Boycott, it turned out that I was not the only person seeking to interview him who was turned down. Most of the rest of the press corps following that tour had the same experience.

It was reported that whilst travelling between match venues, Geoffrey would sit by himself, not mixing with his teammates let alone the journalists who tended to occupy the rear of the coach. The particular sadness and frustration for me was that one of the reasons I had opted to travel to Australia was to interview Boycott.

However, by the end of January, he had made a major decision. With much controversy surrounding him at Yorkshire, including a critical vote of the county's members deciding against reinstating him as their captain, there followed great speculation that he might sign for another county or even play in Kerry Packer's World Series Cricket.

His solicitor Duncan Mutch had arrived in Australia at around the same time as I had. With Mutch's counsel to guide him, he resolved to stay in Yorkshire, citing the support of Yorkshire people whilst calling his home club "the greatest county in the game." In his book, Alan Lee wrote, "For those who were there, Boycott will be remembered on this tour, not for his runs, nor his tantrums, nor his solitude. It will be remembered that he won a battle with himself and went back home to Yorkshire."

Although I was keen to follow the conclusion of the Test Match, I was in New South Wales to interview a couple of the ex-pat Sheffielders who now lived in the Sydney area. The day after that failed attempt to interview Boycott, I recorded an interview with a man from Rotherham who had married a local girl and had settled in Sydney. He had met me at my hotel on his way to work, and after that, I had to find my way on public transport to Manly, a beach-side suburb of northern Sydney.

After anxiously negotiating the local buses, trying to ensure that I was on the right bus and got off at the right stop, I found Christine's house. She was cooking in the kitchen where she made me coffee and reminisced wistfully about what she had left behind in the UK. Despite that element of homesickness, she also spoke with enthusiasm about her new life in Australia, the blessings of its climate and the opportunities that she felt it offered to her children.

As with all my ex-pat interviewees, I asked her to choose a record for me to play on Radio Hallam. Without hesitation, but with a tear forming in her eye, and her voice slightly choked, she asked for "Green, Green, Grass Of Home" by Tom Jones. Although she was born and bred in Sheffield, her late father was Welsh, and it was a song that always reminded her of him, and also of what she described as "the beautiful moors" and the Peak District surrounding Sheffield. She repeated the phrase used by many to describe the Sheffield that existed during the heyday of the steel industry and its associated supply chain.

"A dirty picture in a golden frame," she said. "That's what my dad said Sheffield was. I know it's an old saying, and that it's changing, but that is the image I will always carry."

I left Sydney the following day – Friday, 12th January – and took a flight to Melbourne. I was booked into a hotel in the city centre which, as it turned out, was just a short walk from a local radio station that had agreed to interview me about my trip and about the plans to invite Sheffield ex-pats back to visit Yorkshire.

In what I learned was then the Australian way, the radio station said they did not want me to go into the studio but rather wanted to interview me over the phone, "as it added immediacy".

A touch disappointed with that, as I had been keen to see the inside of their studios, I settled myself into my hotel. I had a wander around Melbourne, had dinner and turned in early, ready for the day ahead.

Just before nine o'clock on the Saturday morning, the phone rang in my room and I was put on hold, ready to go on air. I was soon engaged in a five-minute chat with the two presenters, one male, and one female, who formed their Saturday morning double act. They were looking for humour in every other sentence. While it was not my place to demur from that, I had a clear but serious simple message to convey about Sheffield inviting its former citizens to make a brief visit home.

Whether their audience made sense of what we discussed, I'm not sure, but it underlined to me that the interviewer and interviewee sitting face to face, seeing the whites of each other's eyes, is by far the best way to proceed. Still, as they said goodbye to me and moved into a link for their next record, the young lady said what a pleasant guy I sounded. Some consolation perhaps.

That left me the rest of the day to conduct another ex-pat interview, with the guest again coming to meet me at the hotel. Then I was off to find out what all the fuss was about with Kerry Packer's World Series Cricket.

The match was billed as "Australians v. The West Indians". The established cricket authorities had ruled that Packer could not use conventional cricket grounds, so WSC had hired the Australian Rules football ground, VFL Park at Waverley, to the south of the city. WSC had dropped a carefully prepared 22-yard strip into the middle of the sports field so that bowling and batting could take place on a surface appropriate for cricket.

On an intensely humid afternoon, I took a bumpy twenty-minute train ride, in an open-sided carriage, with no doors. Air conditioning in a literal sense.

One of the significant new elements that Kerry Packer had seized on was day-night cricket, with the final sessions of the day's play taking place in the evening, under floodlights, using a white ball rather than the usual red. Instead of the conventional breaks in play occurring at lunch and tea, the day now started after lunch with the sessions separated by tea and dinner.

I arrived at VFL Park just as the dinner break had started on that Saturday evening, the second day of the Third Supertest. The floodlights were on, but the setting sun still glowed brightly through the huge, glazed wall of the VFL Park Main Stand, onto the diners enjoying the hospitality on offer. The person I had scheduled to interview was looking out through the window as he sat at the main table, alongside the architect of this cricket revolution, Kerry Packer.

He was Yorkshire to his bootstraps, born in Stainton in the West Riding of Yorkshire, and he was a legendary hero of England cricket, but here was Frederick Sewards Trueman enjoying every minute of the opportunity to be part of this chapter of cricket history that his Australian host had created.

The Head Waiter discreetly whispered in Freddie's ear that I had arrived, and he immediately excused himself from the dinner party and joined me at a table on the periphery of the main event.

I had noticed that Kerry Packer and all his guests had been focused on events taking place outside, in the main arena, even though the cricketers were off the pitch during the dinner break.

"It's a punch-up", laughed Freddie. "A couple of lads have swallowed too many beers, no doubt carried in one of those cool boxes no doubt. Kerry told security to let them get on with it, rather than stop them. He and one or two others at the table were wagering bets on which of the fighters would win."

Freddie offered to introduce me to Kerry Packer, which I gratefully accepted, but I asked if we could record the interview first, to which he agreed.

"This World Series Cricket is absolutely fantastic, "Freddie told me. "I know all the boys. I talk to them. I see some fascinating cricket. I believe I'm watching possibly 95% of the best players in the world."

I put it to him that some cricket fans in England regarded it as being possibly freakish, as it was played under lights, with a white ball.

"I don't know why they think it's freakish, because it's not," he replied. "The floodlights are possibly brighter and stronger in candlepower than you would find in floodlit football. The ball is a cricket ball, but instead of being red, it's white. It's exactly the same dimensions and weight. The last of these matches in Sydney was watched by some committee men from Surrey and Sussex, and from Lord's. They saw it for the first time, and they also saw a crowd of approaching 30,000 enjoying it. I asked them what they thought of it, and they all said that it was fantastic and magnificent. 'Without seeing it we would never have believed it', they told me. I believe one day Test Cricket will be played under floodlights."

With that endorsement from a man who, throughout his life was never afraid to say what he thought, I asked him if this was another example of Freddie Trueman setting himself against the Establishment.

"No," he said firmly. "I have always clashed with the Establishment when I thought they were wrong, but I've always agreed with them when I thought they were right. On this occasion, I may appear to be against the

Establishment because I think that not enough of them have been to see this for themselves and understand what's going off."

"Has this not taken the interest away from the Ashes Series?" I asked him. "That, of course, is being played here in Australia at the same time."

"It certainly hasn't taken the interest away for me," he countered. "There's two more Test Matches, and I want us to win 'em. I love being an Englishman in Australia and seeing our boys win. There's nothing I like more than hearing Australians whingeing. I can go back to 1968 when we did 'em in the old city of Sheffield. I tell yer, the Yorkshire boys were absolutely delighted, including me."

We spent the next few minutes chewing over the intricacies of Yorkshire and the prospects for the county side, all invaluable material for me to take back home, and then, the interview done, Freddie repeated his invitation to introduce me to Kerry Packer.

The TV tycoon really was larger than life, an ebullient, big man, but with a grace and charm that genially swept me into his VIP group, even though neither he nor they had any idea who the heck I was. Mr. Packer declined to give me an interview but poured me a glass of red and told the waiter to bring me a steak, or whatever I wanted.

With the resumption of play, Freddie was off to the commentary box and bid me goodbye. After my meal, with all around me intently focused on the cricket, I thanked my host and made my excuses. I was flying to Perth the following day I explained, and before long I was back on that bumpy, dusty train back to my hotel in Melbourne.

Quite an experience, I mused on my journey back. I wondered what Christine's dad, the Welshman who had settled in Sheffield, would have made of this brash, "go for it", country in which his daughter had made her home, and in which one of Yorkshire's greatest cricketers was enjoying the benefits of his legendary status.

I completed my short trip by staying for a few days in Perth, a beautiful modern city, sitting on the Swan River. The city enjoys the wildlife of the outback on one side, and the sandy beaches of the Indian Ocean on the other. All too soon I was flying home, whilst making myself a promise that one day

I would return to Australia, much as I was looking forward to my return to the UK.

That Tom Jones record that Christine had requested came to mind:

The old home town looks the same

As I step down from the train

And there to meet me is my Mama and Papa

Down the road I look and there runs Mary

Hair of gold and lips like cherries

It's good to touch the green, green grass of home

Yes, they'll all come to meet me, arms reaching, smiling sweetly

It's good to touch the green, green grass of home

Claude "Curly" Putman Jr., 1964

© Sony/ATV Music Publishing LLC

My Granddad knew Rasputin ... and I met Elton John

Chapter Eleven

Coventry

The Lord's my shepherd, I'll not want;

He makes me down to lie

In pastures green; he leadeth me

The quiet waters by.

My soul he doth restore again,

And me to walk doth make

Within the paths of righteousness,

E'en for his own name's sake.

Yea, though I walk in death's dark vale,

Yet will I fear no ill:

For thou art with me, and thy rod

And staff me comfort still.

I'm My table thou hast furnished

In presence of my foes;

My head thou dost with oil anoint

And my cup overflows.

Goodness and mercy all my life

Shall surely follow me;

And in God's house for evermore

My dwelling-place shall be.

Psalm 23 : Francis Rous

While I was in Sheffield, both my parents died.

My long-suffering mum, who had spent her later years worrying about her husband's health and well-being, fell ill herself with a failed kidney. She also worried about whatever was to become of me, working in that strange world of broadcasting, surrounded, as she saw it, by all sorts of oddballs and weirdos.

My sister Yvonne still lived at home in Birmingham, keeping an eye on both mum and dad whilst trying to make her own way in the world. It fell to her to keep things together when Mum went into hospital.

With guilt and a heavy heart, I now hold my hands up to the fact that, while I expressed genuine concern, I nonetheless escaped responsibility for what was going on. Rather, I focused on my job and on my life in Sheffield.

After going to Birmingham to visit Mum in Selly Oak Hospital I did not consider her to be seriously ill. That was no doubt an excuse that I allowed myself to believe, but I still did not really get it until my sister called to tell me that Mum had died. She was 61.

My Dad barely survived two years after she had gone. At the age of 63, he died too. Both passed away ridiculously early, but in 1977 when he died my perception was that my dad was an old man, which is what he had become.

I have absolutely no doubt that his heart was broken when Mum passed away but the underlying cause of his demise was smoking. He had reduced the number of cigarettes he smoked each day to zero by the time he was also admitted to Selly Oak Hospital, but they had viciously taken their toll. When he died we were told he had suffered from bronchial pneumonia, and I have no doubt that was true, but I am also certain that his lungs were a complete mess as a direct result of those damned cigarettes.

No one used the words 'lung cancer', and it was quite likely that he had contracted a virus or infection that led to his ravaged lungs submitting to bronchial pneumonia, but his respiratory system was wrecked. What had happened to him all those years before during the war, camping with his regiment on that damp Welsh mountain, had left an inherent weakness. As a consequence, every cigarette he smoked just added to the further destruction of his lungs.

I have never smoked, nor indulged in vaping, largely because of what I observed happening to my father. I abhor both. It has never made any sense to me why any intelligent person would want to put smoke into their body or inhale fumes of any sort, with the associated dirt and the smell that is not only unpleasant but can often lead to fatal consequences. Nor has the sight of someone smoking or vaping ever appeared remotely attractive to me, let alone "sexy" as some might claim.

In response to a call from Yvonne, and very conscious that I had been absent from my mother's bedside when she died, I made a hurried trip down the M1 to be with my dad at Selly Oak Hospital. He had always been slim, but he was now extremely thin. His eyes seemed larger than usual, looking up at me with a soulful resigned expression on his face, his skin an unhealthy pallor. He had never become used to wearing his false teeth, so his sunken cheeks made him look very old and worn out.

His breathing was shallow, and it took a lot of effort for him to speak, but he managed a conversation with me about how I was, how my job was going, and what I was up to generally.

A nurse came by to carry out routine checks, and she suggested that he needed to rest. I said that I would go, and he smiled weakly before beckoning me to bend close to him.

"Look after your sister," he said, before taking a deep breath and adding, "I love you, son. I'm very proud of you both."

The tears that had formed in my eyes just managed to stay put, as I leaned forward and kissed his forehead. He held my hand for a few moments, then drifted off to sleep.

If I was not already aware that he was about to die, my sister said something that brought it home with a thump. She told me that one of the surgeons needed to speak to me about transplanting some of his organs.

"He told me that he wanted that to happen," Yvonne said, "but one of us has to give permission."

The surgeon was there within a few seconds. He quietly explained that my dad was not expected to survive for more than a few days at the most, and they were particularly concerned to use his eyes to help someone else if we would agree.

Very patiently he told me that corneal transplantation is the only effective restoration for the replacement of human tissues in the eyes. He said that the procedure needed to occur within six hours of the donor's death, that only the cornea is taken and not the full eyeball, and that my Dad's eyes could give sight to two different people facing blindness.

Yvonne was weeping but listening. I looked at her and she nodded.

"It's what he would want", she said.

I thought of those beautiful brown eyes that had looked up at me a few minutes before, that would now change the lives of others and agreed to sign the consent form.

Dad died later that night, leaving me with an even greater feeling of guilt that I had not been around anywhere near enough when he and Mum were in their final years. Whilst Dad had looked old to me, and people in their sixties were generally thought of as "old" at that time, it had never really crossed my mind that either of them would leave quite so soon.

Justifying to myself that making a success out of being on the radio would make them proud, I had neglected to spend the time with them that would have made that worthwhile. At the moment of my father's death, I was bewildered and distraught that I had actually let them down and had missed out on myself as a consequence. That my sister had borne the brunt of their demise made it even worse.

"Look after your sister", he had said, and I knew that I had done nothing approaching my share. Selfishly, I felt grief borne out of my own failings as much as Dad's death, and that was to spill over at his funeral.

Yvonne sat quietly while I discussed the service with the vicar of Immanuel Church, Highters Heath, where Dad had been Church Warden. It was the church where I had been head choir boy, where Yvonne remained an active, and by now a senior member, of the Girl Guides, and where my first wedding had taken place.

The vicar gently steered us through what we had agreed should be a simple service, and he asked if we had any particular choices for appropriate music.

"He was a very traditional man, like his father before him," I said, "and I know that his faith meant a lot to him. Combining those two trains of thought, I think that 'Crimond' and 'Abide With Me' would be right."

The vicar smiled.

"Ah yes," he said, "C and A. Just like the store. Popular and reliable favourites."

I smiled weakly at his reference to "the store", C & A being the name of a popular department store that could be found in most UK city centres in the 70s.

C and A it was. 'Crimond' is a hymn based on the 23rd Psalm, with a tune written by Jessie Seymour Irvine, the daughter of a Church of Scotland parish minister who served in the village of Crimond in Aberdeenshire in Scotland. 'Abide With Me', quite apart from its traditional place during the pre-match build-up to the FA Cup Final, always seems entirely appropriate to me as a funeral hymn.

The lines - "Where is death's sting? Where, grave, thy victory? I triumph still, if Thou abide with me," – say everything that should be said on behalf of the departed, particularly someone who had been so proud to serve his country as had my father, like his father before him.

Immanuel Church was full, as the local community, many of them good family friends, came to pay their respects to my father. I am afraid I let him down that day.

Displaying grief and sorrow at the death of your parents is entirely right and appropriate but, as soon as the coffin was placed on wooden trestles in front of the altar, I was uncontrollably overwhelmed with emotion. I started to sob and I could not stop. My sister's face clearly showed the utter disdain with which she quite rightly held my unforgivably undignified display.

I have no doubt that it was the consequence of the guilt that I had built up inside. I had pursued my dream and ignored my family. Alongside that was the realisation that there was so much that I had wanted to say to both my parents in their final days. So much that I should have said.

I should have told them that I appreciated everything they had done for me. I should have told them how grateful I was for the warm loving home that they had created and for the sacrifices that they had made to nurture me, to provide me with a good education and to make my way in the world.

Most of all, I should have told them that I loved them.

Neither of them, particularly my Mum, really understood my ambition to become a broadcaster, and they were both genuinely concerned about a lack of security in my chosen profession. I should have taken the time to sit down and talk to them about it. Instead, stubbornly, I took the view that I would show them I could do it. As time went by, as I rubbed shoulders with famous faces and enjoyed a degree of success, I lost sight of the fact that my life was a million miles away from their understanding of it.

So out poured the tears at Dad's funeral, with regrettably loud sobbing. I felt ashamed afterwards, and I am even more so now, reflecting on it. I hope that what I have done during the passing years, where I have been, who I have met, and all that has happened, has made the point for me.

My greatest sadness is that my parents never met my two sons, their grandsons, nor my sister's daughter brought up so brilliantly by her mother. I just pray that somehow, looking down on us, they know that all is well for me and my family, with me and my sister now blessed by our own grandchildren.

Not long after my dad died, the proceeds of his estate were split equally between Yvonne and me. It was not a huge amount of money, and no amount was equal to what both my parents meant to me, but I spent it as wisely as they would have wanted. I was conscious of using it in a way that my Mum would have approved of as the manager of their resources.

We purchased some furniture for our home in Sheffield. The McIntosh range of furniture was regarded as stylish and trendy at the time, with a dining table and chairs and a matching sideboard with a built-in glass display case. We complemented that with a three-piece suite, two easy chairs and a sofa, and felt quite pleased with how the house looked.

There was still enough in the small legacy for us to realise a dream by going on holiday to America. It was my first trip to the USA and I was determined to make the most of it. One of the original Radio Hallam presenters, Brenda Ellison, had left the radio station not long before as her husband had received a significant job promotion and was operating at a senior level for a company in the supply chain that served the Ford Motor Company in Detroit.

We arranged to stay with them in Detroit and, thanks to the travel industry pioneer Freddie Laker, we and thousands of others were able to fly to the States relatively cheaply. He offered a new concept whereby passengers could buy their tickets on the day of travel as well as buy their own food. His company, Laker Airways, operated the flights under the brand name Skytrain.

Laker's new idea had its glitches. Our departure from London Gatwick to JFK in New York was delayed by 24 hours because of an engine fault on an earlier plane. Passengers had to wait in the Gatwick departure lounge with one or two becoming quite irate at being held up for that length of time. I was not exactly overjoyed either but I was too excited by the thought of going to America to allow myself to be too wound up.

We eventually left Gatwick a day late, and as a result, slept for much of the flight. When we emerged through the clouds above the Hudson River it was to a beautiful sunlit view of Manhattan and, immediately alongside us, the Statue of Liberty greeting us as she had visitors to America since 1886.

Once through the incredibly hectic customs and entry process at JFK, we were in our pre-booked limousine en route to our hotel in New York City. I was in awe of everything I saw and heard. Though I tried hard to present myself as a sophisticated, experienced international traveller I know I failed hopelessly. It was as though someone had taken me as a toddler to the biggest and best playground any child could have, and I was determined to enjoy it.

We stayed for one night in New York before taking a Delta Airlines flight to Detroit Metropolitan Wayne County Airport where Brenda and her husband Malcolm were there to meet us and take us to their lovely home. It was a beautiful wooden-built house in an upmarket area of the city.

That first night in Detroit they took us for a meal at a seafood restaurant, where clam chowder followed by lobster was the popular choice. Highly enjoyable it was too, although my wife caused something of a stir in the car on the way back from the restaurant.

"Excuse me," she said, self-consciously. Putting her hand to her mouth, she went on, "I think I have wind."

"Wind?" exclaimed Malcolm, checking all the controls in his car, "all the windows are shut, I think, and I can turn the air conditioning off if that helps".

Brenda started laughing.

"No," she said, "she doesn't mean that sort of wind. She means she has gas!"

"Ah", I said, "Two countries divided by the same language."

Malcolm joined in the laughter, conceding that he had been in America long enough to have embraced its linguistic terminology.

We stayed in Detroit for a week, before returning to New York, where we set off on a seven-day bus tour. The travel brochure called it "The Eastern Highlights", and it took us into Canada. We went to Toronto and Niagara Falls, through Watkins Glen, the Finger Lakes, and back to New York via Washington and Philadelphia. We stayed in excellent hotels during what was a beautiful trip. The whole experience was made even more so by what local people referred to as the "fall colours" of the forests on the route.

Then it was back to Detroit, with Malcolm and Brenda taking us to see the Henry Ford Museum, an American football match (a college match) at the

Michigan Stadium at Ann Arbor, and to dinner at the home of one of Malcolm's business colleagues.

Malcolm's friend was watching a baseball match on TV as we arrived, with all the guests gathered to follow the action. I was asked if it was like "your English cricket."

"Cricket can't be as bad as this," said a lady, who was obviously not a baseball fan. "This goes on all day and all night sometimes."

"I'm afraid that's nothing," I replied. "Some cricket matches can last five days."

After a gasp of astonishment, there was much laughter and shaking of heads in disbelief. Before I could be quizzed about it, we were called into dinner, although I was called on to elaborate by one or two of those sitting adjacent to me during the meal.

Later our host then asked me if I had ever witnessed the folding of the American flag. I replied that I had only seen it during films and TV programmes, but I had never seen it first-hand. He invited me, and others, to join him in his study, where he picked up a folded flag from a shelf, opened and spread it on his desk. He then carefully demonstrated a series of precise triangular folds.

* * * *

So, within a couple of years, I had been fortunate enough to visit America and Australia. I also enjoyed a settled way of life in Sheffield with little or no intention, nor any incentive, to change it.

In 1979, soon after I returned from Australia, my friend Ian Rufus, who had recruited me for Radio Hallam some five years before, announced that he was leaving his role as the station's News Editor. He was moving back to a part of the world we both knew well, the West Midlands. He was to be Programme Controller for the launch of another new local commercial station, Mercia Sound in Coventry.

Ian left Hallam in the Summer of '79 but then called me a couple of months later. He invited me to lunch and offered me the opportunity to follow him to his new venture. The proposition was that I would be Mercia Sound's Sports Editor but that I would also host my own daily show. The latter would not be sports-related but would be a music show with guests and a few fun elements. The money was a tempting improvement on what I was being paid in Sheffield, so I had much to consider.

Would I be prepared to leave behind what I had spent six years building up in Sheffield, with strong links to all the main sports clubs and organisations and the main characters involved with them? Allied to that was a quite comfortable lifestyle that I had established, socialising with some of the area's key personalities. I went horse riding twice a week, played cricket during the Summer, regularly visited my Uncle and Aunt, and generally embraced the splendours of the many really lovely parts of South Yorkshire and North-East Derbyshire.

My wife's views also had to be considered. Would she be willing to move back to the West Midlands, after returning to the city of her birth where she had also made many friends? She also went horse riding, more often than I did, and she had built up a catering business providing food for weddings, parties and the like.

She made it very clear that she preferred to stay in Sheffield, and that if I really wanted to make the move we would have to work out some sort of arrangement whereby we would live separately for part of the week. We had no children so there was no complication in that regard, but the notion of somehow having two separate homes did not appear to be a pragmatic proposition and held little appeal to me.

I thought about it long and hard. Ian Rufus allowed me some space and time to consider his offer, but he made it clear that he needed an answer sooner rather than later.

Life in Sheffield gave me little reason to complain. I liked the city and the surrounding countryside. I regarded the Peak District as spectacular. Things were far from onerous. My cricket and horse riding sat alongside a busy but hardly demanding workload, one that I had developed into a pleasant and more than manageable lifestyle.

* * * *

Yet the more I pondered, the flipside of all that played on my mind. It seemed to me that comfortable though life in Sheffield may have been, I was actually stuck in a ruck. If I wanted to move on in my broadcasting career I had to look for the next move, and I could not see how that would happen if I remained Sports Editor at Radio Hallam. At some of the other ILR stations, in Liverpool and Manchester for example, the success of the local football teams was putting their sports reporters to the fore in a way that was simply not happening in Sheffield. At least three of my contemporaries elsewhere were on the way to successful careers in television.

I weighed up the sporting environments. The six football clubs in the Sheffield area offered the great plus of enabling me to report without being directly associated with any one of them, but none were flying high. The two biggest clubs, Sheffield United and Sheffield Wednesday, had both found themselves in the Third Division. Other local radio sports editors had benefited from the success of the teams they covered, winning league titles and cup competitions and playing in Europe.

Coventry City, on the other hand, played in the top flight, the First Division. They had briefly flirted with European football, but they had that great romantic story of Jimmy Hill leading them out of the doldrums in the 60s, a story that held great appeal to me. I had always felt an affinity with Coventry City that I am sure was sparked from observing Jimmy Hill's genius.

Added to all that was the fact that I would be returning to a part of the world where I had so many connections. It held an appeal which, the longer I thought about it, the more I resolved it was what I wanted to do.

So I said "yes", despite my wife's reservations. She was adamant that one way or the other, she would not cut her ties with Sheffield. If we were going to move she declared, she would nonetheless be in South Yorkshire several times a week to go riding and to meet her friends.

When it came time to leave, the various farewell events I was asked to attend genuinely surprised me. Several local sports clubs invited me to visit them, presenting me with cards and gifts, amongst them a beautiful, leather-covered riding crop. Speeches were made thanking me for the interest I had shown in them and their activities.

Players from both Sheffield United and Sheffield Wednesday came to the radio station where Ian Rufus's replacement as News Editor, Jim Greensmith, made a speech complimenting me for my contribution to Radio Hallam over the previous six years.

Jim had been Ian's Deputy and he and I had not always got on, although neither had we ever really fallen out. It was a concern for a number of us in the Hallam newsroom that Jim, a Jehovah's Witness, would allow his religious beliefs to colour his news judgement. I have no doubt that it did, but Jim went out of his way, whenever possible, to quite deliberately ensure that others had to deal with stories that might cause such a problem.

He chose his words carefully when making that farewell speech to me, but he took me to one side afterwards and said, "I want you to know that I am genuinely disappointed that you're leaving. We had been planning to offer you an increase in salary and to make changes to the board. As News Editor I am now going to sit on the board, and we were going to invite you to do the same, with share options for you as a director."

For a few moments, I was speechless. I had no idea that any of that would be on the table. There had never been any suggestion that such a package would be on offer for me. I told him I was surprised and disappointed that it had never been mentioned.

"Well," he replied, "that is because you never gave us the chance to offer it to you. You handed in your notice and you were obviously determined to go."

As he spoke, I felt completely vindicated over the decision I had made. The fact that I had received an offer from Ian was not exactly a secret. Jim was certainly well aware of it. He knew that I had been mulling it over for a couple of weeks, so if any serious attempt to persuade me to stay was on the cards it could easily have been made. Had Jim Greensmith really wanted me to stay and work alongside him at Radio Hallam, he had plenty of opportunity to make that clear. Until this moment, however, nothing had been said.

I felt that for him to tell me that was unfair, to say the least. To throw it in my face at the moment of my departure made me quite angry. When he told me that I was "obviously determined to go", I just thanked him and replied quite curtly, "I suppose I was." If ever I had any uncertainty about my decision to follow Ian Rufus to Coventry, it completely disappeared at that moment.

As I reflected later on that conversation, one big question played out in my mind. Had I known that I would receive such a proposition to remain in Sheffield would it have made a difference? I don't believe it would, but I would have had to consider it carefully. It was a decision that not only changed my career path and my future but also had consequences that affected the lives of many other people and influenced events at the radio stations that I would later be involved with.

I might have stayed in South Yorkshire for the rest of my life, and my personal life would have been markedly different. Whilst I am as sure as I can be that the underlying restlessness that drove me towards a new direction and to fresh challenges would have prevailed, there could have been a temptation to stay and become part of the furniture in Sheffield.

The frustration and annoyance that made me reject it stemmed entirely from it being withheld from me until after I had decided to leave for pastures new.

In February of 1980, I moved to Coventry, to start with staying at Ian's house in Kenilworth. Mercia Sound was due to launch in May, four months later. Just as on my arrival at Radio Hallam, the building that would house the new radio station was awash with workmen. It was located at Hertford Place on the edge of Coventry's infamous ring road. Work was underway to fit out the studios on the ground floor, and erect partition walls and a false ceiling on the first floor, where the offices would be.

The building had been a working men's club, with the steward's flat on the top floor. Ian had set up an office in the flat, and I joined him there. In the process, I met his secretary, Susan, and other members of the team.

Alongside the preparations for the launch of the new station, I also spent a fair amount of time looking for somewhere to live. Ian and his wife and children were extraordinarily accommodating, allowing me and one or two others to intrude on their lives and their domestic arrangements, but that could obviously only be a temporary situation.

Sorting through available properties in the area, I was greatly attracted to one in Kenilworth that looked just right. With a garage built under a sloping front lawn, it was a terraced cottage that needed a little improvement, particularly needing more modern taps and basins in the bathroom and in the en suite. It had two bay windows, on either side of the front door, and it looked very attractive. It had a small, manageable back garden, with the added exciting element of a tree house. Not that we had any offspring to climb into it, but it was perfect should that day ever arise.

My wife travelled from Sheffield to see it and was obviously impressed. It had a sizable kitchen with a gas-fired range that would be ideal for her catering business. In one of the two downstairs lounges, or "reception rooms" in estate agents speak, the current owners had a baby grand piano giving the place an added touch of style.

We agreed that it would make a great home if we could afford it. It was going to push us to our limits financially, and it was clear that securing the required mortgage was not going to be easy.

The radio station's launch preparations continued, and other new faces began to arrive. Ian, and the Managing Director John Bradford, had put together an impressive and eager team. The News Editor was Mike Henfield, who had previously been at BBC Radio Birmingham and BRMB, and alongside him a team of reporters who included Peter Lowe, Gary Hudson, Alan Turner, Andy Armitage and Kay Oliver.

Amongst the presenter line-up were Gordon Astley, who would host the Breakfast Show, Dave Jamieson, who lined up for the mid-morning show called "Through Till One", and Tony Gillham who would be Head of Music and would take on the drive-time "Radioactive" show. In addition to my role as Sports Editor, I was to present "Afternoon Delight" from one o'clock until four each weekday afternoon. The line-up was completed by John Warwick hosting the "Night Express" late show at the end of the day, with Andy Lloyd and Jeff Harris presenting weekend programmes.

Although VHF, or FM, listening was growing, an overwhelming number of people listened to medium wave, or AM. So the on-air jingles and car stickers promoted the frequencies: 220 medium wave (1359 kilohertz), and 95.9 VHF in stereo. The jingles made it clear:

Mercia two two oh

Playing on your radio

Something old, something new

Mercia playing just for you.

Music every day

News in every way

Everything you need to know

On Mercia two two oh

What listeners did not realise was that the male singer of those station identity jingles, known as station imaging, was the lead vocalist of The Dave Clark Five, Mike Smith. I am sure when those jingles were commissioned neither Ian Rufus nor Mike Smith knew just how appropriate it was. The Dave Clark Five big hit record "Glad All Over" was one of the anthems regularly played at Coventry City home matches, thus linking Mike's voice with both the football club and the city's first local radio station.

As the new team arrived we got to know each other. Old friendships were renewed, new relationships were formed, and I got on well with Ian's secretary Susan.

The prospect of the house move from Sheffield stalled, with finances to enable the Kenilworth purchase proving to be a serious stumbling block. My wife continued to express her doubts about wanting to leave South Yorkshire.

As we got to know each other, I asked Susan if she would like to see the film "10", starring Dudley Moore, Julie Andrews and Bo Derek, which was showing at a cinema in Coventry. That night I stayed with Sue and, days afterwards, I took my leave of Ian's house and moved into Sue's apartment near Coventry city centre.

My wife never did move from Sheffield. We divorced, and within twelve months of that first date Susan and I bought a house in Nuneaton. I later learned that my wife remarried and moved to another part of Yorkshire. Sue and I were married on November 28th, 1981, my third and final attempt at making matrimony work.

Ian had recruited the Reverend Roger Hall, minister at Warwick Road United Reformed Church in Coventry, to present a faith-based Sunday morning Breakfast Show on Mercia Sound, and it seemed the natural thing to do was for us to ask Roger if he would conduct our wedding ceremony at his church. He readily agreed and I think he was as delighted as we were to find the place packed, not only with friends and family, but also with Mercia listeners. The radio station had been on air for more than eighteen months and its success was borne out by every seat in the church being full, with even a few more kind people waiting outside to wish us well as we left the church.

I had laid on a surprise for my new wife, arranging for a horse and carriage to collect us from the church and take us to the reception, travelling around the city of Coventry. What I had forgotten was that it gets dark quite early at the end of November. Our service started at half past three in the afternoon, so even though the carriage had side lights burning brightly, adding to the romantic image, the groomsman was quite relieved that he was able to guide his horse safely through the dusk and the evening traffic.

Susan had no idea that I had booked the horse and carriage so when she saw it, as we moved out of the church, she exclaimed loudly, "Stuart, you bloody idiot!" to the amusement and delight of those within earshot which, as it turned out, was most of the congregation. She immediately kissed me, however, so I think she was reasonably impressed.

Two years later, we became a family of three, with the birth of our son Nicholas at Nuneaton Maternity Hospital. As the first of the Mercia Sound team to marry and have children, we were featured at home during the pregnancy in the local newspaper, the *Coventry Evening Telegraph*. No more than a day after he arrived a photo of Nick, cradled in his Mum's arms, was featured prominently in the 'paper, his eyes wide open, staring directly down the photographer's lens.

We had moved to Coventry by the time our second baby was born in 1985. Matthew entered the world at Coventry Maternity Hospital at Walsgrave.

It will always be a sadness to me that my parents were no longer with us when Nicholas and Matthew made us a family of four, so the boys never knew one set of grandparents who I know would have loved them hugely. Sue's mum and dad, and the rest of her family, made up for that as we settled in Coventry and made it our long-term home.

Hosting a daily show was great fun. When Mercia Sound went on air in 1980, it was still the norm for the stars of the day to tour the country promoting their wares on local radio and regional TV. The era of the "down the line" interview from London was yet to kick in.

A myriad of star names came to Coventry to see us and to appear on shows across the schedule. I was fortunate enough to have people like Lenny Henry, Lulu, Alvin Stardust, Mike Berry, Godley and Crème, and Gilbert O'Sullivan join me as guests on my show.

Mike Berry was an absolute delight to talk to. His initial foray into pop music in 1960 had given him a top 10 hit with "Don't You Think It's Time", but in 1975 he'd made it to number 2 in the charts with a remake of his 1960 debut song "Tribute to Buddy Holly". When I interviewed him at Mercia, he was in the Top 10 with a song written before the First World War, "The Sunshine Of Your Smile."

Although The Beatles became for me the pre-eminent act in the history of modern popular music, I have always been a fan of Cliff Richard. From the moment that I first heard the instantly recognisable opening guitar riff of his hit "Move It", I was hooked on the voice, and subsequently the versatility of the young singer who was originally billed as a rebellious rock and roll star in the style of Elvis Presley. Many UK pop stars of the late 50s and early 60s, like Tommy Steele, Marty Wilde and Billy Fury, were talked up as 'our answer' to Elvis, but it was Cliff, with his Brylcreemed, quiffed hair and surly, curled lip, who was in the forefront.

In his early years, Cliff was backed exclusively by The Shadows, a four-piece band that developed their own fan following. The original Shadows line-up was Hank B. Marvin on lead guitar, Bruce Welch on rhythm guitar, Jet Harris playing bass guitar and Tony Meehan on drums. They had at first been called The Drifters, but when "Living Doll", their single with Cliff, hit the American charts, they had their name changed to avoid legal complications with the American group also called The Drifters.

It was not, however, The Shadows that played on the original recording of "Move It". That famous opening guitar riff was not played by Hank B. Marvin, although he has since played it countless times in live performances at concerts. What you hear on that 1958 record is session guitarist Ernie Shears.

Cliff Richard went on to enjoy a phenomenal career. Sixty-seven Top 10 singles, fourteen of them being number ones, many top-selling albums, and sharing the record with Elvis Presley as the only act to make the UK singles charts in all of its first six decades, from the 1950s to the 2000s. He is the only singer to have had a number-one single in the UK in five consecutive decades, and although he was never established as a big star in America, he nonetheless had eight US Top 40 singles.

It was a massive moment then for me when my studio guest at Mercia Sound was Cliff Richard. The interview was scheduled to last twenty minutes.

Cliff stayed for an hour. We got on really well, talking about his music, and more besides, both on-air and off. It helps when the guest is easy to chat with whilst you're playing records during the interview, and Cliff was natural and charming during our conversation.

I had met Cliff a few years before at Radio Hallam, but he had been there to renew his acquaintance with Keith Skues, Roger Moffat, Johnny Moran and Bill Crozier, and I had not expected him to remember me. He didn't, but he was a delight to talk to.

He was quietly concerned when we were told that thousands of fans had surrounded the radio station. He took it in good part when I teased him about the fact that they were overwhelmingly female, with many tabloid reports having concerned themselves with any girlfriend he might be seeing.

He was said to have dated tennis star and later TV presenter, Sue Barker, actress and dancer Una Stubbs, and Carol Costa, who had married and divorced Shadows' bass guitarist Jet Harris. He also had a relationship with a dancer from Warwickshire called Delia Wicks.

A few years after I interviewed Cliff, Delia wrote about their 18-month affair. At that time she had retired from show business, worked in a shoe shop in Warwick, and lived in the Warwickshire village of Barford. I interviewed her on Mercia Sound, and she told me that one of her most treasured possessions was a letter that Cliff had written to her to end their romance. She wouldn't show me the letter, nor read it to me, but when she died in 2010 at the age of 71 the letter was published.

"Dear Delia,

I know I haven't written for a long time but I've been so confused in my mind about you and about myself.

I've just had to make, probably, one of the biggest decisions I'm ever going to make and I'm hoping that it won't hurt you too much.

Delia, I want you to try and understand the position I'm in. Being a singer I'm going to have to give up many things in life. But being a pop singer I have to give up one priceless thing — the right to any lasting relationship with any special girl.

Delia, you must find someone who is free to love you as you deserve to be loved, and is able to marry you. I couldn't give up my career, besides the fact that my mother and sisters, since my father's death, rely on me completely. I have showbiz in my blood now and I would be lost without it.

D, all I can say now is goodbye and don't think too badly of me.

Love, Cliff."

So far as I know, Delia was not amongst the horde of fans waiting for Cliff outside the Mercia Sound studios during my interview with him. Police arrived to ensure the safety of all concerned when Cliff left. His limousine was brought to the back door of the building so that he could get into it without being mobbed. The fans were well-behaved, albeit screaming loudly, some in tears, as he was driven slowly away.

Fans, in various numbers, also turned up outside the radio station for visits by stars such as The Bee Gees, Bryan Ferry, Gary Numan, Phil Oakey, T'Pau, Sheena Easton, Bob Geldof, Gilbert O'Sullivan and Shakin' Stevens. Stars with connections local to Coventry and Warwickshire were also featured quite often, high among them The Specials, and the band formed by three of its former members, Terry Hall, Neville Staple and Lynval Golding, who called themselves The Fun Boy Three.

Hazel O'Connor was another, as were The Selecter and its vocalist Pauline Black. The groups Jigsaw and The Fortunes both had members linked to the Mercia Sound area, whilst Vince Hill, Frank Ifield and Don Fardon were all born in Coventry. All were interviewed and featured in programmes on the radio station.

When Phil Lynott, the vocalist and lead guitarist of Thin Lizzy came to the studios the intense interest was more from the female members of the radio station staff, rather than fans outside. They hung over the stair bannister and congregated around the reception area just to catch a glimpse of him. When I asked why they were so keen to see him, the answer was "He's just so dirty".

Mercia Sound launched on 23rd May 1980. Number one in the UK album chart was the LP "Tears And Laughter" by Johnny Mathis, whilst "What's Another Year?" by Johnny Logan was at number one in the UK singles chart, having replaced "Geno" by Dexy's Midnight Runners. That was a tribute to soul singer Geno Washington, performed in a style similar to Geno

Washington's Ram Jam Band. It had been in the charts for a while, with two weeks at number one, and it was played constantly on the jukebox in the Hen and Chickens pub next door to the radio station in the weeks before the launch.

The Mercia Sound team, increasing in number as day one approached, would retire to the Hen and Chickens for lunch. As we got to know each other, those lunchtime gatherings became more and more relaxed and sociable. Pulling together a group of creative people, with a few egos bouncing around, into an effective team is no easy task. Ian Rufus and John Bradford, with different but complementary backgrounds, managed to achieve that with an application of easy, natural charm, good humour and plain and simple common sense.

Ian's experience as a journalist and broadcaster, at the start of ILR, was matched by John's entrepreneurial spirit and wide knowledge of the burgeoning commercial radio industry. John had been a member of the Local Radio Association, a 70s lobby group that campaigned for the creation of local commercial radio. He was the founding Managing Director of Radio Tees, serving County Durham and North Yorkshire from studios at Stockton-on-Tees. It later became TFM.

When he heard that Les Ross had missed out on a job at BRMB, John tempted Les away from Birmingham to be the first Breakfast presenter at Tees. Another member of his on-air team was Tony Gillham who followed him to Coventry.

Ian turned to another former BBC Radio Birmingham colleague Mike Henfield to run the Mercia Sound newsroom, managing the station's journalists. Mike brought significant experience and insightful leadership to the Mercia news team. His twin brother Martin ran BBC GMR in Manchester for 5 years and then presented the BBC North West Tonight regional TV news programme in the 1990s.

Together, John and Ian were the architects of a line-up, a programme schedule, a music format and a news team that wasted no time in getting under the skin of Coventry, Warwickshire and South-West Leicestershire. It was brash, bright and bouncy, and regarded as hugely credible by a local population that immediately fell in love with it.

On day one, I was simultaneously the radio station's Sports Editor and presenter of the early afternoon show. All the shows were given titles. Mine was 'Afternoon Delight', after the hit record written by Bill Danoff, founder member of the American group, Starland Vocal Band. The group had taken the song into charts all around the world and had made it one of the biggest-selling singles of 1976.

I have always felt truly at home in the studio, the place where I really enjoy working. To host my own show, playing the hits and having fun with the audience was really special.

Technologically we thought we were pretty cool. It was 1980, and we played the music from vinyl records spinning on turntables. That had its risks if, for example, the vinyl was scratched causing the record to jump or to get stuck. There was also a potential problem if someone else visited the studio as Sue did on one occasion to give me the sandwiches she had bought for me. She handed me the paper bag across the top of the turntable which, at the time, was playing the record "Oh Lori" by Alessi. The bag just caught the arm of the turntable, causing the stylus to skid across the record and meaning that I had to jump in with a rapid link to the next record and recover from the glitch.

We played the advertisements and jingles off cartridges (carts, as we called them), modelled on eight-track tape machines. Each ad was precisely scheduled to satisfy the requirements of the advertisers and the regulations covering them, so they had to be played at the right time, as listed on a schedule fixed to a clipboard in the studio. As the ad breaks were played, the presenter had to write down the time when they were broadcast on the schedule. No computers in those days, and plenty of paperwork.

There was paperwork involved too for the daily feature "Trading Post". This was an idea copied from other stations. BRMB called it "Tradio". It was effectively a local radio version of a newspaper's classified advertisements, but free of charge. To say it rattled a few cages at the *Coventry Evening Telegraph* is putting it mildly.

Listeners could call us and go on air to detail the item that they wanted to get rid of, usually for a modest price, sometimes for free. The rules were "no animals, no weapons", and only individuals rather than businesses could take part. Sometimes people would call to request something they wanted. The caller gave a 'phone number to enable other listeners to respond.

One or two people complained that they were unable to take part because they did not have a 'phone. I was sympathetic to that and invited people to write in as well, allowing time for it to reach me. One of our advertising sales staff, who had clearly been paying attention at one of the training seminars he had attended before our launch, told me I was wrong to do so.

"We were told," he said, "that we should forget about anyone without a telephone. If they do not have a 'phone, they are not economically active."

I took that piece of sales training hype with a pinch of salt and continued to invite people to write in, but those who did were in the minority. There was no doubt that most people who wanted to take part preferred to do so on the 'phone.

That was how I spent my weekday afternoons, focusing on my show, including Trading Post and the visiting star guests.

My mornings were spent keeping in touch with the news of local sports clubs and personalities, mainly the latest from Coventry City Football Club. The club's manager at the time was Gordon Milne, who had been in the post since 1974.

Coventry City was in the top flight of English football, which was then the First Division but had a reputation for flirting with relegation. The club had done well enough, however, to qualify for Europe in 1970. With Irishman Noel Cantwell, a former West Ham and Manchester United full-back as manager, Coventry City finished 6th in the First Division, their highest League placing, and so qualified to play in the European Fairs Cup. In the second round, City lost 7–3 on aggregate to Bayern Munich, despite winning the second leg 2–1 at Highfield Road.

Two years before Mercia Sound arrived, Gordon Milne had steered them to finish in seventh place in the League table, thanks largely to the strike partnership of Ian Wallace and Mick Ferguson. It was Coventry's second highest-ever final league placing, but this time the club fractionally missed out on a UEFA Cup place.

Gordon Milne was a canny northerner, born in Preston, with a hugely impressive playing career behind him. He had been one of Bill Shankly's first signings for Liverpool after the great man had been appointed to the top job at Anfield. In the 1930s, Shankly had played for Preston North End alongside Gordon's father and fellow Scot Jimmy Milne, and he was well aware of Gordon's talent.

The young Milne went on to become a Liverpool regular during the 1960s, playing a prominent role in the club's rise under Shankly from the old Second Division. Whilst at Anfield, he won a Second Division Championship medal in 1961–62, and First Division Championship medals in 1963–64 and 1965–66. He also played 14 times for England.

Before Mercia Sound launched, the only local media that Coventry City Football Club had to deal with was the *Coventry Evening Telegraph* newspaper. Their man covering the club at the time was Neville Foulger, an experienced and wily reporter who never missed a story, and also a man who knew how to handle a source to whom he had to return, day after day. Neville was a fixture on the Coventry sports scene, and he had written a book "Coventry City: A Complete History Of The Club" in 1979.

National media can hit and run when it comes to most football clubs outside the biggest in the land. Inevitably, the top national reporters are regular visitors to Manchester United, Manchester City, Liverpool, Tottenham Hotspur, Arsenal and Chelsea. They would call in at clubs like Coventry City far less often, so when they do, they don't need to contact the manager again until the story they've written has faded with the passing of time.

In contrast, the local media has to face the manager the following day and be ready to justify anything they have reported. That should not, and rarely does, hamper local reporters from doing their job. It simply makes their relationship with the manager a fundamentally important and often delicate one to manage.

When you arrive out of nowhere, smack in the middle of the carefully developed connection between a manager and a well-established local reporter, treading carefully goes without saying. Gordon Milne, though polite and welcoming, was understandably wary of me, and whilst Neville Foulger was helpful to this newbie, he also had to protect his affiliation with Milne.

It was going to take time to get to know both of them, and that was not going to be easy with the club in the bottom half of the table with Milne under pressure. At the end of March, his team had been beaten 3-1 at home by Wolves at Highfield Road, with the home fans chanting "Milne out".

Local radio was still some years away from the days of live commentary. As at Radio Hallam, our match reports were limited to three updates per half, plus preview, half-time and full-time reports. The first match we covered after our launch was an away match against Manchester United. City lost 2-1, despite a goal from Garry Thompson, with United moving level on points with the eventual Champions Liverpool at the top of the table. City finished 15th.

Over time I got on well with Gordon Milne and learned that he had a keen, albeit mildly sardonic, sense of humour. It was not a long relationship, however. By the end of the following season, Gordon was gone.

The change was made by Jimmy Hill, who had been the club's inspirational Svengali as manager in the 60s, taking Coventry City into the First Division and introducing many novel ideas. One was to change the colour of the kit, making it Sky Blue, which also provided the club's new nickname.

After steering them safely into football's topflight, he fell out with the board and with Derrick Robins, the legendary Chairman who had brought him to Coventry. They could not agree on the terms of the new contract that Jimmy thought he deserved. Jimmy knew, however, that there was keen interest in him from television and that was the move he made.

In 1975 he returned to Coventry City as Managing Director, after nearly ten years hosting TV football shows, first for ITV, then for BBC One fronting *Match Of The Day*. Even after he became the club's Chairman, he continued to host *Match Of The Day* whilst running the Sky Blues.

Jimmy masterminded a redevelopment of the club's training ground at Ryton-on-Dunsmore, including the building of a modern gym and office complex called Sky Blue Connexion. The gym facilities were open to the public, but it also had a suite of offices for Jimmy himself, as well as for Gordon Milne and his staff.

When the Connexion opened in the summer of 1980, Jimmy gave me an interview in which he told me that it was a facility fit for a king. "Gordon Milne is our king, and this is his kingdom. This is where he will reign."

Twelve months later Milne was gone, with former Manchester United manager Dave Sexton taken on to replace him. At the same time, star striker Ian Wallace was transferred to the then reigning European champions Nottingham Forest for £1.25 million, making him one of the world's most expensive players. The joke amongst Sky Blues' fans was that the Sky Blue Connexion should be renamed "the Ian Wallace Memorial Building", suggesting that the player's transfer fee had provided the funds to pay for it.

All of this kept me busy as Mercia Sound's Sports Editor, and it was always exciting to work with Jimmy Hill. He never failed to give me a story every time we met. He would often share with me some of the plans he had for how the game of football could be improved, to make it more enjoyable and a total entertainment product for the supporters.

'JH', as he was called, had carved his own huge slice of Coventry history in the 60s, making Coventry City one of the most exciting football clubs in the land with a plethora of innovative ideas, and great success on the pitch. Now he made my life as the first local radio sports editor in Coventry hugely exciting.

Mercia Sound hit the ground running. Previously the only local stations followed by people in the area were from Birmingham or Leicester, but by definition, they were not local to Coventry and Warwickshire, so they did not serve the area editorially. Reception quality from those neighbouring cities also inevitably varied depending on precisely where you were listening.

When Mercia Sound arrived on locally focused AM and FM frequencies, the impact was massive. In a competitive market in the 2000s, any local station achieving an average weekly audience (called the station's "reach") approaching 30% of the available adult population is doing exceptionally well. Most are below 25%, many less than 20%. When Mercia launched, its first audience figures gave it a reach of 63%.

Admittedly, there was no BBC local station in the Coventry and Warwickshire area at that time. The BBC had said it would launch a station in Coventry in 1980. In fact, it was another ten years before it did. So discounting the neighbouring stations in Birmingham and Leicester, Mercia's only competition came from the national stations, which were then all from the BBC.

Many cities and large towns refer to themselves as being a "large village", implying that everyone there knows everyone else. That was, and remains, particularly true of Coventry. The local community took Breakfast Show host Gordon Astley to their hearts. They loved his risqué sense of humour and his bright and lively manner.

Mid-morning man Dave Jamieson was a class act, an assured broadcaster loved and respected by all. I was grateful to be well received on my afternoon show, and also on the sports programmes. There was a minority amongst the football fans who seemed almost eager to find fault, but I had long since learnt that such so-called supporters exist in all football-following communities.

Tony Gillham was a business-like host of the late afternoon drive-time show. As he was also the radio station's Head of Music there was keen interest in Tony's programmes from local musicians, DJs, and record pluggers both local and national.

The sound of the station was strong and pulled in listeners at both ends of the day. Whilst Gordon Astley's irreverence woke them up at breakfast time, the more subdued but equally cheeky tones of John Warwick saw us all safely tucked in at the other end of the day with the late show. John's humour was effective through its subtlety and, often, its simplicity. He called his car 'Pearl'. When someone asked why, he explained "because it's a Singer."

Like me, John was born and bred in Birmingham, and also like me, he had started in hospital radio and his first job in 'proper' radio was at BBC Radio Birmingham. He loved his food and he was partial to a curry, washed down with a gently chilled lager, just before going on air. I say 'just before' quite literally because John's nightly routine would be to visit the Friend's Corner Indian restaurant on Foleshill Road in Coventry, roughly a six-minute drive to Mercia Sound in normal traffic.

In the early days, John's show began straight after the 9 o'clock evening news bulletin. He had an arrangement with the presenter who was on air before him. In the event that John had not arrived at the radio station in time, the news should be followed by his name-check jingle, and then the first record. By the time the record finished, John was in his seat in the studio and ready to take over. He often missed the news bulletin, but he always got there from Friends Corner in time to back credit that first record. That race from the restaurant probably did nothing for his digestion, but no one listening would ever have known what had occurred.

Weekend shows were also hugely popular. Andy Lloyd on Sunday morning played a perfectly judged selection of soft rock and progressive pop, typified by Al Stewart's beautiful songs "Year Of The Cat" and "Time Passages". For all those who listened at the time, Sunday afternoon on Mercia will always mean Jeff Harris and his Lazy Sunday show, the title inspired by

The Small Faces hit record. Jeff played familiar favourite pop songs programmed to simply relax and enjoy.

All ILR stations were required to present a range of programmes, reflecting different musical genres and, where relevant to the local community, acknowledging the presence of local ethnic groups. Amongst the evening line-up, regional TV presenter Stewart White hosted a country and western show, Alan Perry played big band music, and Sarjit Myrrpurey was the presenter of a weekly show for the Asian community. On Sunday night classical music was in the expert hands of Lyndon Jenkins.

Most stations scheduled their classical music show on a Sunday evening, and for a number, it was hosted by the Managing Director. Mercia took a different line, calling on the cultured beautiful diction of a classical music aficionado. Lyndon was a regular contributor to specialist music journals and a writer of many CD booklets for major record labels. He broadcast regularly on Danish and Finnish radio stations and he received a knighthood from the Queen of Denmark for services to Anglo-Danish cultural relations.

Lyndon had little to do with the live concerts of the music of the Strauss family, or The Last Night Of The Proms, staged for us by the English Philharmonic Orchestra. They were conducted and organised by musical entrepreneur Neil Moore, making money for him, his orchestra and the radio station. They were unashamedly populist, usually selling out at venues like the Belgrade Theatre in Coventry and Bedworth Civic Hall.

They were usually recorded and broadcast as special shows on a Saturday night, but never in place of Lyndon's programme on a Sunday. He did however co-host, with Reverend Roger Hall, a Good Friday concert that I had arranged for us to broadcast live from Coventry Cathedral. It was Bach's St. Matthew Passion, performed by St. Michael's Singers, one of the UK's leading choral societies that took its name from the saint to whom the cathedral is dedicated.

The 2-tone sound, led by The Specials, was putting Coventry on the nation's pop music map. The Specials had released their first album, called "The Specials", in 1979, and had enjoyed several chart hits. The singles, "Gangsters", and "A Message To You, Rudy", were both hits, as was "Too Much Too Young" which gave them their first number-one. As Mercia Sound arrived in 1980, the double 'A' side single "Rat Race" and "Rude Boys Outa Jail" had just entered the top twenty, and that year the group also released "Stereotype" and "Do Nothing", and the album "More Specials".

There was talk of inviting The Specials to mark Mercia's launch by performing on the radio station's roof, in a similar manner to The Beatles' rooftop session in London for their "Let It Be" album ten years before. Whether that plan was ever put to the band became irrelevant because Mercia Sound's insurers were consulted and expressed safety concerns. A particular worry was whether the flat roof of the building was strong enough to take the weight. A balcony one story below the roof level was considered, but it was decided that it was too small. There was also concern about the policing of fans turning up to watch, because of the proximity of traffic on the ring road.

There was no live Specials concert at the radio station, but their music was regularly played on Mercia Sound. There were interviews with members of the band and one or two of them would often pop in to spend time with the presenters and some of the reporters. Other artists who were originally on the 2-Tone label were also featured, such as The Beat, Bad Manners, Madness and The Selecter.

* * * *

The combination of a strong presenter line-up, well-programmed music and top guests, alongside well-researched and presented local news and sport, laid the foundations for a big and loyal following from local people. Mercia Sound got under the skin of Coventry and Warwickshire. What John Bradford and Ian Rufus achieved was the creation of a brand and a product that the people of Coventry and Warwickshire felt they owned. It was their radio station, they loved it and they adopted the on-air team as part of their family.

Local businesses were quick to advertise on the station. The first local advertiser was businessman Joe Elliott, who ran a car accessories company in Coventry that had been founded by his father. Joe and I got on well, and he became a good and close friend. Alongside Joe, the Allen family, who ran local butchers Aubrey Allen and Coventry taxi company Allen's Taxis, were also keen supporters of the station. For years afterwards, and even beyond the time when they were no longer aired on the station, the jingles from their commercials were occasionally sung, and certainly instantly recognised by Mercia listeners.

To be strictly accurate, the main following came from Coventry and North Warwickshire. The towns of Bedworth and Nuneaton sit cheek by jowl with Coventry, and people there also bought into the notion of having their own radio station. It was much harder to win over the South Warwickshire towns such as Kenilworth, Royal Leamington Spa, Stratford-upon-Avon and Warwick.

The radio station's transmission and editorial area was officially Coventry, Warwickshire and South-West Leicestershire. The latter referred specifically to the town of Hinckley, which offered very slim pickings for both listeners and advertisers, but in those early days the effort to win both was put in across all departments of the radio station – Sales, News and Programmes.

The presenters were encouraged to take up opportunities for personal appearances at local events. One or two got to know the owners and operators of local venues who booked them for regular evening DJ sets. I was open to whatever opportunity was chucked my way, as and when time allowed. I received one invitation to compère a local beauty contest, held at the Chesford Grange Hotel near Kenilworth which many years later, in the 90s, was used for the filming of an episode of the BBC TV comedy series "Keeping Up Appearances".

I was asked to interview the beauty contest participants and to introduce the judges, two of whom would become close friends. They were Coventry hairdresser Paul Todd, who was later my best man when I married Sue, and former Coventry City full-back Dietmar Bruck.

Paul and Dietmar had known each other since childhood and were so close that they were almost like brothers. It was a standing joke that Dietmar would admit that he has never paid for a haircut in Coventry in his life.

Paul was Coventry born and bred, whilst Dietmar was born in Danzig, then in Germany, which is now the Polish seaport of Gdansk. He came to England as a child, and he was raised and educated in Coventry. He was part of Jimmy Hill's Coventry City team that took the club into the First Division, winning the Division Two title in 1967.

As co-owner of the Sweeney Todd barber's salon at Gosford Green, a stone's throw from the football club's Highfield Road stadium, Paul cut and styled the hair of that promotion-winning team, and in the 70s gave star striker Ian Wallace an afro perm for his striking ginger hair. With his hairdresser partners Roger Goodrich and Billy Over, Paul made Sweeney Todd one of the most famous hairdressers in the Midlands.

I had met neither Paul nor Dietmar before that beauty contest, but at the first meeting in the bar before the show, we hit it off straight away. The contest promoter had given me a brief biography of both men to aid my introduction, but when I read it I knew we could have some fun with it.

Dietmar had retired from playing and had ventured into coaching and management at non-League level. He was then manager of a local club with the rather flamboyant name Racing Club Warwick. From the notes handed to me by the promoter, it was apparent that confusion reigned over Dietmar's employment.

When the time came for the introductions, I used what I had been given.

"Please welcome award-winning Coventry hairdresser Paul Todd, from Sweeney Todd in Coventry, and former Coventry City star Dietmar Bruck who, it says here, is the manager of Warwick Racecourse."

Paul and Dietmar instantly fell about laughing, as did many in the audience who were clued up about local football.

"That's what it says," I continued, "but Dietmar is, of course, manager of Racing Club Warwick football club."

We had a great time that night, and I made two new and long-lasting friendships.

* * * *

Dave Jamieson was one of the star turns when Mercia Sound launched. His weekday mid-morning show, an easy to listen mix of music and chat, was an instant hit with listeners. He also hosted a late-night show on Saturdays, with the content based around a lateral thinking brain teaser quiz that he called "Six Of The Best". It was, as he put it each week, "six of my best questions and six of your best answers."

Dave gave Mercia two of its most memorable moments, the first of them as we approached Mercia's first Christmas. At 10.50pm in New York, on Monday, 8th December 1980, John Lennon was returning with his wife Yoko Ono to their home in the Dakota Building, on the northwest corner of 72nd Street and Central Park West in the Upper West Side of Manhattan. As they approached the archway entrance of the building, Lennon was shot in the back by Mark David Chapman, who was obsessed with things that Lennon had said.

Lennon had been shot four times at close range. He was pronounced dead just after 11.00pm. It was 04.00am on Tuesday 9th in the UK, and the news broke as radio breakfast shows all over the country were going on air. I will never forget waking alongside Sue that morning in our house in Nuneaton to hear Gordon Astley telling Coventry and Warwickshire what had happened. It was so hard to come to terms with. John Lennon had been an outstanding cultural influence on our generation. It was truly difficult to absorb the enormity of it.

Many people die in tragic circumstances. We mourn their passing and feel great regret. This, though, was different. This was a Beatle.

Gordon's Breakfast Show had included initial tributes and the reaction of shocked fans, music lovers generally and some of Lennon's contemporaries. Of course, Gordon had played some of Lennon's music, including tracks from his album "Double Fantasy", released only three weeks before, but it was Dave Jamieson who captured the moment brilliantly.

As he went on air, Dave's opening link was perfectly judged.

"It's the 9th of December, and as we've heard this morning, the world has been shocked to hear from New York that John Lennon has been shot dead."

He then played Lennon's hit record, "Merry Xmas (War Is Over)", which includes Lennon singing the opening line, "And so this is Christmas…".

The tone from Dave Jamieson was perfect. His words and his intuitive selection of the music were exactly right. The tributes to Lennon were flooding in from all over the world. George Harrison put it best.

"After all we went through together, I had and still have great love and respect for him. I am shocked and stunned. To rob a life is the ultimate robbery in life. The perpetual encroachment on other people's space is taken to the limit with the use of a gun. It is an outrage that people can take other people's lives when they obviously haven't got their own lives in order. I just wanted to be in a band. Here we are, 20 years later, and some whack job has shot my mate. I just wanted to play guitar in a band."

At his trial in a closed courtroom at the Supreme Court in Manhattan, Mark Chapman pleaded guilty to murder. He was sentenced to a prison term of 20 years to life, with a stipulation that mental health treatment would be provided. He has since been denied parole ten times.

Dave Jamieson was again the man on air in 1982 when the name of the city of Coventry was thrust into the global headlines.

In the 1980s if anyone mentioned war in Coventry it was probably in relation to the Coventry Blitz of 1940, during the Second World War. The Vietnam War was quite fresh in the memory with the fall of Saigon in 1975, American troops having withdrawn from the conflict two years before. Separately, there was also bombing on the British mainland in pursuit of the aims of the Irish Republican Army (IRA), the perpetrators no doubt regarding that as a war.

What no one expected was that Britain would find itself involved in an overseas military fight in a year in which other, more innocent issues were to the fore. Tabloid newspapers attracted record readership by introducing bingo to their pages, the Queen celebrated 30 years on the throne, and the Pope was due to visit the UK in the summer. It was war, though, that overshadowed the rest, at least for ten weeks in Spring and early Summer.

On 18th March 1982, an Argentine scrap metal dealer raised the Argentine flag on the island of South Georgia in the Falkland Islands, a British overseas colony.

The day after the flag was raised on South Georgia, Argentinian forces landed on the Island. The British government, led by Prime Minister Margaret Thatcher, regarded the action as an invasion of a Crown colony. Falkland Islanders, who have inhabited the islands since the early 19th century, are predominantly descendants of British people who settled there and strongly favour British sovereignty. The islands became a war zone.

On 5th April, the British government dispatched a naval task force to engage the Argentine Navy and Air Force before making an amphibious assault on the islands. The conflict lasted 74 days, in which time 649 Argentine military personnel, 255 British military personnel, and three Falkland Islanders died.

One of the British ships sent to the Falklands was the destroyer HMS Coventry. She had been on an exercise near Gibraltar, after which she was due to return to the UK before going on an intelligence-gathering mission against Soviet naval forces in the Barents Sea. Her captain was David Hart Dyke, father of the actress, comedian and writer Miranda Hart.

Captain Hart Dyke oversaw considerable success for the Coventry in the Falklands. The ship's helicopter was the first to fire air-to-surface anti-ship missiles in action when under attack from Argentine jets, and she shot down an Argentine assault helicopter.

My time at Radio Hallam meant that the naval battle was brought into sharp focus for me when I heard of the sinking of the Coventry's sister ship HMS Sheffield. On 4th May 1982, the Sheffield was hit by an Exocet missile fired from an Argentinian fighter aircraft. A second Exocet missed, splashing into the sea half a mile off her port beam.

The resulting fire on board the Sheffield was fought for four hours before the captain gave the order to abandon ship. Over the next six days, the burnt-out structure drifted until it was taken in tow to try and reach the safety of port at South Georgia Island. The flow of water into the wreck, whilst it was being towed, was too great and on 10th May 1982, the Sheffield went to the bottom of the sea, the first Royal Navy vessel to be sunk in action since World War II.

HMS Sheffield had 281 crew members. 20 of them died as a result of the attack, with another 26 injured, mostly from burns, smoke inhalation or shock.

Fifteen days later, on 25th May 1982, HMS Coventry and the frigate Broadsword were ordered to take up position to the northwest of Falkland Sound. Their role was to act as a decoy to draw Argentinian aircraft away from other ships. Although successful at first, the ploy failed when Coventry was hit by three bombs fired by Argentinian Seahawk attack aircraft.

Within 20 minutes the Coventry had been abandoned and had completely capsized. She sank shortly afterwards. 19 of her crew were killed, a further 30 were injured, one of whom died nearly twelve months later. Broadsword rescued 170 of the Coventry's crew, and whilst waiting to be rescued they sang the Monty Python song "Always Look On The Bright Side of Life".

When the news of her sinking was flashed up in the Mercia Sound newsroom it was immediately passed to Dave Jamieson to convey to the station's listeners. It's been referred to since as one of the most memorable moments in ILR history.

In a bid for immediate reaction to the tragedy, Mercia Sound reporter Peter Lowe sought out that year's Lord Mayor of Coventry, Councillor Bill Weaver. The interview required judicious editing after the Lord Mayor said, with genuine sincerity, "It gives me a sinking feeling."

The demise of HMS Coventry inevitably cast a huge cloud over the city, but within a few days, an event that had been planned with great precision for some time lifted the gloom. A spiritual uplift came in the form of a historic visit to Coventry by the leader of the worldwide Catholic Church.

On Sunday, May 30th, 1982, 300,000 people stood in blazing sunshine to welcome the Pope to Coventry. Pope John Paul II was given a rapturous welcome as his helicopter arrived at Coventry Airport, next to Baginton village. 100,000 members of the crowd had camped out overnight hoping to catch a glimpse of the 62-year-old Pope.

Ian Rufus asked me to commentate on the event not solely for Mercia Sound but also for the whole ILR network. Together with other members of the media, I was placed in a booth in a portacabin in the middle of the throng. A local catholic priest was alongside me to explain the protocols and nuances of the service. Amongst those in neighbouring booths was Anne Diamond, then a reporter for the ITV regional news programme, Central News.

The limitation of the booth was that the only direct view available was immediately in front, through an open window. That was fine once His Holiness arrived on the giant stage that had been set for him to preside over the service that would follow. On his way there from his helicopter, his journey wound through the massive congregation, many of whom were behind or to the side of the portacabin, out of our direct sight. We had to rely on live TV pictures of the procession, shown on a big screen to the side of the stage.

The sinking of HMS Coventry just days before was very raw in the minds of local people, but here was a man of peace, who had come to share guidance and comfort. His address was inevitably moving, as he referenced the local effect of the Second World War as well as that of the Falklands, describing Coventry as a "city devastated by war but rebuilt in hope".

He also spoke of the city's iconic Anglican cathedral, adding: "The ruins of the old cathedral and the building of the new are recognised throughout the world as a symbol of Christian peace and reconciliation."

In the geography of the Roman Catholic church, Coventry sits in the Birmingham diocese, and many people from across the diocese were involved in the event. 1,000 children took part in a pageant to welcome the Pope, representing the history of Christianity in music and dance. 26 people throughout the Birmingham diocese were confirmed by Pope John Paul that day.

Whilst in Britain, the charismatic Polish-born Pope met the Queen, who of course is the Supreme Governor of the Church of England, and he also visited Canterbury Cathedral and knelt in prayer with Robert Runcie, the then Archbishop of Canterbury.

Nearly a month after the Pope visited Coventry, on Sunday 13th June, I was compèring an event in Rugby, at the town's Benn Hall, when news came through that Port Stanley, the capital of the Falkland Islands, had been recaptured from Argentinian forces by British troops.

It was a dinner event and, as the meal ended, I announced that there was news just in from the Falklands that Stanley was back in British hands. When I said that it was being reported by the BBC that "once again, the Union Flag is flying over Stanley tonight", the packed hall erupted in cheers. The night ended with people singing "Rule Britannia" and "Land Of Hope And Glory".

In those early years, Mercia Sound reinforced its huge initial impact through its coverage of the Falklands War, and of the Pope's visit, and also by keeping local people and community groups in touch with one another through the severe winter of 1981. The snow really did lie deep, very deep, if not crisp and even.

By announcing events that had been called off because of the weather, and messages about how local people were helping each other, we kept the community informed, and we provided a platform for people to talk to others on air. The radio station received countless messages of thanks for its work in keeping people going in a way that no other part of the media was able to.

It was no great surprise to any of us working at Mercia Sound, that local people wanted to be part of the celebrations for Mercia's first birthday party. Ian Rufus, ever alert to publicity opportunities, booked the Locarno ballroom in the centre of Coventry as the venue, knowing very well that it was about to close down for good.

Mercia Sound's first birthday party was the last event ever staged at the Locarno before it went through wholesale refurbishment to re-emerge as Coventry's new Central Library. To ensure that the party went with a swing, Ian booked the duo Chas 'n' Dave as the guest stars, supported by DJ sets from some of the Mercia Sound presenters. It was a sell-out, and an overwhelming endorsement, if it was needed, that local radio had arrived in Coventry and that Coventry quite liked it.

We staged other party nights at Coventry venues over the years, notably at a nightclub that had been at the heart of city centre entertainment since it opened in 1972. Owned by no-nonsense Glaswegian businessman George Hendry, it had been launched under the name 'Mr. George's'. George acquired several properties around Coventry that were then let to local businesses, and he was a highly visible character often seen chewing on a huge cigar and driving around the area in a white Rolls Royce complete with the number plate COV 1.

The Three Degrees, which then had a line-up of Sheila Ferguson, Helen Scott and Valerie Holiday, were the star turn for one sell-out Mercia Sound party. At another the group Modern Romance, who had hits with "Everybody Salsa", "Ay Ay Ay Ay Moosey", and "Best Years Of Our Lives", attracted a mainly female audience.

Whilst Mercia presenters hosted the parties and introduced the acts, I brought a support band into play on each occasion. I had met and made friends with an Irish singer called Bob Brolly whose family was well known throughout the area.

The Irish community in Coventry is large and significant, producing many local politicians, businessmen and entertainers. Like many of the area's Irish families, Bob Brolly had so many siblings and cousins it was hard to keep track of them. He was immensely popular as a singer with his own showband called Calvary and he knew how to work a crowd and keep them entertained. He also had contacts throughout showbusiness, particularly with fellow Irish performers.

For a laugh, mainly at my expense, Bob allowed me to play drums in his band occasionally. I am no drummer, but I managed to maintain a beat. Just about. He learned of my failed attempt at being a singer, so from time to time he also handed me the mic for a brief guest appearance with Calvary. My party pieces were a couple of Buddy Holly songs, "Oh Boy" and the beautiful "True Love Ways", and also "A Groovy Kind Of Love", which was a hit for both The Mindbenders and Phil Collins.

Bob ensured the Mercia parties went with a swing and he would go on to play a significant role on air for Mercia Sound, and later, for BBC local radio in the West Midlands.

In 1981, a concert tour starring the man regarded as the most commercially successful singer from continental Europe arrived in Coventry. Spanish heart-throb Julio Iglesias performed in concert at the Coventry Theatre.

Julio had been a footballer, playing as a goalkeeper in the Spanish second division. His professional football career ended cruelly when he was involved in a serious car accident, which severely damaged his legs. During his recovery, he discovered his musical talent.

The tour brought him to Coventry just as he hit number 1 in the UK charts with "Begin The Beguine". A huge female fan following sought him out wherever he went. When I arrived for a pre-arranged interview in his dressing room at the theatre I had to negotiate my way through a large group of women. There were probably at least one hundred Coventry ladies, all dressed and ready for a night out, all with their tickets for the concert which was still three hours away.

I was ushered into the room where Julio was waiting, very relaxed in a casual shirt, jeans and espadrilles. He spoke slowly during the interview, his Spanish accent flavouring his broken English. From outside the building the chants of his name, coupled with one or two rather colourful suggestions of how much his fans admired him, provided a backing track to the interview.

It prompted me to ask him how he felt about the attention he attracted from female fans.

"How do you respond to that?" I asked.

"If they like my songs, I am happy," he replied.

"I think it's more than just your songs," I said. "What do you say to some of the things those ladies are saying?"

He paused and smiled before answering.

"I am just a simple man," he said.

Local news, the music and chat, and the presenters as local personalities, all became essential parts of everyday life in the area. The advertisements and station jingles were on the lips of many.

I had met and married Sue and we had two lovely sons. Life in Coventry was a genuine delight.

Thinking of you is working up my appetite

Looking forward to a little afternoon delight

Rubbing sticks and stones together makes the sparks ignite

And the thought of loving you is getting so exciting

Skyrockets in flight

Afternoon delight

Bill Danoff, 1976

© BMG Rights Management

Dorothy and Eric Linnell, my Mum and Dad.

Happy chappies in nappies! Cheerful toddlers. My cousin Stephen with the blonde curls, me with the dark hair and the dodgy parting.

With my wife Sue on my right, standing behind my cousins - brother and sister Jane and Stephen.

Three generations - my Dad, my Grandfather and me - outside
Buckingham Palace where my Granddad was about to receive his
MBE from Queen Elizabeth II in 1961.

Receiving my MBE from Queen Elizabeth II at Buckingham Palace in 1994.

After the investiture at Buckingham Palace, with my sons Nicholas and Matthew and my wife Sue.

In Sheffield, with Michael Parkinson.

In Sheffield, with Geoffrey Boycott.

With James Hunt, at Radio Hallam, just before we prompted an invasion of a nearby pub by the local female population, all determined to be in the presence of the Formula One World Champion.

Sebastian Coe, talking to me after breaking three world records in 1979.

Whilst the Breakfast host at BBC WM, interviewing Prime Minister Tony Blair at 10 Downing Street for the BBC Local Radio network.

With my friend and colleague Malcolm Boyden as we both won Sony
Radio Awards for BBC WM.

Interviewing "the greatest", when Muhammad Ali visited Coventry.

In the studio at Mercia Sound with Cliff Richard.

On the pitch at Highfield Road, immediately before Coventry City's final match there. Jimmy about to launch into "Let's All Sing Together".

Bobby Gould alongside me in the Sky Blues' press box.

Enjoying the company of Dave Bennett in the press box.

Interviewing the then Archbishop of Canterbury Rowan Williams for BBC CWR

With the one and only 'Snoz', John Sillett.

At BBC CWR with Pete Waterman and Bob Brolly.

Front page news when my career came close to an untimely end in 2014..

Mum & Dad's pride and joy - me and my sister Yvonne.

Chapter Twelve

A French Heart-Throb

Raindrops keep falling on my head

But that doesn't mean my eyes will soon be turning red

Crying's not for me

'Cause I'm never gonna stop the rain by complaining

Because I'm free

Nothing's worrying me

Burt Bacharach & Hal David, 1969

© Warner Chappell Music, Inc, BMG Rights Management

I love Italian food.

One of my favourite restaurants in Coventry in the early 80s was Quo Vadis, an Italian restaurant in the Coundon district of the city, near to what was then the home ground of Coventry Rugby Club, Coundon Road.

It was run by a great Italian chef, Carmine Chicarella. Like many Italians, Carmine was a keen football fan. He was a member of Coventry City's Vice-President's club which drew its membership from across the city's business community. Most of the Vice-Presidents regularly frequented Quo Vadis, which advertised its services on Mercia Sound.

Whilst Carmine cooked the food, the front of house was run by the disarmingly cheery and very witty Giovanni Zivelonghi. If the handsome Carmine was the culinary genius whose food attracted diners to Quo Vadis,

Giovanni provided the fun, the charm and the ambience that ensured they kept coming back.

Giovanni was born in Verona and he would readily tell you that he was one of the two gentlemen that Shakespeare wrote about. As a young man, he had played professional football in the Italian Second Division, Serie B. A broken leg had forced his retirement, but he remained a passionate football fan and, after moving to Coventry in the late 1950s, he followed Coventry City.

Carmine's wife Jenny completed the cast at Quo Vadis. Whilst Giovanni was the professional host Jenny made it her business to properly get to know people, as she did with Sue and me. She was always bright and cheerful and made you feel really welcome.

So when the French singer and actor Sacha Distel was a studio guest on my show at Mercia Sound, an opportunity occurred for me to give the lovely Jenny the surprise of her life.

The interview covered Sacha's remarkable and eclectic career, including his version of the Bacharach and David song "Raindrops Are Falling On My Head", which was a UK Top 10 hit in 1970. We spoke about his musical background, including his early days as a jazz guitarist working with Dizzy Gillespie and Tony Bennett. The latter had a huge hit with the song "The Good Life", which was written by Sacha Distel.

Sacha spoke frankly about his health, having twice battled cancer. He also chatted easily about his romantic liaisons with Brigitte Bardot, Juliette Greco and Dionne Warwick.

After my interview with him, Sacha was due to go to Birmingham to record a feature for BBC TV. The TV appearance was scheduled for the early evening. When my show ended, Sacha's manager who was travelling with him asked if I could recommend somewhere that they could get something to eat before they left for Birmingham.

I knew it was nearly the end of the afternoon service at Quo Vadis, but I made a quick phone call to Giovanni to check they were still open. No sooner had I mentioned who my guest was and said what I had in mind Giovanni readily agreed to make the necessary arrangements. In their Mercedes limousine Sacha and his agent followed me in my Austin Maestro as we travelled the short distance from the radio station to the restaurant.

Giovanni greeted us with his usual enthusiasm, obviously delighted to welcome the famous guest I had brought with me. The lunchtime clientele had left so we had the place to ourselves. Giovanni steered us to my favourite table in the front corner of the restaurant and took our order, which we kept simple. Spaghetti Bolognese all around, and a bottle of house white.

I had already made sure that Sacha was on board with what I had in mind, having explained that I knew that Jenny was a big fan. I checked with Giovanni that she was not there.

"No," he said, with a slight giggle. "She is not back yet with her shopping. Should be soon though."

It had just started to rain outside, so when Jenny came through the door a few minutes later she was irritated because her hair was wet. The shower had got heavier during the short walk as she'd carried her shopping bags from her car.

Jenny was not a naturally quiet person. When she was around, you probably heard her before you saw her, particularly when she laughed. When she came into the restaurant's reception hall our table was hidden from her view, but we could clearly hear her to Sacha's obvious amusement.

"Bloody rain," exclaimed Jenny, "and they didn't have everything I wanted."

"Never mind," said Giovanni, trying to calm her down, "let me take your coat."

As she took off her damp raincoat, Jenny continued to express her annoyance only for Giovanni to interrupt her.

"Well this might cheer you up," he said. "There's someone here to see you."

Jenny was still not able to see our table, so Giovanni ushered her into the room and gestured towards our corner. She looked across the room where she saw three men looking at her.

Mine was the first face that registered as she saw us.

"Stuart", she said, "how lovely to see…".

She was suddenly silent as she saw who was sitting next to me. She then stifled a scream as she realised that looking back at her across her restaurant, with his tanned good looks, perfect teeth and sparkling blue eyes, was one her all-time favourite stars.

"Oh my God!" she yelled. "Sacha?"

"Sacha!" she yelled again, very loudly, "Sacha! In my restaurant!"

Sacha was on his feet and at her side in a matter of seconds, holding her in his arms, which was just as well as it looked as though she was about to faint there and then.

"How lovely to see you," she managed to say eventually. "What a lovely surprise. The last time I saw you, you were on stage in London. I was five months pregnant."

"Ah," replied Sacha, his French accent underlining his Gallic sophistication, "and what did we 'ave?"

"A girl," laughed Jenny.

At that point, our food arrived, and at Sacha's invitation, Jenny sat and had a glass of wine with us, chatting to her international star guest.

After finishing her drink, she made her farewells, kissing me on the cheek and whispering in my ear, "Thank you, Stuart. That was a lovely surprise. The best ever."

* * * *

Although football, and specifically the Sky Blues, dominated the local sports scene in Coventry, there was plenty of other sport to report on. In 1982, a 29-year-old Coventry-born athlete made international headlines. David Moorcroft, a member of Coventry Godiva Harriers athletics club, had already made his mark as a leading middle-distance runner by competing in the 1500-metres at the 1976 Olympic Games in Canada, winning Gold over the same distance in the 1978 Commonwealth Games, also in Canada, and by running in the 5,000 metres at the 1980 Moscow Olympics. Stomach problems saw him eliminated from that race, but two years later he more than made up for it.

At the Bislett Games in Oslo, Moorcroft broke the 5,000 metres World Record by 5.79 seconds. His time of 13:00.41 stood for three years.

I had got to know David briefly before his record-breaking run, and Mercia Sound followed his story closely. We interviewed him before he set off from Coventry, and on the phone from Norway once he got there. Our race coverage came from network reporters at the event, who also supplied us with reactions and interviews immediately after the race.

David spoke to us again from Oslo before he flew back to the UK, and Mercia Sound laid on a car to collect him from Heathrow Airport and bring him home to Coventry.

By the end of the football season in 1983, Dave Sexton's reign as manager of Coventry City football club was over.

I was sorry to see him go. Dave was not the easiest man to get to know. He kept his private life private, but really his life was football. Once you realised how much the game meant to him, and how important footballers were to him, establishing a rapport became easier. You might think that would apply to all managers, and no doubt it does for many, but I have rarely met anyone who loved the game and those who played it with quite the same intensity and genuine concern as Dave Sexton. By the time he was sacked, we were on good terms, but not before two of the club's young stars had done their best to cause a rift between us.

At the start of the New Year in 1982, Garry Thompson and Tommy English had featured prominently in a front-page story in the *Coventry Evening Telegraph* about them breaking club rules for a late night out. On my visit to the Sky Blue Connexion the next day, I sent a message that I would like to speak to English and Thompson.

The protocol was that you had to wait in the reception area for the players you wanted to talk to, which I did. Within a couple of minutes, I heard a familiar voice shouting at me from the top of the stairs that led up to the offices and the player's canteen.

"Stuart!" yelled a clearly annoyed Dave Sexton. "Thompson and English? Under no circumstances can you speak to Thompson and English. I know precisely what you want to do, and those two are not available. Do you understand?"

I looked back up the stairs.

"Everyone's talking about them Dave," I said. "I just wanted to give them the chance to put their side of the story."

"And it's my job to stop them being a story," he shouted back, before repeating defiantly, "They are not available."

"Is it true you're going to leave them out of the side for the Cup-tie against Sheffield Wednesday?" I asked.

He came down the stairs before replying.

"Yes," he said. "They are being disciplined. They will not play on Saturday."

"Can I talk to you then please?" I asked.

"No," he said, "but you can talk to Gerry Daly."

Turning away, he looked back and added, "And don't try anything like that again."

I duly interviewed Gerry Daly and left with the story that Dave Sexton had carefully given me during our altercation. Thompson and English would pay for their indiscretion by being dropped for the Cup-tie.

Garry Thompson, who I got on with really well and who subsequently became a good friend, was soon back in the side. Tommy English was never a regular in Dave Sexton's starting line-up.

"I don't think Tom was his cup of tea from the off," Thompson told me later. "Tom was quite easygoing with everything, and Dave loved people to be really committed to wanting to work hard and improve, especially on the football side. As you know, Tom was inclined to see the funny side and was quite mischievous. I think our whole attitude to life riled Dave."

I often found myself in Dave Sexton's presence at various events during his time as Coventry City manager and thereafter. He was unquestionably serious about football, and even more so about footballers, and if you kept that in mind he was good company. His approach to me was akin to that of a kindly Uncle once we put the Thompson and English stand-off behind us. On one occasion he spotted me in the audience when he was on a panel with other coaches at a West Midlands football forum, and he made a point of seeking me out as he left the platform.

"Did you enjoy that?" he asked.

"Yes," I replied. "I always enjoy listening to people talking about football".

"I know you do," he replied and handed me a small pouch that bore the FA logo. "Here you go", he said, patted me on the shoulder and went on his way.

In the pouch was an FA leaflet about upcoming England fixtures, a ticket for a youth international and a keyring also bearing an FA logo.

Dave Sexton was a man of few words, but he was an excellent coach and a really lovely man.

In May 1983 Jimmy Hill was forced out as the club's Chairman, with former player Iain Jamieson taking over. It was a turbulent time for the club, and Dave Sexton was sacked.

In his place, the club appointed a manager already well-known to the Sky Blues faithful. He was to become very well known to me and my family thereafter, and I was put in touch with him through another family friend.

Rumours abounded that the new man in charge would be Coventry-born former Sky Blues striker Bobby Gould. Word went around that Bobby had been in the crowd of just 7,437 at Highfield Road watching a desperately poor Sky Blues team lose 2-1 to Burnley in the last match of the season. City finished fourth from bottom, just one point above the three relegated sides, Manchester City, Swansea and Brighton.

That evening in the Mercia Sound newsroom, after I had returned from the match, I received a phone call from a man called Jack Leavers. Jack's second wife was a close friend of my mother-in-law, and the two families got on well.

Jack was something of a legend as a teacher in Coventry. At the time he was a lecturer at Coventry Technical College. Jack had three main loves, his family, educating young people and Coventry City Football Club. He was also a friend of Bobby Gould and he had followed Bobby's progress, from his days as a pupil at Caludon Castle School in Coventry, through the many and various moves of his career.

As a natural goal scorer, Gould had been regularly sought after in the transfer market. He'd found the net 40 times in 82 appearances for Coventry City in the 60s, which led to his first move to Arsenal. Thereafter, he signed for Wolverhampton Wanderers twice, West Bromwich Albion, Bristol City, West Ham United, Bristol Rovers and Hereford United, scoring freely for all of them.

After his playing days he'd been caretaker manager at Chelsea and then, for two years, he was manager at Bristol Rovers. Now he was coming back home, and family friend Jack Leavers was able to put me in touch with him.

"Stuart," Jack said when I took the call, "you can ignore all those people saying that Bobby Gould has been at Highfield Road today. He lives in Bristol, and he's been shopping there this afternoon with his wife."

Before I could say anything in reply, Jack continued, "Do you want his phone number?"

I gratefully wrote down the number, exchanged pleasantries with Jack and thanked him for the call. I went into a recording booth and dialled the number Jack had given me. Bobby Gould answered.

He asked how I got hold of his number, and I told him that it had been passed on by a mutual friend.

"It wouldn't be Jack Leavers would it?" he laughed. "Well done. You found me. What do you want to know?"

"I'd like to record an interview with you please, and ask you a couple of questions."

He laughed again.

"Not now," he said. "No interview tonight, but what were your questions?"

"Were you at Highfield Road today?" I asked. "Will you be in charge of Coventry City from Monday?"

"No, and yes," he said. "I was shopping with my wife in Bristol this afternoon. You can say that, but I don't want to record anything tonight. Be at Highfield Road at half-past nine on Monday morning and I'll talk to you then. Yes, I will be there on Monday."

In fact, Bobby had not been shopping with his wife at all. In his autobiography '24 Carat Gould', co-written with journalist David Instone, Bobby reveals that his departure from Bristol Rovers to take up the Coventry job had been ill-received by Rovers' Chairman Martin Flook. Bobby was leaving Rovers with seventeen months to go on his contract and Flook had banned him from attending their last match of the season against Cardiff City.

Upset by the turn of events, Bobby says he parked his car near to Rovers' Eastville Stadium where he could hear the crowd noise as the match was being played. He had certainly not been at Highfield Road.

The version of events that had him shopping with his wife was what was duly reported, and that Saturday evening's phone call was the start of a professional and personal relationship that has stood the test of time. I duly arrived at Highfield Road on the Monday morning, along with other reporters, and met Bobby in person for the first time.

I was asked to go to the manager's office and wait for him there. It was no more than a couple of minutes before Bobby joined me, and I remember very clearly what Bobby said.

"Good morning Stuart. I have to say that you're the best-dressed reporter I've seen today".

I was wearing a collar and tie and a dark blue blazer. That was fairly normal for me, and I didn't regard it as the least bit special. However the other reporters had been attired, I had apparently impressed the new manager.

"How do you know Jack Leavers?" he asked, and I proceeded to relate the family connection, that my mother-in-law had gone to school with Jack's wife. That made Bobby laugh.

"That's Coventry. Everybody knows everybody else."

There would be several more interviews with Bobby Gould that Summer, as eight players left and eleven arrived. At that first meeting, Bobby had shown me his 'little black book', full of the names and details of players he had assessed, from all levels of the game, in the league and in non-league football. That book was invaluable as he brought in Dave Bennett, Terry Gibson, Trevor Peake, Michael Gynn and Sam Allardyce, amongst others.

Some weeks after the others, Stuart Pearce was signed after Bobby took his wife Marge for a night out. Her treat was to go with Bobby to see a non-league football match at Yeovil because he wanted to watch Pearce play. A defender with a strong left foot, he was an electrician who played as a semi-professional for Wealdstone.

After just a few minutes, Pearce put in a solid challenge that, strongly but fairly, put an opposing player onto the side of the pitch and won the ball.

Bobby told Marge that he had seen enough. They left the match and went for a meal, so Marge had her night out after all.

The next day, Coventry City agreed to a £30,000 fee for Pearce, and on 12th November 1983, he made his professional debut as left-back for Coventry City in a 1-0 home win against Queen's Park Rangers.

That season proved to be every bit the huge challenge that Bobby Gould had told me it would be in that first interview, although it did include one of the club's most famous victories. On 10th December 1983 at Highfield Road, the Sky Blues beat a Liverpool side packed with star names. Bruce Grobbelar, Phil Neal, Mark Lawrenson, Alan Hansen, Kenny Dalglish and Ian Rush were in the visiting team beaten by 4 goals to nil.

An attendance of 20,649 was at Highfield Road that day to see Nicky Platnaeur open the scoring in the first minute. Terry Gibson scored the rest, becoming the first Coventry City player to score a hat-trick against Liverpool.

Despite that historic win, Coventry City again finished just one place above the relegation zone, with a 2-1 win against Norwich City on the last day of the season proving to be just enough to keep them up.

1983 was not only a year of change for the football club, but it was a similar story at Mercia Sound. I received a 'phone call from my former colleague Ralph Bernard, whom I had last been in touch with at Radio Hallam when he sent me in pursuit of Michael Parkinson as a narrator for his documentary series about alcoholism.

As the ILR network expanded Ralph had been appointed as the first News Editor at Hereward Radio in Peterborough, before moving to Wiltshire Radio in Swindon, where he was the launch Programme Director. His 'phone call was to invite me to join him for lunch to discuss something he would like me to consider.

It transpired that Ralph was on the point of being promoted to Managing Director at Wiltshire Radio, based in their Limekiln Studios at Wootton Bassett. He asked me if I would be prepared to join him as his Programme Director. It was a more than pleasant lunch at his home, where his lovely wife Lisa supplied the food before leaving us to chat. Ralph outlined his thinking about how he wanted his station to work, and in particular how the key breakfast and drive-time shows would function, with a DJ and a journalist co-presenting as a team to deliver both music and news in a seamless format.

He gave me a lot to think about, which I promised I would do. I stressed however that the decision would be as much Sue's as mine, as she had her family around her in Coventry. My relationship with Ian was also important to me. Ralph obviously knew Ian well, so I did not have to dwell on that too long.

After a long chat with Sue, who made it clear that she would support whatever decision I made, I slept on it and called Ralph the following day. I thanked him for his offer and told him I had been genuinely impressed and tempted by what he had laid before me. However, I did not think that it was the right time for me to move on and I felt it appropriate to stay in Coventry and continue to work alongside Ian.

Ralph was more than gracious in his response, saying he fully understood and added that my loyalty to Ian was to be commended. From a distance, I then followed Ralph's career as he became one of the most powerful and influential figures in UK commercial radio history.

One of Ralph's first moves after our conversation was to recruit one of my favourite DJs, Johnnie Walker, who had been born in my home city of Birmingham a couple of years before me. I would have relished working with Johnnie, whom Ralph had persuaded to move to Wiltshire Radio from nearby Radio West in Bristol. Soon afterwards Ralph acquired Radio West as well, the Bristol station being ripe for takeover because of serious financial worries. Those two neighbouring stations were both renamed GWR, operating as one entity, and Ralph's impressive career was on the launch pad and about to rocket forward.

What happened next added more than a touch of irony to my decision not to move to Wiltshire. Ian Rufus resigned as Mercia Sound's Programme Controller to launch another yet new ILR station, this time in Hull. He was appointed Managing Director of Viking Radio, which served the East Riding of Yorkshire and North & North East Lincolnshire.

Mercia Sound now had a key vacancy, on par with the job offer I had turned down from Ralph Bernard. It was apparent that John Bradford wanted to make a new appointment as quickly as he could. I think he had discussed it with Ian, but the upshot was that he invited Dave Jamieson and me to join him for, as he put it, "a plate of spaghetti and a bottle of wine."

John had decided to take us to Quo Vadis. My old friend Giovanni welcomed us in his usual inimitable way, asking me "Your usual table Stuart?"

"That would be great Giovanni," I answered. "Thank you."

Whether John was impressed by that display of familiarity from within the local community, particularly with a local advertiser, I have no idea, but I doubt it did any harm.

Dave and I thus faced each other across a table with John Bradford at Quo Vadis. It was certainly a highly unusual way of conducting a recruitment process, effectively interviewing two rival candidates simultaneously in a casual social environment. I am pretty certain that Dave found it an uncomfortable experience, and I was certainly unsure how to play it.

John, I am sure, wanted us both to talk freely and frankly and if he could, lead us towards working together, whoever got the job. He probably also wanted to observe how we interacted with each other. The food, as ever, was excellent but it was the conversation that was much more important.

The following day John called me into his office and offered me the role of Programme Controller. Sue and I celebrated that night by stopping off on the way home at another favourite restaurant, where steaks were the speciality, for a meal and a glass of wine. It would have been a bottle, but I was driving.

My promotion meant an on-air reshuffle and the appointment of a new Sports Editor, but I was determined not to distance myself from the programme schedule and I continued for a time to host the afternoon show.

Inevitably, there were many arrivals and departures in the years that followed. The most significant for the radio station, and for me personally, was the return of Ian Rufus less than twelve months after he had moved to Viking Radio. In fact, Ian made his exit from Viking before it was even launched, when he came back to replace John Bradford who had, in turn, decided it was time to move on.

Ian was installed as Managing Director, and I continued as Programme Controller. The personnel merry-go-round went even further when Dave Jamieson moved to the station Ian had just left, becoming Programme Organiser at Viking Radio in Hull. The revolving door of management and presenter changes made little impact on the public response to Mercia Sound. It was now well established in Coventry and Warwickshire, and continued success looked set to continue.

At Radio Hallam, Ian and I had been part of the radio station's annual charity fund-raising project called the 'Money Mountain.' It was a day-long radio marathon, otherwise referred to as a 'Radiothon', devised to raise funds "to relieve poverty, sickness and physical or mental handicap, particularly amongst children under 18 who reside or whose parents reside in the broadcasting area of Radio Hallam."

It ran close to Christmas, deliberately much closer than the BBC's Children In Need project, which usually occurs in November. It was successful, raising significant funds for its stated causes in Sheffield and adding to the general awareness of the radio station.

At Mercia Sound, we set about doing something similar, but we faced a different dilemma. There was not only Children In Need to consider as a rival fundraiser, but also a Christmas appeal run by the *Coventry Evening Telegraph*. It seemed obvious to me that in an area like Coventry and Warwickshire, it was nonsense for the local radio station and the local newspaper to compete with each other in charity appeals. Both wanted to raise funds to benefit the local community. Ian had similar thoughts and we quickly agreed that we should approach the 'paper and explore whether they were prepared to talk to us about some form of joint venture.

The arrival of a new media entity was obviously an issue for the *Coventry Telegraph*. We were not only pursuing their readers to be our listeners, with consequent competition in the news arena, but we were also keen to persuade their local advertisers to spend money with the radio station. With some justification, the newspaper was not entirely convinced that local advertisers would spend more across both media outlets. Their fear was that to advertise on Mercia, local businesses would simply reduce the amount they spent with the *Telegraph*. When some of the 'paper's advertising sales staff were persuaded to move and recruited to work at the radio station, it added to their concern.

At Mercia Sound, we were also conscious of the competition for advertisers. Several local businesses had successfully used the newspaper over many years, and they would take some persuading to switch their allegiance to this new upstart radio station. Mercia's sales team devised a strategy whereby several seminars were held for specially invited local advertisers. They received presentations from various advertising gurus, some American, some Australian, and some from the UK.

Whilst the object of the exercise was clearly to persuade them to spend their money on the radio, it was always stressed that they would get a better return if they used both branches of the media, and yet more again by increasing their overall spending on advertising. Some responded positively, but others were not so sure and the sales war between the two outlets was occasionally quite intense.

The *Coventry Evening Telegraph* had occupied the patch, without any form of serious local competition, since 1891. In that year, William Iliffe founded the *Midland Daily Telegraph* as Coventry's first daily newspaper. It was at first a four-page broadsheet newspaper, changing its name to the *Coventry Evening Telegraph* in 1941.

The Iliffe family owned the paper and its sister titles in Birmingham for 96 years. A hereditary peerage was bestowed on the family in 1933, with William's son Edward being made the first Baron Iliffe. After such a lengthy monopoly the new concept of commercial local radio presented the 'paper with a new challenge and a major competitor.

With that backdrop, Ian and I sought a meeting with the Editor of the *Telegraph*, Geoffrey Elliott. Geoffrey was widely respected, with BBC radio and TV presenter Jeremy Vine one of those who worked for him. Jeremy cut his journalistic teeth under Geoffrey Elliott in Coventry. In an article in *The Guardian* in 2016, Jeremy said:

"At the time, the editor (Geoffrey Elliott) was like a god. Once a week he would send around this page of A4 about where the paper had gone wrong and what needed to change –I read these circulars intently, I was so keen to learn. One of the things he said was never to use the word incident or situation because they have no meaning. I've always remembered that, and I've never used those words, whether it's on Radio 2 or at Westminster or in Africa."

Geoffrey was a fine and highly regarded journalist, so much so that in 2004 when he was made CBE in the Queen's Birthday Honours, it was noted in the *UK Press Gazette* that he was thought to be the only journalist to have served on the Press Council, the Press Complaints Commission and the Broadcasting Standards Commission. He went on to be head of journalism at the University of Central Lancashire, before retiring to Devon.

We were therefore faced with the task of persuading an impressive and by no means insignificant character in our attempt to create a mutually beneficial annual charity event. Geoffrey listened intently to what we had to say, occasionally chipping in with slightly sardonic comments about Mercia Sound wanting to pin itself to the coattails of the *Evening Telegraph*. He wanted to understand how broadcast journalism worked. He was critical of the way a news story on the radio would be illustrated by a short, single interview clip in a brief bulletin. He felt that as a result, we were not telling the whole story. Geoffrey and Ian spent some time discussing in close detail how radio news worked.

They did not entirely agree, at least not at that first meeting, but I think it was a conversation that led Geoffrey Elliott to understand that Mercia Sound was not a "here today, gone tomorrow" entity, and should be taken seriously. He clearly accepted that we were a credible presence, but he made clear that he would face a difficult debate were he to put forward any plan about a joint charity idea to his fellow executives, particularly with his advertising sales director.

It was at a second meeting with Geoffrey, over lunch at a pub called 'The City Arms' in Earlsdon, that we were able to find the solution that worked for both of us. The newspaper and the radio station would each credit the other when appealing for funds and for public support. We would share the editorial stories of the fund-raising activities of Mercia listeners and *Telegraph* readers, and we would collaborate on how the money was spent.

I suggested the name 'Snowball', to which Geoffrey insisted the word 'charity' was added making it 'Charity Snowball'. Separately to the appeal, and as a deliberately quite distinct entity from either media organisation, The Snowball Trust was formed consisting of leading members of the local community. They included a surgeon, a lawyer, and a bank manager. It fell to them, rather than to us, to decide how the funds would be distributed, working to the criteria that it was for the benefit of chronically sick and disabled children in Coventry, Warwickshire and South-West Leicestershire.

To his immense credit, Geoffrey recognised that Mercia's impact on the region had been by no means insignificant. He also agreed that the newspaper and the radio station, working together, would attract a larger sum from fundraisers than the two would achieve by continuing to work separately.

At the same time, the notion that advertisers would consider that using both would be similarly beneficial was not lost on him either. The principle of enhancing the community was the more persuasive element in the conversation. Nonetheless, the *Telegraph* had an image of itself that if ever a really serious battle for advertising revenue ensued, the newspaper would prevail by virtue of its longevity. That was a view clearly held by the newspaper's senior executives.

So, Charity Snowball was born with fundraising appeals both in print and on the radio put in front of the local populace in 1984. They loved it. Again, it was theirs. It belonged to the people of the area, and all manner of fund-raising activities took place, including the radio station's day-long push, through on-air auctions and a wide variety of appeals, to raise as much cash as possible.

Local auctioneer and property expert Harvey Williams, another link to Coventry City Football Club as their long-standing property adviser, was an invaluable help in co-ordinating the on-air auctions. His incorrigible, persuasive and persistent manner helped us raise thousands.

In the next ten years, Charity Snowball raised one million pounds, something that all those members of the public who contributed, and all the people at the *Coventry Evening Telegraph* and Mercia Sound who worked on it, can be justly proud.

Community was a keyword in all that we did, and many of us accepted invitations to go and talk to local people about what we did and how we did it. Some years after one visit I made to a local school, one of the pupils wrote:

"The first time I met Stuart Linnell was when, for a project, we had to interview a celebrity. We sent off requests to a few media places and Mercia Sound came back and said they would send someone. They sent Stuart. He stayed for what seemed like ages and answered our child-like questions. Feedback to the teacher was that he was a lovely person and that he talked a lot. The teacher said, "It's his job.""

The pupil in question was a young man called Terry Angus who went on to have a successful career as a professional footballer. Terry obtained 'legend' status amongst supporters at Northampton Town, Fulham and Nuneaton Borough. Throughout he remained a fan of his hometown club, Coventry City, though he never played for the Sky Blues. I would go on to meet and work with Terry many years later when he became a matchday pundit for another radio station that I worked for, and we became good friends.

The football club that Terry loved so much continued to struggle. Bobby Gould continued his rebuilding job, with six players leaving as he brought in goalkeeper Steve Ogrizovic, defenders Brian Kilcline and Kirk Stephens, midfielders Martin Jol and Kenny Hibbitt, and striker Bob Latchford. Whilst the manager rang the changes in the dressing room, the directors also went through their own reshuffle, chairman Iain Jamieson being replaced by Coventry-born businessman John Poynton.

John lived in Jersey, where he had founded a highly successful construction company called The Style Group. He made funds available to Bobby Gould for further recruitment. Bobby brought in an Assistant Manager in former Dundee boss Don Mackay.

More new players arrived, and at eight o'clock one morning, I received a call at home. He didn't introduce himself, but I immediately recognised Bobby's voice.

"Stuart are you on air this afternoon?" he asked.

"Yes, Bobby, I am. Why?"

"Would you like to interview our new signing? I can have him in the studio with you by two o'clock."

I did not give it a second thought.

"Yes, of course. Who is it?"

"Wait and see," he laughed. "He'll be with you at two."

The call ended and I was left excited and curious. Two names were being linked with Coventry City, both strikers. One was Alan Brazil, and the other was Cyrille Regis. The latter was the talk of the City fans, although few thought it was likely that he would move from West Bromwich Albion to Coventry. Such a move was ridiculed by national newspaper reporters, who reported the speculation but dismissed it out of hand, suggesting that if Regis was going to move it would be to one of the top six clubs in England, or possibly to somewhere in Europe.

I guessed that they had got it wrong and that Cyrille was going to walk through the door of my studio at two o'clock. There was still considerable uncertainty so I reported what I knew to be the case, that Coventry City's new signing would be revealed on my show that afternoon.

After the two o'clock news, I anxiously checked over my shoulder through the studio window into the radio station's reception area, partly to ensure that a footballer had arrived and also to see for myself who it was. I knew that Bobby would not let me down, and sure enough, the receptionist was about to ask me if she should show my guest into the studio.

Before she could finish, I said "Yes, of course."

Into the studio walked a player who had indeed played for West Brom, but it was not big Cyrille. Instead, arriving in Coventry from Leeds United was England international Peter Barnes. He was a relaxed and entertaining interviewee and his appearance on Mercia Sound instantly had the phones ringing.

Within a week Cyrille did arrive, and presented more conventionally through a press conference at Highfield Road, with a larger than usual press corps in attendance. Many of them from the national 'papers all asked Cyrille the same question, "Why Coventry?"

* * * *

The Coventry City supporters were not bothered by that. Cyrille Regis was the sort of big name signing that they had been waiting for and he was welcomed with open arms. However, it was several weeks before he got on the score sheet, scoring on the same day that Peter Barnes scored his first for the club. It was ironically a 5-2 defeat at their old club, West Bromwich Albion.

Despite Bobby Gould's best efforts it turned into an erratic season of results, and two days before Christmas in 1984, City crashed 5-1 at Leicester, with Bobby so incensed that he marched onto the Filbert Street pitch during the match. To add to City's demise, the referee awarded Leicester a dubious penalty, but City were poor.

When the penalty was awarded, his unbuttoned overcoat billowing either side of him as he strode onto the playing surface, Bobby appeared determined to remonstrate with someone. Thankfully for him, the referee did not see him. Steve Ogrizovic did and gestured urgently to his manager to return to the dugout. Fortunately, our microphones did not pick up what Oggy said.

There were far fewer cameras recording the action in those days, so Bobby got away with that burst of anger, but a 2-0 defeat at Luton in the following match was the last straw for Chairman John Poynton. It was Boxing Day, and Mercia Sound was busy with listeners arriving at the radio station to hand over their money and collect auction items they had secured during the Snowball broadcast. In the midst of it all, I was summoned to the phone. It was Bobby Gould to tell me he was out.

He agreed to be interviewed over the phone and said, in typical Gould fashion, "It's Christmas Stuart. Santa has been and all he had for me was the sack."

Last Christmas, I gave you my heart

But the very next day you gave it away

This year, to save me from tears

I'll give it to someone special

George Michael, 1984

Chapter Thirteen

A New Vision

There won't be snow in Africa this Christmas time

The greatest gift they'll get this year is life

Where nothing ever grows

No rain or rivers flow

Do they know it's Christmas time at all?

Midge Ure & Bob Geldof, 1984

© Warner Chappell Music, Inc.

In 1983 there was another new element in the local media scene in Coventry as Coventry Cable Television arrived.

Across the country cable television was making its mark, quite literally. Roads, footpaths, and in some cases, people's gardens, were being dug up so that cable could be laid underground to deliver multi-channel television to people's homes.

It offered nothing like the range of new channels that have followed since the advent of satellite services and such systems as Freeview, but cable TV was innovative, and to start with it included local content. Coventry Cable Television was run by John Ross Barnard, an experienced broadcaster who had started his career in pirate radio in the 60s. John worked on Invicta Radio, based on one of the former military forts in the Thames Estuary. He was also on board the pirate station Britain Radio before becoming a newsreader on Swinging Radio England.

Later John was appointed Head of BBC video, before becoming chief executive of Coventry Cable Television. When Ian Rufus returned from Viking

Radio he saw the opportunities for cross promotion between the Cable TV company and Mercia Sound. He and John Ross Barnard worked together on developing a local TV channel which they called COLT, which stood for Coventry's Own Local Television.

COLT contributed to the cost of Mercia employing more journalists, and that additional newsroom staffing enabled a 20-minute local news programme to be shown on COLT each evening. Mercia's reporters would take a camera crew with them so that they could produce a filmed version of the stories that they were reporting on for the radio station. At one point, there was a team of twelve journalists based at Mercia Sound, serving both the radio station and the local TV channel.

The news output of the joint radio and TV exercise was highly regarded. Executives from both the BBC and ITN visited Coventry to see how it worked. TV producer Mike Hollingsworth was involved for a time, helping to provide a polished sheen to the news programme, and offering particular guidance to the radio journalists about how to apply their skills to television.

My focus remained on the radio station's output, but I also contributed from time to time with some of the content on COLT. On one occasion, with a COLT camera crew I followed one of the most significant international events of the decade.

* * * *

While we were providing Coventry, Warwickshire and South-West Leicestershire with the area's first local radio station and assisting its local TV channel, there was a major crisis affecting the most populous landlocked country in the world. The second-most populous nation on the African continent. Ethiopia, suffered a widespread famine, made worse by human rights abuses.

Between 1983 and 1985 1.2 million people died. According to the organisation Human Rights Watch, 400,000 refugees left the country, and 2.5 million people were internally displaced. Almost 200,000 children were orphaned.

On 23rd October 1984, a BBC news crew was the first to document the famine, with reporter Michael Buerk describing it as "a biblical famine in the 20th century" and "the closest thing to hell on Earth". Buerk's report on the

BBC Nine O'Clock News that evening on BBC One was picked up on by news programmes around the world.

Photojournalist Mohamed Amin was the cameraman working with Buerk for that report, and he later described it as one of "the most influential pieces of television ever broadcast." It shocked the world, and the initial British response was a flood of public donations to relief charities such as the 'Save The Children'.

Michael Buerk's report was seen by Irish rock singer Bob Geldof whose band, The Boomtown Rats, had hit singles in the late 70s with "Rat Trap" and "I Don't Like Mondays". Geldof, helped by his then partner, TV presenter Paula Yates, contacted an old friend in Midge Ure, the lead singer of the band Ultravox. Geldof said that he wanted to bring together pop and rock artists to contribute in some way to the Ethiopian relief effort. They decided their best option would be to make a charity record.

Geldof set lined up artists who were prepared to be involved, and he also secured promises that everyone would provide their services free of charge. They needed a song. Ure came up with the tune and Geldof the lyrics. The result was "Do They Know It's Christmas?", with its repetitive chorus "feed the world". The group of stars on the record included Sting, Bono, Paul Young, George Michael, Phil Collins, Boy George, Tony Hadley, and Simon Le Bon. Siobhan Fahey and Keren Woodward, both from Bananarama also took part, whilst Geldof and Ure were also amongst the ensemble. They called it Band Aid.

The record was released on 3rd December 1984 and went straight to number one. For a time, it was the biggest selling record of all-time in the UK. That success did not satisfy Geldof. The rock singer was also a campaigner, and he was determined to harness the response that Michael Buerk's report had triggered and that the hit record had built on. He wanted to raise enough money to enable proper change in Ethiopia.

His enthusiasm was matched by singer Boy George, who with his band Culture Club had embarked on a tour of the UK, scheduled to end at Wembley Arena. On the final night at Wembley, an impromptu gathering of some of the other artists from the Band Aid record joined Culture Club on stage for an encore of "Do They Know It's Christmas?". It was so well received it gave George the idea of staging a benefit concert.

Taking George's idea Geldof immediately swung into action, his efforts resulting in the world's biggest stars performing in an event held simultaneously at Wembley Stadium in London, attended by more than 70,000 people, and at John F. Kennedy Stadium in Philadelphia, in America, where the audience numbered exactly 89,484. Concerts were also held in seven other countries on the same day. UK concert promoter Harvey Goldsmith took charge of the concert at Wembley, which was called Live Aid.

Nearly 40% of the world's population watched the Live Aid concert live on television. 1.9 billion people tuned in across 150 nations. Geldof later said, "We took an issue that was nowhere on the political agenda and, through the lingua franca of the planet, which is not English but rock 'n' roll, we were able to address the intellectual absurdity and the moral repulsion of people dying of want in a world of surplus."

It gripped everyone. Sue and I were part of that worldwide audience, watching from home, as Status Quo opened the concert with "Rocking All Over The World." We were absorbed by the whole thing and like the rest of the nation we were stirred by Geldof into realising it was not just a TV show, it was also a fund raiser.

He was unhappy with the amount raised from early donations, so he took matters into his own hands. BBC TV presenter David Hepworth was attempting to give out a postal address for potential donations only to be interrupted by an impatient Geldof who shouted, live on mid-afternoon TV, "Fuck the address, let's get the numbers".

After that outburst the rate and amount of donations increased markedly. The next day Mercia Sound joined other broadcasters in reporting that between £40 million and £50 million had been raised. The figure later reached approximately £150 million, raised directly from the Live Aid concerts.

* * * *

Thrown together incredibly quickly, it inevitably had one or two technical hitches, but Live Aid was not only a fund-raising success, as it also provided some memorable performances. Status Quo, David Bowie, Paul McCartney and Elton John were amongst the stars on stage at Wembley, whilst Phil Collins made history by appearing on both sides of the Atlantic on the same day. He first performed at Wembley, then took a helicopter piloted by TV and radio star Noel Edmonds to Heathrow Airport. There he then caught a supersonic Concorde jet to New York, where another helicopter was waiting to take him to Philadelphia.

Amidst it all the performance that is most remembered from Live Aid was by Queen. Their 21-minute performance was later voted the greatest live performance in the history of rock in a poll of more than 60 artists, journalists and music industry executives. During the set Queen's lead vocalist Freddie Mercury took command of the crowd, leading them as if they'd been rehearsed, in chants and choruses. The group performed 6 songs, opening with a shortened version of "Bohemian Rhapsody" and closing with "We Are the Champions. It was jaw-droppingly stunning, with Freddie Mercury outstanding.

* * * *

After the concerts, Geldof then faced controversies over the realities of using the money in Ethiopia. There were allegations that at least some of it was being diverted from the people who needed it. It was suggested that it had either been retained by corrupt officials and politicians in Africa for their own ends, or even used to purchase weapons.

Radio stations and newspapers from all over the UK were invited to a major PR event in London ostensibly to focus on the success of Live Aid. I went with a camera crew from Coventry Cable TV and we took our turn to grab a word with Bob Geldof.

Quite rightly Geldof wanted to underline the generosity of the artists who had given their time, as well as that of the British public in the financial support they had provided. Despite that, the stories of funds being siphoned off without achieving the intended aim of relieving the famine in Ethiopia had gained traction. Geldof was having none of it and he was ready to deflect and bluntly put down any hint of criticism.

I wanted to get the controversy out of the way and then go on to ask him to expand on the stunning success of Live Aid. It was the wrong tactic. If I had approached it the other way round, I would probably have received answers on all points.

As it was, he became quite angry when I asked him about the structures he had in place to avoid the money ending up in the wrong hands. His response was brusque and dismissive and the interview did not last very long.

It hadn't helped that Geldof was coming under pressure over the issue from some of the tabloid newspapers, particularly the *Daily Express* and the *Daily Mail*.

Much later Geldof toured commercial radio stations throughout the country to thank them for their support for both Band Aid and Live Aid. When he came to Mercia Sound Geldof was interviewed by Jeff Harris, who had taken over my afternoon show, and it was all much more positive. Jeff's questions had centred on the logistics of producing both the record and the concert, and he allowed Geldof to talk about the work that was still needed to help Ethiopia recover.

Ironically, in the course of explaining that, he touched on the difficulties of keeping the money out of the clutches of corrupt elements along the way. Jeff had approached the interview in a much more sensible order than I had.

* * * *

Bob Geldof continues to campaign for equitable and sustainable development in Africa. In 1986, he was made an Honorary Knight Commander of the Order of the British Empire. The "honorary" bit refers to the fact that he is Irish, and thus not a citizen of the British Commonwealth. That has not prevented people referring to him as "Sir Bob."

Oh, oh, oh tell me why

I don't like Mondays

Tell me why

I don't like Mondays

Tell me why

I don't like Mondays

I want to shoot

The whole day down

Bob Geldof, 1979

© Universal Music Publishing Group

My Granddad knew Rasputin ... and I met Elton John

Chapter Fourteen

Cup Winners

Relax, don't do it

When you want to go to it

Relax, don't do it

When you want to come

Relax, don't do it

When you want to sock it to it

Relax, don't do it

When you want to come

When you want to come

Peter Gill, Holly Johnson, Brian Nash, Mark O'Toole, 1983

© Perfect Songs Ltd.

One of the most controversial and most commercially successful records of the decade reached number 1 on the UK charts on my birthday, 22nd January 1984. "Relax", by Frankie Goes To Hollywood, went on to sell 2 million copies in the UK alone, making it the seventh best-selling single in the history of the UK Singles Chart.

Its success was partly borne out of controversy over the song's lyrics. When it first entered the chart in November 1983 it was at number 67, climbed slowly into the Top 30, and then slipped back down again. After an appearance on the BBC TV show 'Top Of The Pops' all that changed, and it smashed its way into the Top 10.

A week later Radio One DJ Mike Read announced on air that because of the overtly sexual content in the lyrics, and what he described as a suggestive sleeve for the record, he was going to refuse to play it on his show. What he did not say was that the BBC had already decided that it would not be played in daytime programmes in any case.

It was played by ILR stations as it hit No. 1 and it stayed there for five weeks, making the whole episode something of an embarrassment for the BBC who had by now also banned it from 'Top Of The Pops'. It reinforced the presence and credibility of the commercial stations as their popularity also grew, many of them providing a serious challenge to Radio One and Radio Two in their transmission areas.

* * * *

Mercia Sound was very aware of the importance of playing current hits, but also of reflecting the interests of the local community. That extended to marking anniversaries such as the 40th anniversary of VE Day in 1985.

Coventry's wartime history, stemming from the Blitz in November 1940, and its consequent legacy of peace and reconciliation are continuing elements of Coventry life. The city is always conscious of the need to mark key anniversaries, so when the time came for the commemoration of Nazi Germany's unconditional surrender on 8th May 1945, the radio station was ready to play its part.

ILR stations were at that time obliged to spend 3% of their revenue on the employment of live musicians. It was part of the deal agreed with the Musicians Union which allowed radio stations to play pop records. Mercia Sound, along with other stations, spent that 3% by staging concerts at local venues.

I booked Coventry's Central Hall, the home of the Methodist Church, for a VE Night 40th Anniversary Concert. Although its primary function was that of a place of worship, Central Hall also served as a community centre and as a performance venue with nearly 1,000 seats. It was perfect for the show I had in mind. The concert would star singer Anne Shelton, who had been one of the favourites of service personnel when she performed at British military bases during the Second World War.

She had performed with Glenn Miller's orchestra and had enjoyed hits with "If You Ever Fall in Love Again", "Galway Bay", "Be Mine" and "Lili Marlene". After the war she was in the charts with "Lay Down Your Arms" and "Sailor". I knew she would go down well in Coventry and the public response was emphatic. It was a sell-out.

It was an emotional night with the audience including many servicemen, past and present, wearing their medals and ribbons, parading their banners. They gave Anne Shelton a standing ovation when she walked on stage and at the end of her performance.

The Lord Mayor of Coventry that year was Councillor Bill McKernan, a Burma Star veteran. Wearing his military medals and his chain of office, he was our guest of honour and he asked me if he could meet Miss Shelton.

She readily agreed and I took Bill backstage during the interval. He very formally shook her by the hand, almost bowing to her which made her laugh, so she put her arms round him and gave him a hug. The hardnosed rugged Councillor, with a reputation for having a stern façade, burst into tears. After he brought himself together, he told Anne that her songs had kept him going in the army when times were tough, and that meeting her that evening was the greatest night of his life.

We recorded the concert and broadcast it that weekend as a special programme. We had a thrilled Lord Mayor, an ecstatic audience, a delighted star performer and an excellent show on tape. All in all it was a memorable night for Coventry and for its local radio station.

* * * *

That same year an historic meeting of two British entertainers occurred at the Mercia Sound studios. It was just before Christmas in 1985, and the Apollo Theatre in Coventry was preparing to stage its pantomime, which that year was Cinderella. In the cast was comedian and TV star Michael Barrymore, Linda Nolan from the Nolan Sisters, and the Roly Polys comedy dance troupe. We also had a TV favourite for the kids, Lenny The Lion, the puppet creation of ventriloquist Terry Hall. Terry was born in Lancashire but by now lived in Coventry.

Michael Barrymore had worked with both the Nolans and the Roly Polys before. He had already had publicity photos taken with the Rolys on the morning that he came to Mercia Sound to appear on the afternoon show. Local presenter Jim Lee, from Nuneaton, was presenting that programme.

The plan was that Michael would be interviewed alongside Terry Hall and Lenny The Lion. Terry was the one member of the cast that Michael had not met before. Michael arrived in good time, about twenty minutes before he was due on air, but when the time came for the interview there was no sign of Terry.

I knew Terry fairly well. He was one of the nicest men you could wish to meet, and he was punctilious in his time keeping. It was most unusual for him to be anything other than early for an appointment. He liked to have the opportunity to take stock of his surroundings and prepare himself for whatever was expected of him.

Time was passing, so I showed Michael Barrymore into the studio and introduced him to Jim Lee. Terry lived a short distance from the radio station so I had my fingers crossed that it would not be too long before he turned up. Jim said he would start the interview with Michael, and we agreed that I would usher Terry into the studio as soon as he arrived, ignoring the red light which indicated that the studio was live.

Sure enough, no sooner had Jim begun the interview with Barrymore that a hot and flustered Terry Hall arrived, full of apologies. He had been delayed for reasons that he started to explain, but I was more concerned about putting him on air than in hearing why he had been held up.

Taking a deep breath he agreed to go straight into the studio. Carrying a suitcase, Terry took the seat I directed him to. I left them to it, quietly closing the door behind me, leaving Jim to introduce Terry and Lenny live on air to Michael Barrymore.

"Is this really the first time you have met?" Jim asked.

"Yes, it is," beamed Barrymore, looking towards Terry Hall.

"I think so," said Terry as if that had not occurred to him before.

"So you won't have met Lenny then Michael?" said Jim.

284

"No not yet," said Barrymore, still focusing his attention on Terry.

Terry said nothing and just sat there. Jim jumped into the silence and also looked at Terry for a response.

"I expect Lenny would like to meet Michael, Terry," Jim said, expectantly.

Still nothing from Terry Hall. I was watching fascinated through the window from the next studio as Jim tried again.

"Is Lenny nearby, Terry, or is he having a rest just now?"

Barrymore looked utterly bemused, as the penny eventually seemed to drop with Terry.

"Yes, he's here," said Terry. "You'd like to say 'hello' to him then?"

"Yes please," Jim replied, and Terry undid the catches of his suitcase. Jim did not even try to explain to his listeners the noise of the suitcase being opened.

Terry's right arm reached into the case, and when it emerged there was Lenny The Lion. With a wholly unexpected burst of energy we heard him speak for the first time that afternoon.

"Hello," Lenny's slightly camp falsetto voice exclaimed. "You must be Michael. I have been so looking forward to meeting you."

Hearing Lenny's voice for the first time, prompted an instant reaction from Michael Barrymore. His eyebrows shot upwards, his face creased in a huge smile. For a moment I thought he was going to collapse in hysterical laughter, but within no more than a couple of seconds he got it. You could see him thinking, "it's going to be OK", as he realised that you would never hear Lenny's voice unless the puppet was present.

"And it's my pleasure to meet you," said Michael, adding, "at last."

He paused before he said, "In fact you are the nicest lion I've met today."

"Aw, don't embawass me!" came back Lenny's famous catchphrase.

Jim managed to stifle his laugh and the interview proceeded without any further hitch, other than a wooden clacking sound every time Lenny opened and closed his mouth. Terry was ensuring that the doll was 'talking' into the nearest microphone.

After the interview Terry was once again full of apologies for being late, and I left him, Lenny and Michael Barrymore in the charge of a producer whose job it was to record them for an advertisement for the panto. Having observed what had happened during the interview, the producer had rigged a dummy mic for Lenny to use to avoid unwarranted extraneous noise.

When you meet your heroes your expectations are often, inevitably, extremely high. So it was when the man who called himself "the Greatest" came to Coventry. He had been born Cassius Clay, but after becoming the heavyweight champion of the world in 1964 he took the name Muhammad Ali.

He was an incredibly handsome man and rightly regarded as a supreme athlete. Ali visited Coventry and Nuneaton as his managers processed him around the world to put him in front of his adoring public, but also to reap the rewards of his fame and notoriety.

So whilst it was a thrill and a privilege to spend just a few minutes in his company, whilst surrounded by hundreds of fans and other representatives of the media, it was also with more than a touch of sadness at seeing him trotted out as little more than a show pony. To add to my angst twelve months later Ali was diagnosed with Parkinson's disease.

So it was a delight to meet him, but it was laced with huge regret.

* * * *

Our first child, Nicholas, was born in February 1983, with younger son Matthew following in July 1985. I was so proud to be a father with two beautiful boys. Sue was a brilliant mum, and the whole family were thrilled at our new arrivals.

Sue's mum and dad loved being grandparents and Sue's brothers, Mark and David, relished the fun of being Uncles. My sister, my Uncle and Aunt in Sheffield and all our relatives embraced our enlarged family.

Sue and I had lived in Nuneaton when Nicholas was born, but we had moved to Coventry before Matthew arrived. Both made their mark in their own ways.

There had been two or three marriages amongst the Mercia Sound team, and ours was the first to produce offspring. The *Coventry Evening Telegraph* asked if they could take a photo of Sue, me and Nick at Nuneaton Maternity Hospital. Right on cue my first-born looked bright eyed directly into the camera as a good friend, *Coventry Telegraph* photographer Bob Coles, took the picture.

Matthew was born at Coventry Maternity Hospital, and I was so excited when the time came to bring him home that I issued an unintended invitation for our house to be burgled. When I received the phone call that I could collect them I was in so much of a hurry to go to the hospital that I raced out of the house leaving the front door wide open.

Fortunately, Sue's elder brother Mark turned up with seconds of me driving away and he was able to keep everything safe and secure. Nick had been with his grandma while all this went on, but before long we were all together ready for the joys of bringing up our two lovely sons.

* * * *

At work the programming of Mercia Sound and the fortunes of Coventry City Football Club dominated my thoughts.

Don Mackay had replaced Bobby Gould as City manager, but just over a year later the likable Don was another managerial casualty. Once again, a survival act was required from the last match of the season. A 4-1 home win against Everton had ensured safety the season before, but this time it was a 2-1 victory against Queen's Park Rangers that did the trick. Once more it was by the skin of those Sky Blue teeth.

The managerial change that followed, in the spring of 1986, was to prove to be one of the most astute made in the history of the club. Two former players were put in temporary charge, before their roles were made permanent at the start of the 1986/87 season.

The fans were sceptical when former captain George Curtis, then the club's Executive Director, and youth team coach John Sillett, popularly known as "Snoz", were announced as the managerial double act. Inevitably the rumour machine had been at full speed suggesting various names to replace Mackay, but Chairman John Poynton decided that the two larger than life characters had something to offer.

Days after appointing Curtis and Sillett, John Poynton invited me and *Coventry Evening Telegraph* football reporter Neville Foulger to join him for lunch. Not just lunch, but lunch near his home on the island of Jersey. At the time a few summer flights from Coventry Airport took passengers to the Channel Islands, and Neville and I found ourselves en route to Jersey.

John had laid on lunch in Jersey at a plush, top-notch restaurant overlooking the English Channel. It had a breathtaking view of the French coast when the weather was kind, which it was that day. Unfortunately my stomach was not in such a generous mood. I had been perfectly fine when we left Coventry, but by the time we arrived at the restaurant I felt decidedly queasy, and I was sadly unable to enjoy the food.

They took pity on me and served me a very light chicken dish, but I struggled even with that. Neville, on the other hand, thoroughly enjoyed his lunch and we were both able to talk to John about his plans and thoughts for the football club. We both came away with interviews and a hugely useful off the record briefing, but whilst Neville flew home with the taste of French cuisine on his palate, I felt hungry, distinctly unwell, and disappointed at missing out on the culinary treat.

* * * *

I reflected a few times on the fact that my move from Sheffield was in part, at least, to seek a more successful football team to report on. My affinity to Coventry City had helped convince me that they would be that team, but the season after season battle against relegation meant that it had proved to be anything but. John Poynton's briefing, and his genuine enthusiasm for the club gave me hope

Meanwhile, away from football, my career progress had pointed me towards a new path. Becoming Programme Controller at Mercia Sound meant I had to become aware of the wider issues affecting commercial radio.

That meant having a full appraisal of how the system had developed. There had been a General Election in 1979, returning the Conservative party to power as the Government of the day. The Conservative leader was Margaret Thatcher who became the UK's first female Prime Minister, in the process removing Labour's James Callaghan from office. The Liberal party finished a poor third under its leader David Steel, after damaging allegations about his predecessor Jeremy Thorpe.

That election result brought a highly significant consequence for local radio. There was an instant expansion of the commercial network. The previous Labour government had approved nine new stations, including one in Coventry which became Mercia Sound. Now a further fifteen were given the green light by the new Government, with the ILR network almost doubling in size.

Audiences were good, local advertisers loved it, but the Achilles heel in the development of ILR was its relative failure to attract significant revenue from national advertisers. The situation was not helped by the network having developed in two tiers, with two different types of station. The big city stations took an aggressive commercial approach to their activities, while the smaller stations serving mainly rural areas put the focus much more overtly on community programming.

At Mercia Sound we fell between the two tiers to some degree. Coventry is a big city, but not of the same size as the likes of Birmingham, Liverpool and Manchester. Mercia included a swathe of rural, partly agricultural, locations within its patch. Localness was key for Mercia Sound and for nearby BRMB, but community content in news and programmes was more of an issue for Mercia than its Birmingham counterpart. Regardless, both felt that their success in attracting audiences warranted a larger share of the national advertising spend than came their way.

Within both tiers, there was general consensus in radio station board rooms across the country that an obstacle to future progress was what was regarded as unwarranted and unnecessary intrusion by the industry regulator, the Independent Broadcasting Authority (IBA). Tony Stoller, the Managing Director of Reading 210, one of the smaller stations, wrote an article in a trade magazine saying that ILR should be largely self-regulating with the role of the IBA being no more than a "guiding hand". He asked if there was any need for the IBA to be involved in almost every aspect of a station's output. Years later Tony Stoller became the Chief Executive of the IBA's successor as regulator, the Radio Authority.

David Pinnell, the Managing Director of BRMB, was amongst those campaigning for things to change. He was a keen advocate of a whole new tier of commercial radio, INR, or Independent National Radio. His theory was that a commercial station broadcasting to the whole nation would widen the appeal of radio advertising to the brands that preferred to use television. The consequence of that, Pinnell suggested, would see an influx of national advertising that would cascade to include local stations.

Pinnell spoke at a so-called "secret" meeting of radio station senior executives, held on 23rd June 1984 at the Sheraton Skyline Hotel at Heathrow Airport. It was known thereafter as the "Heathrow Meeting".

The stations called for a wholly new approach to way in which they were being regulated. They said that ILR was over-regulated, that the government should legislate for the lighter regulation of commercial radio, that there should be a substantial cut in transmitter costs, and that there should be an independent report on the future development of the network.

Changes in UK television played a part in all this. Breakfast television was launched in 1983, after both BBC and ITV had experimented with it. When I was at Radio Hallam I had watched in 1977 when another former BBC Radio Birmingham reporter, Bob Warman, hosted a trial run of Breakfast TV news for Yorkshire Television. It was Britain's first breakfast TV programme, with an experimental nine week run.

Six years later, in 1983, with commercial radio fighting hard to increase its national advertising, regularly scheduled breakfast television began across the UK. The BBC was determined to be first. It was, with the programme 'Breakfast Time' launching on BBC1 on 17th January. The hosts were Frank Bough, Selina Scott and Nick Ross.

ITV's "Good Morning Britain" made it on air on 1st February, with David Frost and Anna Ford in front of the cameras. That the ITV show went through chaos and trauma did nothing to help the commercial radio cause. It was another outlet for national advertisers with yet another new TV service, Channel 4 having launched just a few months before.

That expansion of commercial television had created more opportunities and more air time than ever before for advertisers to consider. The newspaper industry was swift to respond. Local and regional 'papers launched weekly free sheets, delivered free of charge through most, if not all, the letterboxes in their area. The competition for both local and national advertising had never been so intense.

* * * *

All this amounted to pressures and issues that I was aware of but not directly involved with until Ian Rufus once again influenced the direction of my life and career. In 1986 the New Year was welcomed in by heavy snow and sub-zero temperatures, just as Coventry was putting its economic faith in a new car. The Peugeot 309 went on sale in Britain, four months after its continental launch, built at the former Rootes factory at Ryton, some six miles from the city centre.

That ensured that Coventry's economy featured heavily in the news headlines, and made us all aware of the context in which we were making programmes and seeking to attract advertisers. As I and the Mercia team mulled over that, it was announced that David Pinnell had retired at Birmingham's BRMB Radio. After talking it over with Sue, I decided that if I were to make further progress I should apply for the job as Managing Director of the Birmingham station.

For me to get this job it was going to require something more than a convincing conversation in the social setting of an Italian restaurant. With Sue looking over my shoulder and applying her secretarial skills, I wrote a comprehensive and carefully prepared CV with an accompanying letter of application.

In response I received an invitation to attend an interview, which meant that I had negotiated the first hurdle. Sue and I allowed ourselves a tiny celebration, always being aware that actually winning the race was a long way off.

I had no idea who else had applied, and I knew that being Managing Director of a big city station like BRMB was a plumb job that would attract the best the industry could offer. I was also concerned that Ian Rufus would find out that I had applied, whether or not I was successful. In fairness to him, in the light of our long relationship and the way in which our career paths had intertwined, I decided to tell him.

Ian had a poker face. He often used to hide his thoughts in meetings with what appeared to be a vacant expression, when in fact he was actually taking everything on board whilst keeping his views to himself.

When I told him that I felt he should know that I had applied for the job at BRMB, he thanked me and wished me well for it with a typically enigmatic smile.

The interview was held in Birmingham city centre, though not at the radio station. The Chairman of BRMB at the time was John Parkinson, the principal of Solihull College, and he conducted the interview with two other members of his board of directors alongside him, both prominent Birmingham businessmen.

John Parkinson had a lifelong interest in radio, and despite his disarmingly vague and occasionally meandering bearing, which may have stemmed from his academic lifestyle, he was as switched on as anyone I have ever come across when it came to the business of running a radio station. He was also slightly deaf, and although he wore a hearing aid, most people found it necessary to speak to him somewhat louder than usual.

The interview lasted for about half an hour. David Pinnell's secretary had the job of shepherding the candidates in and out of the room. She was ready to guide me towards the way out as my interview ended when I saw and recognised a rival candidate waiting his turn, a man who was already Managing Director of a smaller ILR station in the South of England.

I nodded across to him and he did likewise, whereupon I simply said, "Good luck."

"Oh, luck won't come into it," was the arrogant reply. He was unsuccessful.

* * * *

The BRMB board announced their decision within 24 hours, but not before I received a phone call at home from John Parkinson.

"Sorry to disturb you at home Stuart. Is it a convenient moment?"

"Yes, of course," I replied, feeling somewhat nervous at what I was about to hear.

"Good. Well, first I want to thank you for applying for the job at BRMB and for attending the interview," he said. I was already certain that I knew what was coming next, and I was right, but there was an unexpected twist.

"Let me get straight to the point. You were not successful. We have appointed your current Managing Director at Mercia Sound, Ian Rufus."

That was surprise number one. I immediately thought back to when I had told Ian that I was applying for the job. He had told me nothing about his intentions, but I reasoned that it was hardly surprising that he had kept it to himself.

Before I could respond John Parkinson continued, "I have to tell you that you impressed us greatly and I have just been on the telephone to your Chairman, Jack Butterworth."

He chuckled softly as he spoke.

"Jack and I go back a long way and I knew I could talk to him frankly. I told him that I was about to call you and that I would tell you that although Ian was our first choice that you were a close second. Had we not agreed to appoint Ian, we would have given you the job at BRMB without a moment's hesitation. I suggested to Jack that in my view you are a ready-made replacement for Ian."

He laughed again.

"It's up to him and the Mercia board to make their own decision of course, but from the conversation I have just had with Jack, I think you might hear from him sooner rather than later."

I thanked John for what he had said and for letting me know personally. We chatted for a minute or two more and then ended the conversation.

Sue was in the kitchen and I went through to tell her what had just happened. I had barely finished recounting what John Parkinson had said before the 'phone rang again.

"Stuart?" barked the strident voice of Lord Butterworth.

"Yes Jack. Good evening."

"I hope you have had a call from John Parkinson," he said. It was more of a statement than a question.

"Yes, just a few minutes ago," I replied.

"Good," he said. "You obviously impressed John and his board. I have just had a chat with Phil, Barry, Peter, Brenda, Jean and Doris, and they have agreed that we should not waste any time but rather get on with appointing you, if you are interested."

The names he had reeled off were those of the other Mercia Sound directors. I later learned that they had been meeting that evening without Ian's knowledge, having heard that their Managing Director had applied for another job not long after returning from his foray to Hull.

It turned out that rather than be impressed by Ian's ambition, they had taken a dim view of it. They viewed it as Ian using Mercia as a steppingstone in a bid to climb the executive ladder. What they intended to do about it I have no idea, but the BRMB decision clearly resolved the matter for them.

When Ian had returned to Mercia after going to Hull to set up Viking Radio, we had bought him a boomerang as a welcome back present. Not a toy either, but a pukka polished wood boomerang, mounted in a frame with an engraved brass plate. The boomerang was deliberately chosen after his moves back and forth between Mercia Sound and other stations.

Ian loved it and he had apparently shown it with great delight to the Mercia board of directors. They, however, were not enamoured by it, and particularly so when they found out that he had applied for the job at BRMB.

They were all together in their secret meeting when Jack had received John Parkinson's phone call, the contents of which he relayed to the others. I was already reasonably well known to some of the directors, Lady Liggins, Brenda Price, Peter Davis and Jack's wife Lady Doris. I knew Barry Gillitt and Phil White less well. Once Jack had passed on John Parkinson's comments, they unanimously agreed to offer me the role of Managing Director.

"If you are interested," Jack had said.

Interested? I should say so.

"Yes please," I said, feeling quite shell-shocked at the turn of events.

Jack laughed loudly.

"Good!" he exclaimed. "Now then, I suppose I had better interview you to complete the formalities. Can you come to the house tomorrow?"

The house? What did that mean? His house in Coventry, his home in Gloucestershire or the House of Lords? It soon became obvious.

"Yes, I'm sure I can," I replied, only to be interrupted as, to my relief, he cleared up the confusion.

"I am driving to London tonight. Be at the Peer's Entrance at three o'clock tomorrow afternoon, I will have heard the debate that I am interested in by then and we can chat over tea."

If the turn of events could not be more unexpected, I had been offered the job of Managing Director, not of the radio station I had applied to but of the station where I was already employed. That was now going to be ratified over tea at the House of Lords. To say that both Sue and I were stunned by it all is putting it mildly.

The following day I was booted and suited at Coventry station. I deliberately boarded a train much earlier than I needed to so as not to arrive at the Houses of Parliament later than the scheduled three o'clock appointment.

At Westminster, in Old Palace Yard, I paused and took a breath before entering the stone carriage porch. I gave my name to the police officer and the House official at the entrance and told them that that I was there to meet Lord Butterworth. As I did so I saw Jack approaching from a stairway.

"Your grace," said the official courteously, "Mr. Linnell for you."

"Ah yes," boomed Jack, with what I was to learn was his customary chuckle. "Good. You are on time. Well done. Come on. We'll go to the tearoom."

I had been to Parliament before. There had been a fifth form school trip to the House of Commons, and I had been to functions hosted by local MPs on a couple of occasions, but I had not previously visited the Upper House, and most certainly not its tearoom.

We sat at table and a waiter appeared. Jack asked me what I would like.

"What are you having?" I replied nervously.

"Indian," he replied brusquely.

Trying to sound far more confident than I felt I said, "I will have the same please"

"Will you?" laughed Jack, obviously amused. "How extraordinary!"

The waiter disappeared to get our tea. As he did a figure in religious robes of a purple cassock and a white surplus walked past our table. It was the Archbishop of Canterbury, Robert Runcie. Following him, with a rather hurried but awkward gait, was the unmistakable sight of Lord Longford.

Other famous political faces circled the room, while still more sat enjoying tea and conversation with guests and fellow peers. Jack nodded occasionally in acknowledgement of other members of their Lordships House, whilst casually chatting to me about Mercia Sound and my appointment as its Managing Director.

"You obviously impressed John Parkinson at your interview in Birmingham," he said. "I take it Rufus had not told you that he had applied for the same job."

"No," I replied, "Although I had told him that I had applied for it. Out of courtesy. We have been friends for some years."

Jack laughed again.

"So much for friendship," he said.

"Yes, but I understand why he kept it to himself. He was also my boss, after all."

"Ha!" Jack exclaimed. "Defending him despite his deception. Loyalty. I like that."

Our tea arrived, and Jack poured. A small dark pile of wet tea leaves collected in the strainer as he filled both our cups.

"Lemon or milk?" he asked, taking a slice of lemon for himself.

"Milk, thank you," was my answer, only for it to be met by another huge chuckle.

"My word," he said. "I can see you have a lot to learn. We will get on fine."

Whether he intended to educate me in the etiquette of taking tea in refined circles or in the business of running a radio station was not clear, and I did not ask.

Our conversation turned to his immediate concerns for Mercia Sound and his expectation that, coming from a programming and journalistic background, I would quickly have to learn that by far the most important department in the company was sales.

"Revenue and profit" he declared. "That's what matters."

Referring to his two previous MDs, he added, "Bradford and Rufus have both had the right idea that you earn your revenue by being involved with your local community, but we need to improve the profitability. You will find the board are all behind you if you can do that."

We continued our conversation for another ten minutes or so and finished our tea. He showed me the way out, explaining that the staircase we were using also led to the Prince's Chamber which was used by the Monarch for the State Opening of Parliament. As we reached the stone carriage porch, he offered his hand and asked me one final question.

"Am I right in thinking that you were born in Birmingham?"

"Yes," I replied, "I was."

"Ha," came another exclamation accompanied by the famous chuckle. "Well, you will do alright young man just as long as you remember that the one good thing to come out of Birmingham is the A45 to Coventry!"

Obviously amused by his own joke he shook me very firmly by the hand.

"You'll get a letter," he said, "with all the details about salary and so on. I will see you next week in your office. Goodbye."

I wished him goodbye, and he was already on the first step of the staircase as I walked into the fresh air past the police officer holding the door open for me.

My thoughts were racing. Sue, of course, would ask me what my salary would be let alone any other details of the remuneration package, and it had not even been mentioned in my so-called interview until that final, parting shot. I quickly reconciled myself to the notion that the letter he had referred to would constitute an offer, so that there should be an opportunity to negotiate.

More than that, it would be in the more familiar surroundings of my office and therefore in a more familiar environment than the tearoom of the House of Lords.

* * * *

Even as Managing Director, I was determined to maintain an on-air presence, even if only once a week, so I recorded a weekly hour of music and chat which I scheduled for early Sunday morning. The board determined, as much as a cost saving measure as for any other reason, that I should continue as Programme Controller as well as being MD. I could therefore put my own show wherever I felt it was appropriate in the schedule.

I also contributed very occasionally to the sports output, but I appointed Mike Liggins, from within the Mercia newsroom, to take over as Sports Editor. He did a great job, leading our coverage of one of the most remarkable seasons in the history of Coventry City Football Club.

* * * *

George Curtis and John Sillett enjoyed mixed fortunes as joint managers. Initially Curtis was nominally the manager with Sillett in the role of coach, but the precise determination of who did what was blurred with the two of them always at each other's side and working as one.

The early results gave no hint of what was to follow, and the Sky Blues' fans were not impressed enough to turn up at Highfield Road in particularly large numbers. A crowd of only 11,370 saw them beat Arsenal 2-1 in the first home match of the 1986/1987 season, with goals from Cyrille Regis and Nick Pickering, but only matches against Aston Villa in October and against Spurs in December pushed the attendances up significantly.

That first half of the season was not without its highlights, however. Goalkeeper Steve Ogrizovic scored on a wet and windy day against Sheffield Wednesday at Hillsborough. His huge kick from his own penalty area bounced out of reach and over the head of Wednesday 'keeper Martin Hodge at the other end of the pitch.

The visit of Tottenham at Christmas time pulled in an attendance of 22,175. Two goals from Dave Bennett and one apiece from Keith Houchen and Regis, secure a thrilling 4-3 victory. The real excitement was to follow in the New Year.

On 10th January 1987 the story of that season started to unfold. On a freezing cold afternoon Greg Downs, Regis and Bennett all found the net to defeat Bolton Wanderers 3-0 in the 3rd Round of the FA Cup. A first win in a cup competition always stirs interest with the hope of more success to follow, but that depends on the opposition you are paired with.

When the 4th Round draw was made Coventry fans were simultaneously excited and anxious. The numbered balls drawn from the famous bag at the FA served up the daunting prospect of the Sky Blues meeting Manchester United at Old Trafford. It could not have been a tougher challenge for Sillett and Curtis and their players.

A crowd of nearly 50,000, most of them supporting United, threatened to make the fixture an even greater test. By half-time however it was the visitors who held the advantage. After 20 minutes, Keith Houchen bundled the ball into the United net to score the only goal in the first half to delight the Coventry contingent and raise their hopes.

That's how it stayed, with City's 1-0 victory taking them through with the headline writers and TV pundits, including former manager Jimmy Hill, then hosting "Match Of The Day" on BBC1, describing it as a 'Cup upset' and a 'shock result'. After the match, the Coventry supporters were held in their place on the Old Trafford terraces, behind the red metal fences that kept them off the pitch, until after home fans had left. Not they were in any hurry to leave, as they savoured the win and saluted their heroes.

When the 5th Round placed them at Stoke the demand for tickets meant that 8,000 City fans made the journey to the Victoria Ground. The result was another 1-0 win for Coventry, with Michael Gynn 's 71st minute goal seeing them through to the quarterfinals.

Now everyone in Coventry was talking about the Cup run. Along with the players George Curtis and John Sillett were the most popular men in the city. Everywhere people were asking "could this be our year"? Once more, tickets were at a premium as yet another away match was scheduled with the quarter-final draw sending them to pay Sheffield Wednesday at Hillsborough.

It had extra interest for me, renewing my acquaintance with my former South Yorkshire home and a ground that I obviously knew well. 15,000 fans made the trip up the M1 in high spirits, encouraged by the cheerful banter of Sillett and Curtis. In every interview they passed on to the supporters the same belief that they were conveying to the players that nothing was now impossible.

That belief grew even greater as a great strike from Regis and two goals from Houchen saw them home. The national media was now putting huge focus on Coventry City, their management duo and their players. Tottenham, Watford and Leeds United were the other semi-finalists but throughout the city of Coventry people were stating quite determinedly, "our name's on the Cup".

* * * *

If Hillsborough had not already proved to be a great venue for Coventry City that season, with Oggy's spectacular goal in the League, and that excellent quarter-final Cup win, it was to be the stage for the next part of the adventure. Leeds United were the semi-final opposition. Many Sky Blues fans who were there will tell you it was the best match of the entire Cup run, but not before some half-time jitters.

Of an attendance of 48,000, there were 27,000 from Coventry. The match kicked off fifteen minutes late because of traffic delays on the M1. At half-time Leeds were in front thanks to a goal from David Rennie, who would become a Coventry player six years later. This was the big test for Sillett and Curtis. Could they lift their team in the most critical match of the season so far, or were the FA Cup fun and frolics about to flounder and flop so close to the grand finale?

Midfielder Lloyd McGrath provided the unexpected inspiration. As Curtis and Sillett did their best to gee up his team mates, McGrath started to sing a simple football chant.

"Here we go, here we go, here we go," he sang, just as someone pushed open the dressing room door. The Leeds players were about to run out on to the pitch for the second half, so their door had just been opened too. As McGrath continued to sing, the rest of the City squad joined in, so within seconds the inner sanctum at Hillsborough was echoing loudly to the confident sound of Sky Blues voices.

Before long there was singing and cheering from the Coventry supporters as Gynn and Houchen put them in front. Leeds fought back with an equaliser from Keith Edwards taking the semi-final into extra time. Dave Bennett scored the winner in the 99th minute to set up the football match that everyone in Coventry had dreamt about.

* * * *

We were at Wembley. We were going to play in the FA Cup Final. The opposition would be Tottenham Hotspur who had never lost in their previous six finals. Getting hold of tickets, buying shirts and scarves, and organising transport, were on the to do lists of City fans. The whole city was alive with excitement.

The build up to the Final was extraordinary. City centre shops turned Sky Blue, with a window dressing competition encouraging many retailers to show their support. The local brewery M&B produced bottles of beer with a commemorative label that read 'CUP FINAL Wembley 1987 Coventry City v Tottenham Hotspur'. The Sky Blue' players recorded a specially written song to celebrate their appearance in the Final.

The song, called "Go For It City", was written by Coventry song-writers Steve and Heather Taylor. They had written hit songs for Shakin' Stevens and others, and they set up a makeshift recording studio in their tiny cottage in the mining village of Keresley, on the northern edge of the city. The entire Coventry City squad gathered around the microphones, whilst Steve and Heather put them through their paces, rehearsing them before the recording. TV camera crews were there to film it, and reporters, including me, covered it too.

* * * *

In the week before the Final, George and John took the players away to the New Forest, to stay in a hotel near to the place where John grew up. I spent part of a day with them, doing one or two interviews.

At various times a few people had told me that if I needed tickets for the Cup Final they could be provided. Despite that, I made myself a promise that I would not get involved in trying to obtain tickets should anyone ask me, as I knew that it would probably be a thankless and probably endless task. On my way to the team's hotel, the phone rang in my car. It was one of the Mercia Sound directors, Phil White.

"What's the deal with the Cup Final?" he asked brusquely.

"Just going to meet the team now Phil, so I'll find out soon," I replied. I should have known better than to think he was interested in the team or my reporting of them.

"What about tickets?" he said. No beating around the bush from Phil. "Any chance?"

I hesitated before responding. It was the very thing I wanted to avoid, but he was a key man in the board room. If I said I could not get any I would be lying and I would probably lose face big time.

"How many did you want?" I asked, against my better judgement.

"Just two," he said. "Me and my wife."

One of those who had offered tickets if I needed them was the Chairman of the football club, John Poynton. If I were going to get hold of tickets for one of my directors, it would be the club's Chairman I would turn to. Not that they would be freebies!

"Let me see what I can do," I said, before quickly adding, "but they will be at face value, of course."

I was not at all sure how he would respond to that, but he laughed.

"Expecting me to pay?" he laughed. "Quite right too. The company should not foot the bill. Let me know."

With that the line went dead, and I had to make a call to John Poynton. Two tickets were duly purchased, passed on and paid for. Not just Cup Final tickets, mind you, but tickets located immediately behind the Royal Box at Wembley. Just a few rows in front of Mercia Sound director Phil White and his wife sat Her Royal Highness the Duchess of Kent, Prime Minister Margaret Thatcher and her husband Dennis, senior figures from the Football Association, the Chairmen of both clubs and their wives, and other civic and football dignitaries.

Talking to John Poynton a few days after the match he asked me, having supplied the tickets, if Phil had enjoyed being there.

"Yes," I replied, "I am sure he did. Why do you ask?"

"Well they sat in the VIP restaurant in the main stand behind the Royal Box and kept themselves to themselves. They had even taken their own food and drink."

I later discovered that Phil and Mrs White had taken their own sandwiches and a flask of tea in a supermarket carrier bag. They proceeded to consume that rather than order from the Wembley caterers.

"Yes, of course we did," Phil told me. "I was not going to pay their prices."

That, I thought, is why you are a multi-millionaire. Why spend more than you have to?

* * * *

Saturday 16th May 1987 dawned bright and sunny in London. The Mercia Sound team were located in a budget hotel near the centre of the city. I woke early and made my way to a far grander hotel, the Compleat Angler at Marlow in Buckinghamshire, where the Sky Blues squad were staying.

My driver, in the Mercia Sound radio car, was Tom Wadrop who had for many years been the football club's stadium announcer at Highfield Road. Tom was an incredibly enthusiastic character when it came to radio and football. He was very knowledgeable about both, with a very sharp memory. He had a vague likeness to Tony Blackburn, and he had been thrilled when he interviewed Tony for Coventry Hospital Radio.

With Tom at the wheel, we arrived at the Compleat Angler just at around eight-thirty. I made my way to the restaurant where breakfast was being served. Only a few of the Sky Blues team were up and about, amongst them David Phillips and Michael Gynn.

I ordered scrambled eggs and coffee and joined them whilst Tom went for a look round the hotel to find our Sports Editor, Mike Liggins. I later discovered that the majority of players were emerging slowly from their beds after enjoying a bottle of beer or two the night before, obtained from a local off-licence. Messrs Curtis and Sillett had turned a blind eye.

Mike's brief was to grab some player interviews and then head to Wembley to broadcast them during our build-up to the match. Along the way, he also interviewed a bride and groom whose reception was taking place at the Compleat Angler that day.

John Sillett had arranged for the bride to wear a Sky Blue garter under her wedding dress. Team captain Brian Kilcline was photographed kissing the bride's garter. John said it would bring good luck, both for the happy couple and for the Sky Blues' Cup Final hopes.

That done, his tape recorder carefully placed safely to one side, Mike Liggins was ceremoniously dumped in the River Thames which flowed alongside the hotel garden. Mike must have been expecting it, because he was soon on his way to Wembley in dry clothes.

For Tom Wadrop and me, sampling the relaxed and light-hearted atmosphere in the City camp was part of our reason for being there. It would add to the detail we would be able to report back to Coventry and Warwickshire later during our coverage of the match.

The time came for the team to board their team bus and make their way to the stadium. The bus supplied by Coventry coach and holiday company Harry Shaw Travel, with the company's name proudly sitting alongside the name of the football club.

When they boarded the coach it was the signal for the next part of our mission to kick in. With Tom driving once again the radio car would lead the way to Wembley, with me going on air from time to time to describe the journey.

As the driver started to move away from the hotel we drove to the exit gateway. Tom checked his rear-view mirror and said, "what's going on? They've turned back."

As I looked back to see what was happening, the team bus made three trips round the mini traffic island in the hotel driveway. It turned out that Snoz had seen a magpie just as the bus set off. He told the driver that they could not go anywhere until they had seen another.

"You know the old saying, Stu," he told me later. "One for sorrow, two for joy. I have always been superstitious and having seen one magpie we couldn't carry on until we had seen his mate."

Eventually we were on our way, with Tom studiously obeying the speed limit despite George Curtis, with a huge smile on his face, at the front window of the bus waving at us to go faster. We drove into the stadium along the route referred to as 'Wembley Way', and as we were directed towards our reserved car parking space the team bus carried on through the stadium entrance and parked alongside the dressing rooms.

As Tom parked the car, a sleek, dark green Bentley saloon slid into place alongside us. From the driver's seat emerged Captain Mark Phillips, then married to Her Royal Highness Princess Anne. He was dressed in a smart grey suit, complete with a Tottenham Hotspur tie. He smiled in acknowledgement, so I chanced my arm.

"Looking forward to the match sir?" I asked.

"Yes," he said. "We never lose here, you know."

"Well," I replied, "There's always a first time."

"Not today," he laughed. "Enjoy it."

He marched off swiftly accompanied by his passenger as Tom and I made our way. We headed for the press gallery which hung under the roof of the stand below Wembley's famous twin towers.

* * * *

Mike Liggins led our commentary team at Wembley. I was alongside him together with former City full back Kirk Stephens. Also there, with his manager, was Paul King, the lead singer of the Coventry pop band King whose 1984 hit record "Love And Pride" had become something of an anthem for Sky Blues' fans. At pitch side, to provide us with regular updates about what was happening amongst the coaches and substitutes in the dugout was reporter Ian Woods. Positioned near the photographers behind one of the goals was the youngest member of our team, teenager Rob Gurney.

Ian would go on to be a senior international reporter with Sky News. Rob, after a spell as the main Coventry City reporter and commentator for Mercia Sound and later for BBC CWR, moved to BBC WM in Birmingham to play a key role in the sports team there. Rob returned to CWR many years later, and is held in high regard by Coventry City supporters who rate him, quite rightly in my view, as the best ever Sky Blues' local radio commentator.

Mercia Sound was therefore well covered with the resources to do the job properly and relay the action to those listening in Coventry and Warwickshire. Many who did listen told us afterwards that they watched the TV coverage with the sound turned down and Mercia's commentary accompanying the pictures. After the drama of the semi-final win against Leeds at Hillsborough cassette copies of the Mercia Sound commentary had been rushed out and sold in amazing numbers. The same happened after the Cup Final.

I should also add that top billing in the Mercia Sound team went to the radio station's "Mr. Fix It", Carlton Dale. He had been an advertising sales executive, but in 1987 his job title was Operations Manager. Carlton made things tick. He planned and organised the logistics that enabled all that we did at Wembley and elsewhere. I later learned that it was Carlton, at the behest of some of our directors, who had coordinated and submitted the documentation that led to my being made MBE in 1995. He was the glue that held together so much of what we did, and he went on to be a senior executive at Mercia and elsewhere in the GWR group after I'd left the company.

* * * *

As a contest, the 1987 FA Cup Final had all the excitement, tension and sheer theatre you would want from a major sporting event. BBC TV legendary commentator John Motson described it as one of the best Finals he had seen and probably one of the best ever.

After all the hype, excitement and exuberance that the build-up included, Coventry City supporters knew that, whatever else the day might offer, they could look forward to being part of one of English football's show-piece occasions. Their team was playing at Wembley with an opportunity to win a major trophy. It was a day that many thought they might never see.

After only two minutes, those supporters must have thought that while it was historic, that would be it. Clive Allen scored an early goal for Tottenham and Coventry were 1-nil down. The Cup Final looked like being a match too far for the Sky Blues.

Those that held their faith in the team at this moment had their dreams rewarded as the effervescent Dave Bennett equalised. As the ball came to rest at the back of the net, with Bennett and his teammates enjoying the moment of celebration, the nature of the match and the atmosphere of the entire afternoon was transformed. Tottenham's initial advantage was erased, and we had a contest all over again.

Despite Tottenham scoring again before half-time, the mood in the Coventry camp remained buoyant and in the sixty-fourth minute that buoyancy overflowed. Even the Tottenham supporters had to acknowledge the brilliance of Coventry City's second goal, scored by Keith Houchen.

The move started with a long clearance by Coventry goalkeeper Steve Ogrizovic. It was headed on by Cyrille Regis who found Houchen close to him just outside the Tottenham penalty area. His pass to the right reached Bennett who floated the perfect cross into the midst of the opposition defence. Houchen's long legs propelled him forwards, eventually stretching his body parallel with the ground, his dive ensuring that his head turned the ball past Tottenham 'keeper Ray Clemence to make the score 2-all.

It was the goal of every player's and every fan's dream. It was powerful, dynamic, graceful, balletic and thoroughly thrilling. No one scoring a goal like that deserved not to be on the winning side, and Houchen was rewarded as the match went into extra-time and Coventry scored a third.

For that third, decisive goal the ball was turned past his own goalkeeper by Tottenham defender Gary Mabbutt. He had scored his side's second goal, but now deep into the final stages of the drama Mabbutt was trying to intercept a right-wing cross by Sky Blues midfield star Lloyd McGrath. Mabbutt reached the pass, but it hit him on the knee and spiralled into the net. That part of Mabbutt's anatomy took its place forever in Coventry City folklore. A website, a fanzine and a twitter account all took the name "Gary Mabbutt's Knee".

With a final score of Coventry City 3, Tottenham Hotspur 2, the Cup was ours. Sky Blues fans sang their hearts out including that song written specially for this match, "Go For It City". As the match had gone into extra time, with the scores tied at 2-2, that song rolled off the massed ranks of City fans as they realised that we were enjoying one of the greatest days in the history of this famous club.

Coventry captain Brian Kilcline, who had been injured during extra-time, limped up Wembley's famous 39 steps to lift the trophy to the triumphant cheers and acclaim of the Coventry supporters. Kilcline had been fortunate to avoid retribution from referee Neil Midgley after a badly timed tackle on Mabbutt.

Midgley admitted later that he faced the unwelcome prospect of sending off the Coventry skipper, which after such a superb contest he did not want to do. Before he could take action, he realised that Snoz had told young defender Graham Rodger to get ready to go on as substitute. Kilcline could no longer continue and was carried off as Rodger took his place, so the prospect of a dismissal was avoided.

Kilcline's injury was bad enough for him to need hospital treatment the following day, while the rest of the City squad took themselves of to Magaluf to celebrate. A phone call from Cyrille Regis told Kilcline what a good time they were having, so he checked out of hospital, caught a flight to Spain and managed to avoid the eagle eye of George Curtis.

I have often been asked for my favourite moment covering Coventry City football club, and that FA Cup triumph is obviously at the top of the list.

* * * *

The music industry entrepreneur Pete Waterman was born in Coventry and educated at Whitley Abbey Comprehensive School. He founded the Stock Aitken Waterman song writing team. Another member of that trio, Matt Aitken, was also born in Coventry, but brought up in Manchester. He was already a musical partner with Mike Stock before they joined forces with Pete Waterman, and between the three of them they wrote and produced many hit singles.

Pete came from Stoke Heath in Coventry. He left school at the age of 15 and went to work for British Railways. He was a fireman on a steam train, forming a life-long love of railways. British Railways (BR) also had a financial interest in property in Coventry city centre and contributed significantly to its redevelopment after the war. A young Pete Waterman was amongst the BR workforce set to work tarmacking the surface of the Barracks Car Park.

After a year working for BR Pete made his first move into music. Like so many he was inspired by The Beatles, and he also had a love of American soul music. He built up a significant collection of American import records which he played in clubs and other venues all over the country, generating a fan following that in turn helped him identify the music that was popular with club goers.

He was the first DJ in the UK to pick up on the Philadelphia sound, inspired by the song writing and producing team of Kenny Gamble and Leon Huff. He became the resident DJ at the Locarno Club in Coventry, owned by the Mecca Leisure Group, where he met Neville Staple before Neville became a founder member of The Specials.

Pete introduced Philadelphia group The Three Degrees to the UK, and eventually became one of the UK's leading pop music producers. With Stock and Aitken, and after subsequently splitting from the other two, Pete was the driving force behind more than twenty UK number one singles with acts like Dead or Alive, Kylie Minogue, Rick Astley, Bananarama, Steps, Mel and Kim, Donna Summer, Sinitta, Cliff Richard and Jason Donovan.

He told me his life story when we sat down for a detailed interview in studio 2 at Mercia Sound. One of the most telling revelations from Pete was about Rick Astley's No.1 hit "Never Gonna Give You Up". It was the first Stock Aitken Waterman hit to make No.1 in America, but Pete was remarkably dismissive of it.

"Yes," he told me, "it was a great pop record from a guy who came to us as a shy young man that we hired as a tea boy at the recording studio. He needed to overcome his shyness and we gradually taught him about the recording process. As for that record, it was a big smash hit for a few weeks, but if I had a copy now I'd melt it down to be an ash tray."

We cut the recording of my interview with Pete into six half-hour episodes and scheduled them to go out on Sunday lunchtime from 12 noon to 12.30 under the title "The Pete Waterman Story". The audience reaction was understandably positive, with Coventrians enjoying hearing the life story of one of their own.

The final episode was broadcast on Remembrance Sunday. I was, by that time, Managing Director and Programme Controller at Mercia Sound, and I had been invited to join the Lord Mayor of Coventry and his official party on the dais in the city's famous War Memorial Park. I stood alongside the Lord Mayor as he saluted the massed ranks of service personnel on their march out of the park from the Cenotaph, after the traditional service.

After leaving the service, just after 12 noon, I was on my way home, driving my sky blue Volvo, listening to the last of the six instalments of Pete Waterman's life. The show reached its conclusion, and I heard myself winding it up with a not particularly clever closing link, summarising that Pete was the Coventry kid who had risen from modest beginnings to being one of the richest and most influential figures in modern popular music.

As it played out, I was suddenly filled with great foreboding as I remembered that I had fluffed that link three or four times during the recording. Whilst it was being edited I had been called away to take a phone call and had left the job of tidying it up to one of the younger members of the station's team. Despite his youth, I regarded him as hugely reliable and I was confident that he would not let me down.

However, as the recording continued to be played out on the radio that Sunday I cringed as I heard my first fluff, then another, then another. Eventually the bit I was dreading was transmitted loud and clear across Coventry and Warwickshire, for all to hear, as I committed the cardinal sin for any broadcaster. I had sworn in front of a live microphone.

After the fourth failed attempt to correctly string my words together, I said "oh, fucking hell!".

Mobile phones were in their infancy. They were the size of house bricks, and mine sat solidly in the centre console of my Volvo. When the first fluff played out, I immediately reached for it only for two blinding flashes of realisation to crash into my anxious, confused brain.

One, I would have to find somewhere to pull the car over to hit the keypad on the phone and dial the number (there were no hands-free kits in cars at this stage), and two, even if I got through to the studio, I would not have done so in time to stop the tape.

"Oh, fucking hell!"

The words seemed much louder in my car than any previous part of the programme. I was sure that the Volvo had now turned into a loud hailer on wheels and my expletive was echoing around the streets of Coventry.

They might as well have done. When I got home, my wife said that a reporter from the local newspaper, the *Coventry Evening Telegraph*, had called and asked if I would call back.

When I returned the call it was Steve Chilton, the newspaper's features editor who wanted to talk to me. In answer to his perfectly reasonable questions, I confirmed that I was both Managing Director and Programme Controller of the radio station and, as such, I was responsible for the on-air behaviour of all presenters.

Bearing in mind that I was also the presenter on this occasion, Steve wanted to know what I was going to do? I spluttered something about being sorry for an unforgivable lapse, but that in all work situations mistakes can occur and industrial language is sometimes used, though it should never be condoned. I added that I would have to have a word with myself.

The next day, there was a flurry of telephone messages and one or two hastily scribbled letters from listeners. They were all, inevitably, condemning and complaining about what I had been heard to say. They asked if I realised that young children may have been listening, and did I realise what an appalling example it was for them.

Anyone caught up in such a faux pas will know that you proceed under the assumption, encouraged by a huge amount of hope, that it will all soon fade away. Forgotten in a few days.

Not so.

Thanks to the weekly gossip column published in the *Coventry Evening Telegraph*, under the locally appropriate title 'Peeping Tom', written by Steve Chilton, my agony was prolonged. Steve went on to be an acquaintance with whom I have always been on good terms, but in that evening's newspaper he wrote that from then on I would no doubt be changing my name to Stuart 'Kinnell.

Never gonna give you up

Never gonna let you down

Never gonna run around and desert you

Never gonna make you cry

Never gonna say goodbye

Never gonna tell a lie and hurt you

Mike Stock/Matt Aitken/Peter Waterman, 1987

© Sony/ATV Music Publishing LLC, Universal Music Publishing Group

Chapter Fifteen

Competition and a Merger

All the old paintings on the tombs

They do the sand dance don't you know

If they move too quick (oh whey oh)

They're falling down like a domino

All the bazaar men by the Nile

They got the money on a bet

Gold crocodiles (oh whey oh)

They snap their teeth on your cigarette

Foreign types with the hookah pipes say

(Whey oh whey oh, ay oh whey oh)

Walk like an Egyptian

Liam Sternberg, 1984

© Peermusic Publishing

One Monday morning, a few weeks after Coventry City had won the FA Cup, with the City of Coventry still revelling in the success of its football team, I took a call in my office at Mercia Sound from the Sky Blues Chairman John Poynton.

"What are you doing on Thursday?" he asked.

"I can be free on Thursday," I said, turning the pages of my Filofax. "Why? What did you have in mind John?"

"Would you like to go to Cairo?"

He laughed at my spluttered surprise.

"Having won the Cup", he said, "we've received an invitation from the Egyptian FA to play a match against their national side at Highfield Road when they come here in September. In anticipation of that, and to help seal the deal, I have agreed to take them some of our memorabilia and souvenirs. Scarves, t-shirts, a couple of match shirts, things like that. I wondered if you would like to go."

I was stunned to be invited out of the blue, but I remembered being unable to travel to Argentina with Harry Haslam in 1978 and I had always regretted that, so this time I readily agreed. I phoned Sue and told her that I was going to Cairo for the weekend. Her response was typically pragmatic, suggesting that I should call our doctor and ask for any inoculations I might need.

The GP surgery was, of course, typically busy for a Monday morning, but they squeezed me in for a lunchtime appointment.

"There are a number of things you really should have if you are going to Egypt," said the doctor. "You should have injections to protect you from things like hepatitis A, hepatitis B, typhoid, yellow fever, rabies and tetanus, but you should have had them a couple of weeks before you travel. As you do not have the time, I am going to give you this, but on a sugar lump because it tastes awful."

He procured a sugar lump from a small jar and soaked it in medicinal liquid of some sort. I swallowed it.

"That should give you a level of protection," he said, before adding firmly, "just make sure that, when you are there, you do not drink the water nor have ice in your drinks."

Then, with a knowing smile, he winked and said, "Enjoy it. You will be fine."

I duly made my way to Heathrow Airport on the Thursday morning and sought out the travel guide who I had been told would greet me. I found myself in a group with three others, but there was no sign of John Poynton. The guide appeared ready for my question.

"No, Mr. Poynton is unable to travel, but he forwarded this package for you to take with you to Cairo. I understand someone from the Egyptian Football Association will meet you on arrival."

She then introduced the four of us in the assembled group to each other. Two of whom clearly already knew each other, and it turned out that I was in the company of two music journalists and a travel writer. They were scheduled to meet representatives of the Egyptian government and others to hear about a lavishly expensive production of Verdi's opera Aida, to be staged later in the year at the Pyramids at Giza. It quickly became apparent, despite my declaration that I had been invited to go for an entirely different reason, that I was expected to join in with the Aida excursion.

I could have said "no thank you" there and then and gone back home to Coventry, but my trip was being paid for, so it would cost neither me nor my radio station anything at all. It would also be a visit to a country I had not been to before and might never go to again. I went along with it and boarded the plane to Cairo with the others.

* * * *

Cairo International Airport is situated at Heliopolis, to the northeast of the city. Waiting there, amidst a chaos of movement, a scenario which I quickly established applied to people and vehicles right across Cairo, was a smartly dressed man holding my name on a large card. I thought it odd that someone should have been sent solely with my name with transport for our party, and I soon discovered the reason why.

He was a representative of the Egyptian Football Association, and after a perfectly polite welcome he relieved me of the Coventry City Football Club souvenirs and memorabilia for which I had become John Poynton's courier. The man showed me his identity documents before handing me his business card in exchange for the Sky Blues' goodies.

"Congratulations on winning the FA Cup. I hope you have an enjoyable stay in Cairo," he said, before departing into the night and leaving me in the company of those in search of a story about opera and tourism.

We were taken through a bewildering maelstrom of traffic to a five-star hotel on the banks of the Nile, where the scenes in the reception area were as disconcertingly crowded as the roads outside. Crowded and noisy, because it turned out that almost all of the massed multitude were celebrating a wedding ceremony. The bride and groom were making their way from one part of the hotel to another, to the accompaniment of whooping, wailing and cheering, with a small band of musicians walking alongside them though barely making themselves heard.

Through the hullabaloo we managed to check in and make our way to our rooms, several stories above the wedding ceremony, but still within earshot as it seemed could be the case for most of Cairo. Fortunately, the hotel had a restaurant some distance from the festivities where we were invited to have dinner. It was an opportunity for the four of us to get to know each other, or more specifically, for them to get to know me, the stranger in the mix.

Over the next two days we interviewed Egypt's Ministers of Tourism and Culture in their respective offices, and we were taken to see the Pyramids at Giza. I say "we" interviewed them, though for the most part I listened to the others working until literally having my elbow nudged to contribute a question. This despite the fact that I had little, if any, knowledge of Verdi, even less of opera generally, and my awareness of Egypt and the antiquities was scant to say the least.

My interest in proceedings picked up when we were taken to the former home of the American ambassador to Egypt, Alexander Kirk, where the 1943 Cairo Conference had been held. There we saw, carefully wrapped in protective transparent plastic covers, the chairs on which Winston Churchill, the President of the United States Franklin Roosevelt, and Generalissimo Chiang Kai-shek of the Republic of China, had sat whilst they discussed the Allied position against Japan during World War II and made decisions about post-war Asia. So much fascinating history set before us, in the extraordinary setting of the pyramids and, beyond them, the Sahara Desert.

The Museum of Egyptian Antiquities was on our itinerary, allowing us to see artefacts from the Valley of the Kings, in particular those from the tomb of Tutankhamun. We then headed to an impressive ranch-style country club where a number of hugely expensive racehorses were stabled and trained. The club was positioned on the edge of the Sahara.

We had lunch in the club house, watching the horses being schooled in the paddock. A few hundred yards beyond the equestrian facility the greens of three immaculately manicured golf holes protruded incongruously into the desert sand. An entire 18-hole course was being built there, we were told, which would be completed within the next two years. To add to the bizarre but spectacular view, we could make out a camel train on the horizon, as it pursued its ponderous path across the Sahara dunes.

On our last night we were treated to dinner on a boat on the River Nile. Entertainment was laid on with brash, noisy illustrations of local culture. We were required to cast aside our British reserve and join in. Despite the reason for me being there, I hadn't seen a football kicked, or even the inside of a stadium, but I had been encouraged to revel in the gyrations of a belly dancer.

As the merriment unfolded, I made my big mistake. I had, to that point, been scrupulously careful in following my doctor's advice, "don't drink the water, and don't have ice in your drinks". That evening I garnished my plate of food with salad, failing to realise that at some point prior to it arriving in front of us the green leaves and the tomato slices had been washed in Egyptian water.

It was just over twelve hours later, on the packed and uncomfortably warm flight home, that I started to feel the consequences. The bubbling in my stomach developed into something extremely uncomfortable by the time we returned to Birmingham Airport. Fortunately I had managed to contain my affliction until that point, but I went on to suffer badly for the best part of the next ten days.

Medication from my doctor, alongside an already self-imposed nil-by-mouth regime saw me survive a most unpleasant experience, for me as well as for Sue and the children. That short but memorable trip abroad was followed by more than a week off work.

Some two or three weeks later, after I had thankfully made a full recovery, I popped home briefly one lunchtime to find a lady I did not recognise waiting at our front doorstep. Before I could say anything, she introduced herself as a senior officer from the local public health department.

"May I come in?" she asked, in a tone of voice that was clearly making a demand rather than seeking permission.

Once inside the house we sat in the lounge as she explained that as I had been suffering from a notifiable disease it was necessary to check all was well, particularly as there were children living there. To say I was surprised is an understatement..

"Notifiable?" I queried.

"Yes," she said, "You have had cryptosporidium, often caused by contaminated water or food. It is highly contagious, and children can be specially at risk. Do you know how you caught it?"

"I was in Egypt a couple of weeks ago," I explained and went on to tell her about the salad on the boat on the Nile.

"May I see your fingernails?" she said, holding out her own hand.

She examined my fingers and then asked if she could have a quick look round the house, particularly where the boys slept, as well as the bathroom and kitchen. When she had finished, she smiled before announcing her conclusion.

"I can see all is well," she said. "I am sure you appreciate that we have to check these things."

Sue was at work, but as soon as our surprise visitor had left, I called her to tell her what had happened.

"Thank goodness the place was tidy," she said, causing me to smile at the thought of Susan ever leaving her home in a state that would appear less than tidy to any visitor.

As I made my way back to my office, it occurred to me that my life had embraced yet another rich experience entirely due to Coventry City Football Club.

* * * *

As both Managing Director and Programme Controller of the radio station, I wanted to make my mark on the business. It was important to me to maintain the continuing popularity of Mercia Sound's programmes to which so many talented and hard-working people had contributed. I had to focus on the company accounts and balance sheet, but also on the audience figures. All were pretty healthy, but it irritated me that we made successful and popular programmes, yet we never seemed to be amongst those receiving wider recognition. Others seemed to figure in the annual rounds of prize- winning, but radio's awards seemed to elude Mercia Sound.

Everyone likes winning prizes, and if we could pick up one or two it would be just reward for the presenters and certainly do us no harm when making our sales pitches to advertisers. It always occurred to me as incongruous that amongst those who were often amongst those celebrating at the nationally acclaimed Sony Radio Awards was BBC Radio 3.

I had nothing against Radio 3, but a study of the audience figures quickly revealed that its audience was often so small that it barely registered. Should it ever be revealed, my doubtless naïve reasoning would immediately cast me as a cultural heathen. Yet my thought process at the time screamed that it was wrong and wholly unfair that programmes of Radio 3, with its infinitesimally small audience should collect trophies when ours, consistently hitting high ratings, did not.

My thoughts along those lines appeared in a interview I gave to a weekly industry newspaper, the result being that I was invited to contribute to a debate with the well-respected radio critic Gillian Reynolds. Gillian was held in high regard as a former commercial radio programme controller herself, as well as in her then current role as the radio critic of *The Daily Telegraph*. I soon realised that equating popularity with winning awards was not as obvious as I had considered it should be.

The debate took place in the august surroundings of the Council Chamber at Broadcasting House, or 'BH', in London. To say it is a room steeped in history is putting it mildly. As descriptions of the interior of BH will tell you, it is a semi-circular room, lined in Tasmanian oak. It was designed to be a "dignified room intended for meetings of bodies such as the BBC's Advisory Councils, and enabling, for instance, representative international committees to meet in London, under the BBC's own roof."

Gillian Reynolds is nothing if not a strategist, and if she intended that the location for our debate would prove intimidating for a local radio kid from the sticks she was right. She invited me to make my case.

Taking a deep breath, I asked the assembled, and quite large, group of national network producers, researchers and noteworthy BBC luminaries, with a smattering of presenters amongst them, if they realised that at certain times of the day no-one was listening to Radio 3. I told them that I had seen the figures, so I knew it was true. Taking an even deeper breath I drew the conclusion that they were therefore only making the programmes to impress the awards judges and win prizes. Why else, I reasoned, would they bother?

What followed was the unleashing of controlled fury and utter disdain as my effrontery at even making such a suggestion was dismantled, disgraceful proposition after appalling thought. A lady who turned out to be one of Radio 3's most senior producers maintained a steady rhythm with her knitting needles, with a dark blue woollen creation spilling round her knees. She did not drop a stitch, and I do not recall precisely what she said, but in could easily have been "vengeance and retribution require a long time; it is the rule", as she took on the visage of Madame Defarge.

It certainly felt as though her knitting was sealing my fate, and the coup de grace was delivered by none other than the producer of John Peel's Radio One show, Paul Walters. Paul was one of my radio heroes, and to be on the receiving end of his excoriating critique of my theory left me reeling. I mumbled something barely understandable about still believing that the relationship between awards and audience figures was unfairly skewed. before adding a feeble apology if I had upset or insulted anyone. As I uttered the words I was looking directly at John Walters, as if pleading for forgiveness.

Having departed the scene of what I had foolishly thought might be a meeting of minds with Gillian Reynolds, I was surprised and privately delighted to be selected to be the commercial radio representative on the Sony Radio Awards Committee. That committee did not decide who won what, but rather was a group of broadcasters who oversaw the awards system and the annual show-piece presentation event. As such I attended the glamorous black-tie event, held at the Grosvenor House Hotel on Park Lane in London for a number of years thereafter, mixing with the great and good of the industry. I lived in hope of Mercia Sound winning a Sony, let alone receiving one myself. Eventually I did, but it was many years later, sometime after I had left commercial radio and that committee.

* * * *

Mercia Sound was an award-winning radio station, but we had to go nearly 3,500 miles to achieve it. We submitted an entry two or three years running to the New York International Radio Festival. The second time we did, we struck gold. Our entry demonstrated the breadth and depth of the whole of Mercia's output, and won Gold for having the best eclectic format. The story got very slightly lost in translation when it was reported by the *Coventry Evening Telegraph* that we had won gold for the best "electric" format.

It was a thrill to fly to New York for the festival and collect the medal. Thoroughly enjoyable, too, to go there with presenters Bernie Keith and Chris Radley. Neither had been to America before and New York was a massive culture shock for both, but one they soon took in their stride. They both suffered from jet lag, and so slept through their first few hours in Manhattan.

Chris, from Coventry, knew his rock music. Bernie arrived at Mercia via a cassette tape. Like other radio station programmers, I received tapes from would-be presenters every day. I did my best to listen to them all, sometimes in the office, sometimes in the car. It did not require hours of listening. It was usually possible to decide within 30 seconds if it was worth hearing more.

Bernie sent me his tape from Plympton in Devon, where he lived with his parents. I not only listened to it, I did so more than once. I asked my secretary Kathy to invite him to come and see me. After the first 30 seconds of the tape, that was test number 2. Was he keen enough to come to Coventry and meet me?

He did. A diminutive figure, wearing large spectacles that seemed almost too big for his face, he was clearly nervous when he joined me in my office. He was very nervous and extremely polite, but clearly full of enthusiasm. It was quickly apparent that he really wanted to be a radio presenter. He told me how he had presented his own show for his family at home, and that his ambition was to be on air for real.

I was very impressed and offered Bernie a job. He became Mercia's late show presenter, eventually taking on the breakfast show. He was irreverent and funny on air, and very popular. I recruited other presenters from audition tapes, but Bernie was without question the most talented and proved to be the most popular. His frequent use of double entendre in his humour meant that once in a while he pushed right up against what might be seen as appropriate. As a result, I had to ask him to tone it down once or twice, which he always accepted. When we had those conversations however, he always won the day, making me laugh out loud when the point of the exercise was for me to rein in his naughtiness.

* * * *

As Breakfast Show host, Bernie found himself on the receiving end one day when we staged an on-air stunt aimed at stealing the headlines from a rival.

The BBC had been due to launch one of its local radio stations in Coventry in 1980, at around the same time that Mercia Sound first went on air. For reasons of their own, they ended up being ten years late. It was 1990 before BBC CWR finally arrived, serving Coventry and Warwickshire.

Its launch managing editor was Mike Marsh, with whom I got on very well. I contacted him soon after he arrived in Coventry and took him to lunch. We went to one of my favourite restaurants, the Grandstand Restaurant at Coventry City Football Club's Highfield Road ground. He told me about his programme plans and how he intended the station to be complementary to, but competitive with, Mercia Sound.

After our meeting, I realised that however the station sounded, its launch would be a big story locally and would be extensively reported on by the *Coventry Evening Telegraph*. We needed a spoiler, a stunt designed to steal the headlines. We needed an imaginative idea, so a brainstorming session of one or two members of the Mercia management team was tasked with creating a plan.

Critical to making it work, and always working hard by my side in those days, was Carlton Dale. He had joined the station as an advertising sales executive, but his brilliant organisational skills made Carlton the perfect choice to be the station's Operations Manager. He earned the nickname "Mr. Fix It", because he always could.

The plan we came up with included raising funds for Charity Snowball.

Former Radio 1 DJ David 'Kid' Jensen was then the host of Capital Radio's drivetime show in London. and he was also the host of ILR's first nationally networked show, "The Network Chart Show". Sponsored by Nescafé, it ran on Sunday afternoon at the same time as Radio 1's Top 40.

Not all stations were happy to drop their own local programmes to accommodate a national show, but the deal was that we all had to. I took the view that if that was the case we should promote it as much a part of our own output as any other show. Doing just that was part of our stunt to steal the limelight in Coventry from the launch of BBC CWR.

I had got to know Kid Jensen when he sat alongside me as a member of the Sony Radio Awards Committee. I called him and briefed him on our plans, and he readily agreed to take part. The only person in the dark was Bernie Keith. That said, Bernie was very excited when I told him he would be interviewing Kid Jensen at Mercia on the Breakfast Show to promote The Network Chart Show.

David checked in to a Coventry hotel the night before, and on the morning of Wednesday, 17th January, just after 8 o'clock, he was on air with Bernie. 10 minutes into the interview, Carlton Dale walked into the studio, live on air, with Sergeant Bob Esslemont and two constables from Coventry's Little Park Street Police Station alongside him. With the microphones live, the Sergeant told Bernie they wanted to question him and that he had to go with them, there and then.

A genuinely shocked Bernie was escorted from the studio, with David Jensen telling the Mercia Sound audience that he would have to take over and host the remainder of the Breakfast Show. David soon revealed to listeners that Bernie had known nothing about it, but he would be held in a cell at Little Park Street until people pledged cash for Charity Snowball to have him released.

The phones rang immediately and continued to do so throughout the day. After the Breakfast Show, Carlton Dale took Kid Jenson to meet Bernie in the police cell at Little Park Street police station in Coventry city centre where the two radio hosts had their photos taken.

It worked. We made the front page of the *Coventry Evening Telegraph*, thousands were raised for Snowball, and the shine was taken off the launch of BBC CWR.

I am not sure that Bernie has ever properly forgiven me for that stunt, but we have remained good friends. Nearly 20 years later he helped me extend my career with a return to work behind the mic.

* * * *

Whilst continuing to oversee Mercia's programmes, and whilst continuing to watch Coventry City, my working days became more and more consumed by the rapidly changing nature of the radio industry.

Once more Ian Rufus was a leading light as corporate interests made their presence felt. Ian, and John Parkinson, still the Chairman at BRMB, approached me and Lord Butterworth with a view to a merger of the Birmingham and Coventry stations. The rationale behind the move was to satisfy the demands of shareholders by improving the profitability of both companies. That improvement, they argued, would be achieved by presenting the combined broadcast areas of the two stations as a single entity, making them more attractive to national advertisers than they were separately.

I had personal evidence of the attitude national advertisers were taking towards even successful local commercial radio stations. At our board meetings, directors like Phil White were constantly pushing for increased revenue, reduced costs and thus improved profits. The local sales team were under no illusions that more was expected from them, highlighted daily in my meetings with Sales Director Nick Rushbrooke.

Whilst Nick constantly reminded me what his staff were facing when they went into battle every day with the long-established *Coventry Telegraph*, and one or two less high-profile competitors, he nonetheless worked tirelessly to devise new, innovative ideas to attract local advertisers. Nick was also a past master at glad-handing local businessmen, taking them to lunch, playing golf with them, focusing on those who would best respond to that approach.

Nick also involved me in regular visits to London, to the offices of the company that was contracted to present Mercia Sound and other stations to national advertisers. He had worked there for a while before moving to Coventry, and he knew the people involved very well. Nick also knew many of the key decision makers from the major national brands and he suggested that we invite some of them to visit us at Mercia to see and hear the station for themselves.

One of the obstacles we faced in securing the national ad money our audience numbers warranted was that the people making those spending decisions were based in London. They were therefore unlikely to hear our programmes or have any sense of how the station sounded. They were supplied with myriad charts and graphs detailing audience figures, but it would be hard to judge just how good the station was from a bald page of statistics.

The former working men's club that had originally occupied the building that had become Mercia Sound had housed the club steward and his wife in a small, one-bedroom apartment. It was there, in what had once been the living room of the steward's apartment, that we held our board meetings, and it was there that Nick Rushbrooke and I hosted top media buyers representing Coca-Cola, Mars and one or two other major brands.

We gave our guests a guided tour of the studios, with a couple of our main daytime presenters lined up and briefed to flatter and impress. It was received reasonably well, although there was a slightly patronising air from some of the more senior of our visitors. It was as if having to visit Coventry, let alone the rest of the rigmarole that we provided, was an unnecessary diversion from their more important metropolitan lifestyle.

I put such thoughts to one side and did my best to be the genial host during dinner. We hired a local catering company, and they delivered excellent fare. Nick usually appointed himself wine waiter for the night, ensuring that the glasses were regularly replenished.

After the meal the caterers took their leave, and we pushed hard how our excellent audience figures warranted more national advertising revenue than was forthcoming. The response was immediate and not what we wanted to hear.

"Stuart, you obviously have a well-run, excellent radio station that your local population clearly loves," said Peter, a leading media buyer whose demeanour had left me particularly concerned, "but you have two problems in trying to secure more of our money."

Neither Nick nor I said anything but sat in expectation of some home truths. I bit my tongue as Peter continued.

"First, as I am sure Nick will understand, we rarely buy airtime on individual stations, so to some large degree you need to make your case to other stations and persuade them that they should give Mercia a larger share, if you think you're entitled to it. That said, you have a particular issue here in Coventry."

"Which is?" I asked.

"The nature of almost all of our advertising is to promote our brand and persuade people that, for example, they should drink Coke rather than Pepsi. It is aimed at an essentially young audience who are in the process of making decisions about their favourite brands, decisions that will probably live with them for most of their lives. The Coventry population, and therefore your audience, is mainly older than the age group we want to target. They have already made their brand decisions."

I tried to argue that we included programming within our schedules that was specifically aimed at younger listeners. The response was that they would not buy airtime within individual programmes, instead expecting to be included throughout the main daytime output.

Peter, and our other guests, thanked us profusely for dinner and "a most enjoyable evening", before heading off back to London. Before he left, however, Peter took me to one side and offered me what he obviously regarded as a word of encouragement.

"I know you will be disappointed by what we have said tonight, and I do understand your frustration. It should not be the end of the story. I know that your industry is about to change. It has to. We want to use radio more than we do, but radio has to help us do that. Talk to your neighbours."

"Things will change," he said again, shaking my hand. "They have to."

He was right. There would be changes, the first of them being the merger between BRMB and Mercia Sound that Ian Rufus and John Parkinson had proposed.

* * * *

The deal on the table was hugely favourable for Mercia Sound. We were, in business parlance, cash rich. Jack Butterworth and John Bradford had established the business in 1980 in such a way that it had the means to withstand a rainy day should it ever prove necessary. It never had, and the monthly contest that ensued at our board meetings was whether I was able to show that we had made more money from our advertising income than Phil White, who had taken on the role of investing the cash, had from his adept ability to profitably move the money around. It was often a close call, but I always won, much to my own satisfaction and the huge amusement of the Chairman.

BRMB wanted to get their hands on our cash, but the deal I struck, with Jack Butterworth's support and Phil White' encouragement, ensured that they did not get it cheaply. Rather than a takeover of Mercia by its Birmingham neighbour, it was almost a 50-50 deal, and it was regarded by both boardrooms as a genuine merger. As part of it, I acquiesced to Ian becoming Managing Director of the new enlarged company, whilst I became Deputy MD with an overview of all programming.

Ian was my friend. We had known each other a long time, and I was keen that our personal relationship should remain strong. It was tested though when Ian proved to be reluctant to alter the BRMB management structure, which I knew would cause a problem in future months as hardly any cost savings resulted from the merger. I was sure that Phil White, who now joined the new group board of directors, would want to know why. I effectively remained at Mercia, running the Coventry part of the business much as before.

Not that the deal went through entirely on the nod. Phil had won himself a deserved reputation as a man whose business acumen and insight was amongst the best there was. So much so that he had become an adviser to the merchant bank Barings. He had earned many millions running a scrap metal business from a small office at a scrapyard at Hinckley in Leicestershire, and from investing his money astutely.

Yes, he was an adviser to Barings. This, however, was ten years before the collapse of the bank through unauthorised derivatives trading involving the trader Nick Leeson. When the merger between BRMB and Mercia Sound was taking place Barings was one of the most stable international investment management firms with sovereign connections, pension funds and charitable institutions amongst its clients. Phil White was one of its most trusted advisers, so when Phil asked Barings to run their eye over the deal, and with a peer of the realm as the chair of one of the participants, they could not have been more receptive.

In the week before the merger was due for completion, Lord Butterworth and I found ourselves in the main board room at Barings, in the heart of the City of London. An imposing view of the corporate edifices that housed some of the world's top businesspeople lay below us, including the Lloyd's Building and the Bank of England, as we looked down from the 25th floor.

A superb lunch was provided and the Chairman of Barings, Sir John Baring, was an ultimately polite and very correct host. He was described by the author Stephen Fay, in his book "The Collapse Of Barings" as a melancholy man of gravitas. "You are not supposed to know what he is thinking," wrote Fay, "and certainly not to question whether he is thinking at all."

Other members of the Barings family, the brothers Nicholas and Peter Baring, joined us for lunch, as did three of the bank's senior executives. Lord Butterworth was in good form, grandly exuding bonhomie. His enthusiasm for our hosts was expressed long and loud.

Jack, however, had a problem. It was one that Ian Rufus had warned me about when I took over as Managing Director at Mercia Sound. Jack was prone to nod off at a moment's notice.

It was, we thought, a form of narcolepsy and I knew that Lady Butterworth was more than a little concerned about it when Jack was driving. Fortunately, it did not seem to occur when he was at the wheel, but when I was briefing him before a board meeting his head would nod, his eyes close, and he was apparently no longer present.

He had done the same with Ian, who told me that it made him extremely uncomfortable. Ian's answer was to simply stop talking until Jack woke up. I decided that I would do the opposite. I carried on talking, if anything speaking more loudly than I had been. Regardless of what either of us did, Jack would wake after maybe a minute, sometimes slightly longer, with a very loud cry of "Oh YESSS!", as if he had been following all along.

During the lunch at Barings all was proceeding well, with Jack engaging in discussion with Sir John Baring over the state of the economy, the movement of interest rates and so on. Without warning his eyelids drooped and the distinctive voice of Lord Butterworth stopped. Jack had, to all intents and purposes, fallen asleep.

Around the table, concerned faces turned their gaze on me. Sir John raised his eyebrows and had started to ask, "is Lord Butterworth OK?". He had got as far as "Butterw..." when Jack opened his eyes, raised his head, and cried out "Oh YESSS!"

Sir John's anxious look relaxed slightly.

"I suppose it can be quite tiring in the House of Lords," he said to Jack.

"No," replied Lord Butterworth firmly, "why on earth would you think that?"

I managed to break the embarrassed silence that followed by raising the issue of the merger which is, after all, why we were there.

"Have you formed a view for us, Sir John?"

"Oh, it is perfectly fine," he replied, "Phil White said he thought it was OK, but that he wanted our opinion. If Phil White thinks it is fine, it is certainly fine with us."

Nodding heads and smiling faces around the table acquiesced and we finished our lunch without any further disturbance.

* * * *

For all his wealth, Phil White liked to present himself as a fundamentally down to earth man of the people. Rarely in a suit, his favoured jackets and trousers were nonetheless obviously purchased from quality outfitters. He made great play of "only" driving a Saab. It was a Scandinavian brand, and nowhere near the biggest selling car of the day, but it enjoyed a reputation for excellent, reliable engineering and its top of the range model, which Phil owned, had a sizable price tag.

When we reported at the board meeting what Barings had said about the merger, Phil clearly bathed in the glory of the moment. He took me to one side that evening, after the meeting.

"Sir John Baring told me what happened," he said. "He said he was impressed with you and the way you dealt with it."

He paused before continuing.

"Jack will have to stand down soon, won't he?"

"The IBA regulations say he has to retire at 80", I replied. "That's in just over twelve months."

"Do you think anyone else would want it?"

I realised what was behind his question and I knew I had to be careful in my response.

"Peter would be interested, I think, and possibly Barry, but I take it you would be too."

"What do you think?" he said. Before I could answer he patted me on the shoulder and said, "keep me informed."

* * * *

The issue of Jack's retirement came up a couple of meetings later, the IBA having written to him, copied to me, advising us that we should consider putting a process in place to elect and appoint a new Chairman. Jack was less than happy.

I had to place it on the agenda for the board to discuss, but Jack shut down any debate by declaring that he would be writing to the IBA to demand they reconsider. He argued that competency rather than age should be the critical factor.

The room fell silent, which annoyed me. None of the other directors seemed ready to stand up to him. Maybe they thought if it was left it would go away. I felt the minutes of the meeting had to reflect something other than Jack's fit of pique.

Taking a deep breath, I said that I did not think if he wrote such a letter it would be the least bit helpful. I added that I had already had a conversation with the IBA, and they remained adamant that the rule would not be altered in any circumstance.

As I spoke Lady Butterworth looked at me and raised her eyebrows. Doris knew what was coming. The other directors just stared at me and Jack.

"Butterworth will not be silenced!" he yelled at the top of his voice. "If I want to write to them, I will do so."

The others looked stone faced. Lady Liggins was the first to speak.

"I am sure that Stuart has sounded them out properly Jack," she said, "and a rule is a rule, but if you feel that you have a case to make Jack, then of course you should write to them."

Jack grunted and, to the relief of all concerned, he moved us on to the next item. He did write to the IBA, but he tempered his view, and instead of raising an objection it was an acknowledgement of their letter to him. He included a paragraph to the effect that age was a brutal arbiter, but he did not demur from their requirement for him to stand down.

Lord Butterworth retired from the Chairman's role of the radio company he had founded. His wife remained on the board, and Phil White replaced Jack. Peter Davis, a local lawyer and a keen supporter of the everything Mercia Sound did, made a pitch for the chair, but Phil's financial connections saw him secure the support of the other directors.

* * * *

Covering sport, and particularly football, I was acutely aware of the irritation caused to broadcasters and listeners alike of the changes made to our regular schedules whenever we covered a fixture at any time other than on a Saturday afternoon, for example on midweek evenings. The BBC was able to be more agile, putting football on one frequency whilst keeping a regular show on another.

Peter Baldwin, the Director of Radio at the IBA, consulted with station managers to establish to what extent this was an issue. He phoned me to discuss it, and to gauge my response to another proposition called 'incremental radio'. The idea was that a second station, providing specialist interest programmes, would be licensed in the transmission area of an already established station. I replied that if such a service was introduced in Coventry, Mercia Sound should have an increase in signal strength to help provide better reception in the Leamington and Warwick areas, where the topographical dip in the land meant that the current signal was poor.

I also stressed that we should also have the right to put different programmes on our medium wave frequency to those we had on FM. This would allow us to compete directly with the BBC by putting football match coverage on medium wave whilst regular programmes continued on FM. As for an incremental station within the same patch as Mercia Sound, I was confident enough that our audience figures were strong enough to live alongside a station serving a specific community.

Peter asked me to submit a proposal for a trial run of separate shows on AM. We already included programmes for Asian and Polish listeners in Coventry and Warwickshire, and I turned to one of Coventry's well-known characters and a good friend, Irish singer Bob Brolly, to see if he would host a weekly show for the many people in the area whose heritage lay in the Emerald Isle.

The point was made. We demonstrated the separate outputs could be readily laid on and Mercia Sound was soon running different evening programmes on FM and AM.

Splitting frequencies was so successful that in 1989, the combined AM transmitters of BRMB and Mercia Sound were taken over by a new station, devoted to golden oldies music, called Xtra-AM. Les Ross, moved from hosting the Breakfast Show on BRMB to broadcast, again at breakfast time, across the West Midlands on the new station.

I will admit to being slightly miffed that Xtra was to be run from Birmingham, under the management of a member of the BRMB team, Phil Riley. I got on with well with Phil, and I had no gripe with him personally, but it felt that part of my little empire had been taken away. I probably sulked like a spoiled child for a day or so, but there was no choice but to accept it and get over it. Phil steered Xtra to great success from its launch.

Twelve months later, a new station, after the model of the incremental service described to me by Peter Baldwin, was launched to serve Coventry's Asian community, called Radio Harmony. At the same time Mercia Sound added a second FM frequency, aimed at Leamington Spa and Warwick, to overcome the issue of the weak signal strength.

* * * *

Although I had forsaken direct coverage of the Sky Blues because of the demands of running the business, I had a season ticket to watch the team at Highfield Road. After the '87 Cup Final victory, John Sillett was placed in sole charge of the team, and over three seasons he kept the club in the top half of the table. In fact, they finished seventh in 1988/1989, although that season was overshadowed by the complete opposite of their FA Cup triumph from two seasons before, when they were beaten 2-1 in the Third Round by non-league Sutton United.

David Phillips scored the Coventry goal that day as the Sutton victory was hailed as the day's top performance on BBC TV's 'Match Of The Day.' I had travelled to Sutton with my brother-in-law David that day, and we stood and watched amongst the contingent of 2,300 City fans. To our surprise, alongside us was a member of the team who had won the Cup at Wembley, full-back Greg Downs. Greg was not a happy man at Sutton, having been left out of the side. His mood was made worse by watching his team-mates lose, as he chewed on a big cigar, wincing at every missed tackle, and groaning at every uncompleted pass.

* * * *

Covering first-class cricket at Mercia Sound was slightly more complicated than covering football, in that our local team, Warwickshire, played their home matches at Edgbaston in Birmingham. There were many very able reporters who ensured that we maintained our coverage, but it meant that with my daily commitments in Coventry I could not be as close personally to the players and the club as I could with local football.

Warwickshire had, historically, played some fixtures at other grounds in the county, including venues in Coventry, Nuneaton and Stratford-upon-Avon. In the early 80s, they had played at the Griff and Colton Ground in Nuneaton and at Courtaulds Ground in Lockhurst Lane, Coventry, but had not ventured out of Birmingham since. I understood why.

The club had a major investment in the County Ground at Edgbaston and that is where the majority of the members, who had paid for the privilege, expected to see their team play. However, I felt that this was not wholly fair to those who regularly incurred the cost of travel to and from Birmingham from other parts of the county.

The Warwickshire captain at the time was Andy Lloyd, with whom I got on well. He agreed with me that it should not be impossible for at least one home match a season to be played elsewhere, which was something other counties seemed to manage.

So it was that for a few years in the early 90s, Warwickshire played once a year at the Bulls Head ground at Binley Road, Coventry, the home of Coventry and North Warwickshire Cricket Club. I took great pride in having played a tiny role in encouraging that move. They have since staged one-off matches in Stratford and in Rugby, the last of which was in 2015.

Since 2010 Edgbaston has been developed into one of England's premier cricket stadiums, arguably second only to Lord's. It thus seems likely that few, if any, Warwickshire matches will now be played anywhere but Birmingham.

* * * *

In November 1990, John Sillett was sacked as manager of the Sky Blues, despite being on his sick bed on the day it was announced. Former England star Terry Butcher, his playing career nearing its end, was recruited as player-manager, with the club once again desperately trying to battle clear of the relegation zone.

John Sillett went on to be manager of Hereford United, where he'd been in charge prior to his time in charge of the Sky Blues with George Curtis. John's second stint at Hereford lasted for just one season, after which he worked as a pundit for ITV in the Midlands, and for me at Mercia Sound. He travelled with me to most Sky Blues' away matches, with my brother-in-law, David Cleobury travelling with us.

Most of our trips to away matches were made by train, with Dave taking on the role of carrying the broadcast kit. That amused Snoz hugely, prompting him to give Dave the nickname "pack", as in "pack animal". We enjoyed some great trips together, all the more so because Snoz was instantly recognised wherever we went.

He joined in and loved the banter with the fans on the trains, all of whom wanted to talk to him and share jokes and stories with him. Most were inevitably Coventry City supporters, but everyone, football fans or not, were thrilled to see and meet him. They were the days before mobile phones with cameras, otherwise I am sure there would have been a clamour to grab photos with him too.

* * * *

Covering the fortunes of the Sky Blues and running a radio station probably occupied more of my time than they should, but the care and welfare of my family were the most important things in my life. Too often, my work priorities got in the way, but I was more than fortunate that Sue was a strong and brilliant mother, overseeing the growth and development of our two sons. Nicholas and Matthew were lively, lovely boys, and Sue, together with our extended family, ensured that they had a happy childhood.

Marrying Sue meant I became part of a loving family that readily embraced me into their midst. Her Mum and Dad, Eileen and Des, welcomed me from the start, as did Sue's brothers, Mark and David. My sister and her daughter, together with my cousins and their offspring, were also part of a superb family. I was truly blessed.

Mergers and takeovers, however, became the priorities for the radio business, so that's where my main focus had to be.

It was a time of change and unrest across commercial radio. Nothing stays the same for ever. The world turns, and things move on. You either move with them or you stand still, and the latter was not what our directors and shareholders were prepared to settle for. The issue for me and for Ian Rufus was identifying which move would prove to be most beneficial, to the company and to us as individuals.

Rock and roller cola wars, I can't take it anymore

We didn't start the fire

It was always burning

Since the world's been turning

We didn't start the fire

But when we are gone

Will it still burn on, and on, and on, and on

We didn't start the fire

It was always burning

Since the world's been turning

We didn't start the fire

No we didn't light it

But we tried to fight it.

Billy Joel, 1989

© Universal Music Publishing Group

Chapter Sixteen

The Palace and Pebble Mill

The best things in life are free

But you can give them to the birds and bees

I want money

That's what I want

That's what I want

That's what I want

Janie Bradford & Berry Gordy Jr., 1959

© Sony/ATV Music Publishing LLC

The merger of BRMB Radio in Birmingham and Mercia Sound in Coventry and Warwickshire set our newly formed Midlands Radio Group on a positive, exciting platform. It also alerted the rest of the UK commercial radio network that there were deals to be done and that the West Midlands was pushing that agenda forward.

Ian Rufus had been in touch with Colin Walters, one of the leading figures in the early years of UK commercial radio, who with his launch Managing Director Philip Birch had made Piccadilly Radio a huge success in Manchester. I was brought into the discussion with the notion of putting the stations serving the West Midlands and Greater Manchester together. It made perfect sense. The logic behind it, creating a unit that would more than hold its own alongside London's Capital Radio, fell naturally into place.

Every radio station outside London had a story to tell of being unable to realise what each regarded as their fair share of national advertising revenue. Capital effectively called the shots with national advertisers for the whole network, and It was becoming ever more obvious that local stations existing through local advertising alone was not sustainable. The demands of shareholders for increased profitability were increasing, so the pressure for change was building.

Colin Walters was also concerned by a predatory approach that he knew was being prepared by the Red Rose Radio Group, owned by businessman Owen Oyston. He was also the owner and Chairman of Blackpool Football Club. Oyston had set out to be an actor in his teens, but failed to make his mark.

He was more successful, very successful in fact, as an estate agent. He pioneered the concept of "no sale, no fee", initially in and around Blackpool. He built Oyston's Estate Agents into the largest firm of family-owned estate agents in the United Kingdom. In 1987, he sold it to Royal Insurance for a sum in excess of £35-million.

Now he was intent on achieving similar riches from radio and he wanted Piccadilly Radio. Knowing Oyston's intentions, Ian and I, together with John Parkinson and Phil White, put together a bid that we knew would be supported by the Piccadilly board of directors. Similar to the deal between BRMB and Mercia, it would take the form of a merger, rather than a takeover. Ian would remain in the West Midlands and run that part of the enlarged business, Colin Walters would move to London to oversee the push for greater awareness and an improved return in national revenue, and I would relocate to Manchester to run things there.

Things moved forward smoothly. The boards of both Midlands Radio and Piccadilly Radio approved the deal. Everything was in place. The final step was for Piccadilly shareholders, meeting at the Midland Hotel in Manchester, to give their assent.

John Parkinson, Ian and I travelled to Manchester to attend the meeting as observers, ready to toast our new venture afterwards. When we arrived we were met by Colin Walters and his chairman. Both looked anxious.

Their concern was well founded when they explained that Owen Oyston had in recent days purchased sufficient shares in Piccadilly that would enable him to prevent the deal going through. However, to do so he would have to turn up at the meeting and cast his vote.

With five minutes to go there was no sight of him. The room was packed with Piccadilly shareholders and some of the station's staff, including some of their front-line presenters. Behind a table, set on a raised dais, sat their board of directors, the Chairman in the middle. He kept checking his watch.

I sat with John Parkinson and Ian Rufus on one side of the room, wondering just how this was going to turn out.

"I think we'll be OK," whispered Ian. "He's not going to show."

As the seconds ticked away, the clamour of gossip and chatter across the room gradually died away. Everyone seemed to be looking at the time. Eyes began to focus on the dais, waiting for the meeting to be called to order.

Less than a minute remained when the room's large double doors were flung open. A tall, striking figure strode into the room. He was wearing a black fedora hat and over his smartly tailored suit, a long black cape, which was buttoned across the chest by a shining gold chain. He positioned himself on a row of empty seats close to the dais.

The entrance could not have been more flamboyant. Drawing on his thespian days, Owen Oyston clearly relished the moment. He undid the cloak and whirled it expansively round his shoulders before placing it alongside him on one of the vacant seats. The hat followed, unleashing long blond if slightly greying locks, matching the moustache and goatee beard.

Few in the room failed to recognise him. One or two of the Piccadilly team shook their heads and put their hands to their foreheads. They were already anticipating what would follow. It seemed to me that was more because they knew that they could trust Colin Walters, but they now realised that life was set to be very different for their radio station.

"You were nearly too late Mr. Oyston," said the Chairman. "I was about to start the meeting."

"In that case Mr. Chairman," came the reply, delivered in vibrant, stentorian tones, "I am right on time. Just in time too, I feel."

The Chairman duly opened proceedings and read a prepared prologue to the motion proposing the merger. Owen Oyston then got to his feet and asked to address the room. The vote that followed was academic, as Oyston's shares enabled him to block the deal. His Red Rose Group subsequently acquired Piccadilly Radio, and soon after renamed their business Trans World Communications.

After the meeting, Ian Rufus and Colin Walters left together for a pre-arranged meal, whilst John Parkinson and I were about to make our way to the railway station and head back to the Midlands when we were, to our surprise, invited to have lunch with Owen Oyston. He was extremely gracious, and once more I found myself in conversation with someone who had taken the time to find out quite a lot about me. I wondered who he had been talking to.

I knew a few members of both the Piccadilly and Red Rose teams, particularly Piccadilly Sports Editor Tom Tyrrell and Red Rose Programme Controller Keith Macklin, who was well known as a TV rugby league and football commentator. I somehow doubted that Oyston's information had come from them, but whatever his source, he had a remarkable insight into where I had worked and what I had done. He stopped short of offering me a job, but it seemed that could be the next move.

John Parkinson, in fact, intervened to joke that Mr. Oyston should not try to poach one of Midlands Radio's executives in front of its Chairman. The comment was well received and a genial Oyston told me to contact him personally should a move appeal to me. That call was never made.

Friends and colleagues who worked at Red Rose had previously offered me their thoughts about him, and his colourful private life. The latter was revealed very publicly a few years after that Manchester encounter, and it became apparent that that I hand been wise to steer clear.

There was no reason to suppose that I would have been affected by his various legal and alleged criminal activities, but they did impact on his radio interests. He was known to have a herd of bison on the land around his home at Claughton Hall, near Lancaster, which apparently straddled the Pennines. His personal net worth was estimated to be in excess of £100-million, so I am sure that working for him would have been interesting but it was not a route I wanted to pursue.

* * * *

After the Piccadilly drama, at Ian's insistence the Midlands Radio group quickly made another move. Ian was determined that we should not stand still, and

I am sure he was right, but what he had up his sleeve did not sit comfortably with the team at Mercia Sound.

Ian's plan was for us to join forces with the Radio Trent group in the East Midlands. Their group included Radio Trent itself, serving Nottingham and Derby, and Leicester Sound, a radio station that Trent had rescued after its original company, using the name Centre Radio, had failed.

The antipathy towards the Trent Group stemmed from the notion that if we were not going to merge with what was perceived to be a big station like Piccadilly, the West Midlands entity should instead seek a take-over of its own. The perception was that another merger, particularly with a group not regarded as of a similar status to the BRMB-Mercia combination, was not the direction we should consider.

It was fully accepted that the Trent stations had a fine track record of excellent programming and had launched some stellar careers. Yet there was concern, in part focusing on Trent's Managing Director Ron Coles. Few, if any, in the West Midlands knew Ron, but his reputation was that he had a strong, charismatic personality, and so was likely to take the lead in any negotiation or policy planning. Nothing wrong with that, but he was not "our" man.

I will not deny that to some degree I shared those concerns, though I did not wholly agree with them. Ron very likeable and I always got on well with him, but I did wonder whether Midlands Radio should be considering other targets or partners. Ian Rufus, however, had a single-minded approach, and he convinced me that putting the West Midlands and the East Midlands together made sense.

Once again there was something of a cliff-hanger involved in the meeting that finally settled it. I had been contacted by Alan Mullett, Managing Director of Beacon Radio in Wolverhampton, another station that had enjoyed mixed fortunes since it launched. Alan was concerned that as a West Midlands station, Beacon would be on the fringe of any new enlarged enterprise across the rest of the region. He asked if we would be interested in a counter proposal.

I discussed this with Phil White, who said if Beacon were serious they should put their bid on the table. If they did he would ensure that it would be considered. I communicated that to Alan, who promised an offer would follow.

By the day of the meeting that was scheduled to sign off on the merger with the Trent Group, there was no sign of any bid from Beacon. The Piccadilly debacle was still fresh in my memory, but John Parkinson told Phil White that he had received a call from Beacon's chairman. He confirmed they planned to make a bid.

The meeting with Trent was held in Nottingham. I drove there with Phil White. En route the phone rang in my car. It was Alan Mullett checking what time it was due to start. I told him, and at Phil White's prompting, added that if he was going to make a move he needed to "get on with it"!

John Parkinson was in the chair as the directors and executives of the Midlands Radio group and the Radio Trent group gathered round the table. Phil White had already told John that he understood that Beacon were likely to make contact before we began, so John engaged in inconsequential small talk with those sitting near to him until it was time to start. Just as he called that the meeting to order, Ron Coles' secretary walked in to say that the Chairman of Beacon Radio was on the phone, wanting to speak to Mr. Parkinson.

John looked at his watch and fleetingly caught my eye.

"Please tell him that we have started our meeting", said John. "If he will leave his number I will call him back when we have finished."

Ian Rufus and Ron Coles exchanged glances. The meeting proceeded and the merger was done. Whatever subsequently occurred between John Parkinson and the Beacon chairman was never passed on, but if Beacon had been genuinely interested they had missed their chance.

The new enlarged group took Midlands Radio's name, with Ron Coles becoming Managing Director and Ian as his number two.

My role reverted to running Mercia Sound. I was asked to simultaneously run Leicester Sound with my immediate future therefore involving regular journeys up and down the M69. Phil White's office at his scrapyard at Hinckley, was midway along the motorway. I made regular visits to see him and discuss the business.

* * * *

Phil's main concern in life was making money. He knew that to do so he had to have the right people in the right place. He was astute enough to raise the issue of staff morale with me, recognising that the ownership changes we had been through could have an effect. I told him that there were quite a few people at Mercia who were, to say the least, uncertain about it all, and that although I had no first-hand knowledge of it I had heard that there were similar feelings amongst the team at BRMB.

At Leicester there were one or two who were distinctly unhappy and had made no secret of it. I was welcomed by many there, but that was by no means a united view.

"Well," said Phil, as frankly as ever, "you have to manage that and keep on top of it. You do know that this is not the end of it, of course?"

I asked him what he meant.

"There will be other deals," he said. "Who knows who will make the next move, but you can be sure that someone, somewhere, is planning it right now."

What he said next surprised me.

"Ian did not exactly emerge with glory from this, did he? To settle for being number two hardly sounds ambitious. He was too worried about doing a deal, any deal, to properly gauge where it was going."

I jumped in to say that I thought that was a rather harsh assessment.

"I have known Ian a long time," I said, "and in my experience he has always acted with the next move very much in mind. Yes, I am surprised and disappointed that our side has not come through as top dog in this merger, but I assume he has something else in mind."

"If he does," said Phil, "you can be sure that it will benefit him not the company, nor you. Stuart, your loyalty is commendable, but you need to look after yourself in situations like this."

Phil had given me food for thought about what the next move might be. He was proved to be correct, as the process of restructuring commercial local radio by way of mergers and acquisitions had only just begun.

* * * *

Ron Coles steered the group through a successful launch on the full stock exchange in 1990, but he also made some decisions that alienated Phil White. At Radio Trent group, Ron had been at one with his board of directors. They backed him with little, if any, dissent and he was very much the king of his castle.

Running Midlands Radio was something else again, and the man you really did not want to fall out with was Phil White. Achieving stock market status was something that Phil applauded, but when Ron went on to make an investment in a multi-ethnic station in London, serving many diverse communities with a variety of foreign language programmes, things took a very different turn.

Spectrum Radio was an important venture, attempting to satisfy the inevitably challenging requirements of many different ethnic groups. It devoted a few hours per day to each community. That was always going to be daunting. There were many and varied fingers in the management pie, and the word was that they did not always see eye to eye.

Ron recognised that there was huge kudos to be had for anyone making it a success. For Phil White it was an irrelevant dalliance and, more significantly, bad business. When Ron told the board what he had done Phil was apoplectic.

He was about to spend Christmas at his family home in the Isle of Man, and he asked me to meet him at his office near Hinckley. When I arrived, he was briefing his secretary about issues to be aware of whilst he was away. As I entered his office he immediately raised the issue of Ron's investment in Spectrum Radio. I suggested that Midlands Radio could afford to speculate in the interests of the growth of the ILR network.

"One of these days," he said quietly, in a quiet tone laced with obvious irritation, "you will need to sort out the winners from the losers. Never mind how much is involved, you never just give money away. You need think twice about who you hitch your star to. I understand that you keep on supporting your friends Stuart, but this is not a game."

* * * *

It certainly was not a game to Capital Radio. Its dominance of the network and its proximity to national advertising decision makers in London, had provided much of the impetus for the mergers and acquisitions. Capital proceeded to purchased Midlands Radio plc for £18-million. Soon afterwards, in 1993, they sold Radio Trent, Leicester Sound, and Mercia Sound. The buyer was the emerging force of Ralph Bernard's GWR in 1993. Capital retained ownership of BRMB, so they now had London and Birmingham.

One early GWR decision was that Mercia Sound's 1359 kHz medium wave frequency would cease to be Xtra-AM and would instead be rebranded as GWR's own oldies service, Classic Gold. Under Capital's management Xtra-AM continued in Birmingham, with its presenters urging Coventry listeners who wanted to continue to listen to Xtra-AM to retune to the Birmingham frequency. That prompted GWR to pull the plug on Xtra-AM in Coventry earlier than they had originally planned.

Phil White's forecast about a proliferation of other deals was proving correct. GWR made changes almost immediately. The irony was not lost on me that had I accepted Ralph Bernard's offer to work with him in Wiltshire at the very beginning of the GWR adventure, I might have been leading those changes and imposing my ideas on the newly acquired stations. Instead it was Steve Orchard, who under Ralph's guidance had been schooled by Australian radio programmers into what was required, who led the charge.

Steve effectively rebranded Mercia as the "all new Mercia FM", which was its on-air identity for nearly two years. It was effective, although it irritated presenters and listeners alike, many of them asking me how long it was going to be referred to as "new".

At first, Ralph Bernard decided to leave me in my post in Coventry, but before long I was seconded to the East Midlands to oversee the launch of a new station. Radio Trent had served both Nottingham and Derby as one entity, but in 1994 it was decided to separate them and give Derby a station of its own.

I was given the role of 'launch director', working with Steve Orchard and the team at Derby to create RAM FM, as the station would be known. It used the legendary, or possibly mythical, Derby ram for its name. Former Radio 1 DJ Dave Lee Travis was a star guest on air that first morning to launch the station from studios under the Assembly Rooms in Derby Market Place.

The staff at RAM FM were a small but talented team, including news presenter Anne-Marie Minhall, who I was not surprised to see move soon afterwards to Classic FM where she became one of the main presenters. Just over ten years later, Capital Radio returned to the area, merging with GWR, as a consequence of which RAM FM was reconnected to Radio Trent. This time it was also connected to Leicester Sound to form one programme stream called Capital FM East Midlands. By that time, I was no longer involved with the commercial radio ownership merry-go-round.

* * * *

In 1995 I was thrilled and delighted to be made MBE for services to broadcasting, receiving my medal from Her Majesty Queen Elizabeth II at an investiture at Buckingham Palace. Sue was able to attend, as were Nicholas and Matthew, the two boys smart in morning suits that matched mine. At 12 and 10 years of age respectively, I know that they found the proceedings somewhat tedious, but I hope that they can reflect on having been at such a special place on such a special day that meant a huge amount to me.

Apart from being a huge honour in itself, to receive the same award that had been bestowed on my Grandfather was very special. Even more so, to receive it from the same monarch, some 33 years later, was just extraordinary.

Nick and Matt were repeating the role that I had enjoyed on that day in 1961 when I sat with my dad at Buckingham Palace, watching the Queen place the medal on my Granddad's lapel.

You are never told who nominates you for an honour, nor the reason why, other than the simple citation. Mine read "for services to broadcasting" which is great, but that does not really tell you much. As time passed, I gathered that I had been nominated by at least one of the former Mercia Sound directors and others, for my work at the radio station and in the wider community. A major element was that Charity Snowball achieved the sum of £1-million in 10 years. The real thanks for that go to the listeners and the wider population of Coventry, Warwickshire and South-West Leicestershire. They raised and donated the money, so my MBE was as much a reward for all those who had contributed.

* * * *

Shortly before my investiture, Sue and I were invited to join all the other GWR executives and their partners for dinner at the magnificent Le Manoir aux Quat'Saisons in Oxfordshire, owned by the French celebrity chef Raymond Blanc. A wonderful meal was complemented by an overnight stay. Not just any overnight stay. The room Sue and I had been allocated was the beautiful 15th Century Dovecote. After a splendid breakfast the next morning we headed home as I wondered precisely what Ralph Bernard had in store for me.

By now I had returned to Coventry from my role as launch director of RAM FM, but Carlton Dale had unsurprisingly been running the Mercia ship very successfully. Carlton had readily bought in to the GWR ethos.

Surplus to requirements, regardless of the MBE, it seemed inevitable that I faced redundancy. Ralph was not so brutal, however, and he asked me to explore the idea of establishing a sports production unit. It would provide original sports programming that could be syndicated across the GWR stations, and maybe the rest of the commercial radio network.

Working from home, it did not take long for me to realise that there was one huge obstacle to be faced. At that time the BBC held almost all the major sports contracts, and that meant that very few doors would open to any other broadcast organisation. History states that later, when Sky waived huge cheques around all that changed, but I did not have a cheque book to reach for let alone significant sums to go with it.

The dining room table at home became my desk. By this time, Sue was pursuing a career in teaching, as a member of staff at the Montessori School that both our boys had attended. So I had the house to myself. This was long before the now widely accepted notion of working from home. I found it a lonely and frustrating time, particularly as it proved difficult to establish whether any opportunities existed for sports coverage outside the BBC and ITV.

Whilst I made many calls, it was a rare day that I received one in return, so when the 'phone rang one morning, it made a pleasant surprise. Even more so when the voice at the other end belonged to a former colleague from the Radio Hallam newsroom.

It was David Robey, Assistant Managing Editor at BBC WM in Birmingham, the station that had originally been BBC Radio Birmingham, where my professional life as a broadcaster had begun. David asked if I was available to host a show on WM whilst one of their regular presenters was away on holiday. How did he know that I might be? I never found out, but it seems Ralph Bernard may have had something to do with it, the three of us having been at Hallam at the same time.

I said that I would be interested, but that I would have to ensure that GWR had no objections. Perhaps not surprisingly, since I was unproductively taking a salary from them, they were happy for me to proceed. It was quite bizarre to return to the studios at Pebble Mill, where I spent a thoroughly enjoyable fortnight sitting in for WM's mid-morning presenter Malcolm Boyden who would become a good friend.

Malcolm's producers looked after me brilliantly, and my two-week run on the show seemed to go well. I also renewed acquaintances with Ed Doolan, the Australian who had become an adopted Brummie and a local legend after years on BRMB before moving to BBC WM. I had briefly known Ed years before. Malcolm Boyden's show was on air each day immediately before Ed, so I handed over to him every day throughout the fortnight.

At the end of the two weeks, David Robey introduced me to the station's Managing Editor Tony Inchley, who had been away for most of the time I was there. He had been listening though, and he thanked me for what I had done and said how much he had enjoyed it. David's parting shot was that he looked forward to us linking up again soon.

I thought no more about it until, a week or so later, WM's Programme Organiser Tony Wadsworth 'phoned me. He invited me to meet him at Pebble Mill to discuss an opportunity that he hoped might interest me. Tony was hosting the WM Breakfast Show himself, with his wife Julie presenting the regular travel updates during his programme.

When we met Tony explained that he had only intended to take on Breakfast on a very short-term basis after the departure twelve months before of the previous host, the legendary former BRMB Sports Editor Tony Butler. Ever since, the station had been looking for a new, regular Breakfast Show presenter. The opportunity he had on offer was for me to take on that role if I were interested.

We got as far as talking terms, at which point Tony Inchley joined us. He and I chatted privately and readily agreed on the fee that matched my GWR salary. That left me to talk to GWR, and Ralph Bernard was generous in every way, agreeing to my move and wishing me well.

Ralph had been good enough to keep me on when others might have shown me the door, but I knew that I had stepped away from any meaningful role in ILR some months before. The move to BBC WM marked the end of 21 years in commercial radio.

Radio is a sound salvation

Radio is cleaning up the nation

They say you better listen to the voice of reason

But they don't give you any choice 'cause they think that it's treason

So you had better do as you are told

You better listen to the radio

Wonderful radio

Marvellous radio

Wonderful radio

Radio, radio

Elvis Costello, 1977

Chapter Seventeen

Moving On

Nothing to do to save his life call his wife in
Nothing to say but what a day how's your boy been
Nothing to do it's up to you
I've got nothing to say but it's okay
Good morning, good morning
Going to work don't want to go feeling low down
Heading for home you start to roam then you're in town
Everybody knows there's nothing doing
Everything is closed it's like a ruin
Everyone you see is half asleep
And you're on your own you're in the street
Good morning, good morning

John Lennon & Paul McCartney, 1967
© Sony/ATV Music Publishing LLC

Presenting a Breakfast Show was not a wholly new experience for me. I had sat in at Mercia Sound when the regular presenter was away on holiday, but the BBC WM Breakfast Show was different. At Mercia, music was an essential part of the show, but BBC Local Radio required an all-speech format.

I was offered plenty of advice. Malcolm Boyden, whose show now followed me, said "you know your football, so you'll be fine at WM. It's not brain surgery, is it?"

David Robey, who I soon learned was preparing himself to replace station manager Tony Inchley on the latter's anticipated retirement, told me, "enjoy yourself. You don't need me to tell you how to do it, but we do not expect, nor want, you to be another Tony Butler. Just be yourself. Your producers will advise you."

I very rarely saw Tony Inchley. The word was, accurately or otherwise, that he was not in the best of health. From senior management, however, I was welcomed by the West Midlands Head of Regional and Local Programming (HRLP) Nigel Chapman. Of all the senior executives I have met within the BBC Nigel was the most open and approachable.

Within that giant corporation there is inevitably quite a mix of different persona; some truly human and genuine individuals with whom it is easy to get along, but also a few who convey the feeling that they are doing you a favour by giving you the time of day. I have met, for example, three of the BBC's Director-Generals. All no doubt good, sincere men, each with their own notion of how to do the job. All interesting men, but from my perspective, none presented themselves as a leader for whom you would lay down and die.

Not so with some of the managers who were closer to what was happening day to day. Some, and I stress the word some, were more inspiring. Nigel Chapman was one such. He spelled out clearly what was expected of me as Breakfast Show host at BBC WM.

"It's a difficult challenge," he said. "I am sure from your background, you know how the audiences stack up and what station does what. We need BBC WM to be popular but not to the extent of being trivial. WM has tried that, and it did not deliver what we wanted. Your job is not to copy Terry Wogan on Radio 2, nor to imitate the 'Today' show on Radio 4, but to fit somewhere in between. We think you can do that. You are aware of the news agenda, but you also appear to be at home playing records. That fits the bill for us. Good luck."

If nothing else, that at least told me what they were not looking for. The added element for me was, despite my highly critical perspective of my home city that I had held since moving to Sheffield some twenty years before, I now felt immense pride in being the local BBC Breakfast Show host for Birmingham.

My sporting affiliations and immediate family connections were firmly established in Coventry, and my time in Sheffield had provided many happy memories and invaluable experience, but being given the opportunity to broadcast every morning to Birmingham, the city where I was born and grew up, still meant a huge amount. I thought of my parents and grandparents, particularly my Mum, my Dad and Granddad Charles, and wished fervently that they had still been around to share it with me.

In the first few months one or two old schoolfriends made contact, asking if I was the Stuart Linnell that they had known at Kings Heath High School or Kings Norton Grammar School. There was also contact from one or two former colleagues from my days working for Birmingham City Council. It was great to hear from them, and in a couple of instances it proved helpful as I built up contacts to whom I could turn for items in the show.

My producer, Gemma Walker, proved to be one of the best in the business; certainly, one of the very best I have ever worked with. Her contacts book was full of all the right people, and she was not afraid to call them at that early time of day, whilst we were on air, regardless of whether they were in the bathroom, having breakfast, or at whatever stage of their day's preparation they had reached. Sometimes she even made those calls before the show started at six o'clock, which meant that she woke many of those she called. Such was her skill and charm at knowing just what to say and how to say it, few turned her down.

Most of our stories were set up the day before by afternoon and evening producers working on the following morning's news agenda. We were nothing if not reactive, however, to how a story had developed overnight, or to material that emerged fresh that morning. To do so, with the show on air between 06.00 and 09.30, we inevitably disturbed people at precisely the time of day that many least appreciated it, but Gemma managed to achieve it with great aplomb, a disarming laugh and just the right turn of phrase.

* * * *

One of the joys for me of working at BBC WM was properly getting to know Ed Doolan and his wife Christine. Ed and I had been passing acquaintances for a few years, but working at the same station, sometimes on different aspects of the same story, meant we became much closer.

Popular though he was with the listener, Ed could be difficult to work with. His show majored on consumer affairs, taking the part of many of those who wrote to him or 'phoned his show asking for help in dealing with the frustrating bureaucracy of local councils, or unscrupulous rogue traders. He was uncompromising in his professionalism, and the brusque approach he took during his show with people he deemed were not playing fair with his audience occasionally surfaced off air in the office.

To avoid confrontation with Ed some of the organisations and companies he pursued would respond in writing by sending a fax or an email, but Ed would refuse to read those messages on his show. He would study them off the air so that he knew what was being conveyed, but he would never reveal the contents during his programme.

"It's no good sending me a fax," he would declare. "A fax can't answer my questions."

It would be fascinating to know how Ed would handle the world where social media rules so overwhelmingly, though I have absolutely no doubt that he would have adapted his approach.

At least one of the other members of the WM team once confessed to me "I can't stand Doolan. I'm sorry if he's your friend, but he's not my cup of tea." Whilst I understood that, I enjoyed Ed's company, on the air and off, and Sue and I often enjoyed dinner and attending social events with Ed and Chrissy.

Ed's family heritage was part Jewish and part Irish. He was born and brought up in Australia. After working as a schoolteacher, first in Sydney and then in London, he worked in Germany for the broadcaster Deutsche Welle. He took all that experience to the West Midlands, and in his many years at BRMB and BBC WM he became, by common consent, an adopted Brummy.

All that prompted many an opportunity for humour, to which he readily contributed, about his affiliations. On St. Patrick's Day he was Irish, when England played Australia at cricket or rugby he supported the winning side, he hailed the ability of German footballers to regularly beat England on penalties but called the 1966 World Cup Final result a triumph, and when the opportunity arose he was partial to a bacon sandwich, "but don't tell the Rabbi."

He had friends and contacts throughout the worlds of show business and politics. He often interviewed fellow Australians such as Clive James and Barry Humphries. The latter would appear sometimes as himself, whilst on other occasions adopting the role of either Dame Edna Everage or Sir Les Patterson. Rolf Harris was another old friend from Australia, and members of the West Midlands' showbiz glitterati, like Jasper Carrot, Don Maclean, Noddy Holder and Tony Iommi would often appear on Ed's show. Amongst his other guests, many appearing with him more than once and always keen to return, were

Telly Savalas, Leonard Nimoy, Jim Davidson, and HRH Princess Anne. Once, when Ed was unwell, Jim Davidson came to Pebble Mill and was drafted to appear on my show instead. Whilst Jim readily answered my questions, his over-riding concern was for Ed's well-being. "Just you make sure to tell him I asked after him," he said, very purposefully.

Ed regularly took a couple of weeks leave from BBC WM to be the stand-in host of 'The Jimmy Young Show' on Radio 2 when Jimmy was on holiday. He also often appeared on the regional TV news show 'Midlands Today' on BBC1. His three-hour Christmas Show on BBC WM, broadcast live from Birmingham's Symphony Hall, became an eagerly anticipated annual event filling the hall to its 2,000-plus capacity.

He was particularly proud of the fact that in his lifetime he interviewed every British Prime Minister since Sir Alec Douglas-Home in 1963, with the exception of Harold Wilson. If you asked him who was his favourite interviewee, he would not hesitate before giving you two names that he could not choose between, those of Margaret Thatcher and Nelson Mandela.

The Radio Academy honoured Ed with a place in the UK Radio Hall of Fame. He was awarded Honorary Doctorates by Birmingham's three universities, becoming the first person to be recognised by all three. Thereafter, whenever we met or spoke on the 'phone I would refer to him as "Doctor, Doctor, Doctor Doolan" which quite amused him.

Ed kept recordings of almost everything he did on air, as well as an archive of many other radio and TV shows, which enabled his broadcasting career to be extended by three or four years after he was diagnosed with dementia. Long after my time at WM, Ed stopped presenting his live daily show, instead spending one day a week at the studios recording links to some of his most memorable interviews, which were then edited into a weekly Sunday lunchtime programme.

Ed died in 2018, and Sue and I were amongst the mourners at his funeral in the February of that year. Jasper Carrot, Les Ross and Ed's agent Paul Vaughan, all made very moving speeches about an exceptional, singular, one-off broadcaster.

* * * *

In 1997 Ed used one of his many local contacts to assist Malcolm Boyden and me when we both found ourselves in line for one of UK radio's top awards.

After spending many years arguing the case for local radio to be properly recognised at awards ceremonies, I found myself amongst the Sony Radio Awards nominees.

My BBC WM show had been nominated in 1996 in the Best Speech-Based Breakfast Show category. At that stage, the Sony's did not allow for discrimination between national and local stations, so we were up against the 'Today' show on BBC Radio 4, amongst others. It meant a trip to London to the awards ceremony, and to my absolute delight I found myself allocated a place on the same table as one of my all-time favourite cricket commentators Henry Blofeld.

I was not quite so delighted to discover that Henry and I were sitting apart, although directly opposite each other, on a circular table of ten in the midst of the Great Room at the Grosvenor House Hotel on Park Lane, where the awards ceremony was held every year. The room was packed with the great and the good of UK broadcasting, and the conversation during dinner from more than a hundred tables was so loud it was impossible to even attempt to talk to anyone other than those immediately either side of you.

Henry Blofeld had been placed next to Paul Brown, Head of Programming at the IBA. Both clearly enjoyed each other's company, but Paul, knowing my sports background and sensing my enthusiasm to meet Henry, was kind enough to introduce us before we sat down to eat. Being greeted with a warm smile, those twinkling Blofeld eyes, and the infamous trademark phrase "my dear old thing", made my night.

We didn't win Gold that night but instead took Silver, which in that company I took as a compliment. I think Nigel Chapman must have seen a confidential copy of the embargoed press release giving details of the winners, because on our journey to London when someone gave vent to speculative thought about how we would do, he said, "oh, I think we probably travel in hope rather than expectation."

Twelve months later it was a different story. My show had been nominated again, and this time Malcolm Boyden was also in the running in another category, that of Radio Personality of the Year. This is when Ed Doolan stepped in. He appointed himself transport manager for the big event. Ed told us he had laid on two stretch limousines, courtesy of a friend who ran a business supplying such vehicles.

Boyden and I sported black bow ties and dinner jackets, and our female colleagues, including my producer Gemma, were appropriately glamorous as we set off at lunchtime on the fateful day down the M1 to the Grosvenor House. What Ed had omitted to tell us, or in fairness maybe didn't know himself, was that these luxury limos were regularly used for transporting relatives to funerals, so their engines had been adapted accordingly. Their top speed, even on the motorway, was 45 miles per hour. It was a long journey.

So much so that, having been on air at 6 o'clock that morning to host the Breakfast Show, I had nodded off long before we reached the outskirts of London. Like my habitual lateness, my ability to fall asleep at the drop of a hat in any given situation is an accepted part of Linnell family life. On this occasion my early start, added to the monotony of the drawn out, painfully slow excursion, lulled me into a fairly deep slumber. I was told afterwards that, much to the great amusement of all present, I had snored quite loudly during the journey, something else my wife in particular would acknowledge as an all-too common occurrence.

Whether someone nudged me to silence the snoring, or whether the car stopping and re-starting as we made our way through London did the trick, I don't know, but I re-entered the world of consciousness just as we passed the end of a road bearing the name 'Stuart's Close'. I pointed it out and muttered, more to myself than anyone else, "I wonder if that's an omen." Nigel Chapman, who had travelled with us again, said "Who knows? This time, it might be."

I later mused on the fact that once again Nigel must have seen the embargoed press release, because this time I won Gold. Michael Aspel was the host of the awards, and when he announced that my show had won, I grabbed Gemma's hand and took her on stage with me. Nick Ross, presenter of BBC TV's 'Crimewatch' programme, presented me with the trophy, and with Gemma alongside me I made my acceptance speech, trying to remember to mention everyone on our team. In doing so, I failed to refer to my wife, which was unforgivable, given that she had to put up with me getting up to go to work at four o'clock every morning. Sue has reminded me of that ever since.

To the delight of the entire WM entourage, Malcolm Boyden also won Gold. More than a few celebratory glasses were enjoyed before the end of the awards show at which point one of our number stumbled towards the stage where Michael Aspel was gathering his script before walking off. Michael looked down at the commotion occurring in front of him, only for the miscreant to look up glassy eyed at the legendary TV star and utter, in inebriated delight, "double fucking Gold!", before passing out.

We managed to gather all the members of our party, albeit in a state of euphoria, and set off on our ponderous journey home in the Doolan ordered lazy limousines. Before we left London, however, someone decided it would be a good idea to share our good fortune with Her Majesty, or whichever member of the Royal Family may have been spending the night at Buckingham Palace. The cars duly drew up outside the Palace gates, depositing Boyden and I, and one or two others, onto the pavement still clutching our Sony Awards.

The duty police officer was not impressed, but despite the provocation of our behaviour, resisted the temptation to deal with us too severely. He managed to persuade us that we would be better off returning to the vehicles and making our way home, rather than disturb the royal peace.

* * * *

I slept at Pebble Mill that night. We made it back sometime after one o'clock in the morning, and as I needed to be in the studio at five, or thereabouts, ahead of the six o'clock start of the Breakfast Show, the logical thing would be to kip there. On the ground floor, near to the TV studios there were a few lockable cubicles with a small bed or couch that presumably doubled as dressing rooms. I was provided with a key for one of those, and access to a nearby shower. My 1997 Sony Gold award 'slept' with me.

* * * *

My interviews with politicians, national and local, on the WM Breakfast Show, brought me to the attention of the BBC's West Midlands Political Editor Patrick Burns. He asked me to have a cup of coffee with him one morning, during which time he offered me the opportunity to present the weekly live TV show "The Midlands At Westminster". It was usually shown on BBC1, but would move to BBC2 from time to time according to the needs of the schedule. Patrick explained that I would alternate in the presenter's chair with Stephen

Le Fevre. One week Stephen would host the show, the following week it would be my turn. The show included filmed reports compiled by the politics reporters, and the presenter would conduct live studio interviews with MPs, local Councillors and other guests.

Patrick asked me to think it over. That took, at the most, thirty seconds, and I went on to enjoy sitting in front of the cameras every other weekend. One unexpected consequence was that during the General Election campaign of 1997 I was flown back to the UK from holiday in the Canary Islands to host an Election Special on Midlands regional TV with candidates from the main parties as studio guests. I left the family at the villa we were renting in Lanzarote whilst I travelled to Birmingham to host the show, returning to the beach the following day.

* * * *

For three days in May 1998, the world's focus was on Birmingham as the 24th G8 Summit was held in the city. The G8 was the forum which brought together the heads of the richest industrialized countries. The political leaders of France, Germany, Italy, Japan, the United Kingdon, the United States, **Russia and the President of the European** Commission, all gathered in England's second city.

Part of the backdrop to the summit was the scandal that hit the American presidency of Bill Clinton. It had been revealed that the President had an affair with a White House intern called Monica Lewinsky. It lasted for 18 months, ending in 1997, the year before the summit. That served to heighten the already hugely significant awareness of the event. Security was everywhere in Birmingham, with an international media presence following everything that was said and done.

The setpiece event of the summit was a dinner at which the Presidents and Prime Ministers would sit down together to explore what they could tell the world what, if anything, they had resolved during their time in Birmingham. It was held in the ornate banqueting suite at Birmingham Council House, the home of Birmingham City Council. Before the dinner a reception was held, where the great and the good of the West Midlands could meet the world leaders. Amongst the invited guests at the reception were Ed Doolan and Stuart Linnell from BBC WM.

So Doolan and I shook hands with Helmut Kohl, the Chancellor of Germany, with Jacques Chirac, the President of France, with the Prime Ministers of Japan, Italy and Canada, with our own Prime Minister, Tony Blair, and with Bill Clinton. The only one we did not meet was Boris Yeltsin, the President of Russia.

Yeltsin's presence was fraught with concerns for the organisers of the summit, particularly for the UK as host nation. There were rumours that he might not show up for the dinner, and Tony Blair was constantly excusing himself from the gathering, apparently to oversee whatever was happening to ensure the Russian President was safely escorted to the event.

America's First Lady, Hilary Clinton, was there, and after we'd hovered for a few minutes on the edge of a throng of people attempting to grab a word with her husband, Ed nudged my elbow and said, "let's go over there." He nodded in the direction of a smaller queue.

Within a few minutes we were chatting to Mrs. Clinton. Our conversation lasted only a few minutes, but in that short time I was captivated. The room was crowded, but when she turned towards you with those deep blue eyes, it was as if there was no one else present. It is a rare skill, but Hilary Clinton is brilliant at making you feel, for the brief time we had with her, that nothing else mattered.

No sooner had Mrs. Clinton worked her magic than Ed steered me toward an adjacent room. One of Ed's contacts within the City Council had ushered us towards the exclusive area of the banqueting suite where the leaders would dine. A beautifully laid oval table sparkled and shone as we were allowed to look, but not touch, the porcelain, cutlery and glassware that would shortly be used when this historic dinner was served.

We soon had to leave the scene as word arrived that Boris Yeltsin had finally made it. Having got him there, Tony Blair was clearly anxious to get the dinner underway and the other principal guests were invited to make their way into the dining room at which Ed Doolan and I had just been allowed to take a privileged peek.

I had met Tony Blair in Drowning Street soon after he had led Labour to victory in 1997. One of his key policies was, as he put it in a speech at the 1996 Labour Party Conference, "education, education, education."

Amongst his initiatives was to establish a reading hour every day for primary schools. I was asked to interview the Prime Minister about the scheme for BBC Local Radio.

So I found myself walking through that famous imposing shiny black front door, with the words 'First Lord Of The Treasury' inscribed on its letter box. I caught a glimpse of the Downing Street Press Secretary and the Prime Minister's Official Spokesperson Alistair Campbell addressing his team in an office adjacent to Tony Blair's just as the Prime Minister came to join me and the BBC producers who were with me.

I had been given a stereo tape machine to use, with a microphone with which I was unfamiliar. Mr. Blair was unsurprisingly bouyant so soon after taking office, and the interview went well.

However my lack of knowledge of the mic resulted in the Prime Minister's voice being heard loud and clear, whilst mine was sounded distinctly distant. The end product was usable but didn't include much of the interviewer. An unforgettable day, but not my greatest radio moment.

* * * *

In 1999, I was surprised and delighted to receive an honorary degree from Coventry University. The University's Vice-Chancellor at the time, Michael Goldstein, invited me to his office to talk about my career and to tell me that I had been selected for the Honorary MA because of my broadcasting and my contribution to the community in Coventry and Warwickshire. In part, the purpose of the conversation was to provide Michael with the information he require to compile the citation he would deliver in Coventry Cathedral at the awards ceremony at which the degree would be conferred. To say that I was thrilled for my work to be recognised in this way is an understatement. Michael is also a keen Sky Blues supporter and he and I often compare views and opinions about our favourite team.

That year ended with the celebrations for the end of the second millennium. They were promoted around the world as the end of the 20th century and the 200th decade, and the start of the third millennium, the 21st century and the 201st decade. There has been much debate, however, about the accuracy of the date with many mathematicians and academics suggesting that it should all have been commemorated twelve months later.

As it was the world had fun with major events held at the end of 1999 on New Year's Eve, including the opening of the Millennium Dome, later renamed as the O2 Arena, built at Greenwich in southeast London. Sue and I were among those invited to be at the huge event held there that night, with Her Majesty Queen Elizabeth II and the Prime Minister Tony Blair in attendance

Having driven from Coventry, we took a London tube train to the London Town of Stratford where all those attending were handed their admission tickets. We then had to queue to travel back along the same line to get to the Dome. The queue was large and slow moving. I spotted the former jockey Willie Carson and his wife being hurried by security officers through the line of people. Having met and interviewed him once I grabbed Sue's hand as I called out "Do you know where we're going Willie?".

He turned to see who was calling him. Whether or not he recognised me I don't know but he gave me that famous cheeky smile and winked back as he replied "I don't, but someone does. Come on."

As he spoke he waved us to follow him, so we did and soon boarded the train which took us to the party. All the pre-packed airline type meals had gone by the time we got there, but we found our seats opposite the Queen in time to watch an aerial ballet and other entertainments, before joining in with 'Auld Lang Syne', followed by the chimes of midnight.

* * * *

Life at BBC WM was never dull, and I thoroughly enjoyed every minute of being part of it until it was dramatically cut short. It was the result of the vindictive actions of a former BBC presenter carrying a grudge against Midlands broadcasters who continued to work after he had lost his job.

John Clarke, an old friend from Coventry who ran a PR agency involved me from time to time in presentations to some of his clients. It was a very loose business arrangement, and I was always careful to avoid any issue that might compromise my role as a BBC presenter. Few of the clients of the PR company had any interest in the area covered by WM, so that rarely posed a problem.

My PR friend forwarded a letter he received, addressed to me, asking for advice about media training. Offering tuition or guidance in how to face a media interview or enquiry has always been a vexed matter for the BBC and

I was well aware of that. I replied by simply suggesting that if the correspondent provided me with precisely what they required I would offer avenues they might pursue that might help. I knew, for example, of companies and individuals not employed by the BBC who could deliver what was needed, depending on what it was the letter writer required.

The following week I was summoned to a meeting by regional BBC management at Pebble Mill who threw a copy of my reply at me across the desk telling me that it was proof that I was providing media training without BBC permission to do so. It came out of the blue. I was astonished and totally at a loss of what to say or do.

I was asked if I denied writing and sending the reply. Naturally I did not, but I did not understand why or how my letter was now in the hands of members of management. I accepted that of course I had written it and tried to make it clear, as I believed the letter did in any event, that I was merely replying out of politeness, trying to ascertain what the person who had contacted me wanted so that I could recommend how they might proceed further.

My protests went unheeded and within a very uncomfortable thirty-minute meeting I was told that my contract, which had just a few months left, would be paid up but not renewed. I was told that I should remove any personal items from the offices and studios immediately and that I should not return. It being Friday, someone else would do my show from the following Monday morning.

In retrospect I wish I had gathered my wits sufficiently to fight and challenge that action through tribunals or the courts. All I could think of however was that I had a wife and two young sons to worry about. A few months money was available to me and I feared losing that.

My anxiety was fuelled when I left Pebble Mill that afternoon. As I made my way out of the reception area, one of the security staff approached me and, clearly embarrassed, asked me to hand over my entry pass to the building. He also asked if I was taking any BBC property with me, or if all the items I was carrying belonged to me. I assured him that I had nothing that wasn't mine. He then looked me in the eye and smiled kindly.

"Just doing my job Stuart, as I'm sure you realise. I don't know what's happened, but I'm sorry to see you go. Take care of yourself. I hope we see you again sometime."

I shook his outstretched hand and thanked him. I tried to smile, but inside my stomach was doing somersaults.

The severity of the moment hit home hard. I had been sacked. It was brutal and it was wrong. I knew it was wrong, but my contract was about to expire. I knew that if, in any event, they had chosen not to renew I would be gone anyway.

That weekend Sue and I were in some turmoil, to say the least, over what to do. Ed Doolan was the first to offer support and he carefully pieced together what had happened and, without total proof, soon worked out who it was who had plotted against me. Ed had previously been the target for a former BBC colleague with an axe to grind, as had our mutual friend Bob Warman, the veteran presenter of the regional ITV news programme Central News. Both had seen off the attempts to at least denigrate them in the eyes of their employers, their colleagues and the listening and viewing public, but it had been a distressing and unpleasant experience.

Ed had been determined to discover who was behind it, and he uncovered a considerable amount of evidence pointing to an unemployed veteran of Midlands broadcasting as the person responsible. The individual in question died in 2010, so in identifying him I do not put him through the embarrassment and angst that he had inflicted on me. I take no pleasure in revealing that Barry Lankester was the man that Ed identified.

Barry, born and educated in Coventry, had played a hugely significant role in the development of broadcasting in the Midlands. During his career Barry was an actor, news presenter, news and sports reporter, sports commentator and a skilled producer. He had a cultured distinctive voice, always perfectly modulated with perfect diction. His work in the BBC's regional programming helped lay the foundations for local radio in the Midlands.

I never found out what lay behind his departure from the BBC, but Ed maintained that he knew the story and that it was, at least in part, related to drink. Ed said that Barry had always held a grudge after being required to leave the BBC, and in a warped sense of injustice he was determined to wreak his vengeance against the likes of Bob Warman and Ed. They became aware of what he was doing and were always on guard against his activities, looking out for such clues as letters signed by anagrams of his name, whereas I blundered into the not very sophisticated trap that he set, and fell victim to it.

Ironically, some years before, I had employed Barry on a one-off basis to appear on Mercia Sound, sitting alongside me as a co-commentator for the 50th Anniversary of the bombing of Coventry on November 14th, 1990. Together we had described Her Majesty, Queen Elizabeth, the Queen Mother receiving the Peace Bell from the President of Germany at Coventry Cathedral. Barry had found Mercia Sound's style of broadcasting slightly more informal than he had previously experienced at the BBC, but we had worked together well with no apparent indication of him displaying any animosity towards me.

Nonetheless I became his target. Barry's efforts succeeded in so far as my contract with BBC WM was not renewed and in 2001, aged 54, I was left frantically looking for a new job.

* * * *

Difficult years followed, even after I successfully applied for a role with a commercial radio company that established a remit of operating small local stations on some of the original principles of UK Independent Local Radio. The company was always struggling for adequate investment and was therefore constantly under-funded.

Rather than providing me with gainful employment, the promised salary, share options and the like never materialised. It cost me a considerable amount of money, substantially eating into our personal cash reserves. On more than one occasion, despite having no remuneration from the company myself, I paid the wages of staff out of my own pocket. A chastening time which also cost me friendships, broken fences that remain unrepaired.

* * * *

Freeing myself much later than was sensible from that arrangement, I once again cast around for new opportunities. Now in my sixties I was very aware that it would not be easy, but I set about sending emails to BBC local radio station managers, offering my services as a freelance presenter hoping that my name might be recognised by some and that my experience might count for something.

Thankfully, one or two replied positively and I found myself hosting occasional shows for BBC Hereford and Worcester, BBC Radio Oxford, and BBC Radio Derby. Closer to home, BBC Coventry and Warwickshire provided me with a regular weekly show, hosting the faith-based Sunday Breakfast Show.

* * * *

My absence from being a regular on-air presence also meant for a few seasons my involvement with the reporting of Coventry City Football Club was also put on hold. The club stepped in and involved me as their regular match-day stadium announcer, and I'll always be grateful to the then club secretary Graham Hover for his friendship and support.

My brother-in-law David was also involved, orchestrating events in and around the tunnel area, where players, sponsors and special guests would emerge on to the pitch. David also worked closely with the Coventry City Former Players' Association, the CCFPA, particularly on their annual Legends Day. The CCFPA work really hard, keeping the football club in touch with its heritage.

David and I have some great memories of being part of the match-day stadium team, but the best of all for sheer entertainment, history and, of course, the result, was the final match at Highfield Road on 30th April 2005, against Derby County. Two goals from Gary McSheffrey, two from Dele Adebola, and one apiece from Stern John and Andy Whing saw the Sky Blues bow out of their famous stadium with a 6–2 victory.

There was a memorable hour building up to the kick-off, started with the West Midlands Police band marching and playing on the pitch. A parade of City legends, including John Sillett and Bobby Gould, followed, ending with Jimmy Hill running out to a huge ovation. I had introduced the legends from the centre-circle, and when he arrived Jimmy took the microphone from me and led the crowd in a rousing version of "The Sky Blues Song".

After that tremendous result, the City fans celebrated for one final time on the Highfield Road pitch, with the record "Time To Say Goodbye" by Andrea Bocelli and Sarah Brightman playing over the loudspeakers.

* * * *

Football also provided me with another opportunity, when the League Managers Association (LMA), working with other partners like the Professional Footballer's Association (PFA) and the FA, decided to develop and provide training courses for would-be managers. I had a meeting with John Barnwell, who was then the Chief Executive of the LMA, and who I knew from his time as manager of Wolves. John asked if I would be interested in creating an element of the course that would help the delegates learn how to deal with the media.

The courses were held at Warwick Business School, based in Coventry at the University of Warwick. Thanks to John's introduction, and with the assistance of Professor Sue Bridgewater from the Business School, I put a course together, involving presentations from TV presenter Bob Hall and *Coventry Telegraph* reporter Adam Dent. It was a fascinating time, advising coaches who I had enjoyed watching as star players, such as Paul Ince, Brian McClair and Chris Hughton.

One who proved to be a very keen and able student would go on to become one of the most successful and popular managers of Coventry City. His name is Mark Robins. Many years later, when I thought Mark would have forgotten my involvement in the course, he let me know that he hadn't. His success as a manager had little to do with me, but I take a small sense of pride that he attended one of my courses.

* * * *

My involvement with the LMA and with the Sky Bkues helped keep me going as I pursued whatever freelance radio work that I could find, but then came a real lifeline. To my surprise and eternal gratitude, Bernie Keith re-entered my life.

One of the stations that I had contacted looking for presenting opportunities was BBC Radio Northampton, where Bernie had become the station's star turn. On receiving my email the station's managing editor had mentioned it to Bernie who instantly provided me with a glowing endorsement. It resulted in the opportunity to sit in for Bernie himself, hosting his show when he was on holiday, and a few weeks later I was invited to the take over from host of the lunchtime consumer show when he was away.

When my email arrived, the managing editor was about to take maternity leave, so by the time I had completed my second session for BBC Radio Northampton the station had acting managers in charge. They invited me to meet them and asked if I would be interested in taking over the lunch show on a regular basis. The current presenter was moving on and the opportunity to replace him was mine if I wanted it.

A brief conversation with Sue endorsed my decision to accept the offer, and so in 2009 I began a return to being a front-line daily presenter. I was now 62 and provided with an opportunity that had seemed remote a few months before. I found myself working with a highly professional team that included some very experienced and talented broadcasters. It was quite a contrast with one or two of the other stations I had worked at, where the age group of the staff was generally younger.

Whilst it is always good to see young people being given their chance, it was also reassuring to work within a more mature team at a station where experience was valued. That was demonstrated perfectly by the station's two main news presenters. Andrew "Radders" Radd, whose regular shift covered the morning, from the Breakfast Show until lunchtime, and Sarah Foster, who steered the station through the afternoon.

They were both highly professional, trained journalists who expertly compiled the hourly bulletins with the benefit of great awareness of the national news agenda combined with massive local knowledge. That Radders is also a cricket lover of considerable repute, contributing to Wisden, and knowing everything there is to know about Northamptonshire County Cricket Club, was a huge plus for me.

* * * *

As I took stock of my new opportunity Ed Doolan's influence once again came into play. My new brief was to be BBC Radio Northampton's consumer champion. I drew on the Doolan play-book of how to pursue the issues and difficulties that listeners presented to us. With two delightful producers, Ally Grant and Ellie Frost, we formed a great team that was a joy to be part of. Ally and Ellie knew each other well, having worked with my predecessor on the show, but they readily made me welcome, and we very quickly forged a working relationship that was more akin to being part of a family than a workforce.

As their Christian names sounded so similar, they had already created on-air identities as "Ally and Miss Frost" to avoid confusion for the listener. We had great fun together and hopefully found solutions to the problems encountered by Northamptonshire listeners.

After a couple of years, the station's long-serving breakfast presenter also decided that the time had come to move on. After ten years on breakfast shows in Northampton and elsewhere, he wanted to realise his aspirations to move into BBC management. I was offered the role as host of the breakfast with a small increase in my pay rate and in the duration of my contract.

Over the next seven years, we woke Northamptonshire each weekday morning with a diet of news, interviews and features, a little inconsequential chit-chat to lighten the load and, at either end of the show, a little music. BBC policy, approved by the regulator Ofcom, was for BBC local radio stations to play no music on weekday mornings between 07.00 and 08.30, with the exception of Bank Holidays. So we made the most of the first hour of the show, from 06.00 to 07.00, with some familiar tunes, and then ended the show each day with one track chosen to provide an appropriate bridge from the all-speech, news-based content of Breakfast into the somewhat less reverent approach of Bernie's mid-morning show.

At breakfast time we pursued and steered the local news agenda and covered the major national and international stories. We enjoyed strong, though occasionally tetchy, relations with the local MPs, Councillors and other key decision makers, we reflected the views of Northamptonshire people and did our best to entertain at the same time. Those three key elements of good broadcasting, entertainment, information and education, were always at the heart of what we did, whilst always trying to remember that the most important person in the equation was the listener. Did it all make sense and mean something for Mr, Mrs or Miss Scoggins? That was always the test we measured ourselves against, and hopefully most days we came out OK.

I thoroughly enjoyed hosting the BBC Radio Northampton Breakfast Show, despite that drama of being knocked down by a police car, as described at the start of my story. The real ignominy of that event, for me and for the police officer driving the vehicle, is that she wasn't even going fast! Thank God she wasn't.

* * * *

During my time at Northampton three friends died. In December 2015, the football world said goodbye to Jimmy Hill, the great innovator, and the man who converted the club to Sky Blue and led them to the top-flight of English football, at the age of 87. Jimmy was not only a hugely influential in the history of the game, he also transformed its television coverage.

A magnificent celebration of his life was held at Coventry Cathedral, attended by hundreds, including the then Chairman of the FA Greg Dyke, and Roy Hodgson, who was then the England manager. Also there were PFA Chairman Gordon Taylor, several other managers from across the country, the Sky Blues manager at that time Tony Mowbray, and many City players, past and present.

TV commentator Barry Davies was there, and much as the purpose of the evening was to pay tribute to Jimmy, I was thrilled to grab a selfie with Barry, who has always been one of my broadcast heroes.

There were speeches from Jimmy's son Jamie Hill, from Bobby Gould and from commentator John Motson, who was very funny with his stories of working with Jimmy at matches and in the studio. West End star Dave Willetts sang, accompanying himself on ukulele during "I'll See You In My Dreams". The event concluded with everyone singing "The Sky Blue Song."

It would be wrong of me to claim that Jimmy was a close friend, but in his time as Chairman of Coventry City he was always generous with his time, and he was always ready to discuss football with me. Whenever we met, he always ensured that he gave me a story.

* * * *

Three years later, I received a message whilst on the air in Northampton that I struggled to comprehend. It was with deep shock and disbelief that I learned that Cyrille Regis had died at just 59 years of age.

* * * *

There were many tributes to illustrate the respect with which Cyrille was held. That he played with distinction for four different West Midlands clubs, West Bromwich Albion, Coventry City, Aston Villa and Wolverhampton Wanderers, and is regarded with fond affection by fans of all four, underlines his status as a real legend. You will get no argument from those supporters that he deserved more than just five international caps for England.

I first met Cyrille when Bobby Gould signed him for the Sky Blues in October 1984, and he went on to star in that historic FA Cup victory three years later. His death meant that great squad was without one of its heroes. Everyone's thoughts turned to his wife, Julia, and his family.

Cyrille was elegant on and off the pitch. He was a true gentleman and, like the other members of the '87 fraternity, he was my friend. He was always approachable, and always measured when expressing his thoughts and opinions about football.

He once lost his temper with me, when I questioned on air whether he warranted his place in the team based on his goalscoring form at that time , but it was quickly forgotten. However, he could never dismiss so readily the racism and racist abuse to which he and other black players had been subjected. When the issue came to the fore, as it did on air during an interview one evening, his anger was controlled but deep. He firmly spelled out the unforgivable hurt and insult that resulted from the ugly taunts, gestures and actions of prejudiced and ignorant people.

Of all the clubs he played for, Cyrille's first love was West Bromwich Albion. A celebratory event in memory of Cyrille was held at their home ground, The Hawthorns. I sat alongside Dietmar Bruck as coaches, players and fans saluted his distinguished career, all expressing great disbelief that he had died at only 59.

He was a huge, influential, figure even after his playing days came to an end. Amongst the many paying tribute was his former West Brom teammate, Brendan Batson, who simply said, "we will miss him."

* * * *

The day after Cyrille died we lost Ed Doolan. Like Cyrille, Ed was truly a legend. He invented consumer broadcasting in the UK, long before the likes of Watchdog and Rogue Traders weighed in on TV. He was the Citizen's Advice Bureau of radio.

He was the voice of people who thought they had no voice. No one who needed help was insignificant so far as Ed was concerned. He usually went straight to the top, and woe betide any organisation, company, local council or individual who failed to respond or take it seriously.

He was the mediator, the referee, the problem solver and the wise counsel, but always with a keen awareness that he was hosting a radio show, an entertainment. It was never, ever boring.

He spoke with equal authority and enthusiasm to Prime Ministers and Peers, and one of his proudest moments was when he met and interviewed Nelson Mandela. The mutual respect between the two said as much about Ed as it did about the great statesman.

Ed the man was as sharp, as entertaining and as witty as Ed the broadcaster. I am proud to have worked alongside him, and to have called him my friend.

We always enjoyed spending time with with Ed and his wife Chrissy. She was described as his "rock" through his later years when he was battling dementia.

Ed Doolan was a colleague, a friend, and someone I admired hugely as a broadcaster and a man.

As the years go by and friends pass away the value of keeping family close takes on particular significance. My sister and I have steadily grown closer and she has become a Mum and a Grandmother.

My cousin Steve does not live close by but we have kept in close touch and Sue and I often visit his sister, my other cousin, Jane. When circumstances allow family gatherings provide the opportunity to catch up and share our memories, with food and drink usually involved.

* * * *

One of the Northampton breakfast shows that will live long in the memory was a live broadcast from Belgium on Monday, 31st July 2017. BBC Radio Northampton Sports Editor Graham McKechnie graduated from Oxford with a degree in history, and his special interest was the First World War and those who went to fight. Graham was particularly keen to marry his two loves of history and sport, even more so if the wartime combatants played Graham's favourite code, rugby union.

On that chilly July morning my show, produced by Graham, came live from Shrewsbury Forest at the Ypres Salient, the area around Ypres in Belgium which was the scene of some of the biggest and bloodiest battles of World War 1. The date was the 100th Anniversary of the death of Edgar Mobbs, the English rugby union footballer who played for and captained both Northampton Saints and England.

On 31st July 1917, Mobbs was killed in action at Shrewsbury Forest during the Third Battle of Ypres, also known as the Battle of Passchendaele, whilst attacking a machine gun post. With the brilliant expertise of the military historian Jon Cooksey, and the input of Saints' and England player Phil Dowson, who later became Saints' director of rugby, we told Mobbs' story. We spoke to members of his family as, that morning, they installed a large wooden cross in the forest to mark the spot where the great man fell.

Walking through the forest that morning, whilst on air, Jon Cooksey told me that in the hiatus and trauma of the battle soldiers from both sides were left where they fell, as the bullets and shells ripped through their ranks.

"When you say they were left where they fell," I said to Jon, "what does that mean? Were the bodies then gathered for burial after the battle?"

"Oh no," he explained earnestly. "They literally lay dead or dying on the forest floor. Over the years they have been covered by woodland detritus, but skulls and fragments of bones surface from time to time, as do remnants of ammunition and armaments."

It suddenly dawned on me what Jon meant. I felt a chill down my spine. Phil Dowson later told me he had the same feeling at that same moment as the meaning of Jon's words registered.

"So what are we walking on?" I ventured, trying to sound much calmer than I felt. "Are we walking on a war grave?"

"It's not a designated war grave as such," Jon said, "but, yes, the woodland floor we are now walking on has grown over the bodies of those who died here."

Towards the end of the show a local man who lived nearby, and who fortunately spoke good English, said that he walked his dog through the forest every day and often discovered artefacts from the war.

"Only yesterday," he said, "I found a skull that we think was that of a young man, as well as a couple of spent grenades nearby."

That gave us plenty to think about, and more than a few moments of quiet contemplation, as we made our way back from Belgium through the Channel Tunnel.

* * * *

The more immediate contemporary battle being fought by Northampton, as well as other towns and cities in the UK, was that of a significant decline in its retail economy. It had endured the closure of several major town centre stores, including House of Fraser, British Home Stores, and Marks & Spencer. Alongside that, homeless people sleeping rough, some in shop doorways, contributed to an image of the town that many felt was distinctly uninviting.

Other places in Northamptonshire were similarly affected, so to highlight the issues we focused on the need for the regeneration of the centre of the county town. In an attempt to provide the platform of a positive approach, BBC Radio Northampton launched an initiative using the title and hashtag "Love Northampton". On 28th November 2018, the radio station held a debate, open to the public, which I hosted in All Saints' Church in the town centre.

By now, after seven years of being woken by my alarm at 04.00 every weekday morning, I had handed over the Breakfast Show baton to one of Northamptonshire's own, Annabel Amos. I took on the other end of the working day, hosting the late afternoon drivetime programme. The "Love Northampton" content emerged from that show, with a series of weekly studio based round table discussions on Monday evenings.

With plenty of lively and engaged input from listeners our conversations ranged around local history, Northampton's creative and cultural life, anti-social behaviour, the provision of public transport and how to re-energise retail activity in the town. The weekly debate provided a spark for action and further discussion within local organisations and community groups. It was readily acknowledged that it had been initiated, fostered and encouraged by the radio station.

The arrival of the Covid-19 pandemic in 2019 brought much of it to a shuddering halt, but hopefully not for ever.

* * * *

In 2012, before the pandemic entered our lives, I became embroiled in a complex issue turning on how broadcaster's pay was treated by Her Majesty's Revenue and Customs, and how it was dealt with by the BBC. The taxman wanted to be sure that anyone who claimed freelance status, whatever their line of work, were genuinely entitled to be treated as freelance.

I became a member of an inner circle within a WhatsApp group, representing local radio presenters. Even though they were household names on their patch, regarded as local stars, they were paid nowhere near the large sums attributed to nationally known broadcasters. I compiled a document that became known as the "dossier of despair".

The stories ranged from that of a morning show presenter in the North of England who worked as a taxi driver in the afternoon to keep the wolf from the door, to a mother of three who regularly went without a meal herself so that her children could eat. There were many such stories in the dossier, all from presenters whose listeners would have been horrified to hear how they were having to live their lives. Their professionalism and their love of the job meant that those listeners would never have guessed.

The dossier was presented to the most senior level of BBC management at one of a series of meetings that I attended at Broadcasting House in London, travelling there from my home in Coventry. National network presenters were also affected, and a group of five of us attended a meeting of the Digital, Culture, Media and Sport Select Committee of MPs, giving evidence to them at the House of Commons.

* * * *

Alongside my work in Northampton, I continued to be part of the BBC Coventry & Warwickshire sports team, covering the fortunes of Coventry City Football Club. Off the pitch, the club went through a torrid time.

On 14th December 2017, with the club in the second tier of English football, the Championship, it was taken over by a Mayfair-based hedge fund called Sisu Capital. It was reported at the time that the club was half an hour from administration when the deal was done. Administration was regarded as something to desperately avoid. The Football League imposed penalties of league table points deductions on clubs that took that route, so it meant relegation to League One, or the Third Division as it used to be called, would have been highly likely.

As it was, the excitement and anticipation of new investment and a new dawn under the new owners soon disappeared. It translated into despair and disenchantment as the club slipped further and further down, eventually into League Two, the old Fourth Division. Whilst it had been in the Premier League, surviving relegation battle after relegation battle, fans would say "if the Titanic had been painted Sky Blue, it would not have gone down."

That proved to be a sad joke as Coventry City sunk lower and lower, with some fearing it might even end up as a non-League club. Sisu pointed out just how serious and how much worse the club's financial position has turned out to be when they started to examine it closely. "Basket case" was the phrase they used.

There was no doubt that there had been a significant element of mismanagement over a number of years. Like many other clubs, Coventry City had spent much, much more than it could afford on players as it tried in vain to compete with high-flying club such as Manchester United, Liverpool and Arsenal. It all seemed a far cry from the day when George Curtis and John Sillett had led the legends of '87 to that famous Wembley FA Cup triumph over Tottenham Hotspur.

The saga that followed Sisu's acquisition of the Sky Blues was painful and protracted. The finger of blame was pointed at former directors, at Sisu, at Coventry City Council, at Wasps rugby club who went on to own the Ricoh Arena, at the Football League, and very often at all of the above.

Through it all, the fans of a proud and famous club were the ones who suffered most. Disputes over the Arena, exacerbated by the involvement of Wasps, saw Coventry play its "home" matches at Northampton Town and at Birmingham City, yet the fans continued to support it whilst praying and dreaming it would all reach a sensible conclusion.

The supporters did not go entirely unrewarded, as they watched their team win the Football League Trophy Final at Wembley, beating Oxford United 2-1 on 2nd April 2017, and then secure promotion back to League One with a 3-1 victory over Exeter City on 28th May 2018, again at Wembley. I was fortunate enough to be part of the BBC Coventry & Warwickshire team covering both matches.

* * * *

The Covid-19 coronavirus pandemic delivered bad news and good news for Coventry City Football Club. As it hit the UK the pandemic forced an early end to the football fixtures of the 2019-2020 season. When the consequent tally was taken, Coventry City were declared Champions of League One, and were thus promoted to the Championship.

The club was by no means equipped financially or with players who could seriously contemplate further elevation back to the Premier League. Following promotion "home" matches were played in Birmingham, but the club's future soon looked a little brighter. The pandemic caused fatal damage to the finances of Wasps rugby club, resulting in the collapse of its attempt to use ownership of the Ricoh Arena as a means of survival. It was forced to quit the Premiership, the top league of English rugby. Soon after Wasps' exit, the hugely disliked Sisu also departed the scene.

After a complex round of legal wrangles, with the involvement of administrators, the Arena had new owners. It was purchased by the retailers, the Frasers Group. At the same time, Coventry City Football Club was taken over by Stratford based businessman Doug King.

It looked, tantalisingly, as though he had brought the club good luck as well as a new approach. Within a few months of acquiring the club, Doug King proudly occupied prime seats at Wembley on 27th May 2023. The Sky Blues played Luton Town in a match that offered the winner the riches of playing in the Premier League. Literally, riches.

The contest ended 1-all before being decided by a penalty shoot-out, won by Luton. I watched amongst the Sky Blue Army of City fans as Coventry's hopes disappeared with a penalty that was launched into mid-air and over the crossbar. We went home disappointed and dismayed, but with immense pride in having seen the club, under the management of Mark Robins, take us to the edge of a return to the Premier League. Mark later steered us through a superb FA Cup run in 2024, culminating in a defeat, again on penalties, in the semi-final against Manchester United. The match had ended 3-all at the end of ninety minutes, but Coventry supporters will always consider that their team should have won the match with a goal in the last minute of the additional time, only for it to be ruled out by a highly dubious offside decision made by the VAR officials.

* * * *

Sport is a huge part of life in Northamptonshire and particularly in the county town. Northampton Saints rugby club, Northampton Town football club and Northamptonshire County Cricket Club, all have their home grounds in Northampton. Just a few miles out of town there's the Silverstone motor racing circuit, and Towcester Racecourse.

All have their own significant chapters in the history of British sport, with names I readily recall from my youth such as Dickie Jeeps, Dave Bowen, Colin Milburn and Graham Hill. There are, of course, many more.

Rugby union is the predominant sporting interest in Northampton, and during my time as a BBC Radio Northampton presenter, Saints were Premiership runners-up in 2013, before winning the title the following year. They also regularly contributed to the international scene, with players such as Courtney Lawes, Dylan Hartley and Tom Wood playing for England, and George North for Wales. I was delighted to make contact with Tom Wood, who was born in Coventry and started his career at the local club side Barkers Butts. It was a pleasure to interview Tom, and his father Andy, who also played for Barkers Butts.

Northampton Town Football Club, knicknamed "The Cobblers" because of the town's association with the shoe industry, had their ups and downs whilst I was working there. In September 2010, Northampton Town was the only League Two side to reach the Third Round of the League Cup, then sponsored by Carling, beating the mighty Liverpool at Anfield on penalties, after drawing 2-2 after extra time. To say the town's population was euphoric the following day is putting it mildly.

In my youth, the Cobblers played at the County Ground in Northampton, sharing the venue with Northamptonshire County Cricket Club, who continue to play there. The football club moved to its own stadium, Sixfields, in 1994, and in my time in Northampton the ground and the rebuilding of one of its stands was at the heart of a major scandal, involving the club and the local council.

It became a drawn-out affair, which had a parallel with Coventry City whose 27-match exile at Northampton occurred whilst I was a BBC Northampton presenter. I regularly found myself presenting my daytime show in Northampton and travelling back there to cover the Sky Blues for BBC Coventry and Warwickshire, either on a Saturday or a weekday evening.

Amongst the Cobblers players at that time were Ivan Toney and Dominic Calvert-Lewis, both of whom became stars in the Premier League. One of their managers was Chris Wilder. He was a guest on my breakfast show at BBC Radio Northampton one morning, and after our interview he said he thought he recognised my name. I replied that it might be from my time at Radio Hallam in Sheffield. The penny dropped, leading to his response that he used to listen to me when Hallam started in 1974, when he was seven years of age!

A former Northampton manager, who I remembered from years gone by, is Graham Carr, who often visited BBC Radio Northampton, and I would occasionally bump into him in the street in the town centre. A Cobblers' legend, Graham played for the club as well as managing them. I knew him from my Mercia Sound days, when he was manager of Nuneaton Borough. He used to take his young son to watch the Borough play. His son, by the way, had little interest in the football. He grew up to be the comedian Alan Carr.

In something of a contrast with the Saints and the Cobblers, Northamptonshire County Cricket Club provided a welcome, calming environment, where I occasionally spent a quiet hour watching a few overs before heading back home up the M1. Not that the club failed to make its own contribution to the local rosta of top sportsmen. Amongst those who played there at the time were Ben Duckett, David Willey and Alex Wakely.

Working in such a sports rich town provided me with some great personal highlights, such as having my photograph taken with rugby union's Premiership trophy, being driven in a high-performance car around Silverstone, and meeting former England rugby international Roger Uttley.

I also met football manager Sean Dyche, who was born in Kettering in Northamptonshire, and played for the Cobblers before going into management. Sean, who was manager of Burnley at the time, had been interviewed by the radio station's sports reporters, and we fell into conversation as we both left the building. When he learned I was a Sky Blues supporter he told me how impressed he was by the job Mark Robins was doing as City manager.

* * * *

During my time at BBC Radio Northampton, I had returned to covering Coventry City matches for BBC CWR, which meant I was working six days a week. That became seven days of week for a time, because for a couple of years I also continued to host CWR's faith-based Sunday Breakfast Show. From wondering if I would ever work again, I found myself being on air every day of the week, which eventually proved unsustainable. CWR resolved that conundrum by deciding to take its Sunday morning show in a new direction, engaging Coventry born broadcaster Justine Greene, who was well established as the main newsreader on BBC Radio 2 and BBC 6Music.

When the pandemic hit we all moved in a new direction. The pandemic and its associated public lockdown had a profound effect on all walks of life. Hardly anything or anyone was untouched. A significant consequence was that people learnt to work from home, including broadcasters, thanks to some clever kit swiftly assembled by BBC engineers. Just as long as you had a strong wifi signal, you could do your job from wherever was appropriate in your own home.

A couple of years prior to that I had made the decision to scale back on my work and "take a break", as I put it, from regular daily broadcasting. On 29th March 2019, after ten years at BBC Radio Northampton, I hosted my final regular daily radio show. My Northampton colleagues gave me a superb send-off, with a buffet lunch at a local town centre restaurant. A local cakemaker had designed and baked a beautiful cake in the shape of a record player, and I was presented with a glass microphone on which a plaque bore the inscription "Stuart Linnell, the voice of the county." That flattered me, to say the least, but it was a delightful momento of ten hugely happy years.

Speeches were made, and after returning to the studio for my last show it was invaded by the same lovely people who had attended the lunch. They gave me one final farewell, complete with a moving address by my old friend Bernie Keith, live on air.

I had been wrestling with what record to play to sign off, settling in the end for The Beatles. The words of the Lennon and McCartney song "In My Life" seemed wholly appropriate, not just as a way to call time on regular day time broadcasting but also to say, "au revoir" and thank you to the county of Northamptonshire which had provided me with a truly enjoyable, rewarding and wholly unexpected swan song.

Despite leaving Northampton my plan had been to continue on air in Coventry, for a short while at least, as part of the BBC CWR sports team, but the pandemic intervened. Using that home broadcasting kit supplied by the BBC, I was able to host CWR's Friday night Sky Blues 'phone in from the back room of my house. We operated like that for the best part of a season, but it couldn't last. The changes wrought by Covid 19 prompted a fundamental rescheduling of programmes and presenters, and my employment by CWR came to an end. Eventually, my career seemed to be over, once and for all.

* * * *

I enjoyed a long lie-in on the Monday morning after my Northampton farewell. During the following week, Sue and I spent most days taking things easy, going for meandering drives into the Warwickshire countryside, and enjoying a couple of relaxing lunches.

The following Monday, after a leisurely breakfast, my wife applied her intuitive logic and mapped out a potential new route forward for me.

"How do you feel?", she asked.

"Rested", I replied. "I hadn't realised how tired I'd become."

"Well,", she said, "Don't think you're going to get under my feet all day. What are you going to do?"

Before I could summon up a sensible response she put a copy of a local community newspaper in front of me, open at a page carrying an advertisement inviting applications for the role of volunteer Chair of Healthwatch Coventry. It described itself as "your local health and social care champion". It added that Healthwatch makes sure that NHS leaders and other decision makers hear the voice of patients and the wider public, using that feedback to improve care. I had often interviewed local Healthwatch representatives in the past, so I had a smattering of understanding about it.

I applied for the post and, to my surprise, was appointed. That was the start of a process through which I began to learn just how the NHS functioned and what the public thought of it. One of my new Healthwatch colleagues told me I was about to play a significant role in the local health economy. I also had to learn the meaning of the many acronyms that litter the jargon that pervades health and social care in the UK. Far too many acronyms and far too much jargon.

* * * *

If I thought I was finally putting my career at the microphone behind me, I have to thank an old friend and acquaintance, David Lloyd, for helping me to continue to make radio shows. David had supported a former colleague of his, Andy Marriott, to form a station called Serenade Radio, aimed at serving an audience that others were ignoring with music that had been phased out by established stations. Andy says that Serenade is loosely based on the old Light Programme where, as he puts it, "quality and a sense of warmth and old-fashioned values were paramount".

Serenade is heard online, so to listen to it you do so via a computer or similar device, such as a mobile phone, a tablet, a smart speaker or an internet radio. David Lloyd introduced me to Andy who knew enough of my background to offer me a weekend show in his programme schedule. As I thanked David for his support he offered a gentle observation about Serenade.

"I'm pleased to help Stuart, but in case you hadn't realised already, there's no money it. Everyone does it for free, for the love of the music, and for the fun of doing it. I think you'll find that at least it scratches an itch".

It's true. No one is paid at Serenade. It carries no advertising, nor any news or weather bulletins. It is programmed around easy listening music, and it covers its costs, like the electricity bill and copyright fees, from listener donations. I was therefore now in the world of the volunteer, at both Healthwatch Coventry and at Serenade Radio.

David Lloyd went on to enjoy huge success as one of the founders of Boom Radio, which to some large degree borrowed Serenade's notion of providing programming that the BBC had deserted. David found a willing business partner in Phil Riley, who had been the driving force behind Xtra-AM all those years ago when Mercia Sound and BRMB had merged. Phil had subsequently become one of the most successful entrepreneurial executives in commercial radio. At Boom, Phil and David put together a team that quickly claimed a major place on the UK broadcasting map.

* * * *

In July 2021, Coventry City football club lost one of its great heroes with the death of George Curtis, one half of the duo that had taken the Sky Blues to FA Cup glory in 1987. I was honoured to be asked by George's wife Inger to deliver the eulogy at George's funeral service, held in Coventry Cathedral. George was a friend, as well as a sporting hero to me and thousands of others, so I was anxious to do my best in his memory and to do my best for Inger and the Curtis family.

It was well received, and it was reassuring in no small measure to be congratulated and thanked after the service by the Curtis family and by some of the club's former players and managers, including Gordon Milne, my old friend Bobby Gould and the other half of that '87 Cup Final management team, John Sillett, who had been in poor health himself for some time. Snoz was in a wheelchair at the funeral, and at the wake that followed at a local hotel.

* * * *

Sue and I celebrated our 40th wedding anniversary that year, with a family party at the lovely setting of Nailcote Hall Hotel at Berkswell. Whether it was, in part, because I was a touch emotional I'm not sure, but during my speech that day, despite all my careful preparation I forgot to mention some of our relatives, even though they sat staring me in the face. I rambled through things that I wanted to say in a completely bizarre and random order. Probably by far the worst speech I ever made. Still, it was a party and a celebration, and we were surrounded by people who mattered to us.

Sue and I marked the anniversary with a short break in Cornwall, staying at the Headland Hotel at Newquay. On previous visits to Cornwall we'd often commented how nice it looked, with its imposing views over the Atlantic Ocean. It is beautiful and it did not let us down.

Whilst we were there, I took an early morning phone call from BBC CWR. Had I heard that John Sillett had died. Was I available to go on air, there and then, to pay tribute to Snoz? I had only a few minutes to gather my thoughts before being interviewed over the 'phone by CWR Breakfast Show presenter Phil Upton about a man who, like George Curtis, had been a good friend as well as being a Sky Blues legend.

George and John died within weeks of each other, leaving a huge legacy having made their mark on the history of Coventry City Football Club and the city of Coventry.

* * * *

With the passing of old friends you reflect on your own "dash", as it's referred to in the famous poem by Linda Ellis, the dash being what you have done in the years between your birth and death. For much of my dash I presented regular, daily radio shows. In later years I took on a role within the local health economy, as well as having the opportunity to compile and present a weekly online radio show.

In my retirement I purchased a season ticket to follow Coventry City football club as a supporter, no longer concerned with having to describe or comment on the performance. My elder son Nick has done the same, with Matthew, my younger son, joining us occasionally. We sit alongside each other to watch the matches, something that couldn't happen during the many years when match days meant I was working, occupying a seat in the press box. I am immensely proud of our family, and Sue and I have beautiful grandchildren, so life is never dull.

World-wide travel is by no means uncommon for many people, but a long association with the brilliant people at the Elite Travel Group consortium of High Street travel agents has taken me to some wonderful and exciting locations. With Elite, and on family trips, Sue has been with me as we visited places like Malta, Morocco, Cyprus, Turkey, Portugal, and many parts of Spain, including several holidays in the Balearic Islands. We have also been to the Canary Islands, Belgium, Jersey, Ireland, Italy, Germany, Greece and France, plus long-haul trips to Australia, New Zealand, and many places in the USA.

All who travel with have their own special memories, and amongst ours are attending an audience with the Pope at the Vatican during a holiday in Rome, and also a great surprise during a week in New York for our 30th wedding anniversary. We were there for the Thanksgiving Day parade, and atop one of the floats was a singer whose voice I recognised instantly. Neil Diamond.

I have met some remarkable people, famous and not so famous. I have mixed with Prime Ministers, Presidents and Royalty. I have been honoured by the monarch, and I have visited and worked at historic sporting locations, like Wembley, Twickenham, Silverstone, and Lord's, as well as many of the UK's famous football and cricket grounds. I have been blessed with good friends and a great family.

Not bad really, even if Mum was right about my chosen career. It's not a proper job, but despite her anxieties, I have been fortunate to enjoy a life that has been rich in variety, and satisfying in achieving things I might not have even encountered had I pursued another route. I hope Mum and Dad would have been proud of the path I trod along the way, "to be a pilgrim", in the words of my old school song.

Though I know I'll never lose affection
For people and things that went before
I know I'll often stop and think about them
In my life, I love you more.

John Lennon & Paul McCartney, 1965
© Sony/ATV Music Publishing LLC

My Granddad knew Rasputin ... and I met Elton John

www.ingramcontent.com/pod-product-compliance
Ingram Content Group UK Ltd.
Pitfield, Milton Keynes, MK11 3LW, UK
UKHW021940250725
7084UKWH00007B/582